Mastering Terraform

A practical guide to building and deploying infrastructure
on AWS, Azure, and GCP

Mark Tinderholt

Mastering Terraform

Group Product Manager: Preet Ahuja

Publishing Product Manager: Surbhi Suman

Book Project Manager: Ashwin Kharwa

Senior Editor: Runcil Rebello

Technical Editor: Nithik Cheruvakodan

Copy Editor: Safis Editing

Proofreader: Runcil Rebello

Indexer: Subalakshmi Govindhan

Production Designer: Joshua Misquitta

DevRel Marketing Coordinator: Rohan Dobhal

First published: July 2024

Production reference: 1120724

Published by Packt Publishing Ltd.

Grosvenor House

11 St Paul's Square

Birmingham

B3 1RB, UK

ISBN 978-1-83508-601-8

www.packtpub.com

To my Mom and Dad, thank you for investing in a family PC, recognizing my talent, believing in me, and giving me a gentle push in the right direction.

Foreword

Cloud computing has transformed the way applications are built and delivered. In the early days of the public cloud, the services available were generally low-level infrastructure. Today, the hyperscalers provide a broad range of services, including specialized data stores, application middleware, and many compute platforms for virtual machines, containers, and functions. Applications can be quickly built by composing together services. Scaling with demand becomes totally elastic without complex capacity planning.

While building applications is easier, our infrastructure is now more complex than ever. Infrastructure as Code is broadly adopted to manage the complexity of cloud infrastructure by allowing users to simply codify the resources required to support their application. HashiCorp Terraform is the de facto standard for Infrastructure as Code, driven by an extensible ecosystem that supports thousands of integrations spanning public cloud providers, **Software as a Service (SaaS)**, hardware systems, and more.

This new book on Terraform provides a pragmatic, hands-on approach covering real-world scenarios. The author, Mark Tinderholt, deeply understands cloud environments as a principal architect at Microsoft Azure. For readers new to Terraform, the book provides a foundational overview to understand Terraform, the **HashiCorp Configuration Language (HCL)**, and how to use the extensible providers. From there, the author covers the key concepts needed for cloud-based applications and patterns such as GitOps and CI/CD.

Going from the basic concepts, the author then dives into real-world examples of using Terraform to manage virtual machines, containers, and functions across AWS, Azure, and GCP. This takes the core concepts and applies them, to enable you to quickly do the same. This hands-on approach enables you to better understand how to apply Terraform outside of simple examples.

The book ends by providing guidance on best practices in production environments, how to adopt Terraform for existing infrastructure using the import mechanisms, and finally, how to continue learning through Terraform certifications. There are multiple levels of Terraform certifications, with tens of thousands of people certified. The certifications are useful both to test your knowledge and competence with Terraform and to share with prospective employers.

This book is a great resource for anybody hoping to learn more about Infrastructure as Code with HashiCorp Terraform and quickly get an understanding of how to use it to build applications in the major cloud providers. The author brings a depth of understanding as a senior engineer with a first-hand understanding of how cloud providers are built, having spent years working with Terraform.

Armon Dadgar

Co-Founder and CTO of HashiCorp

Contributors

About the author

Mark Tinderholt has over two decades of experience as a software developer and architect. With a solid foundation in application development and a pioneering role in cloud technology adoption, he has led diverse teams across numerous industry verticals on multiple cloud platforms. As an expert in cloud technology, Mark embraced Terraform early on to empower his development teams with greater control over their application environments. He organizes his local **HashiCorp User Group** (**HUG**) and is a HashiCorp ambassador. He also hosts a popular YouTube channel called *Azure Terraformer*.

I want to thank all those who have helped support and shape me as a person and professional—my parents, teachers, mentors, colleagues, and my loving family.

About the reviewers

Maksim Muravev is a talented DevOps engineer with over 10 years of experience. He is currently enhancing game technology at Wargaming in Cyprus. His expertise spans AWS, Terraform, Kubernetes, and **continuous integration/continuous deployment (CI/CD)** systems. Maksim's contributions to the professional community include founding Hackathon Raptors, winning DevOps-related hackathons, and sharing his knowledge through blogs and workshops. His work has been recognized in technical and academic circles, underscoring his commitment to bridging practical applications with theoretical insights.

In this journey of bytes and dreams, I extend my deepest gratitude to the communities and individuals who've been the lighthouses in the vast ocean of technology. Your wisdom and camaraderie have been my compass. Thank you to my family, whose patience and love have been the bedrock of my persistence. This book is a testament to the collective spirit of innovation and support that fuels our industry.

Nikolay Malykhin started to work as a system administrator at university and, after finishing his master's degree in computer networking, continued to work as a control system and equipment engineer more than 10 years ago.

All these years, he has not only been a husband, father of two boys, and friend but has grown up as an engineer.

Today, he works as a software engineer in the delivery division at Ness, one of Israel's largest and most prominent information technology and digital service providers.

I want to thank my friends and Packt Publishing for giving me this amazing opportunity to review this book and help create something for engineering and IT, which I like so much.

I would also like to thank my wife – without her support, it wouldn't have been possible to find time for this book between family and work.

Table of Contents

3

Harnessing HashiCorp Utility Providers 69

Part 2: Concepts of Cloud Architecture and Automation

4

Foundations of Cloud Architecture – Virtual Machines and Infrastructure-as-a-Service 93

5

Beyond VMs – Core Concepts of Containers and Kubernetes   105

6

Connecting It All Together – GitFlow, GitOps, and CI/CD   135

Part 3: Building Solutions on AWS

7

Getting Started on AWS – Building Solutions with AWS EC2   155

8

Containerize with AWS – Building Solutions with AWS EKS   197

9

Go Serverless with AWS – Building Solutions with AWS Lambda   233

Part 4: Building Solutions on Azure

10

Getting Started on Azure – Building Solutions with Azure Virtual Machines 259

11

Containerize on Azure – Building Solutions with Azure Kubernetes Service 291

12

Go Serverless on Azure – Building Solutions with Azure Functions 313

Part 5: Building Solutions on Google Cloud

13

Getting Started on Google Cloud – Building Solutions with GCE   335

14

Containerize on Google Cloud – Building Solutions with GKE   363

15

Go Serverless on Google Cloud – Building Solutions with Google Cloud Functions   379

Part 6: Day 2 Operations and Beyond

16

Already Provisioned? Strategies for Importing Existing Environments

17

Managing Production Environments with Terraform

18

Looking Ahead – Certification, Emerging Trends, and Next Steps   437

Preface

Infrastructure as Code has emerged as the de facto method for provisioning and maintaining cloud infrastructure. While this approach has been around for a while, it has matured and refined over the years. Initially, it followed largely imperative programming models and employed agents to facilitate change. However, with the advent of API-based cloud services, it has transformed into a primarily declarative configuration of desired states that are translated into cloud services and their configuration—of which Terraform is the gold standard.

Terraform is crucial for both application development teams, who create applications and services that delight end users, and platform teams, who empower enterprises and organizations with smooth and efficient operations. As a result, Terraform has become the preferred way for these teams to build and manage the environments that support their goals.

This book, *Mastering Terraform*, recognizes that to truly master Terraform, one must first have a deep understanding of the cloud services and architectures that will be automated through the use of Terraform and Infrastructure as Code. Throughout this book, the focus will be on solving real-world problems—whether by building new environments or managing existing ones—using Terraform.

We live in a multi-cloud world. That's why each of the largest hyperscale clouds—AWS, Azure, and Google Cloud—will receive equal treatment within this book. No matter which of these clouds you plan on working with—one, two, or all of them—this book will treat you as a first-class citizen.

Another reality embraced in this book is that Terraform is not the only tool in the tool shed. Practitioners often need to integrate multiple tools to accomplish their goals. Therefore, we'll explore three different cloud computing paradigms: virtual machines, containers, and serverless. Each has its own design characteristics, deployment mechanics, and toolchain dynamics that you need to be aware of when working with them.

Who this book is for

This book is intended for cloud, DevOps, platform, and infrastructure engineers, SREs, developers, and cloud architects who want to use Terraform to automate cloud infrastructures and streamline software delivery. You will benefit from having a basic understanding of Infrastructure as Code (such as Terraform, Ansible, and AWS CDK), cloud architecture, development tools, and platforms. This foundation will help you elevate your skills through the concepts and practices covered in the book.

What this book covers

Chapter 1, Understanding Terraform Architecture, provides an in-depth look at the core tenants of Terraform's architecture, focusing on Terraform state, modularity, the command-line tool, and the configuration language that make up what we know as Terraform.

Chapter 2, Using HashiCorp Configuration Language, provides an in-depth look at the critical language structures used by Terraform's functional language, **HashiCorp Configuration Language** (**HCL**). It shares best practices and real-world use cases for common scenarios.

Chapter 3, Harnessing HashiCorp Utility Providers, provides an in-depth look at the utility providers that extend Terraform core and your cloud provider of choice. It shares the best practices and common use cases to help you streamline common cloud-agnostic operations no matter what cloud platform you're using.

Chapter 4, Foundations of Cloud Architecture – Virtual Machines and Infrastructure-as-a-Service, provides an overview of core concepts needed to start designing and building Infrastructure as Code solutions using Terraform. These critical concepts transcend cloud platforms, which will help prepare you to automate this category of solution no matter what your cloud of choice.

Chapter 5, Beyond VMs – Core Concepts of Containers and Kubernetes, provides an overview of core concepts needed to start designing and building Infrastructure as Code solutions that integrate with Docker and Kubernetes—a scenario that is becoming more and more popular these days. The chapter explores Docker and Kubernetes integration strategies using both native client tools and relevant Terraform providers for Kubernetes and Helm.

Chapter 6, Connecting It All Together – GitFlow, GitOps, and CI/CD, provides an overview of software development processes using GitFlow and the impact of this approach on Infrastructure as Code operations. Finally, we explore using GitHub Actions to implement CI/CD pipelines for virtual machines, Kubernetes, and serverless workloads.

Chapter 7, Getting Started on AWS – Building Solutions with AWS EC2, provides an end-to-end solution developed for AWS using virtual machines powered by EC2. The chapter explores the usage of Packer to automate OS-level configuration, Terraform to provision the infrastructure and deploy the workload, and finally, GitHub Actions to automate the entire process.

Chapter 8, Containerize with AWS – Building Solutions with AWS EKS, provides an end-to-end solution developed for AWS using Kubernetes powered by EKS. The chapter explores the usage of Docker to automate OS-level configuration, Terraform to provision the infrastructure and deploy the workload, and finally, GitHub Actions to automate the entire process.

Chapter 9, Go Serverless with AWS – Building Solutions with AWS Lambda, provides an end-to-end serverless solution developed for AWS Lambda. The chapter explores the necessary application code changes to conform to AWS Lambda's framework, Terraform to provision the infrastructure and deploy the workload, and finally, GitHub Actions to automate the entire process.

Chapter 10, Getting Started on Azure – Building Solutions with Azure Virtual Machines, provides an end-to-end solution developed using Azure Virtual Machines. The chapter explores the usage of Packer to automate OS-level configuration, Terraform to provision the infrastructure and deploy the workload, and finally, GitHub Actions to automate the entire process.

Chapter 11, Containerize on Azure – Building Solutions with Azure Kubernetes Service, provides an end-to-end solution developed for Azure using Kubernetes powered by AKS. The chapter explores the usage of Docker to automate OS-level configuration, Terraform to provision the infrastructure and deploy the workload, and finally, GitHub Actions to automate the entire process.

Chapter 12, Go Serverless on Azure – Building Solutions with Azure Functions, provides an end-to-end serverless solution developed for Azure Functions. The chapter explores the necessary application code changes to conform to the Azure Functions framework, Terraform to provision the infrastructure and deploy the workload, and finally, GitHub Actions to automate the entire process.

Chapter 13, Getting Started on Google Cloud – Building Solutions with GCE, provides an end-to-end solution developed for GCP using virtual machines powered by GCE. The chapter explores the usage of Packer to automate OS-level configuration, Terraform to provision the infrastructure and deploy the workload, and finally, GitHub Actions to automate the entire process.

Chapter 14, Containerize on Google Cloud – Building Solutions with GKE, provides an end-to-end solution developed for GCP using Kubernetes powered by GKE. The chapter explores the usage of Docker to automate OS-level configuration, Terraform to provision the infrastructure and deploy the workload, and finally, GitHub Actions to automate the entire process.

Chapter 15, Go Serverless on Google Cloud – Building Solutions with Google Cloud Functions, provides an end-to-end serverless solution developed for Google Cloud Functions. The chapter explores the necessary application code changes to conform to the Google Cloud Functions framework, Terraform to provision the infrastructure and deploy the workload, and finally, GitHub Actions to automate the entire process.

Chapter 16, Already Provisioned? Strategies for Importing Existing Environments, provides an in-depth look at different approaches for bringing existing resources and environments under Terraform management. The chapter explores the usage of built-in import capabilities as well as strategies using third-party tools and provides real-world recommendations for when and how to use them and what the trade-offs are to employing these techniques.

Chapter 17, Managing Production Environments with Terraform, provides in-depth guidance for how to manage long-lived environments using Infrastructure as Code with Terraform. The chapter explores different real-world operating models that help organizations better coordinate Infrastructure as Code at scale. Then, it delves into Day 2 operations with best practices for managing change and break-fixing when things go awry.

Chapter 18, Looking Ahead – Certification, Emerging Trends, and Next Steps, provides a practical guide to preparing for and sitting for a Terraform Certification exam. The chapter also explores emerging trends and potential next steps for those of you who want to take your mastery of Terraform to the next level.

To get the most out of this book

You should be comfortable using a command-line interface on either Windows or Linux, a code editor such as Visual Studio Code, and a Git source code repository such as GitHub.

While the book offers a conceptual overview of cloud computing concepts such as virtual networks, virtual machines, Docker, and Kubernetes, familiarity with these technologies will help fill in gaps and enhance your learning experience.

Additionally, a basic understanding of an imperative and object-oriented programming language such as Java, C#, or Python will be useful for the serverless chapters.

Software/hardware covered in the book	Operating system requirements
Terraform v1.8.4	Windows, macOS, or Linux
Packer v1.10.3	Windows, macOS, or Linux
Kubectl v1.26.2	Windows, macOS, or Linux
Helm v3.13.2	Windows, macOS, or Linux
.NET 6	Windows, macOS, or Linux
AWS CLI v2.15.58	
Azure CLI v2.58.0	
Google Cloud SDK v469.0.0	

Download the example code files

This book provides three comprehensive end-to-end solutions, one for each major cloud platform: AWS, Azure, and Google Cloud. Each solution is accompanied by its own dedicated GitHub repository, containing all the necessary code to help you get up and running quickly with each platform:

- Amazon Web Services:

  - Chapter 7 - Virtual Machine Solution: `https://github.com/markti/aws-vm-demo`

  - Chapter 8 - Kubernetes Solution: `https://github.com/markti/aws-k8s-demo`

  - Chapter 9 - Serverless Solution: `https://github.com/markti/aws-serverless-demo`

- Microsoft Azure:

  - Chapter 10 - Virtual Machine Solution: `https://github.com/markti/azure-vm-demo`

  - Chapter 11 - Kubernetes Solution: `https://github.com/markti/azure-k8s-demo`

  - Chapter 12 - Serverless Solution: `https://github.com/markti/azure-serverless-demo`

- Google Cloud:

  - Chapter 13 - Virtual Machine Solution: `https://github.com/markti/gcp-vm-demo`

  - Chapter 14 - Kubernetes Solution: `https://github.com/markti/gcp-k8s-demo`

  - Chapter 15 - Serverless Solution: `https://github.com/markti/gcp-serverless-demo`

You can download the additional example code files for this book from GitHub at `https://github.com/PacktPublishing/Mastering-Terraform`. If there's an update to the code, it will be updated in the GitHub repository.

We also have other code bundles from our rich catalog of books and videos available at `https://github.com/PacktPublishing/`. Check them out!

Conventions used

There are a number of text conventions used throughout this book.

`Code in text`: Indicates code words in text, database table names, folder names, filenames, file extensions, pathnames, dummy URLs, user input, and Twitter/X handles. Here is an example: "When you run `terraform init`, Terraform transforms the current working directory into the root module of the workspace."

A block of code is set as follows:

```
app_settings = {
  "SCM_DO_BUILD_DURING_DEPLOYMENT" = "false"
  "WEBSITE_RUN_FROM_PACKAGE"       = "1"
```

When we wish to draw your attention to a particular part of a code block, the relevant lines or items are set in bold:

```
app_settings = {
  "SCM_DO_BUILD_DURING_DEPLOYMENT" = "false"
  "WEBSITE_RUN_FROM_PACKAGE"       = "1"
```

Any command-line input or output is written as follows:

```
terraform import 'ADDRESS["key"]' ID
```

Bold: Indicates a new term, an important word, or words that you see onscreen. For instance, words in menus or dialog boxes appear in **bold**. Here is an example: "The two major cloud platforms, **Amazon Web Services** (**AWS**) and **Microsoft Azure**, had already adopted resource typing in their respective IaC solutions."

> **Tips or important notes**
> Appear like this.

Get in touch

Feedback from our readers is always welcome.

General feedback: If you have questions about any aspect of this book, email us at `customercare@packtpub.com` and mention the book title in the subject of your message.

Errata: Although we have taken every care to ensure the accuracy of our content, mistakes do happen. If you have found a mistake in this book, we would be grateful if you would report this to us. Please visit `www.packtpub.com/support/errata` and fill in the form.

Piracy: If you come across any illegal copies of our works in any form on the internet, we would be grateful if you would provide us with the location address or website name. Please contact us at `copyright@packt.com` with a link to the material.

If you are interested in becoming an author: If there is a topic that you have expertise in and you are interested in either writing or contributing to a book, please visit `authors.packtpub.com`.

Share your thoughts

Once you've read *Mastering Terraform*, we'd love to hear your thoughts! Scan the QR code below to go straight to the Amazon review page for this book and share your feedback.

`https://packt.link/r/1835086012`

Your review is important to us and the tech community and will help us make sure we're delivering excellent quality content.

Download a free PDF copy of this book

Thanks for purchasing this book!

Do you like to read on the go but are unable to carry your print books everywhere?

Is your eBook purchase not compatible with the device of your choice?

Don't worry, now with every Packt book you get a DRM-free PDF version of that book at no cost.

Read anywhere, any place, on any device. Search, copy, and paste code from your favorite technical books directly into your application.

The perks don't stop there, you can get exclusive access to discounts, newsletters, and great free content in your inbox daily

Follow these simple steps to get the benefits:

1. Scan the QR code or visit the link below

https://packt.link/free-ebook/9781835086018

2. Submit your proof of purchase

3. That's it! We'll send your free PDF and other benefits to your email directly

Part 1:
Foundations of Terraform

Before we begin our journey, we need to establish the conceptual model, architecture, and capabilities that define Terraform and how it can be harnessed to develop and maintain your cloud architectures.

This part has the following chapters:

- *Chapter 1, Understanding Terraform Architecture*
- *Chapter 2, Using HashiCorp Configuration Language*
- *Chapter 3, Harnessing HashiCorp Utility Providers*

1

Understanding Terraform Architecture

At its core, **Terraform** is a simple command-line program that evaluates source code, which describes what a desired state should look like, compares it against what the actual state is, constructs a plan to transform the actual state into the desired state, and can execute the plan. But don't let its perceived simplicity fool you. Terraform's internal complexity manifests itself in its external simplicity.

Terraform is a large, source-available project written in Go that maintains the command-line executable. It provides baseline functionality such as **HashiCorp Configuration Language** (HCL) parsing, state management, plan creation, and execution.

Terraform is extremely powerful, yet ironically, it does very little by itself. But here's the exciting part: Terraform's superpower comes from its extensibility, a power that is not limited to its creators. The actual Terraform executable, by itself, can't do much, but when bundled with one of its plugins—called **providers**—Terraform can do quite a lot! This extensibility is a testament to the collaborative nature of the Terraform community, where everyone can contribute to its growth and capabilities.

In this chapter, we will cover the following topics:

- Understanding Terraform architecture
- Understanding Terraform state
- Understanding how to build and consume modules
- Understanding how to use the **command-line interface** (CLI) effectively

Terraform has four superpowers that distinguish it from other tools: *planning, extensibility, configuration language*, and *modularity*. Some tools may share some of these, but they don't have them all. With these powers combined, Terraform is a game changer in cloud automation.

Understanding Terraform architecture

The biggest differentiator of Terraform is that, well, Terraform plans ahead. Let's look at how Terraform handles planning in detail.

The plan

When working with Terraform, you will be following a process where Terraform is used to analyze the existing environment. In doing this analysis, Terraform is determining what (if any) changes in the code need to be applied to the actual environment to bring it up to date. Terraform itemizes these changes as actions within the plan. While Terraform does this analysis on our behalf, produces the plan, and is fully capable of executing that plan against the environment, we are still responsible for reviewing the plan and determining if the planned changes are what we intended:

Figure 1.1 – Terraform resources are straightforward machines with inputs and outputs

Terraform represents every component in your environment as a resource in this analysis. Resources are extremely simple machines. They take inputs and produce outputs. They also can be chained together, thus creating explicit relationships between the components within your environment. These relationships inform Terraform's analysis of your environment and the sequence of actions enumerated in the plan.

Once we have decided that this plan is what we intended, we ask Terraform to execute it. Terraform will then apply that plan to our actual environment. The outcome of this process is that Terraform will bring our environment up to date with the description in the code.

Terraform's design encourages developers to repeat this process. Therefore, as the developer updates their code, with each iteration of the code applied to the environment, we will continually assess the current state and determine the future state to match the environment our code describes. Each time we run Terraform to assess the environment, it will produce a plan. This plan was generated at a point in time when evaluating the differences between the actual environment and the code base.

On *Day 1*, since the environment does not exist, everything Terraform must create the developer described within the code. On *Day 2*, however, things are more complex. On *Day 1*, we started cleaning. However, on *Day 2*, we are still determining where we are starting because Terraform has already provisioned the environment once before. Many things could have changed since *Day 1*. We could have intentionally modified the code base to change the environment. Likewise, *gremlins* could have altered our environment during the night, thus introducing drift into our environment and requiring us to roll back their changes.

To analyze the existing environment, Terraform consults two sources of information: **Terraform state** and the environment itself—via the provider (which is also informed by Terraform state). If the Terraform state is empty, then Terraform assumes the environment does not exist and creates a plan that will create everything:

Figure 1.2 – Resource plan, Day 1: everything needs to be created

If Terraform state exists, things will get interesting, and Terraform will have to earn its paycheck. Terraform will use the Terraform state to analyze the environment by querying the provider (s) about the health and configuration of each resource declared within. Based on these results, Terraform will construct a set of instructions. Once Terraform executes these instructions, the current environment will match the desired environment—as described in the code. However, after the first time Terraform has executed your plan successfully, if you ask Terraform to create a plan again, it will consult the Terraform state and use the providers to consult the actual environment and see that no changes are needed:

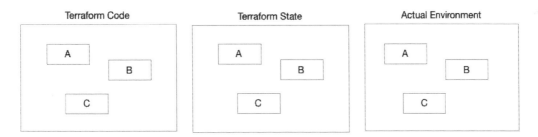

Figure 1.3 – Resource plan, Day 2: no changes in your environment

To create such an instruction set, Terraform must generate a complete dependency graph of the resources within the environment to determine what order it must execute the instructions. The relationships between the resources infer these dependencies. If one resource takes in, as an input variable, the value of another resource's output variable, Terraform will determine that there is a dependency between these resources:

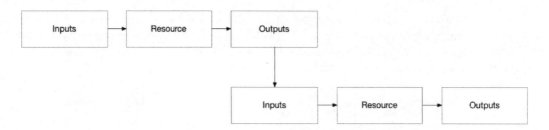

Figure 1.4 – Dependencies: one resource's inputs is another resource's outputs

Sometimes, Terraform will only know the results of instructions after executing them. Hence, the obligatory warning message `known after apply`. However, this dependency graph and the subsequent plan are the crux of the Terraform machine.

This process makes Terraform an idempotent tool, meaning it can be applied multiple times without changing the result beyond the initial application. Idempotence is not necessarily unique to Terraform across automation tools, as some tools operate similarly. **Ansible** is a great example, also ensuring that repeat operations do not alter the state unless changes are necessary.

Execution phases

Terraform's core workflow follows a three-stage process: *initialize*, *plan*, and *apply*:

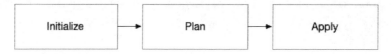

Figure 1.5 – Terraform execution phases

Let's examine each stage to see what parts of our code base are being utilized and what actions Terraform is taking.

Initialize

First, initialize the Terraform workspace using the `terraform init` command, which loads and configures all referenced providers and modules:

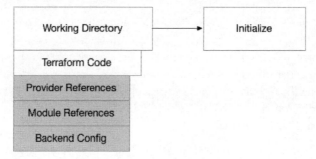

Figure 1.6 – Terraform initialization loads provider and module
dependencies and verifies backend connectivity

Plan

Once a Terraform has initialized its workspace, it can generate a plan using the `terraform plan` command. Although the command seems simple, this is a very complex process.

First, a dependency graph is built of all resources using the implicit (and sometimes explicit relationships between them). Then, Terraform checks the state file to determine if it has already provisioned the resource. Suppose the resource exists in the state file. In that case, Terraform will communicate with the resource via its respective provider and compare the desired state with the expected state as stored in the state file and the actual state reported by the provider. Terraform makes note of any differences and creates an action plan for each resource. The action can be *create*, *update*, or *destroy*:

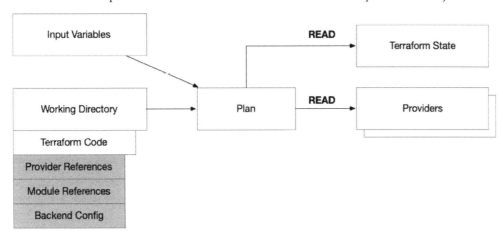

Figure 1.7 – terraform plan evaluates the current code base with a set of input variables and compares it against the workspace's Terraform state

Apply

Once a Terraform has generated a plan, it can optionally execute it against the actual environment using the `terraform apply` command. Using the dependency graph, Terraform will execute each resource action in sequence. If resource actions are not dependent on each other, then Terraform will execute them in parallel. During this phase, Terraform will constantly communicate with each provider, initiating commands and checking the status of the relevant provider. As Terraform completes resource actions, it will continually update the Terraform state:

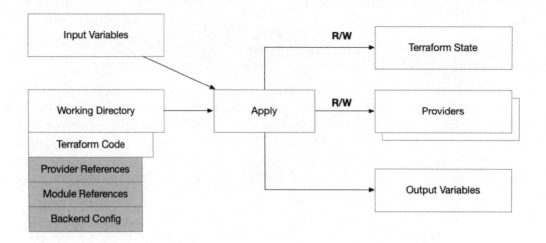

Figure 1.8 – terraform apply executes the plan through communication with the providers, updates the Terraform state, and returns output variables

Resource actions

When Terraform generates a plan, it evaluates each resource to determine if change is required to achieve the desired state of the infrastructure. There are several different situations where Terraform will determine action is needed on a particular resource.

Create

A create action can occur in three situations:

- The resource is completely new
- Something outside of Terraform deleted the resource
- The developer updated a resource's code in such a way that the provider requires it to be destroyed and re-created

Here's what adding a new resource looks like:

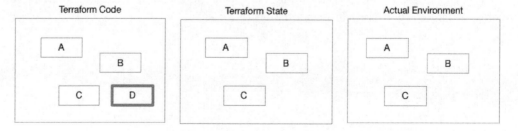

Figure 1.9 – Adding a new resource

When a resource is entirely new, it doesn't exist in the Terraform state file. For example, we want to create a **virtual machine** (**VM**) named vm001. If this is the case, Terraform doesn't use the provider to check if the resource is there. As a result, you can run into situations where the plan will generate successfully, but when Terraform executes the plan, it will fail. This situation usually boils down to resource naming conflicts when another user has provisioned another unrelated resource with the same name as the one Terraform plans to create (that is, somebody has already provisioned a VM named vm001). This situation can occur if someone creates a resource manually or even when a resource is created through Terraform but in a different Terraform workspace and, consequently, a different Terraform state file.

A prime example of the concept of **drift** is when someone manually deletes a resource outside of Terraform:

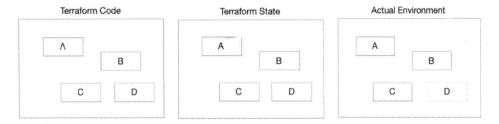

Figure 1.10 – Drift

When a developer changes a resource, sometimes the provider requires it to be destroyed and then re-created. For example, we want to change our VM's hardware profile from 4 CPU cores and 16 GB RAM to 8 CPU cores and 32 GB RAM. This logic exists in the provider's code base at the resource level. It would help if you carefully check the documentation of the resources you are using to ensure you are aware of any potential disruptions or data loss that could occur when updates force a resource to be destroyed and re-created.

Change

A change action can occur in two situations:

- The resource has changed in code
- The resource has been modified outside of Terraform

Here's what changing an existing resource looks like:

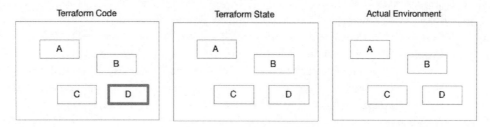

Figure 1.11 – Updating an existing resource

This change won't require the resource to be destroyed and re-created. This could be something simple such as changing the tags of a resource. These types of changes can also be introduced by drift. For example, someone adds a new tag manually using the cloud platform's management portal without updating the Terraform code base.

Destroy

A destroy action can occur in two situations:

- The developer deleted the resource from the code
- The developer updated a resource's code in such a way that the provider requires it to be destroyed and re-created

Here's what removing an existing resource looks like:

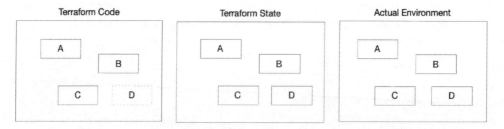

Figure 1.12 – Removing an existing resource

This could be as simple as removing an unused—or, more likely, no longer used—resource. For example, removing an unnecessary **network security group** (**NSG**) rule—such as one that grants access to port 22 to the entire internet—is probably a good idea!

Resource action plans can have a cascading effect. Naturally, dependent resources are also new if a resource is entirely new. However, it would be best to be mindful when the resource needs to be destroyed and re-created. This action is called a **drop-create** action. When a resource plays a critical role within the environment, it is very common that when a drop-create action occurs, there will be a large swath of the resource graph that will also be destroyed and then re-created—usually, any resource dependent on the resource being drop-created.

Configuration language

When Terraform was first only a glimmer in the minds of Armon Dadgar and Mitchell Hashimoto, the industry had two paradigms of **Infrastructure-as-Code** (**IaC**): imperative, which dominated under the names of Chef and Puppet, using traditional programming languages such as Ruby and Python. However, there were declarative approaches, but most were an exercise of crafting large and complex JSON documents.

The two major cloud platforms, **Amazon Web Services** (**AWS**) and **Microsoft Azure**, had already adopted resource typing in their respective IaC solutions. AWS CloudFormation and **Azure Resource Manager** (**ARM**) templates leveraged a consistent schema to describe resources of various types. Each resource type had a standard set of attributes that helped the platform target the appropriate resource provider to handle the request. Likewise, each resource type had its own custom attributes and schema to configure its unique nature. But the solutions were silos within the respective cloud platforms.

So, in many ways, the industry was primed and ready for a solution that would adopt a resource type-based approach and thus knock down the silos between cloud providers enabling, at the very least, a tool that could describe resources on multiple clouds within the same context. There were challenges with both imperative and declarative approaches.

Imperative approaches resulted in overly complex code, nested structures, and elaborate state-checking logic made for difficult-to-maintain code bases that could quickly descend into spaghetti code. Also, programming language and platform heritage could stoke religious rivalries between developer camps.

The declarative solutions, on the other hand, relied on industry-standard document formats such as **JSON** and **YAML**. These formats encouraged a simple top-down approach and induced no tribalism due to their neutral nature. However, they made it difficult to represent complex expressions and implement simple iterations and loops, and even simple things such as annotating code with code comments were not possible or overly cumbersome.

Terraform brought the best of both worlds by bringing elements of an imperative language, such as expressions and looping, and fusing it with the best of the declarative model that encouraged a simple top-down approach to defining resources within an environment.

HCL uses simple block definitions that allow for a more concise representation of resources than other declarative solutions but a more code-like syntax, all linking between blocks that acknowledges the resource type-driven nature of cloud computing in its bones:

```
resource "random_string" "foo" {
  length  = 4
  upper   = false
  special = false
}
```

A block's definition has three parts: the **block type**, the **resource type**, and the **reference name**. In the preceding example, the block type is `resource`, the resource type is `random_string`, and the reference name is `foo`. To create dependencies between resources, we use the reference name and type to access output values from the resource:

```
resource "azurerm_resource_group" "bar" {
  name     = "rg-${random_string.foo.result}"
  location = var.location
}
```

In the preceding code, we create an Azure resource group by referencing the `result` output value from the random string named `foo`.

This simple pattern describes how we can combine dozens, sometimes hundreds, of resources to build sophisticated cloud architectures:

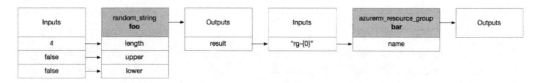

Figure 1.13 – Chaining of Terraform resources, where the outputs of one resource act as inputs to another

Using this preceding pattern in HCL allows Terraform to determine the relationships between our resources and construct a plan to provision them all. The funny part and the sheer brilliance of the whole thing is that it's just a fancy game of connecting the dots.

Modularity

Everything lives in modules. When you make your first Terraform project, you inadvertently create your first Terraform module. That's because every Terraform project is a root module. In your root module, you declare providers,

One ubiquitous pattern within Terraform is that when you code resources, modules, or data sources, you work with inputs and outputs. Each Terraform resource and data source works in this manner, as does your entire Terraform workspace, allowing Terraform to be embedded neatly into a toolchain within a pipeline to provision an environment.

The root module doesn't have to be the only module that you write. You can create reusable modules that are designed to encapsulate reusable aspects of your solutions that can be shared across root modules. The difference between a root module and a reusable module is that the root module is designed to be the entry point for deploying one or more environments. Reusable modules are simply components that define useful patterns or best practices and allow you to save time having to re-create them whenever you want to create a new environment or a similar solution.

Now that we have taken a high-level look at Terraform's architecture and understand the core technology, we know that it comprises the Terraform command-line application and the HCL functional language. We also know that Terraform's superpower is that the design of the core technology is highly extensible by leveraging providers to adapt the technology to a multitude of extremely diverse platforms and technologies and the built-in modularity that enables practitioners to easily create simple or sophisticated IaC solutions that can be packaged and made to be reusable across teams and organizations.

Next, we'll delve into a critical subsystem that enables Terraform to achieve consistent, idempotent IaC motion across various platforms and technologies.

Understanding Terraform state

Terraform uses the state to remember what was previously provisioned in a given workspace. Some critics of Terraform, when they compare it to AWS CloudFormation or ARM templates, point out that these technologies don't rely on this concept of maintaining state in an externalized file. Of course, this is only true because these tools only support a single target platform and can tightly couple to the proprietary nature in which those platforms maintain state. However, Terraform—with its flexible plugin architecture—can't assume anything about the platform and the resources that it provisions to each target platform. Therefore, Terraform needs to drop to the lowest common denominator and ensure that it knows what it has provisioned before in a uniform and consistent fashion.

This approach to maintaining the state provides a couple of benefits. First, it uniformly records what Terraform has provisioned across platforms that maintain their internal state and those that don't. Second, it allows Terraform to define a boundary between managed and unmanaged resources.

This problem is the classic **Jurassic Park problem**. In *Jurassic Park*, they had genetically engineered all these dinosaurs. They engineered them with population control in mind—so that they couldn't mate—or so they thought. In the park, they had all these sophisticated systems to track where all the dinosaurs were and how many of them there were. However, the big flaw of their design was that they programmed their systems to only look for dinosaurs that they genetically engineered. So, their system worked flawlessly and showed them where all the dinosaurs they created were. Wouldn't you know it? The number of dinosaurs always matched the number they expected to see. That's bad for Jurassic Park because, due to this flaw, they were unaware of a defect in their genetic engineering that allowed the dinosaurs to mate. Jurassic Park had too many dinosaurs, and things got—well—a little out of hand:

Figure 1.14 – The Jurassic Park problem

Terraform only looks for resources that it has provisioned. It can do that because it maintains a state file. The state file is just like the list of dinosaurs that Jurassic Park thinks it has. This approach was terrible for Jurassic Park. But for Terraform, it's a good thing:

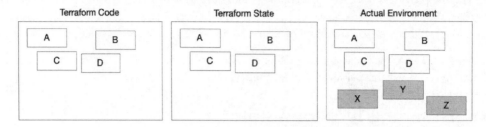

Figure 1.15 – Terraform ignores resources provisioned externally, even if those resources draw dependencies on resources provisioned by Terraform

Why? Because not all resources are going to be—or need to be—created and managed by Terraform. By clearly scoping what Terraform is responsible for (and what it's not), it allows Terraform to be flexible in allowing organizations to choose their level of involvement with Terraform. Some teams and organizations will start small and only deploy a few things with Terraform. At the same time, others might go nuts and provision everything with Terraform. Still, there will very likely be things that are happening that Terraform doesn't know about. The Terraform state is constructing guard rails to keep Terraform in its box and let it know what it's allowed to touch. Doing so enables Terraform to play well with others and gives freedom to teams and individuals to use whatever method or tools they want to control aspects of an environment.

State file

Terraform state is a JSON data file stored somewhere Terraform knows how to find it. This file maintains a list of resources. Each resource has a resource type identifier and all configurations for that resource.

The state file mirrors what we describe in our code but is much more verbose than what we declare in our code. The following code generates a random string with a length of four characters, no uppercase characters, and no special-case characters:

```
resource "random_string" "foo" {
  length  = 4
  upper   = false
  special = false
}
```

After running `terraform apply`, Terraform will produce a state file containing the same resource but with more context:

```
{
  "mode": "managed",
```

```
      "type": "random_string",
      "name": "foo",
      "provider":
"provider[\"registry.terraform.io/hashicorp/random\"]",
      "instances": [
        {
          "schema_version": 2,
          "attributes": {
            "id": "vyoi",
            "keepers": null,
            "length": 4,
            "lower": true,
            "min_lower": 0,
            "min_numeric": 0,
            "min_special": 0,
            "min_upper": 0,
            "number": true,
            "numeric": true,
            "override_special": null,
            "result": "vyoi",
            "special": false,
            "upper": false
          },
          "sensitive_attributes": []
        }
      ]
    }
```

The `provider` and `type` instances help identify which resource type this resource is and which Terraform providers the developer uses.

The `schema_version` parameter of the resource attribute helps identify whether the current resource is compatible with the current version of the provider. If it is not, it can help give the provider an indicator of how to upgrade it to the latest version of the schema.

Partial resource management

Due to Terraform's nature as a piece of **open source software** (**OSS**) and the built-in assumption that these cloud providers are their own piece of software that is evolving over time, at a different pace than the Terraform providers, there will be periods of time where the cloud providers will have features that Terraform is unaware of.

When this happens, we don't want Terraform to fight with the cloud provider to turn them off just because Terraform isn't aware of them. This scenario is extremely common as it presents itself naturally when an environment is being managed by Terraform and a specific version of the Terraform provider. As the Terraform provider has new features added to keep pace with the target cloud platform, the provider version is not always kept up to date in the Terraform code—nor should it have to be.

Let's say we provide an environment using Terraform and v1.0, our favorite cloud platform's Terraform provider. The next day, our favorite cloud provider added this amazing feature, Feature X. We still have the same code and the same Terraform state file, but we are extremely eager to try out Feature X. However, we are using the latest version of the Terraform provider—v1.0—and it has no support for Feature X.

What can we do? Well, we can wait for our friendly internet strangers who contribute to the Terraform provider's open source project to add support for Feature X. However, we don't know when that will be.

Did we mention we were extremely eager to try out Feature X? If we just can't wait, we could just enable Feature X directly on our favorite cloud platform. *Wouldn't this create drift*, you say? In normal circumstances—yes—as we're modifying our Terraform-managed resource using our favorite cloud platform web interface. Normally, the next time we run `terraform apply`, Terraform will detect that changes have been made to that resource outside the environment and revert our changes. However, since we are on v1.0 of the Terraform provider, Terraform is happily ignorant of Feature X. Thus, any changes we make to the configuration of Feature X will go unnoticed by Terraform. This also means that if you delete that `terraform destroy` resource and re-create it, you'd have to go out to the portal and manually reconfigure Feature X all over again.

That is, until we upgraded to v1.1 of the Terraform provider, which was released the day after we manually set up Feature X on our resource. Now that we are using v1.1 of the Terraform provider, the resource Terraform is using to provision that service to our favorite cloud platform is now aware of Feature X. If our code is still the same, it's going to think that Feature X shouldn't be enabled at all and should remove it.

To avoid this, we'll need to carefully run `terraform plan` with v1.1 of the Terraform provider to see what changes Terraform is planning using this upgraded version of the provider. Then, we'll need to update our code to configure Feature X just as it is configured. Once we do that, Terraform will see that no changes are required, and Terraform will bring Feature X under management:

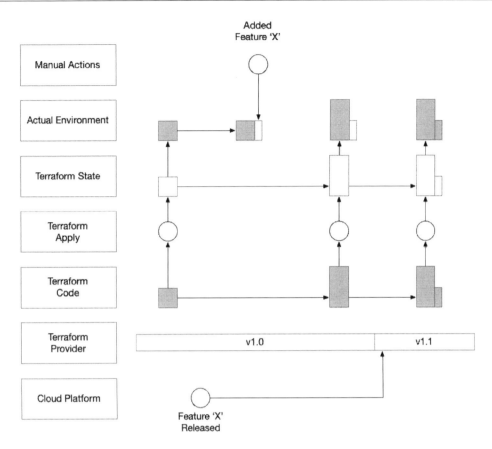

Figure 1.16 – Managing the perpetual change that occurs as a new cloud platform's capabilities are created, exposed through the Terraform provider and adopted in your Terraform codebase

Now that we have looked at how Terraform maintains the state and how this aspect of its architecture affects how Terraform creates and executes plans, let's move on to the more practical topic of developing and consuming modules.

Understanding how to build and consume modules

One of Terraform's most powerful capabilities is its ease of organizing and packaging reusable code, which increases the maintainability of your code base and improves the reusability of common patterns in your architecture.

Traditional developers have it easy—you must simply create a new method to encapsulate a reusable code block. In other IaC tools, doing the same thing is a challenge. In Terraform, all you need is a new folder.

Terraform scopes every module within a folder. When you run `terraform init`, Terraform transforms the current working directory into the root module of the workspace. You can use modules stored in other folders within the same repository just by using a relative path to reference the module. It is a standard convention within the Terraform community for storing local modules in a `modules` directory near the root module's directory.

Consider this folder structure:

```
/terraform
    /modules
        /rando
    /root
```

The path to the root module is `/terraform/root`. The path to the `rando` module is `/terraform/modules/rando`.

Consider the contents of the root module:

```
main.tf
outputs.tf
variables.tf
versions.tf
```

The preceding list of files is a typical convention for the file structure of a module. In the `versions.tf` file, you should declare the `terraform` block, which contains both the Terraform version and each of the referenced Terraform providers and their corresponding versions.

In the `variables.tf` file, you should declare all the input variables this module expects. It's essential to keep all input variables declared in one place to make it easier for the module consumer to understand the contract for this module.

Likewise, in the `outputs.tf` file, you should be used to declare all the output values that this module will produce.

Since it is possible to declare input variables and outputs in any `.tf` file within the folder, nothing prevents you from following this approach. However, you don't want to make other developers scan every file in your module's folder for a `variable` block to get a good understanding of the module's interface.

In the `main.tf` file, you should declare the *meat* of your module. This file is where the magic happens. However, you are not limited to just one file. At your discretion, you can create additional `.tf` files to better organize more complex modules into relevant sections or groupings of related resources.

We need to understand the relative path to get to the `rando` module to reference the `rando` module from the root module. This relative path is calculated based on the root module's working directory. Therefore, a declaration of the `rando` module would look like this:

```
module "foo" {
    source = "../modules/rando"
}
```

The `source` meta-argument is a required attribute for every `module` block. You'll notice that declaring a module differs slightly from declaring a resource or a data source. For example, when declaring a module, the resource type is omitted. That's because a `module` block is both a block type and a resource type. Therefore, besides the module block definition, we only need a reference name.

We can reference our module's output values simply by recognizing that `module` is the resource type:

```
locals {
    dynamic_name = "foo-${module.rando.result}"
}
```

As you can see in the preceding code, we are referencing the `result` attribute on a module called `foo` because modules are not as descriptive of a type; therefore, it's even more important to give more detail in the reference name.

Now that we understand the basics for creating and referencing our custom modules, let's look deeper into the module design question.

Module design

In many ways, the decision to create a module in Terraform is the same as deciding to write a new method when writing in a traditional programming language such as Java or C#.

Just like in a traditional programming language, you could write all your code from start to finish in a single file using a single method, and if there were repeated parts, you would copy and paste them to repeat them.

Just like in a traditional programming language, there are reasons to write methods encapsulating repeating blocks of code. Otherwise, if you didn't encapsulate that code into a method, you'd have to copy and paste it repeatedly.

The decision about when to create a module versus just putting it in the root module is an important one. You should have good reasons for creating a module. You should always focus on value. When someone uses your module—which could be just yourself or your team—does it make their life easier by using it?

Root modules

There are many different ways to set up your root module in Terraform. The debate continues, with some vehemently advocating one method over the other. It's important to be aware of the different approaches so that you can recognize them when you see them and evaluate which approach works best for you.

Folder per environment

One common technique for structuring a root module is setting up a different folder for each environment you want to provision and maintain. In this approach, there is a folder for each long-lived environment. This folder contains a root module that can stand alone from the other environments. Consider the following folder structure:

```
/terraform
    /dev
        main.tf
        versions.tf
        variables.tf
        terraform.tfvars
    /test
        main.tf
        versions.tf
        variables.tf
        terraform.tfvars
    /prod
        main.tf
        versions.tf
        variables.tf
        terraform.tfvars
```

The preceding folder structure has three environments: dev, test, and prod. Each environment has its own root module that is completely isolated from other modules. It has its own required_ providers block and defines its own provider declarations. This approach has strong isolation between each environment—so much so that practically every aspect of the deployment could be altered from environment to environment. The version of Terraform, the version of the providers, and the version of the other modules used within the solution, the input parameters, and their values are all customized within the files within the corresponding folder for the environment.

This approach is more common where the practitioners aren't comfortable using GitFlow and maintaining other branches and following a **software development life cycle (SDLC)** where infrastructure updates are promoted from less mature-level branches (for example, develop) to more mature branches (for example, main—where production code exists).

Variable file per environment

Another technique is to maintain a single Terraform code base and multiple input variable files for each environment. This approach is focused on maintaining consistency and compatibility between environments. It is more difficult with this approach to make massive structural differences between the environments as it becomes difficult to merge changes from branch to branch.

Consider the following folder structure:

```
/terraform
    /modules
        /solution
            main.tf
            versions.tf
            variables.tf
    /env
        dev.tfvars
        test.tfvars
        prod.tfvars
    main.tf
    versions.tf
    variables.tf
    terraform.tfvars
```

As with the previous approach, where we had explicit folders for each environment, this approach still allows the same variation between environments but requires you to maintain long-lived branches for each environment as you make changes to the core structure of the root module. This aligns more with a software development process called GitFlow (more on that in *Chapter 6*).

The key characteristics of this approach are that environmental differences are captured in different input variable values stored in the corresponding .tfvars files. The goal is that any variation between the environments will eventually be stored within these files, and the code bases for each environment—stored within several long-lived source code branches—will eventually mirror each other. This allows us to have different sizes and counts in our production environment versus our development environment and maintain consistency between the architecture and configuration deployed across each environment.

Reusable modules

Now that we have our root module under control, it's time to start thinking about when to create reusable modules that can be utilized in our root modules to produce sophisticated cloud architectures that will power our applications and solutions.

Encapsulation of complexity

The number of resources you plan to encapsulate within the module is an important metric, as it can indicate if you are reducing complexity by creating a module or adding more (spoiler alert: adding more is bad). Modules can range from one resource to dozens—even hundreds—of resources. When considering the number of resources you put into your module, you should consider the value you bring when someone uses the module.

If your module only encapsulates one resource block, your code would likely be simpler by directly referencing the resource. In this situation, the module adds a layer of abstraction on top of the underlying resource you are provisioning. If that's all it's doing, then you need to reduce the complexity more to justify the creation of a module.

Suppose your module encapsulates a few tightly related resources that are highly dependent on each other and have limited integration points with other resources. For example, when creating an NSG and a collection of rules. Creating a module encapsulating these tightly coupled resources might be a good idea because it will make it easier and more concise for the developer to create an NSG. In that case, this is the sweet spot for creating a module. You are likely trading one or two additional input variables for one or two additional corresponding resource blocks. That's a good trade-off:

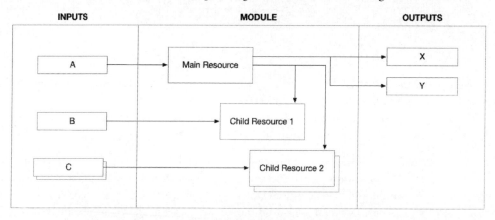

Figure 1.17 – Module design: encapsulation of complexity

The preceding diagram shows that this module is provisioning three resource types. Our module defines a single interface that will provision this cluster of resources. Some simple inputs, A and B, are passed to the main resource and child resource 1. A more complex input object, C, which happens to be an array, is passed in and used to construct a resource block for each item in the list.

Repeating patterns

Another common scenario is when you have many resources that you want to be repeated based on the size of a collection (either a list or a map). In this situation, you should tell each resource how many copies of it you want and pass in all the input variables to satisfy its requirements:

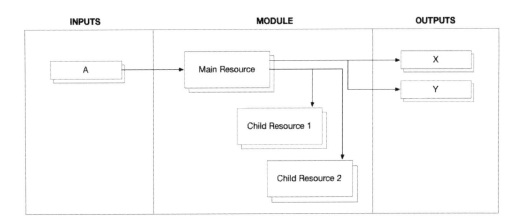

Figure 1.18 – Module design: repeating inside the module

However, if you encapsulate the repeating resources into a module, rather than repeating every resource, you repeat the module. This approach can significantly enhance the readability and maintainability of your code:

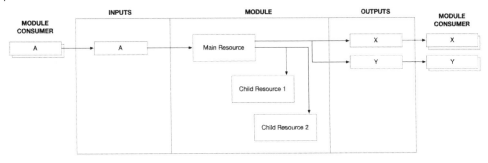

Figure 1.19 – Module design: repeating outside the module

The outside consumer of the module is responsible for introducing iteration on the module resource itself:

```
module "foo" {
  source = "../modules/rando"
  count  = 5
}
```

By applying the iterator to the module itself, we achieve the same outcome as if we adorn every resource declared in the module with a count and pass in the number of resources as an input variable to the module. However, working with every resource inside the module becomes more difficult.

When you design your module to be repeated by a parent module, your module doesn't have to think about the complexity of how many resources the parent module wants to create across all items in the collection. Each module instance only has to worry about one instance of each resource.

Does it flatten or simplify the resource in a way that can make the resource easier to use?

If you are starting from scratch, it's best to let those patterns emerge over time. The code in the method is, by its very nature, a rather opinionated piece of code. Once you identify one, all it takes is a destroy, refractor, and re-apply, and you're using your new module.

Destroying the entire environment and starting over isn't always an option. This approach can only be used in a development or testing environment. In production environments, you will need to take a different approach.

Sometimes, you can write a method you can use in many scenarios. This approach is most common when developing framework code that tackles a horizontal problem space. But sometimes methods are intended to do very particular things.

This same principle applies to Terraform module design. Some modules are highly flexible and designed in a framework, while others are more like *Hey, I want to do this specific thing, and I want to keep it simple*. With a scenario-driven module, the interface to the module will be very, very simple because it's only about shepherding dependency inputs into the module's scope that the module needs and doesn't have on its own within its scope.

A framework module typically has a much more complex interface; as a result, it will have many more levers that the module consumer can pull. Sometimes, those inputs are no longer straightforward primitive types (`string`, `bool`, `number`); they are complex objects you construct and pass in. As the number of scenarios your module supports increases, so does the complexity of your module. You have to pass in a lot more parameters to configure it. It will become much more tedious and error-prone to pass those complex objects as you may have to implement more object construction logic using local variables.

Most Terraform providers have resources that do not require you to construct complex objects to use them. You will use primitive types, sometimes collection types, and nested blocks.

However, when building modules, you do have the ability to create complex objects as input variables. You should avoid overly complex data structures because of the complexity that it adds. Frequently, the dependencies between resources are relatively small. So, if you only need small pathways to connect two objects, why create massive **data transfer objects** (**DTOs**) to pass context from one object to another? It makes the code easier to understand and easier to maintain. Future authors and your module consumers will be cursing your name, just like in poorly written traditional software.

I've seen software where there have been methods where instead of using the correct primitive types such as `bool` and `number`, everything is a string. Will that work? Sure. But does that make it easy to understand? Does that inject additional complexity, such as constantly type-casting the input values back and forth between strings into their proper type? You should use the correct type and simplify the interface.

We have to strike a balance between using complex types and having too many input variables on a module because having too many input variables affects cyclomatic complexity, making it difficult to maintain. However, unlike other languages, working with HCL is challenging when using complex objects. Developers could be more efficient when constructing and transforming large, complex data types. HCL is excellent for developers when declaring and associating resources by piping output variables into input variables.

Consuming modules

Now we understand the design considerations for when and how to design sound modules, let's look at how we can consume and manage modules, from small scenario-driven modules to strongly versioned framework modules.

Local modules

Local modules can maximize code reuse within your Terraform solutions without incurring the overhead of setting up and maintaining a separate module repository.

Using local modules for application-specific patterns, such as components or layers within your architecture, can be a great way to organize your Terraform code. One typical pattern when deploying to the cloud is active-active, multi-region deployments. In this situation, you should design the module to provision the application to a single region, and then this module should be deployed to a configurable set of regions using the count or for_each meta-argument:

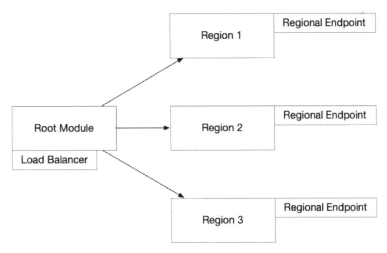

Figure 1.20 – Using Modules to encapsulate resources provisioned to a single region of a Cloud platform

With this approach, you can create load-balancing resources in the root module to distribute traffic across the regional endpoints, coupled with multiple instances of the regional deployment module in the desired number of regions.

This consumption approach is ideal when only the module is used within the current project. This scenario can manifest in layered or multi-region architectures.

Remote repositories

Using external modules is the best way to capitalize on highly reusable patterns within your architecture. Terraform allows you to reference a module that is not stored in your project's source code repository. The most common way of referencing a remote module is via a Git repository. This method works with any Git-compatible repository, from GitHub to Azure DevOps to GitLab.

Publishing your modules publicly on the open internet makes it extremely easy to reference them from any source code repository, whether public or private. However, in some enterprise scenarios, public repositories are not allowed—corporate governance may only allow private repositories. In these situations, you must select an authentication mechanism to access those modules as an end user and from within your pipelines. You can authenticate with your private, remote Terraform module repositories using an SSH key or a public access token.

Once you have secured your authentication to the Git repository that stores your modules, you must reference the module from your source code:

```
module "foo" {
    source = "git::ssh://git@ssh.dev.azure.com/v3/{AZDO_ORG}/{AZDO_
PROJECT}/{AZDO_REPO}//{MODULE_PATH}"
    }
```

The preceding examples show how you reference a specific module hosted in a Git repository on Azure DevOps. Using this approach, you will access the default branch for the Git repository, which will most likely be `main`, and it will take the latest commit from that branch—never a good idea.

The proper way is to specify a reference for a specific module version. When using the `ref` query string parameter for your Git repository URL, you can target a specific tag, branch, or commit within the Git repository:

```
module "foo" {
    source = "git::ssh://git@ssh.dev.azure.com/v3/{AZDO_ORG}/{AZDO_
PROJECT}/{AZDO_REPO}//{MODULE_PATH}?ref={AZDO_TAG}"
    }
```

Tags are the ideal method to guarantee a specific version because creating a tag within a Git repository doesn't require changing your branching strategy. Once you are done testing the module, you can push a tag and rest assured that you will always receive that exact version of the module when you specify that tag as the `ref` parameter.

Terraform registry

HashiCorp provides a mechanism for third-party module publishers to distribute their modules. This repository is accessible via `registry.terraform.io` and houses a tremendous wealth of Terraform modules in a publicly accessible, stable, and versioned environment. When you publish modules here, you must meet specific requirements to allow you and others to reference the module using a simple name and version:

```
module "caf" {
  source  = "aztfmod/caf/azurerm"
  version = "~>5.5.0"
}
```

The Terraform module registry ultimately uses GitHub under the hood, so you are referencing a module in a GitHub repository. However, it allows you to use a simplified module name and version without the additional complexity of the GitHub repository's information.

Now that we know how we can use modules to build more manageable IaC solutions and understand that modules can serve different purposes under different contexts, let's move on to understand the CLI better so that we can build automation around Terraform to integrate it with our release pipeline and CI/CD process.

Understanding how to use the CLI effectively

Now that we understand Terraform's core architecture, let's examine its CLI and how to interact with it. There are many different commands, but we'll focus on the important ones for implementing the core Terraform workflow. I'd encourage you to explore HashiCorp's documentation for some of the more obscure ones, and later in *Chapter 17*, when we discuss managing existing environments using Terraform, we'll be covering some more commands useful in that context.

init

This is an important command and probably the first one you will ever execute when working with Terraform. The reason is that Terraform works within a working directory instead of other tools that operate on a single file (such as ARM or CloudFormation) or an entry point file (such as Ansible). Terraform also relies on hidden directories to load important context about the workspace. This approach is very similar to how Git works when you clone a repository. Therefore, we must allow Terraform to set things up so that everything it needs is in the right place and makes itself at home. The `terraform init` command does just that:

```
terraform init
```

The Terraform initialize command accomplishes a few things:

- Provider installation
- Module installation
- Backend initialization

Provider installation

First, it analyzes the directory and searches for provider declarations and downloads and installs those providers. It doesn't connect to the providers, so a successful `init` process doesn't indicate that your provider credentials are good. It suggests that the providers and specific versions of those providers you specified exist, and it installs them. As an extension of Terraform, each provider is just a Golang executable that Terraform interfaces with. Therefore, Terraform needs to download and stage that executable somewhere to know where to execute it when the time comes.

Each provider's binary is downloaded and stored in the hidden directories created during the `init` process. These hidden directories and their contents enable other Terraform operations to function. Still, they are not files that need special protection, so you should not be too concerned if you delete them accidentally—or on purpose. To bring them back, one must rerun `init`, and Terraform will re-generate them as before.

Module installation

Second, it analyzes the working directory and searches for module declarations within the code base. It then downloads and installs those modules from their respective source locations. It doesn't matter if you reference modules using a relative path or a remote GitHub repository; a local copy of the module folder will be downloaded and stored in the hidden directories that Terraform uses for execution. As with the provider binaries, these module files must be there for future Terraform operations to succeed. Again, just like the provider binaries, these files do not require protection as Terraform will also bring them back with a single call to `terraform init`.

If you are developing reusable modules, you are most likely simultaneously using those modules in a root module that you use to test them. You run `terraform init` on the root module's folder, and that root module references your reusable module. It's important to note that if you change your module, simply rerunning `init` will not automatically bring in those updates. If the version of the module reference has stayed the same, Terraform will check the folder in which it loaded the modules and see that it has already downloaded that module version. To force it to download a new copy of your modules, you will need to either increment the version of the module (which can be tedious during module development) or manually clear the modules by deleting them from the `.terraform` directory.

Backend initialization

Lastly, Terraform will look for a `backend` block within the `terraform` block of your working directory's `.tf` files. Most backends require some configuration settings to work. Ultimately, a Terraform backend provides a location for the Terraform state file, so these configuration settings guide the Terraform backend on how to get to the Terraform state file.

For example, to use the ARM backend, you must specify a way to triangulate to the correct Azure Blob Storage account container state file. Terraform will pass several landmarks along the way on the journey that Terraform takes to get to the location of the desired state file: first, the resource group where the storage account lives, then the storage account where the storage container lives, then the storage container where the state file lives, and finally, the name of the state file, which Terraform locates using the `key` value and the current Terraform workspace name.

A fully populated Terraform backend configuration for Azure would use the `key` value and the current Terraform workspace name.

A fully populated Terraform backend configuration for Azure would look like this:

```
terraform {
  backend "azurerm" {
    resource_group_name   = "rg-foo"
    storage_account_name = "stfoo"
    container_name       = "tfstate"
    key                  = "foo.tfstate"
  }
}
```

The Azure backend will use `resource_group_name`, `storage_account_name`, and `container_name` to get to the place on Azure where files are stored. Then, `key` and the workspace name are used to formulate the name of the state file. If you are using the default workspace, then the name of the state file will be the value of `key`. However, if you use a named workspace, the Azure backend will generate a state file name that looks like `foo.tfstate:env:prod` for a workspace named `prod`.

Each Terraform backend plugin will have a different strategy for reading and writing state files and its logic for generating the state filename where the state is ultimately stored. Getting to know your provider, the available backend, and how to configure it is essential.

validate

`terraform validate` is a helpful method that is essentially the closest thing to a compiler. It analyzes all code files within the scope and verifies references and syntax. If there are any broken references to data sources or resources, running this command will help you find them without having to initialize your backend. As a result, the `validate` command is a helpful command to execute as an early warning to detect any problems with your code before you move on to other steps.

workspace

`terraform workspace` is about creating forks of the same Terraform solution to have different instances or forks of the Terraform state. Just like in source code, when you create a fork, the idea is that you will modify the code, and those modifications will remain long-term. Therefore, you may never merge the newly forked code base into the `main` branch.

Whether you realize it or not, you are using Terraform workspaces. You just aren't using a custom-named workspace. You can find this out by running the `terraform workspace show` command, which will say `default`.

Creating a new workspace for each long-lived environment is a good idea—even if you plan on segmenting your backend.

Running `terraform workspace new dev` will create a new workspace for your development environment. You can run the same command for your production environment, such as `terraform workspace new prod`. From then on, any Terraform operation that utilizes the state will use the state file for the selected workspace. You can change back and forth between these state files by changing the workspace like this: `terraform workspace select dev` or `terraform workspace select prod`.

With workspaces, you might create a workspace to test something out with the intent of eventually making those same updates in the original workspace.

Workspaces represent utterly different environments because the dev environment will always differ slightly from the test, staging, or production environments. These environments will live in isolated workspaces and have the same isolation within their state file.

The common thread is that the workspaces work off the same code base. The idea is that you will have the same code base and deploy multiple environments with it—most likely long-lived environments, but not necessarily so.

plan

`terraform plan` is a read-only operation that requires access to your backend state and requires you to have executed `terraform init` prior. Also, if you use a non-default workspace, you should select your workspace before you run `plan`. `terraform workspace select` allows you to do that.

`terraform plan` will perform a read-only operation, checking the state file and checking in with every resource in the state file. This process can take a while, depending on how many resources are in your state file and how long it takes for the provider to get a response from whoever it's talking to. So, to keep your Terraform projects lean and fast, consider how much scope you want to keep within a single Terraform workspace.

You may consider splitting those chunks into sub-workspaces if it's too big. I've seen projects where an entire solution is in one Terraform state file, and it takes 45 minutes to run a plan. Having too broad workspace isolation can be extremely painful, and I would highly advise you to consider the boundaries of the components of your system and organize your Terraform workspaces so that you have smaller, semi-dependent workspaces. It's okay to have dependencies between workspaces. Still, you need to call out those dependencies using data sources so that you don't get into a situation where you can make a circular reference between two Terraform workspaces.

Terraform needs you to set all your input variables before you can run the `plan` operation. You can do this in three ways: through an individual command-line argument, a variable file, and environment variables.

An **individual command-line argument** is helpful for small projects with interactive command-line sessions. Still, it quickly becomes unmanageable when the environment grows more complex or you want to use a pipeline tool—a scenario on which we will spend the bulk of this book.

The **environment variable** approach is instrumental in the pipeline tool approach because it allows you to execute Terraform commands without modifying the arguments to the command you run.

apply

`terraform apply` is the most crucial operation in the arsenal. Before execution, this command requires `terraform init` to have been executed successfully. Selecting the correct workspace corresponding to the input parameters you specify will also be essential.

`terraform apply` is also unique compared to other operations: you can execute it by pointing at a single file rather than a working directory. The `terraform plan` command outputs the plan file. If a plan file is not specified, `terraform apply` will execute a plan before the `apply` stage.

It is best practice to execute `apply` by always passing in a plan file. Doing so will ensure that you don't have any surprises when you execute. However, there is still a chance that something changed in the environment between when you last ran `plan` and when you finally executed `apply`.

This is particularly important when working on a team of multiple people that might be introducing change to the environment, either using Terraform locally or through a CI/CD pipeline. Changes could also be introduced outside of Terraform through manual changes within the cloud platform's management portal. Using a Terraform plan file when you run `terraform apply` will help keep the plan you execute exactly how you intended with the best information available at the time of provisioning.

As with `plan`, input variables can set their values in many ways.

destroy

`terraform destroy` is how you can completely eradicate your entire environment. The ability to do so is advantageous when your solution spans multiple logical groups within the target platform or when using multiple providers.

Logical container deletion

Some platforms make it easy to manage the life cycle of related resources. For example, Microsoft Azure resources every resource to be provisioned within a resource group, and on **Google Cloud Platform** (**GCP**), every resource is provisioned within the context of a project. The Azure resource group and Google Cloud project are logical containers you can use to clean up after yourself quickly with a cascading delete operation. Platforms that lack this feature can make it extremely tedious to clean up after yourself, such as in AWS, where you must navigate to many different portal pages to ensure you delete everything. Savvy command-line power users can string together their clean-up scripts using a well-planned tagging scheme. Still, tools such as Terraform add a lot of value in just being able to delete every resource you provisioned with a single command.

Cross-platform deletion

Even on cloud platforms with logical containers, to collectively manage the life cycle of related resources, you still need help with associated resources that you provision in tangential systems or platforms.

Summary

In this chapter, we took an in-depth look at Terraform's architecture. We primarily focused on two critical architectural components: state and modularity. Having a sound understanding of Terraform's architecture is vital for you to be able to use Terraform to its fullest effectively. Finally, we ended by looking at Terraform's CLI, which will enable you to, when you're ready, integrate Terraform with your own CI/CD pipelines. In the next chapter, we will explore HCL so that we can lay the foundation on which we can start building IaC using Terraform.

2

Using HashiCorp Configuration Language

In the first chapter, we examined Terraform's architecture. It is a simple command-line tool that takes in code and creates a plan that it can later execute at the user's behest. In this chapter, we will examine how to leverage Terraform's language—**HashiCorp Configuration Language** (HCL)—to define infrastructure as code so that we can build sophisticated cloud-based architectures using Terraform.

The chapter covers the following topics:

- Resources and data sources
- Locals and types
- Variables and outputs
- Meta arguments
- Loops and iterations
- Expressions
- Functions

Resources and data sources

Resources and data sources play a critical role in Terraform and are probably the most important language constructs to understand as they allow you to access existing and create new resources.

Resources

Resources are the most common block that you use when coding in HCL. The `resource` block is what Terraform is all about. You can think of each resource as a digital twin of something Terraform will provision in the real world:

```
resource "random_string" "foobar" {
  length  = 4
  upper   = false
  special = false
}
```

A block's definition has three parts: the **block type**, the **resource type**, and the **reference name**. In the preceding example, the block type is `resource`, the resource type is `random_string`, and the reference name is `foobar`. To create dependencies between resources, we use the reference name and type to access output values from the resource:

```
resource "azurerm_resource_group" "foobar" {
  name     = "rg-${random_string.foobar.result}"
  location = var.location
}
```

In the preceding code, we create an Azure resource group by referencing the `foobar` random string's output value, `result`.

Each resource within a Terraform provider is a tiny semi-independent computer program designed to manage a particular underlying system architecture. These resources define a schema that allows you to control the configuration of those underlying components. Sometimes, this schema is straightforward; at other times, it can be very complex, composed of primitive type attributes and additional custom block definitions nested within the resource block.

These nested blocks allow you to declare one or more sub-resources within a resource. The resource dictates the number of each type of nested block it expects. Sometimes, resources allow many instances of the same nested block, while at other times, they may allow precisely one.

For example, the Azure Cosmos DB service allows you to create hyper-scale NoSQL databases and quickly set up replication across multiple geo-locations. Each geo-location is a nested block within the Cosmos DB `resource` block:

```
resource "azurerm_cosmosdb_account" "db" {

  name                = "cosmos-foobar"
  location            = azurerm_resource_group.foobar.location
  resource_group_name = azurerm_resource_group.foobar.name
  offer_type          = "Standard"
  kind                = "MongoDB"
```

```
    consistency_policy {
      consistency_level = "Eventual"
    }

    geo_location {
      location            = "westus"
      failover_priority = 0
    }

    geo_location {
      location            = "eastus"
      failover_priority = 1
    }


  }
```

As you can see, the geo_location block is repeated multiple times within the azurerm_
cosmosdb_account block. Each instance of the geo_location nested block tells this Cosmos
DB account where to replicate the MongoDB databases and the failover priority.

Data sources

In its most primitive form, Terraform is about provisioning resources, but as we saw, there is a lot
more to it than that. Once Terraform provisions the resources, then what? What happens when you
provision a resource by some other means? Can you still reference it from Terraform? Resources create
something new. Data sources access something that already exists.

Data sources are less prolific but still play a critical role. First, they allow you to reference resources
provisioned outside the current Terraform workspace no matter how they were provisioned—through
a GUI, another automation tool, or another Terraform workspace:

```
data "azurerm_resource_group" "bar" {
  name     = "rg-foo"
  location = "westus"
}
```

Like the resource, a data source block's definition has three parts: the block type, the resource type, and the reference name. In the preceding example, the block type is `data`, the resource type is `azurerm_resource_group`, and the reference name is `bar`. To create dependencies between resources and data sources, we use the reference name and type to access output values from the data source just like we did with a resource, but we also need to prefix the reference with `data` to clarify to Terraform whether this reference is to a new item or an existing one:

```
resource "azurerm_storage_account" "fizzbuzz" {
name                        = "stfizzbuzz"
resource_group_name         = data.azurerm_resource_group.bar.name
location                    = data.azurerm_resource_group.bar.location
account_tier                = "Standard"
account_replication_type = "GRS"
}
```

In the preceding code, we create an Azure Storage account by referencing the `bar` Azure resource group's output values: `name` and `location`.

Now that we understand the core components that Terraform is responsible for (resources and data sources—something new and something old), let's look at the data types we will use for internal and external data structures.

Locals and types

After resources and data sources, the next most important thing to be familiar with is how to work with locals, which allow us to create internal variables and types that allow us to manipulate data within our Terraform solution.

Locals

Terraform allows you to perform sophisticated operations on a variety of types. Sometimes, it's necessary to use intermediate values that store a calculated value you can reference across your code base. It's essential to understand how to do this, and what data types are available when working with internal data inside a module and when defining the contract between your Terraform modules.

The `locals` block allows you to declare local variables. You can think of these as member variables in a class or local variables in a function, except they merge into one construct within the flattened scope of a Terraform workspace.

You can define a local variable anywhere in your HCL code simply by declaring a `locals` block and declaring and defining a local variable within it. You must specify a value when declaring a local variable:

```
locals {
  foo = "bar"
}
```

The preceding code declares a local variable called `foo`. Terraform infers the type to be `string` simply by the use of double quotes.

You can declare as many `locals` blocks as you want in any `.tf` file. As in other languages, you can nest local variables inside the value of other local variables. You can do this by using the `local` object prefix. Using the element's type to reference it from elsewhere in the code is similar to referencing resources and data sources:

```
locals {
  foo = "foo"
  bar = "bar"
  foobar = "${local.foo}${local.bar}"
}
```

It can be tricky to remember, but locals are always declared in a plural block name (`locals` versus `local`) and referenced in the singular, `local.*`. The mixture of singular and plural terminology can seem strange as most other blocks in Terraform are declared in a singular block and referenced in the singular.

Primitive types

By design, HCL supports a limited number of data types. This design encourages simplicity in your code and avoids overly complex logic around type conversion. In principle, you should avoid doing complex logic in HCL and rely on the consistent input-output model ingrained into Terraform's modular architecture to do any heavy lifting outside of Terraform and pass in a known good value as input in one of the supported types.

There are only three primitive types: `string`, `number`, and `bool`.

String

While there are `number` and `bool`, their use or function is not very complicated. However, `string` can become very difficult very quickly. If you go spelunking in GitHub for HCL code, you will see a predisposition for complex string manipulation operations embedded in the code. Just because you can doesn't mean you should. This is the way.

Avoid complex string manipulation where possible, and when it is necessary, encapsulate it into a local value so that it can be easily output for testing purposes before you run `apply`.

String interpolation

String interpolation is a pervasive operation, but try to avoid it where possible. Avoid using a complex expression when you can pass in a reference to a single `string` object:

```
resource "aws_vpc" "main" {
  cidr_block       = "10.0.0.0/16"

  tags {
    Name = "${var.application_name}-${var.environment_name}"
  }
}
```

In the preceding example, we pass in two variables and concatenate them to construct the Name tag, commonly used by the AWS console:

```
locals {
    name = "${var.application_name}-${var.environment_name}"
}
```

Alternatively, we can declare a local that constructs the name and directly sets the tag with the value of the local:

```
resource "aws_vpc" "main" {
    cidr_block        = "10.0.0.0/16"

    tags {
        Name = local.name
    }
}
```

It simplifies our resource block for the AWS VPC by eliminating the string interpolation syntax (consisting of two double quotes, ", and two interpolation blocks, ${ ... }). It also creates a reusable local that we can use to tag our resources consistently. This can improve the readability and, ultimately, the maintainability of the code, especially if the string needs to be reused across multiple resources.

A string that spans multiple lines

Depending on the provider and resource you use, sometimes you must embed large strings spanning multiple lines. Terraform uses a heredoc style of declaring multi-line strings:

```
locals {

    shopping_list = <<EOT
apples
oranges
grapes
bananas
EOT

}
```

String content can be structured or unstructured. If HCL supports the structure of your string, you should consider using native syntax to represent the content. The most common cases of structured content embedded in HCL are JSON or YAML formatted strings because many cloud platforms have services that define their configuration schema that you must supply in either of these two formats. In this case, you should use the jsonencode or yamlencode functions to convert objects declared in native HCL into the appropriately formatted string. More on this later in this chapter.

Another consideration is if there is an excellent reason to maintain the content in its original string format. Here are a couple of situations where this might be the case:

- **Too large**: If the content is substantial and thus quite laborious to convert into HCL, it may not be cost-effective to do the conversion.

- **Reusable artifact**: If you are trying to share the content between two tools, you'll want to maintain it in the original format (either JSON or YAML). Keeping two copies of the same configuration in HCL and one in the original format won't make sense. In this situation, you can have both tools use the same content—in its original form—by having Terraform reference the content from a file using the `file` function.

Collection types

HCL supports only two collection types: `list` and `map`.

List

If you have done any development before working with Terraform or programming with HCL, you will no doubt be familiar with the concept of an array. Every programming language uses different syntaxes, types, and classes to represent this concept. A **list** is an ordered list of objects where items in that list can be accessed using the index of the desired item:

- **C# and Java**:   `string[] array = { "westus", "eastus" }`
- **Go**:   `array := [4]string{"westus", "eastus"}`
- **Python**:   `array = ["westus", "eastus"]`
- **JavaScript**:   `var array = ["westus", "eastus"];`
- **HCL**:   `array = ["westus", "eastus"]`

Notice any similarities with any of the languages we've looked at? Python is the clear winner in the similarity contest. JavaScript is a close second—simply with some extra semi-colons and such.

As might be expected, items contained within an HCL list are accessed similarly across all of these languages:

```
a = array[1]
```

The value of a would be `eastus`.

The `list` object type is fantastic for situations where we want to provision a corresponding resource for each item in the list.

Map

Like the concept of an array, a map in HCL corresponds to another prevalent collection type that goes by many names in other programming languages. From `Dictionary` to `KeyValuePair` and back to `map`. They all share this concept of a key—guaranteed unique within the collection—and associated with a corresponding value. To look up the value, you don't access it with its index within the collection; you can access it with the `key` value:

```
networks = {
  "westus" = "10.0.0.0/16"
  "eastus" = "10.1.0.0/16"
}
```

When we want to access the value for the particular network, we specify the region name we are using:

```
a = networks["westus"]
```

The value of a would be `10.1.0.0/16`.

This solution only works when the collection's key is unique. In the preceding example, this allows us to quickly set up one network for every region we choose; however, with the current design, we cannot do that if we want to set up two networks for the same region:

```
networks = {
  "westus" = "10.0.0.0/16"
  "eastus" = "10.1.0.0/16"
  "eastus" = "10.2.0.0/16"
}
```

We can't because adding a second entry for any region would produce an error. The error would be subtle. When we attempted to access `eastus` values in our map, only their last matching entry would come back. Therefore, it is the same as if `10.1.0.0/16` did not exist. Having such a discrepancy in your code and what Terraform provisions can lead to confusion and misaligned expectations, so remember that when working with `map`, you should reserve it for situations where the key is unique.

Complex objects

HCL is not object-oriented; therefore, it does not have a mechanism for defining classes like other languages that represent complex types. However, it does support complex objects. It uses dynamic types, meaning Terraform will evaluate the object's type at runtime.

Dynamic typing can be a blessing and a curse. It is a blessing because we don't have to conform to strict structures of objects. If we need another attribute, we can quickly add it. It is a curse because it means we need an official source of truth for how the object should be structured, and we'll have to rely on reference tracing when refactoring the structure of objects passed from one module or resource to another:

```
network_config = {
  name    = "westus"
  network = "10.0.0.0/16"
}
```

Defining an object is as simple as declaring the object reference and setting it to the value of a block—as indicated by the { and } symbols. This block can contain any number of primitive types, collections, or complex objects.

Now that we understand the data types that Terraform recognizes and how to use them to construct internal `local` variables, we can look externally to see how we can define the data contract between our module and the outside world: its inputs and outputs.

Inputs and outputs

Next, let's look at how to get data into and out of Terraform using input variables and outputs.

Inputs

As we learned in the previous chapter, Terraform operates within the context of a module. That module is scoped physically within a directory. The **root module** is a special case where its directory is the same as Terraform's working directory. Whenever you are writing HCL, you are writing within the context of a module, whether the root module or some other module; therefore, you need to consider how to get data into your module and how to get data out of it.

Input variables are an essential design consideration because Terraform modules are simple machines that take inputs and produce outputs.

The input is all about what information the module needs to provision itself, and those inputs can come from wherever. As you design inputs, they should be atomic.

The module should be able to take the input without any additional manipulation or logic to parse the input variable's value. You should parse the value outside of the module. That doesn't mean that inputs can't be complex objects or collections, but keeping the interface as simple as possible is a good idea. The more complex your inputs are, the more complex your module will be—whether it's your root module or reusable modules that you share across workspaces.

Your root module will likely have the most complex inputs. Consider your input's structure for root modules based on how you inject the parameter into the variable. If you use a variable file written in HCL, using complex types that span multiple lines, whether a list, a map, or a complex object, is effortless. However, suppose you plan to use a **Linux environment variable** or command-line argument method to pass in the parameter. In that case, you should reconsider using complex objects as inputs, as they can be challenging to troubleshoot and verify that you are getting the correct value into that input.

When you use Linux environment variables, it's important to remember they are not very good at storing structured data with complex schema. The most complex schema you see in a Linux environment variable is some delimited text. PATH is an excellent example of this, as it is a delimited text value. You could use a delimited text value as an input variable to simplify injecting the value. The downside is that you'll have to parse the value after you get it into Terraform.

In the case of a root module, this could be desirable because it reduces the complexity of the interface of the two tools: Terraform and other executables. This sort of integration is widespread within automation pipelines where separate pipeline tasks execute different tools, and you pipe the output from one tool into the inputs of the other. Passing values into Terraform from the command-line interface is similar to how we pipe the outputs of one module into the inputs of another module. However, this is more seamless within Terraform because HCL can be used to transfer the value. In contrast, with command-line tools, you would need additional parsing steps to transform the value into the desired format for Terraform to consume quickly:

```
variable "foo" {
    type        = string
    description = "This is the value for foo. It is needed because
'reasons'. Its value must be less than 6 characters."
    }
```

In the preceding code, we declare an input variable, foo, with a type of string and provide some guidance to the user of our module on how to use this input variable within description.

Sensitive data

Sometimes, you may need to input sensitive data such as a password, connection string, or access key. You must annotate your input variables to ensure that Terraform knows not to display them in its output, as this can lead to secret leakage through the operational logs that Terraform emits:

```
variable "super_secret_password" {
    type        = string
    description = "Password that I get from somewhere else"
    sensitive   = true
}
```

In the preceding code, we are annotating our super secret password with the sensitive attribute to prevent this secret from being output by Terraform.

Optional

When building modules that can support many scenarios, you will often need to provide input variables to support the data needs of each scenario. Each supported scenario may only require a subset of the input variables to be specified. In this situation, we should make our input variable optional.

For primitive types, you can accomplish this quite simply by setting the default value to `null`:

```
variable "totally_optional_field" {
  type        = string
  description = "Yes, No, or Maybe"
  default     = null
}
```

In the preceding code, we set `default` to `null`, allowing the user to ignore this input variable completely.

Setting an input variable to be optional can be more complicated when working with complex objects, as we may want the entire object or its attributes to be optional.

Consider the following code:

```
variable "person" {
  type = object({
    first_name  = string
    middle_name = string
    last_name   = string
  })
}
```

In the preceding code, we declare a variable called `person`. Unfortunately, not only is it a non-optional input variable, but every attribute on the `person` object needs to be specified.

Let's see whether we can loosen things up:

```
variable "person" {
  type = object({
    first_name  = string
    middle_name = optional(string)
    last_name   = string
  })
  default = null
}
```

In the preceding code, notice that adding `default = null` on the `person` variable block allows users of this module to ignore this input variable completely. Additionally, if the user supplies a `person` object, the `middle_name` attribute is not required. Now, the supported inputs are much more flexible for the user.

The following value sets the entire object to `null`:

```
person = null
```

The following value sets the input variable to an object but omits the `middle_name` attribute:

```
person = {
  first_name = "Keyser"
  last_name  = "Söze"
}
```

Lastly, we set the input variable to an object and specify values for all attributes:

```
person = {
  first_name  = "Keyser"
  middle_name = ""
  last_name   = "Söze"
}
```

Thanks to the inclusion of `default` and `optional` within our input variable declaration, all are equally valid parameter values for our module.

Validation

When creating modules you will use more broadly in your organization, consider adding some basic validations to your modules' inputs. The `validation` block provides a way to add primitive data validation on incoming input variable values.

Adding validation can significantly reduce apply-time failures that can plague your user if an input value has requirements from the underlying provider that may not be evident through your module's interface. For example, a cloud platform may impose naming conventions on resources such as alpha-numeric only, all lowercase, less than 30 characters, and so on. Unless the consumer of your module is aware of the platform-specific constraints, they could encounter difficulties using your module as they attempt to figure out how to get the correct set of values as inputs—especially if your module abstracts the underlying cloud platform's resources in any way:

```
variable "name" {
  type        = string
  description = "Name of the thing"

  validation {
    condition     = length(name) < 30
    error_message = "Length of name must be less than 30"
  }
}
```

In the preceding code, we specify a condition that checks that the length of the input variable is less than 30. We could use any valid Boolean expression. We are good if it returns either `true` or `false`. We can use any number of functions that Terraform supports. However, prior to version 1.9.0 of Terraform, we can only reference the variable that the `validation` block lives on—meaning, we can't reference other variables to create complex multi-variable input validation, nor can we make validation conditional on other elements declared within Terraform, be they other variables, resources, data sources, locals, or otherwise. This all changed in version 1.9.0 of Terraform, where input variable validation was opened up to referencing other blocks within the module. This allows you to implement much more sophisticated validation using locals and data sources that might be useful to verify inputs.

Outputs

Output variables are an essential consideration as well. It's crucial to only output values that you will need. You should avoid putting unnecessary outputs—this is a pretty easy rule to follow within the root module. Still, when authoring reusable modules, it becomes more difficult because it is harder to predict what the consumer of your module will need:

```
output "foo" {
  value       = "bar"
  description = "This is my output for foo"
}
```

In the preceding code, we declare an output called `foo` that returns a constant value of `bar`. While this example could be more practical, its simplicity will be instructive. Namely, that output values can be any valid expression in HCL. I draw your attention to this because you will no doubt encounter dozens of examples that output an attribute on a resource, but the output block is much more potent than that. Coupled with all the tools available within HCL—many that we'll get into later in this chapter—you can construct any value you need. Knowledge of this capability is crucial in enabling you to smooth the edges between how you integrate Terraform and other tools.

It is a good practice to annotate your outputs with a `description` attribute to inform the consumer of your module (whether it is a user using your module via the command-line tool or from within another Terraform module) of what you intend the output to be and its purpose and what type of data they can expect.

Sensitive data

Sometimes, you may need to output sensitive data such as a password, connection string, or access key. Most resources will define which attributes are considered sensitive, so Terraform will warn you if necessary:

```
output "super_secret_password" {
  value        = "NewEnglandClamChowder"
  is_sensitive = true
}
```

In the preceding code, we annotate our super secret password with the `is_sensitive` attribute to inform Terraform that this is not data that we would like it to shout to the world from the rooftops!

Now that we understand how to declare inputs and outputs within our Terraform modules and the basic structures—resources, data sources, and locals—that we work with so frequently, we are ready to move on to some more complex structures in the language. Our first stop is meta-arguments. Sounds fun, right?

Meta-arguments

Meta-arguments are attributes that you can set on any resource block. They allow you to control different aspects of the resource related to its context, dependencies, and lifecycle. Each meta-argument enables finer-grained control over that resource by allowing the developer to give very focused resource-specific instructions to Terraform.

Provider

The `provider` meta-argument is a reference that allows you to specify under which provider context you would like to deploy the resource. The scope of the context is dependent on the provider you are using. The two most common scopes are which region you are deploying to within a public cloud and what authentication credential you are using.

You will need to understand the specific scoping mechanism of your providers. This book will use the `aws`, `azurerm`, and `google` providers. Each provider defines its scope differently. The scope of the AWS provider is an AWS account and an AWS Region. The scope for the GCP provider is a GCP project and a GCP region. The Azure provider is scoped only to an Azure subscription:

```
provider "aws" {
  region = "us-east-1"
}

provider "aws" {
  alias  = "secondary"
  region = "us-west-1"
}
```

Then, when attaching to resources, if you do not specify the `provider` meta-argument, all the resources you declare will be provisioned by Terraform using the default `aws` provider:

```
resource "aws_instance" "foo" {

}
```

When you want to provision to the `secondary` instance of the `aws` provider, you will need to declare it using the `provider` meta-argument on the `resource` block itself:

```
resource "aws_instance" "bar" {

  provider = aws.secondary

}
```

Therefore, when using AWS and GCP to do multi-region deployments, you will see the `provider` meta-argument to provision resources to different AWS and GCP regions. However, on Azure, you'll only see the `provider` meta-argument to provision across multiple subscriptions—a very exotic deployment type.

Depends on

Sometimes, when Terraform is planning, it needs help to get the dependency graph right. That's because Terraform can only detect explicit dependencies—but sometimes, you can have implicit dependencies, depending on the provider and the resource within that provider. These implicit dependencies occur when a resource requires another, but there is no direct relationship between the resources:

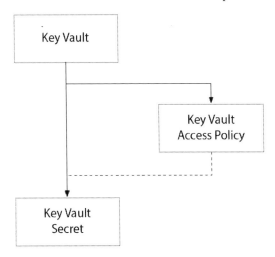

Figure 2.1 – Implicit dependency between the Key Vault secret and Key Vault access policy

A great example is whenever you use Azure Key Vault. You need permissions within the key vault itself before creating secrets. Therefore, by default, the identity running Terraform does not have access to create secrets within the key vault it just created:

```
resource "azurerm_key_vault" "top_secret" {
  name       = "kv-top-secret"
```

```
    sku_name = "standard"
}

resource "azurerm_key_vault_secret" "foo" {
  name         = "foo"
  value        = "bar"
  key_vault_id = azurerm_key_vault.top_secret.id
}
```

The preceding code will fail. You need to explicitly grant the identity that Terraform is running under access to Key Vault to create secrets. You can do this by adding an **access policy resource**:

```
data "azurerm_client_config" "current" {}

resource "azurerm_key_vault_access_policy" "terraform" {
  key_vault_id = azurerm_key_vault.top_secret.id
  tenant_id    = data.azurerm_client_config.current.tenant_id
  object_id    = data.azurerm_client_config.current.object_id

  secret_permissions = [
    "Get", "List", "Set"        ]
}
```

Unfortunately, after adding this access policy resource, my code still won't work. When I run `apply`, it will tell in my code! Because there is no explicit dependency between the secret and the access policy, Terraform thinks that both can be created in parallel—thus creating a race condition that will inevitably fail when Terraform attempts to make the secret.

Therefore, we need to make sure that we define the dependency of the secret on the access policy so that Terraform knows that it needs to create the access policy before we attempt to create the secret:

```
resource "azurerm_key_vault_secret" "foo" {
  name         = "foo"
  value        = "bar"
  key_vault_id = azurerm_key_vault.top_secret.id

  depends_on = [azurerm_key_vault_access_policy.terraform]
}
```

By explicitly declaring the dependency between the secret and the access policy, we will solve the problem in our Terraform plan that creates a race condition between them.

Lifecycle

The `lifecycle` meta-argument is a block that can appear on any resource block and is used to alter the control of that resource's—well—lifecycle. That is the resource's creation and deletion—the birth and death. Each option allows you to handle edge cases where you want Terraform to behave differently than usual.

Create before destroy

This situation reminds me of that classic movie scene from *Indiana Jones and the Raiders of the Lost Ark*, where Indy is in a booby-trapped Peruvian temple. To acquire the golden statue, he must replace it with something. First, Indy has to create a bag of dirt to replace the golden statue. Then, he must delicately replace the golden statue with it. The situation that our hero, Indy, finds himself in is the essence of `create_before_destroy`. In these situations, you need the new thing before you get rid of the old. There are many examples of this scenario. It can apply to certificates, security groups, and the like.

Lock resources

For some resources, you don't want to take the chance that a less-than-careful administrator will blow them away without thoroughly analyzing `terraform plan`—an unfortunately common occurrence. This situation is where `prevent_destroy` comes into play. By adding this meta-argument to your resources, you are adding yet another gate that the user must explicitly remove before they can destroy the resource. Many cloud services natively support this feature, but not all. Therefore, Terraform allows you to enable this feature within your HCL code on any resource vital to the environment's health or may contain stateful data that you would lose in the case of destruction.

Ignore changes

Sometimes, Terraform is one of many tools that operate in an environment, or you want to allow manual administration of a particular feature after deployment. In this case, the `ignore_changes` option will enable you to provision the resource with Terraform but ignore changes made outside of Terraform:

```
lifecycle {
  ignore_changes = [
    tags
  ]
}
```

Ignore changes is an array of object references relative to the `resource` block you defined. You can imagine `this` before any reference within the list. You will get an error if you attempt to reference an external resource.

Replace triggered by

Many Terraform resources already know what circumstances should cause Terraform to trigger a replacement. The cause is usually a change in the value of a critical attribute. However, sometimes, there are situations where you want Terraform to replace the resource when another resource is updated or replaced. Often, this can happen when there is no direct dependency between the resources, making it difficult for Terraform to determine that a destructive action is taking place.

For example, with an Azure Virtual Desktop host pool, the host pool and its **virtual machines** (**VMs**) are declared independently. Still, they are associated with a third resource called a VM extension that will initiate the joining of the VM with the host pool. In this scenario, Terraform knows about the VM's relationship with the VM extension and the VM extension's relationship with the host pool. Still, because you create the host pool's relationship with the VM through an attribute in the VM extension, it does not cause a replacement if it is updated. Therefore, the VM will never be reattached to the host pool if it changes:

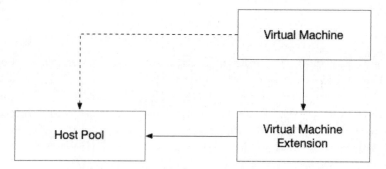

Figure 2.2 – Implicit dependency between the host pool and VM prevents
Terraform from replacing the VM if the host pool changes

Now that we understand how to modify Terraform's default behavior using meta-arguments, we can handle better edge cases specific to the cloud resources we plan on provisioning with whatever providers we want to use. Now, it's time to scale things up by learning to turn Terraform into a resource factory—pumping out complex configurations without all the copypasta!

Loops and iterations

There are three different ways to iterate within HCL. The most common are two meta-arguments, `for_each` and `count`, which operate on a resource, module, or data source block. At the same time, the third option uses the `for` expression, which operations on any collection.

Count

The `count` meta-argument is Terraform's oldest method of iterating resources: an oldie but a goodie. The `count` meta-argument is excellent when you want to provision the same block multiple times and have no unique identifier to key off of. In this situation, you will use the item's index in a list to determine its uniqueness. This approach can pose challenges in the future if the items in the list need to change in such a way that would cause the indices of each item to change.

The best way to manage this is to treat your list as append-only, as this will avoid replacing related resources. Adding or removing items from the middle of the list will cause all the items below that item to shift their index, resulting in destruction and recreation.

For example, if you want to provision a five-node cluster, you wouldn't remove a specific node from the cluster when you scale down. You would reduce the number of nodes. You don't care which nodes get removed. You only care how many there are. In this situation, it is ideal to use `count`:

```
resource "aws_instance" "node" {

  count = var.node_count

  # the rest of the configuration

}
```

For each

An alternative to `count` is the `for_each` meta-argument, which allows you to create multiple blocks from a map collection. This approach can be a distinct improvement over the `count` technique because the order of the items in the collection does not matter—only the key. If you update the code to remove the key, Terraform will remove the corresponding item. If the item changes order with other items in the collection, it will not affect Terraform's plan.

This approach is only possible with a map collection as the source of the iteration because, with a map collection type, each item must have a key that uniquely identifies it amongst its peers.

As a result, using `for_each` works well when deploying to multiple regions as, typically, you wouldn't have more than one deployment in the same region; hence, the region name makes an excellent unique key for the map that drives the `for_each` loop. You can add or remove regions without worrying about shifting the index of the items in the collection:

```
locals {

  regions = {
    westus = {
      node_count = 5
```

```
      }
      eastus = {
        node_count = 8
      }
    }

  }
```

Consider the preceding `map` configuration. Using this as the collection, we can drive any number of resources, data sources, or modules:

```
module "regional_deployment" {

  for_each = local.regions

  node_count = each.value.node_count

  # the rest of the configuration

}
```

In the preceding code, we see that we are setting the `for_each` source to be the map stored in `local.regions`. We then can use the `each` prefix anywhere within the module block to access either the key or the value using `each.key` and `each.value`, respectively. No matter the value's type, we can address it how we normally would, using `each.value` as a reference to the object.

For expressions

The `for` expression is a way of iterating within Terraform that does not require you to attach it to a block (i.e., resource, data source, or module). You can use the `for` expression to construct in-memory objects to apply object transformations to streamline block-based iteration or for output.

Iterating over a list

When iterating over a `list`, you must specify only one parameter to the `for` expression. This parameter will represent each item within your `list` so that you can access each item within the output block:

```
region_names_list = [
for s in var.regions :
upper("${s.region}${s.country}")]
```

In the preceding example, we are iterating over all the objects in `var.regions`. As we do, during each iteration, the current value is accessible in the `s` parameter. We can use the output block to generate any object we desire to be created in the new list that this `for` expression will create.

Iterating over a map

When iterating over a map, you must change how you structure your `for` expression. You must specify two instead of one parameter declared immediately after the `for` keyword:

```
region_array_from_map = [
  for k, v in var.regions :
  {
    region        = k,
    address_space = v.address_space
    node_count    = v.node_count
  }
]
```

In the preceding example, you'll see that we specify two parameters for the `for` expression: k and v. We chose these names as a convention to help us remember what these variables mean within the scope of the `for` expression. k represents the map's key, while v represents the value. The value can be any type, be it a primitive, collection, or complex object. If we want to access the `value` object, we access it based on its type. In this example, the value is a complex object with two attributes. In the `for` expression's output block, we specify the structure of the object we want each item in the resulting array to have.

In this case, we are creating an array of objects with three attributes: `region`, `address_space`, and `node_count`, essentially flattening the original map into an array of objects. The output looks like this:

```
region_array_from_map = [
  {
    "address_space" = "10.0.1.0/24"
    "node_count" = 5
    "region" = "eastus"
  },
  {
    "address_space" = "10.0.0.0/24"
    "node_count" = 8
    "region" = "westus"
  },
]
```

Outputting a list

The `for` expression will always output either a `list` or an object. You can select the output type you want by the character in which you wrap the `for` block. If you wrap the `for` expression in square brackets, then the expression will output a `list`:

```
region_list = [for s in var.regions : "${s.region}${s.country}"]
```

The preceding `for` expression will produce the following output:

```
region_list = [
  "westus",
  "eastus",
]
```

Sometimes, the names of the module or resource outputs don't align precisely with other resources' desired inputs. Therefore, using a `for` expression and outputting a list can help transform these incongruent output values into a format convenient for consumption within another part of your code.

Outputting an object

Wrapping the `for` expression with curly braces will output an object:

```
locals {
  region_config_object = {
    for s in var.regions : "${s.region}${s.country}" =>
    {
      node_count = s.node_count
    }
  }
}
```

This approach will output an object with attributes for each item in the list of regions in the `regions` input variable. Each attribute will take the name of the concatenation of the region and country names, and its value will be an object with a single attribute called `node_count`. The output will look like this:

```
region_config_object = {
  "eastus" = {
    "node_count" = 8
  }
  "westus" = {
    "node_count" = 8
  }
}
```

Outputting an object can be very useful in scenarios where you need to generate a JSON or YAML payload. You can reference this payload in another resource or output it so another tool can extract that value from Terraform using the `terraform output` command.

Converting a list to a map

One common problem is converting a list into a map. This is needed because, while a list is sometimes the most concise way of storing a simple collection, it cannot be used with the `for_each` iterator.

Therefore, if you want to have your cake and eat it too, you need to convert that list into a map. This can be done with a simple `for` expression that iterates over the list in memory and outputs a map:

```
locals {
  foo_list = ["A", "B", "C"]

  foo_map = {
    for idx, element in local.foo_list : element => idx
  }
}
```

In the preceding code, we are invoking the `for` expression and outputting an object using curly braces ({ }). We are taking each element within the list and setting it as the key of our `map` and taking the element's index within the `list` and setting it as the value. It's important to note that this will only work when the items in the `list` are not duplicates.

Now that we know how to loop, swoop, iterate, and cross-mojinate, we can avoid the pitfalls of copypasta by leveraging Terraform's three extremely powerful iterators—`count`, `for_each`, and `for`—to build dynamic collections of resources, data sources, or anything really!

We are nearing the end of our journey into the depths of HCL. Next, we will look at a few more language expressions that help us cope when we want to use dynamic collections and conditional logic to jazz up our modules!

Expressions

The HCL has some unique expressions to handle complex scenarios such as conditional logic, referencing dynamic types, and iterating nested blocks. We will learn about these final language structures before we delve into the library of functions available to us within the language.

Conditional expressions

In other languages, this technique is called a ternary conditional operator—namely, of the imperative variety. That's fancy talk for an `if` statement in HCL. Typically, an `if` block spans multiple lines of code and uses some method for scoping the two conditions:

```
if (x == 5) {
  // do something
} else {
  // do something else
}
```

This classic example shows how a conditional statement manifests in an imperative language. The curly brackets provide scope for the code that the computer will execute when the Boolean expression is `true` or `false`. In imperative code, you can do anything inside these scoped regions.

The difference between this approach and using a **ternary conditional operator** is that, with the former, the goal is always to produce a value.

With a ternary conditional operator, each condition must return a value. Consider the following expression:

```
y = x == 5 ? x * 10 : 0
```

The preceding expression will set the value of y to be 50 when x is 5, and it will set the value to 0 for any other value of x. The equivalent imperative code would look like this:

```
int y;
if (x == 5) {
   y = x * 10
} else {
   y = 0
}
```

The difference between this imperative alternative and the ternary conditional operator statement is that the developer can do other things in the scope regions that are either related or unrelated to setting the value of y appropriately.

Splat expressions

A **splat expression** is another way of accessing an attribute of each item in a list of objects. You can use this expression to access a single attribute from a resource or module block with the count or for_each meta-argument attached:

```
resource "aws_instance" "node" {

   count = var.node_count

   # the rest of the configuration

}
```

Consider this collection of AWS EC2 instances. This block uses the count meta-argument to create a dynamic number of these resources from 0 to n, where n is the value of var.node_count. As a result, we can't just access output values from this resource like we usually would if it were singular. We need to access it using an index to specify which instance of the resource block we want to access:

```
locals {
   first_instance_id = aws_instance.node[0].id
}
```

In this case, we specify the index of 0 and access its `id` attribute. But what if we wanted to get all of the values of `id` for every EC2 instance simultaneously? Using a `for` expression, we could iterate over the list of `aws_instance` resources. However, there is a better way—using the splat expression:

```
locals {
  all_instance_ids = aws_instance.node[*].id
}
```

Using * instead of an actual numeric index tells Terraform that we want to activate a splat expression. Instead of accessing a single object, we want to access all the objects in the array. Once done, `id` returns a `list` containing all the `id` values for our EC2 instances.

Dynamic blocks

We know that Terraform represents the objects it provisions as `resource` blocks, which, as we know, support nested blocks within them. When a nested block supports many instances, it can sometimes be helpful to declare them dynamically using an approach called **dynamic blocks**. With this approach, you essentially drive the number of nested block definitions within a `resource` block based on a collection of objects.

Let's take the example of our Cosmos DB account that needs to replicate its databases across multiple geo-locations. We can add as many `geo_location` nested blocks as we want and configure them accordingly, but this can get tedious—especially if the configuration for each block is relatively uniform:

```
resource "azurerm_cosmosdb_account" "db" {

  name                  = "cosmos-foobar"
  location              = azurerm_resource_group.foobar.location
  resource_group_name   = azurerm_resource_group.foobar.name
  offer_type            = "Standard"
  kind                  = "MongoDB"

  geo_location {
    location            = "westus"
    failover_priority = 0
  }

  geo_location {
    location            = "eastus"
    failover_priority = 1
  }

}
```

We can accomplish the same thing using a dynamic block. Suppose we declare a map that defines the regions we want to replicate across and the failover priority of each region. In that case, we can use this map to drive a dynamic block that sets up our Cosmos DB account correctly—and concisely:

```
locals {
  regions = {
    westus = 0
    eastus = 1
  }
}
```

Now, with the map configured with our replication region settings, we can use a dynamic block to instruct the Cosmos DB resource on how to set up its geo_location nested blocks:

```
resource "azurerm_cosmosdb_account" "db" {

  name                = "cosmos-foobar"
  location            = azurerm_resource_group.foobar.location
  resource_group_name = azurerm_resource_group.foobar.name
  offer_type          = "Standard"
  kind                = "MongoDB"

  dynamic "geo_location" {
    for_each = local.regions
    content {
      location          = geo_location.key
      failover_priority = geo_location.value
    }
  }

}
```

Notice that geo_location becomes a reference to each item in local.regions as we iterate through it, and because local.regions is a map, that means that geo_location is an item within this map. That means that each geo_location is a key/value pair, and we can use key and value to access the respective values when we set location and failover_priority on the content of the nested block.

That's it! We have completed all the concepts, syntax, and modifiers within HCL. We are ready to start rocking the Terraform world, right?

Hold up—before we do that, let's pack our **bat belt** with tools to help us out of many tricky situations: functions!

Functions

HCL includes dozens of functions that you can use to help develop your infrastructure with Terraform. However, I don't plan on draining the ocean on every single function because I think many of them cover concepts that are outside the scope of this book. I will focus on the most pertinent and practical functions of developing excellent cloud infrastructure. Another exciting new feature that is available in Terraform 1.8.0 is the introduction of provider-specific functions. This allows provider authors (e.g., `aws`, `azurerm`, etc.) to create functions that provide useful functionality that is specific for that provider. This could be for common utilities such as parsing and AWS ARN or an Azure Resource Identifier.

Numeric functions

Numeric functions operate on objects of the `number` type. The usual suspects are present—everything from absolute value, ceiling/floor, min/max, and so on.

Given that these functions cover fundamental concepts in math, they are primarily outside the scope of this book. I'd encourage you to check out the excellent documentation provided by HashiCorp on these functions.

String functions

String functions operate on objects of the `string` type. Like the numeric functions, the usual suspects are present.

There are several functions related to string manipulation, such as `split`, `replace`, and `join`.

Split

The `split` function can be helpful when working with comma-delimited values that you might pass in as input variables. You can use input variables of the `string` type to pass in a collection of values. Using environment variables or command-line arguments makes it difficult to reliably pass in complex structures such as `list`, `map`, or `object`. Therefore, it is widespread to simplify those complex structures into multiple comma-delimited `string` input variables.

Several functions are used for cleansing data of unnecessary whitespaces, which can occur when you do string manipulation.

Format

The `format` function can be a cleaner way to perform string manipulation without really nasty string interpolation—which can degrade the readability of your code with all the extra $ { } symbols added to separate object tokens:

```
locals {
  foo = "rg-${var.fizz}${var.buzz}${var.wizz}"
}
```

You can replace the preceding code with this:

```
locals {
    foo = format("rg-%s%s%s, var.fizz, var.buzz, var.wizz)
}
```

The `fizz`, `buzz`, and `wizz` values are passed into the corresponding `%s`. The `%s` symbol is a token to inject values passed in with specific formatting instructions. There are different verbs for different data types and formatting options.

A variant of this function called `formatlist` does the same thing but operates on `list(string)`. It is a convenience function that avoids the additional complexity of wrapping a `format` function in a `for` expression.

Replace

The `replace` function is another commonly used string function. Many cloud services have particular requirements for naming conventions, so `replace` is very useful when you want to cleanse your names of invalid characters when naming conditions are incongruent across different services:

```
locals {
    full_name = "foo-bar"
}
```

For example, Azure Storage accounts do not allow hyphens in their names, while Azure resource groups do. Therefore, if you pass in an input variable to set a common prefix across all your resources and include a hyphen, you will run into trouble when Terraform attempts to provision the Azure Storage account:

```
locals {
    storage_account_name = replace(local.full_name, "-", "")
}
```

Replace can be used to eliminate this naming convention faux pax quickly.

Collection functions

Collection functions are an assortment of functions that let you work with objects of the `list` or `map` type. These contain everyday set-based operations, Boolean checks, and accessors.

Length

The `length` function is probably the most common collection function. It is often used with the `count` meta-argument as it provides a simple and dynamic method for obtaining the number of items in a list:

```
locals {
    fault_domains = [1, 2, 3, 4, 5]
```

```
    fault_domain_count = length(local.fault_domains)
}
```

In the preceding code, we calculate the number of fault domains using the `length` method on the `fault_domains` list. This approach will produce a value of 5 for the `fault_domain_count` local variable.

Range

The `range` function can be useful for taking a count and creating an array of indices for them. There are three overloads, but the most useful of the overloads is the one that follows:

```
range(start, limit)
```

This overload of the `range` function takes a `start` number and a `limit` number. This capability is helpful because cloud platforms often have deployment boundaries that are important to how we structure our architecture. These boundaries significantly impact the resiliency of our architecture—such as regions, Availability Zones, fault domains, and so on—so we must take them seriously.

A common problem we face when working within and across these boundaries is that our deployments often need to be very specific about which area to target within a boundary. For example, I need to specify that my subnet is in Availability Zone 2 or that my VM needs to be in fault domain 3.

The problem arises because cloud platforms often don't have a uniform or consistent way of telling us the domain of values for a particular boundary. For example, rather than giving us a list of *Availability Zone 1*, *Availability Zone 2*, and *Availability Zone 3*—the values we need to target our resources to the target area correctly—the cloud platform might give us a more cryptic *"This region has 5 Availability Zones, Good Luck!"*. When we need to be specific, they are generic. This incongruence does not produce ideal outcomes.

If we are hardcoding our resources, this would be fine. Still, when you want to provision to a dynamic list of Availability Zones, which allows you to iterate across the list of Availability Zones and provision some resources to each, you need to somehow convert a range into a discrete list of elements such that you can align each item in that list. Queue the music; here comes `range` to the rescue!

```
locals {
  max_fault_domains = 5

  fault_domains = range(1, local.max_fault_domains)
}
```

In the preceding code, let's pretend the cloud platform provided the hardcoded number of fault domains. We need to create a list that we can iterate across to provision a VM to each of the fault domains. Thanks to `range`, we can produce the following list:

```
fault_domains = [1, 2, 3, 4, 5]
```

With the preceding list, we can quickly iterate to create a VM in the correct subnet using the `count` meta-argument and the length of the `fault_domains` list.

Flatten

The `flatten` function can be helpful when you have homogenous data elements stored within different arrays. This situation might occur when you have a module return a collection of sub-resources:

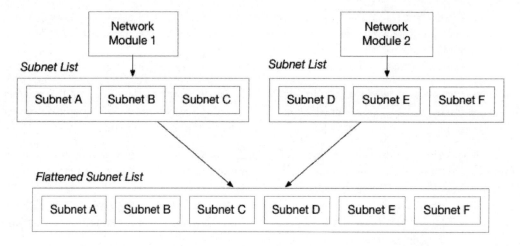

Figure 2.3 – The Network module; each produces its list of subnets
that you need to aggregate into a single list of subnets

In the preceding diagram, we can see that we have a module that provisions a network. This module outputs a list of subnets. Often, we want a module to encapsulate relevant sub-resources that are tightly coupled with the primary resource of the module. While this approach makes the code more maintainable, it also creates difficulties upstream if we want to act uniformly across all the sub-resources it outputs.

With `flatten`, we can collapse the list of lists into a single flattened list with each subnet as an item. Doing so will enable us to work uniformly with all of the subnets from the consuming module we are developing.

Transpose

The `transpose` function is also beneficial when working with hierarchies of objects with complex relationships with their children:

Figure 2.4 – Resource VMs associated with a collection of security groups

For example, in the preceding diagram, two VMs are associated with a collection of security groups. We have set this up as a `map` collection in this situation. The key would be the VM and the value of a collection of security groups.

This `map` works excellently when we want to iterate over the top-level object—the VMs—but what if we're going to iterate over the child objects, the security groups? We flip this relationship upside down using the `transpose` function on this map!

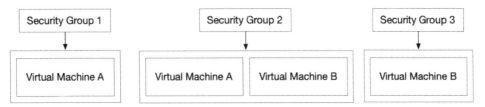

Figure 2.5 – Security groups associated with a collection of VMs

The preceding diagram shows that instead of having the top-level object be the VM, it's now the security groups. The `transpose` operation has also replaced child objects with VMs. However, you'll notice that the function has maintained the relationships between parent and child—we're just looking at the relationship through a different lens.

Zipmap

The `zipmap` function is handy when you have two `list` objects, one containing the keys and the other containing the corresponding values. Both list corresponding items in the same index, and the lists must be the same length.

The name is interesting as it is an attempt at word painting. Imagine the construction of a zipper: two independent but parallel lists of notches, but when the zipper is applied sequentially, each notch on the left side is attached to the corresponding notch on the right side:

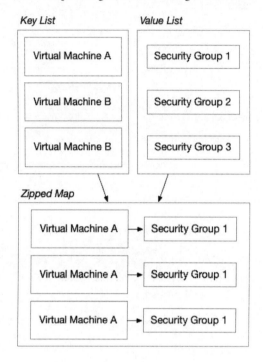

Figure 2.6 – VMs list and a corresponding security group list

In the preceding diagram, we have two lists, one containing VMs and another containing security groups. With the zipmap function, we can create a new map object that creates an association between each element in the VM and security group lists.

Encoding functions

Encoding functions let you work with text of various encoding formats and convert back and forth between them. These include string-based operations such as Base64 and string-to-object encoding formats such as JSON and YAML.

Many services will often require input data to be encoded in Base64 to simplify the transmission of complex data, and the two corresponding encode and decode functions work as you would expect them.

The JSON and YAML encode and decode functions work like typical serializers, with the encode functions taking in an object and producing a string—while the decode functions take in a string and produce an object.

Filesystem functions

Filesystem functions provide a set of utilities that make it easier to work with local files, which can come in extremely handy if you need to drop a config file for the next step in your automation pipeline or if you need to access files containing content needed for resource provisioning.

File

The `file` function simply loads the contents from the file at the specified path on the disk into a string. The `path.module` special variable is used to specify the current working directory of the current module. This is useful during module development because it allows you to embed and use files to store content needed within your module:

```
locals {
  template_content = file("${path.module}/template.json")
}
```

This method is commonly used in conjunction with the `jsondecode` and `yamldecode` functions to take the string content and convert it into an object that can be used more easily within HCL:

```
locals {
  template = jsondecode(
    file("${path.module}/template.json")
  )
}
```

Template file

The `templatefile` function works just like the `file` function but with a twist. It allows you to pass in parameters to be replaced with corresponding placeholders in the file specified:

```
locals {
  template = jsondecode(
    templatefile(
      "${path.module}/template.json",
      {
        hostname   = "foo"
        ip_address = "10.0.1.8"
      }
    )
  )
}
```

The parameters of `hostname` and `ip_address` indicate the tokens that should be replaced in the file with their corresponding values, `foo` and `10.0.1.8`, respectively. If the contents of the file contain the `${hostname}` or `${ip_address}` tokens, they will be replaced with the corresponding value. This can be a very convenient way to drop important configuration details into your infrastructure that is only available after Terraform has executed its plan.

Date/time functions

Date/time functions provide a set of utilities for creating timestamps. These functions can help set expiration dates for short-term access tokens or transform a date/time string into the correct format expected by the specific resource you use.

When working with time in Terraform, it's important to note that there is no explicit date/time type. Terraform handles date/time values using the `string` type. The default format that Terraform uses is the RFC 3339 format, which looks like this:

```
2023-09-14T13:24:19Z
```

The preceding value has the following format:

```
{YYYY}-{MM}-{DD}T{HH}:{mm}:{ss}Z
```

This behavior is essential to understand because all the date/time functions that are available will either take in or produce a timestamp in this format.

Hash/crypto functions

Just like the encoding functions, there are several options when it comes to hashing and cryptographic functions. These functions implement a variety of hashing algorithms such as MD5 and SHA and encryption algorithms such as RSA. There are also corresponding file-based operations that allow you to read content from a file.

It's important to remember that hashing is not the same thing as encryption and that when using encryption, you should secure the keys you use both inside and outside of the Terraform state.

IP network functions

The IP network functions make it easier to work with CIDR blocks to split address spaces into subnets.

Although Terraform's networking functions support IPv4 and IPv6, we'll look at IPv4 addresses in our examples to make it easier to understand.

An IPv4 address is a 32-bit value with 4 octets and 8 bits per octet. We construct CIDR blocks to identify a range of IP addresses to allocate to a virtual network or a subnet within that virtual network.

Terraform has the `cidrsubnet` function, which calculates these CIDR block ranges, making it easier to generate CIDR block ranges dynamically rather than hardcoding them or using string manipulation to construct them:

```
cidrsubnet(prefix, newbits, netnum)
```

The `prefix` argument is the network space you want to split up. The `newbits` argument is how big we want the chunks that the prefix splits into to be—its value has an inverse relationship with the size of the address space chunks. As the `newbits` value goes up, the size of the chunks decreases. As the value of `newbits` goes down, the size of the chunks increases:

```
locals {
  cidr_block_start    = "10.0.0.0/16"
  cidr_chunk_size     = 8
  cidr_block_list     = range(0, 4)
  dynamic_cidr_blocks = [for i in local.cidr_block_list :
cidrsubnet(local.cidr_block_start, local.chunk_size, i)]
}
```

In the preceding code, we are splitting up the address space of `10.0.0.0/16` with chunks that have 8 additional bits. That means we are looking for chunks with the size of `/24`—or 256 IP addresses. If we used 6 instead, we would be looking to split into chunks of `/22`—or 1,024 IP addresses. As you can see, the fewer additional bits, the more IP addresses in each chunk, and the fewer chunks we can fit into the primary address space:

```
resource "aws_subnet" "subnet" {
  count      = 4
  cidr_block = cidrsubnet(var.cidr, local.chunk_size, count.index)
}
```

In the preceding code, we can use this function to construct the address space for each subnet within an AWS VPC. Thanks to the `count` meta-argument, we don't need the `for` expression to construct a list of address spaces. We can use `count.index` to specify the `netnum` input to select which chunk we want our subnet to use.

Type conversion functions

Explicit type conversions are exceptionally rare in Terraform, but several functions are available to aid you if necessary, e.g., `tonumber`, `tobool`, `tolist`, etc.

Summary

In this chapter, we took an in-depth look at the language that powers Terraform: HCL. We looked at its core structures: resources, data sources, locals, and modules. We looked at inputs and outputs that will help us design better contracts between our modules and the outside world. We looked at language structures that allow us to build dynamic collections of resources—helping us scale our code without all the copypasta. And lastly, we looked at an arsenal of functions that can help us when coding in HCL to solve complex problems quickly and efficiently.

In the next chapter, we will explore the utility providers HashiCorp publishes that provide critical cross-platform functionality to our Terraform solutions.

3

Harnessing HashiCorp Utility Providers

As we discussed in the first chapter, when we learned about Terraform's architecture, Terraform was designed to be extensible. In the previous chapter, we spent a lot of time looking at the **HashiCorp Configuration Language** (**HCL**), which provides many tools that we can use to help us define our **infrastructure as code** (**IaC**). However, these language devices are not always sufficient. That is why HashiCorp has built a set of utility providers that provide a kind of base class library, or a set of reusable features that are helpful to specific scenarios, no matter what cloud platforms you are using to build your IaC solutions.

This chapter covers the following topics:

- Working with reality
- Adaptation and integration
- Filesystem
- Operating system and networking

Working with reality

When building our architecture with IaC, the product is not the code but living and breathing environments. While the code lives in the abstract realms of our minds, these environments operate within the real world, and just like how our best-laid plans get smashed by reality—so do our environments.

Therefore, we need some tools to prepare our environments to meet and come to grips with reality. The `random` and `time` providers allow us to avoid conflicts between our resources and our environments— whether it's the name of something or when something expires. These are all critical elements of our solution design that can make or break our architecture when it encounters the real world.

Randomizing

The `random` provider offers several ways to add randomness to your Terraform solution. Each `random` resource type may generate different types of random values and have other attributes to control the output. Still, all of them—with only a couple of exceptions—generate the random value through a single output called `result`. They also all have at least one attribute called `keepers`, which triggers Terraform to recreate the resource. This attribute can be helpful to set when you have transient resources that get replaced often, and you need to ensure there are no name conflicts when destroying and recreating the resource.

Random strings

Generating random strings can be a great way to guarantee uniqueness across deployments, especially in situations where you are dynamically generating short-lived environments. Depending on the case, there are two ways to generate strings—one for non-sensitive data, such as resource names, and another for sensitive data, such as access keys and passwords.

Generating non-sensitive dynamic names can be done using `random_string`. At the same time, `random_password` can create sensitive values you should protect from leakage by marking them as sensitive if you output them and by securing your state, since Terraform will store the resulting value in state:

```
resource "random_string" "name_suffix" {
    length          = 6
    special         = true
    override_special = "/@£$"
}
```

The preceding code generates a random string that can generate unique resource names within projects. Using short random strings to embed within the names of your resources is a great strategy when working with resources with minimal name length constraints, as it can be challenging to create a coherent naming convention across all your resources when one or two of the resources require abnormally small name lengths. This situation is common when resources need to have globally unique names, such as S3 buckets or Azure Storage accounts:

```
locals {
    resource_name = "foobar${random_string.name_suffix.result}"
}
```

When you couple a random name suffix with part of your naming convention, you can still have a relatively rational resource name:

```
resource "random_password" "database" {
    length          = 16
    special         = true
```

```
    override_special = "!#$%&*()-_=+[]{}<>:?"
}
```

Unique identifiers

You can also generate a **Universally Unique Identifier** (**UUID**), also known as a **Globally Unique Identifier** (**GUID**), using `random_uuid`. This can be helpful when your resource supports very long names, as these non-case-sensitive, alphanumeric values take the following format: `00000000-0000-0000-0000-000000000000`. You might need this to generate a unique correlation identifier to link resources within your deployments using a common tag.

Just for fun

There is also a fun little resource called `random_pet`, with a nod to the age-old jest of *pets versus cattle*, where you can generate pet names. This resource is probably not useful for production but can be helpful in development or lab environments where you can be more creative with resource names. The `random_pet` resource's `id` output will generate names with an adjective-noun format. Here are some sample values I came up with using the sample included in this chapter of the book:

- `notable-coyote`
- `quiet-parakeet`
- `pure-woodcock`
- `healthy-monkey`
- `mint-foal`
- `pet-serval`
- `ideal-lab`
- `special-urchin`

You can see that almost all of them don't make much sense, but some can be funny.

Random numbers

Generating random numbers can also help generate random names or generate a random index from an array. `random_integer` offers a simple solution that allows you to pick a number between specified `min` and `max` values.

Consider the following array of AWS availability zones:

```
locals {
  azs = [
    "us-west-1a",
    "us-west-1c",
    "us-west-1d",
    "us-west-1e"
  ]
}
```

If we wanted to pick a random availability zone from this `list`, we could use `random_integer` to generate a random index from it:

```
resource "random_integer" "az" {
  min = 0
  max = length(local.azs) - 1
}
```

The preceding code would allow us to generate a random integer between 0 and the length of the `list` minus 1, which would be 4 - 1 = 3. Therefore, we would randomly generate either 0, 1, 2, or 3.

We can access the random availability zone using the following code:

```
locals {
  selected_az = local.azs[random_integer.az.result]
}
```

Finally, we could use the availability zone name to configure our AWS resources:

```
resource "aws_elb" "foo" {

  availability_zones = [local.selected_az]

  # ... and other aws_elb arguments ...
}
```

Beyond simple integers

When simple integers aren't enough, you can use `random_id` to generate more sophisticated outputs. The only input is the `byte_length` to control how large the random number generated can be. This resource differs from other `random` providers' resources as it does not have a `result` output, but has several others that present the random number in various formats, including decimal, hexadecimal, and Base64:

```
resource "random_id" "foo" {
  byte_length = 8
}
```

The preceding code generates a random number with a length of 8 bytes. Examples of the output values of the different formats are listed as follows:

- **ID**: `IpVgeF7uUY0`

- **Decimal**: `2492004038924456333`

- **Hex**: `229560785eee518d`

- **Base64 standard**: `IpVgeF7uUY0=`

- **Base64 URL**: `= IpVgeF7uUY0`

Again, depending on your naming conventions, this can be useful for creating names or tags that uniquely identify your resources.

Shuffle

Using the previous example, when selecting availability zones from a list, we would have to generate various `random_integer` resources if we wanted to select multiple items from that list at random. Attempting to do so with `random_integer` is already pretty cumbersome, but it becomes more challenging if we have requirements to ensure that the second instance of `random_integer` isn't the same as the first one.

Luckily, an alternative approach to using `random_integer` to select the index of an array is to use a built-in resource for the specific task of choosing a random subset of items from a `list`. You can achieve this approach using the `random_shuffle` resource, passing in the `list` and the number of items you want using the `result_count` attribute. The output `result` will be a `list` of strings that you can use. This approach dramatically simplifies our solution if we want our AWS **Elastic Load Balancer** (**ELB**) to span multiple availability zones.

Consider the following array of AWS availability zones:

```
locals {
  azs = [
    "us-west-1a",
    "us-west-1c",
    "us-west-1d",
    "us-west-1e"
  ]
}
```

We would use `random_shuffle` to generate two availability zones for our ELB:

```
resource "random_shuffle" "azs" {
  input        = local.azs
  result_count = 2
}
```

Finally, we set the `availability_zones` attribute using the `result` of `random_shuffle` because its output is the correct type of `list(string)`:

```
resource "aws_elb" "foo" {

  availability_zones = random_shuffle.azs.result

  # ... and other aws_elb arguments ...
}
```

This resource is useful, but you need to watch out when using it as it can cause your solution to become non-deterministic—meaning that Terraform won't be able to figure out how to create a plan until the `random_shuffle` resource has been created. This could require you to use targeted `terraform apply` operations to avoid first-time-apply failures.

Working with time

In Terraform, the `time` provider offers several capabilities that make it easier to handle various scenarios where resource life cycle management is dictated by time.

While most cloud providers offer much better solutions for resource scheduling, there are still cases where time plays a crucial role in the provisioning of resources. This situation often involves certificates, where you need to set a fixed or rolling window for the certificate to expire. In this situation, you can use either a specific date/time in the future or one that is relative to the current date/time.

Current date/time

Sometimes, you want to capture the current date and time, which you may like to use for the effective date of a secret's value. There are two methods to obtaining the current date in Terraform—a function and the `time_static` resource:

```
locals {
  option1 = timestamp()
}
```

The preceding code demonstrates using the `timestamp()` function. The following code shows how to use the `time_static` resource from the `time` provider:

```
resource "time_static" "current_time" {}
```

Both approaches will generate the current date/time on the first time you run `apply`. The difference is that the `timestamp()` function will always generate a current date/time stamp on every subsequent `apply`. This makes it more ideal for scenarios such as tagging a resource with its last modified date, which could be useful to determine the last time the resource was touched by Terraform. Another common scenario is triggering resource updates that you want to happen every time, but try to avoid this because this creates perpetual churn in your solution.

At the same time, the `time_static` resource will maintain, in State, the original date/time stamp at the first Terraform `apply`. This can be useful for life cycle management of the resources to determine when the deployment was originally created or for setting policies for backups, scaling, or decommissioning based on age.

Fixed date/time

A string representation of the date/time can be used to create a specific time in the future using an absolute date/time:

```
locals {
  future_date = "2024-05-04T00:00:00Z"
}
```

The preceding code will set the expiration date to May 4, 2024. The format of the string representation of date/time is `YYYY-MM-DDTHH:MM:SSZ`.

Another option is using the `time_static` resource and setting the `rfc3339` attribute, which is rarely used due to its limited value over simply setting a local:

```
resource "time_static" "may_the_fourth" {
  rfc3339 = "2024-05-04T00:00:00Z"
}
```

Time offset

A specific time in the future using a period relative to the current date can be created using `time_offset`:

```
resource "time_offset" "certificate_expiration" {
  offset_years = 1
}
```

The preceding code will set the expiration date to exactly one year in the future. There are different attributes to adjust the offset date/time stamp by years, months, days, hours, minutes, and seconds. You can set the `base_rfc3339` attribute to change the date/time to which the offset is relative. This can be a great way to dynamically set certain expiration dates. However, you need to ensure that you routinely run Terraform to keep the target date in the future.

Rotation

You may need to recreate resources on a regular cadence in several situations. This secret could need to be updated every 90 days or XXX days. In these situations, the `time_rotating` resource provides an advantage over its static siblings, both `time_static` and `time_offset`.

Time offset seems like the solution for rotation as it is relative to the current date, but just like `time_static`, it is just another way of calculating a static date/time stamp that Terraform will store in State. The `time_rotating` resource's superpower is that when the `rotation_days` period expires relative to the original date, you will see that the resource triggers a replacement:

```
resource "time_rotating" "certificate" {
  rotation_days = 90
}
```

This also requires you to regularly run Terraform to keep the values in the future. If you utilize resources like this, make sure you coordinate with your change management procedures, as they can sneak up on you when you execute a `terraform plan` only to discover you've passed the magic date.

In this section, we learned how to randomize the names of our resources using the `random` provider, and even generate secrets that we can use to fully automate an environment with resources that need you to set passwords before Terraform can provision them. We also learned how we could use the `time` provider, when to use it versus the `timestamp()` function we looked at in *Chapter 2*, and other advanced scenarios of creating time periods and windows of rotation.

Next, we'll look at some utility providers that help us overcome some limitations of Terraform whenever we encounter a situation in which Terraform doesn't already have a built-in solution or an existing provider that tackles the problem.

Adaptation and integration

As we've discussed, Terraform and its providers are open source projects, so there may be limits to what it can do or what is available. As a result, we often need to find ways of overcoming these limitations—even temporarily. In this section, we'll look at several providers that help Terraform reach outside and take advantage of external programs and systems that can enhance Terraform and help it overcome situations lacking a built-in solution.

Accessing external resources

Like many utility providers, the `external` provider is tiny. It only has one data source of the same name as the provider: `external`. As the name implies, this data source allows you to integrate with third-party components. It enables you to execute a local program, pass its input, and process the output. This capability can be advantageous when you want to obtain dynamic configuration from an external source, perform complex transformations on inputs you receive from other providers, and integrate with third-party tools that you want to integrate with Terraform.

This provider is very particular about the runtime requirements of the program that you specified. First, the program must run successfully by exiting with an exit code of zero. If the program returns a non-zero code, the provider will sound the alarm and scramble an error message to Terraform. Second, the provider expects both the input and the output to be in JSON format.

Using the `external` provider works perfectly when your third-party program fulfills all these requirements. It is a happy coincidence indeed! If you are integrating with such a program, that's great. However, this provider is the right choice when you author custom scripts or programs that explicitly meet these contractual obligations.

To be as cross-platform as possible, the ideal programming language to write these custom scripts would be Python or Go. With these programming languages, you can create a lightweight script, designed and built, that is fit for the purpose of talking to the external system of your choice and providing Terraform-friendly outputs and error handling:

```
data "external" "example" {
  program = ["python", "${path.module}/example-data-source.py"]

  query = {
    # arbitrary map from strings to strings, passed
    # to the external program as the data query.
    id = "abc123"
  }
}
```

In the preceding code, we are executing the Python program on the local machine–this could be our laptop or the build agent of our **continuous integration/continuous delivery** (**CI/CD**) pipeline.

When you want to make something from nothing

Terraform and its providers are open source projects. That means that we are at the mercy of friendly internet strangers who are keeping pace with the changes made to the platforms and technologies that we hope to automate. While Terraform has fantastic coverage across a wide set of public cloud platforms and technologies, sometimes, it needs a little help. There might be a small feature that lacks support that you can't configure natively through the resources available in the provider. Sometimes, those small tweaks play a critical role in configuration, and we need to draw dependencies on them from other resources that can be provisioned natively through the Terraform provider. That's where the `null_resource` comes into play.

Null resource

The `null_resource` allows us to leverage meta-arguments such as `provisioner` to perform local and remote script executions. This allows you to execute critical command-line scripts that must be completed before Terraform can continue its plan. As a result, the `null_resource` has no attributes such as other Terraform resources. Its only attribute is a `list(string)` called `triggers`. When any strings within this array change, the `null_resource` is replaced. This is an important life cycle control that you need to consider when configuring the `provisioner` blocks you attach.

Time sleep

There is another technique of doing nothing. There can be situations where the action you try to trigger is non-deterministic, meaning you won't know exactly when it finishes. This could be out of context or a true technical limitation of the resource or shim you use. The `time` provider offers a resource called `time_sleep`, which lets you create a sleep timer. You must declare `depends_on` meta-arguments to ensure that the sleep timer is invoked between the required resources:

```
    # This resource will destroy (potentially immediately) after null_
resource.next
    resource "null_resource" "previous" {}

    resource "time_sleep" "wait_30_seconds" {
      depends_on = [null_resource.previous]

      create_duration = "30s"
    }

    # This resource will create (at least) 30 seconds after null_
resource.previous
    resource "null_resource" "next" {
      depends_on = [time_sleep.wait_30_seconds]
    }
```

Delayed `destroy` can be done using a different attribute called `destroy_duration`.

Making HTTP requests

Sometimes, you can access data from external sources without using a local script or command-line utility, by directly accessing a REST API endpoint. This approach is advantageous when you want to fetch configuration information staged at a static HTTP endpoint, access information about resources managed outside of Terraform, integrate with a cloud provider or external services directly through a REST API, and integrate health checks into your Terraform process.

The `http` provider provides a single data source called `http`, allowing you to make an HTTP GET operation. The only required input is `url`, but you can provide several attributes you would expect to set on an HTTP request, such as HTTP request headers and body content:

```
    data "http" "foo" {
      url = "https://foo"
    }
```

After Terraform makes the HTTP request, you can access the HTTP response status code, headers, and body content.

In this section, we learned how to integrate with all sorts of external components—local programs or scripts, a remote server, and nothing at all.

Next, we'll look at some utility providers that help us work with creating and accessing files. We've already encountered some functions that enable some of these scenarios, but some additional scenarios are only possible when we use utility providers.

Filesystem

When building IaC solutions using Terraform, there are many situations where we need to either use existing files or create new ones. In this section, we'll look at the utility providers that enable more advanced scenarios that move beyond the `file` and `templatefile` functions and when we should use the providers versus using the functions.

Reading and writing local files

There are many situations when reading or writing files can be very useful to simplify how Terraform integrates with other tools by creating configuration files, scripts, or any other artifact required for your infrastructure deployment. To produce the desired output, you can define the content using templated files, input variables, or other expressions within your HCL code.

Terraform has a utility provider called `local` that provides this functionality. This provider has two resources and two data sources named `local_file` and `local_sensitive_file`.

Why not just use the function? Functions do not participate in the dependency graph, so when you use the `file` or `template_file` functions, you cannot use them with files generated dynamically during a Terraform operation. Therefore, if you plan on generating and using a file within Terraform, you should always use the `local` provider's resources.

Writing files

The `local_file` resource (and the corresponding `local_sensitive_file` resource) allows you to create a new file at a target location specified in the `filename` attribute. There are several options for sourcing the content, either by using dynamically generated content inside Terraform or an existing file:

- `content`: This attribute allows you to pass any string as long as it is UTF-8-encoded, using simple strings from resource outputs, local variables, or functions to generate a string.

- `content_base64`: This attribute allows you to pass binary data as a Base64-encoded string.

- source: This attribute allows you to pass a path to an existing file from which you want to read the contents. When using this attribute, you copy the original file to a new location.

In the following code, we are setting the content attribute to a simple constant string and using the ${path.module} special token to specify the current module's working directory as the output location for a file with the name of foo.bar:

```
resource "local\_file" "foo" {
  content  = "foo!"
  filename = "${path.module}/foo.bar"
}
```

Be careful when destroying, especially if you dynamically generate the file's contents inside Terraform using a jsonencode, yamlencode, or any other method—you may run into issues because of the way Terraform handles dependencies on this resource type.

Also, be aware when writing sensitive data to files, as it can pose a security risk. Likewise, filesystem access or I/O failures can create opportunities for additional points of failure when executing Terraform.

Given these common pitfalls, generating file contents using Terraform can still be extremely effective. One such scenario is generating YAML inventories for Ansible, which can be an excellent way of integrating Terraform and Ansible as part of a broader maintenance process for long-lived environments that need configuration management changes at the operating system level.

Reading files

The local_file data source (and the corresponding local_sensitive_file data source) allows you to read the contents of an existing file and output its contents in a variety of formats that you can use as inputs to other resources and modules within your code base. This capability is similar to what the file function can do but provides a few advantages.

First, it can create a standalone block referenced multiple times from multiple resources without repeating the filename's path in the equivalent function call. Creating a central reference to the local file can make your code more maintainable by making the dependencies on the file more apparent to both Terraform and humans.

Second, by leveraging the data source, you immediately have several ways to output the data, including Base64-string, SHA, and MD5 options. By leveraging these output options, you can avoid additional nested function calls to perform the same encoding operations.

In the following code, we access an existing file within the module's current directory with a foo.bar filename:

```
data "local_file" "foo" {
  filename = "${path.module}/foo.bar"
}
```

We can then access the file's raw content by using the `content` output of the data source or any of the other encoding options mentioned earlier.

Templating files and directories

In the previous chapter, we covered templating files and surveyed HCL's built-in functions, including the function called `template_file`. You should use this function when working with a single file, but the `template` provider offers a resource that you can use to apply templating across all the files within a given directory.

The resource takes input files from the `source_dir` attribute and, for each file, substitutes the specified input variables for the corresponding placeholders, writing each output file to the established `destination_dir`. Using this resource is a great way to update configurations that span a multitude of files. Still, you must stage all files with a consistent set of placeholders for the templating engine to replace in the same fashion as the `template_file()` function operates.

Generating file archives

Sometimes, it's necessary to package outputs from Terraform into compressed archives that you can use for several different purposes, such as efficiently transferring configuration to the next stage in the application deployment pipeline, bundling configuration for easy distribution to other external repositories, and generating documentation or other artifacts to track deployment history, environmental changes, or snapshots of configuration as they change over time.

You should avoid this approach when working with secrets or sensitive data, as more appropriate solutions exist for those scenarios. Metadata related to the infrastructure generated by Terraform and needed by another tool in another format is the ideal scenario for this approach.

The `archive_file` resource generates a ZIP file at the specified `output_path` and includes one or more files, using either existing files or dynamically generated files.

Including existing files

When you want to reference either existing files that are stored in your Terraform module directory or files generated by Terraform using the `local` provider, you should use `source_file` or `source_dir` to include a single file or an entire directory of files within the archive, respectively:

```
data "archive_file" "init" {
  type        = "zip"
  source_file = "${path.module}/foo.txt"
  output_path = "${path.module}/files/out.zip"
}
```

Including dynamically created files

When you want to output content that's dynamically generated by Terraform using object construction in local variables or other means, you need to use one or more `source` blocks and specify the `content` and the `filename` of the file to include it within the archive:

```
data "archive_file" "dotfiles" {
  type        = "zip"
  output_path = "${path.module}/files/out.zip"

  source {
    content  = "foobar"
    filename = "foo.txt"
  }

}
```

Optionally, if you only want one dynamically generated file in the archive, you can use the top-level `source_content` and `source_filename` to have a single file:

```
data "archive_file" "dotfiles" {
  type        = "zip"
  output_path = "${path.module}/files/out.zip"

  source_content          = "foobar"
  source_content_filename = "foo.txt"

}
```

The preceding examples produce the same output, but the latter is slightly more concise for the single-file archive scenario. At the same time, the former allows you to add as many files to the archive as you like in the future using additional `source` blocks.

It's important to note that each method for including files within the archive is mutually exclusive, so you must choose one—and only one—approach.

In this section, we learned how to leverage the `local`, `archive`, and `template` providers to handle more robust filesystem access scenarios where leveraging the existing functions may not be ideal.

Finally, we'll look at some utility providers that help us work with setting up operating system configuration, security, and network access control.

Operating system and networking

HashiCorp created Terraform's utility providers to solve common problems that span cloud platforms. As a result, some utility providers solve problems relating to common architectural scenarios you will encounter when setting up or connecting to servers.

Generating certificates and SSH keys

In Terraform, the `tls` provider offers general capabilities related to **Transport Layer Security (TLS)** and cryptography. You should use this provider with a certificate authority to generate signed certificates for production workloads. Still, several features are very helpful in development and lab environments to streamline productivity.

SSH keys

When working with virtual machines, an everyday use case is the need to generate **Secure Socket Shell (SSH)** keys that you can use to access your Linux-based virtual machines. Of course, you can create and pre-stage a key on the public cloud of your choice using standard command-line tools such as `ssh-keygen`, but Terraform has a provider with resources for this very task, which makes it extremely easy and convenient to encapsulate the same SSH key generation with the infrastructure that is going to use it. It's a perfect tool for short-lived lab environments to kick the tires on, but when using this approach, you'll need to lock down your Terraform state:

```
resource "tls_private_key" "ssh_key" {
  algorithm = "RSA"
  rsa_bits  = 4096
}
```

Now that Terraform has generated your resource, you can drop it into the secrets manager of your choice:

```
resource "azurerm_key_vault_secret" "ssh_private_key" {
  name         = "ssh-key"
  value        = tls_private_key.ssh_key.private_key_openssh
  key_vault_id = azurerm_key_vault.main.id
}
```

In the preceding example, we drop the `private_key_openssh` value into an Azure Key Vault secret, allowing us to use the SSH key from the Azure portal to connect to the machine directly or use Azure Bastion.

RSA is the most popular algorithm used for SSH keys. It is tried and true, but you should use a key size of at least 4,096 bits. Newer algorithms such as ECDSA and ED25519 are also supported, but you should ensure your clients support these algorithms before wider adoption within your organization.

When you generate the SSH key, you don't need to save it to the filesystem. You should save it to a certificate management service such as **AWS Certificate Manager** (**ACM**), Azure Key Vault, or Google Cloud's Certificate Manager.

Due to the way Terraform planning works, for Terraform to know whether or not the SSH key resource exists and whether your certificate manager has the resource, it needs to maintain critical attributes in the state file. Many of those key attributes are highly sensitive information, including the public and private keys. Therefore, securing your Terraform state's backend will be crucial to prevent unauthorized access. It's not an impossible or difficult task in its own right, but until you've got a secure backend strategy in place, this approach is probably good to skip for production workloads.

Certificates

When generating a certificate, you typically need to generate a **certificate signing request** (**CSR**) to a **certificate authority** (**CA**), which would include a private key (usually in the form of a PEM file) and details about the certificate subject, including human-friendly information such as the organization name, physical address, and network address information such as domain names or IP addresses.

Terraform has a resource, tls_cert_request, that can generate the CSR. Like the tls_private_key resource that generates an SSH key, this resource performs a task a human operator would perform by using a graphical or command-line interface to generate the CSR. The output of this resource would then need to be passed to a CA to generate a signed certificate.

You can use the foo resource to generate the certificate locally. The CSR provider will attempt to process it on the local machine running Terraform.

First, you need a private key, which you can create using the tls_private_key resource we used to generate an SSH key:

```
resource "tls_private_key" "foo" {
  algorithm = "RSA"
}
```

Then, we need to generate the CSR using the tls_cert_request resource:

```
resource "tls_cert_request" "foo" {
  private_key_pem = tls_private_key.foo.private_key_pem

  subject {
    common_name  = "foo.com"
    organization = "Foobar, Inc"
  }
}
```

Finally, we can generate a certificate using the private key and the CSR:

```
resource "tls_locally_signed_cert" "vault" {
  cert_request_pem = tls_cert_request.foo.cert_request_pem

  ca_key_algorithm   = tls_private_key.foo.algorithm
  ca_private_key_pem = tls_private_key.foo.private_key_pem
  ca_cert_pem        = tls_self_signed_cert.foo.cert_pem

  validity_period_hours = 17520

  allowed_uses = [
    "server_auth",
    "client_auth",
  ]
}
```

Generating CloudInit configuration

Cloud Init is an open source, multi-platform tool for providing startup configuration to cloud-hosted virtual machines. It configures the new instance using metadata from the cloud and user data. For example, you can set the hostname, set up users and groups, mount and format disks, install packages, and run custom scripts.

Basic usage

Sometimes, you can use data sources to generate content rather than talk to an external system. The `cloudinit_config` is a perfect example of this. It is designed with a schema to help simplify generating the sometimes-verbose Cloud-Init configuration file passed as input to newly created virtual machines.

Cloud-Init supports several different part types. Each type infers a different schema and format for passing in content, sometimes using JSON, YAML, bash scripts, or raw text. The full scope of what Cloud-Init can do is out of the scope of this book, but I'd encourage you to look into the online documentation for further details. I'll cover a few everyday use cases to show how you can use your existing Cloud-Init knowledge and apply it while using the `cloudinit` Terraform provider:

```
data "cloudinit_config" "foo" {
  gzip          = false
  base64_encode = false
}
```

To attach the output as user data to a new **Elastic Compute Cloud (EC2)** instance on AWS, we would use the following code:

```
resource "aws_instance" "web" {

  # other ec2 attributes

  user_data = data.cloudinit_config.foo.rendered


}
```

Loading external content

When you have a large amount of external content you want to download to the instance, you can use x-include-url and x-include-once-url:

```
data "cloudinit_config" "foo" {
  gzip          = false
  base64_encode = false

  part {
    content_type = "text/x-include-url"
    content      = "http://foo.com/bar.sh"
  }
}
```

Using custom scripts

When you want to execute custom scripts stored within the Terraform module directory, you can use several different part types to run the scripts under other conditions:

- x-shellscript: This script will run whenever the instance is booted. That is, it will execute every time your instance starts up, whether it is the first boot after creation or a subsequent reboot.

- x-shellscript-per-boot: This is the same as x-shellscript. It will also run on every boot of the instance.

- x-shellscript-per-instance: This script will run only once per instance. That is, the script will run on the first boot after the instance is created but will not run on subsequent reboots. This part is helpful for initialization tasks that only need to be done once for each instance, such as setting up software or users that persist across reboots.

- x-shellscript-per-once: This script will run only once across all instances. If you create multiple instances with the same script, this script will only run on the first instance that boots. This part is helpful for tasks that only need to be done once in a set of instances, such as setting up a database or a leader node in a cluster.

Consider the following script, which is stored in a bash script file called `foo.sh` in the Terraform module's root folder:

```
#!/bin/bash
sudo apt-get update -y
sudo apt-get install nginx -y
echo '<h1>Hello from Terraform Cloud-Init!</h1>' | sudo tee /var/
www/html/index.html
```

We can embed this in a `cloudinit_config` data source to generate the user data we pass to a newly created virtual machine:

```
data "cloudinit_config" "foo" {
  gzip          = false
  base64_encode = false

  part {
    content_type = "text/x-shellscript"
    content      = file("${path.module}/foo.sh")
  }
}
```

Cloud config files

Cloud-Init supports a custom schema for performing various everyday tasks. Several different part types are supported, enabling you to include cloud config data in multiple formats in your Cloud-Init packages:

- `cloud-config`: This is the most commonly used content type for standard cloud-init YAML configuration files. You can use the `cloud-config` content type for general-purpose instance configuration tasks, such as setting up users and groups, managing packages, running commands, and writing files.

- `cloud-config-archive`: This content type provides multiple cloud-config parts in a single file. A `cloud-config-archive` file is a YAML file that contains a list of cloud-config parts, where each part is a map containing a filename, a content type, and the content itself. You should use this when applying multiple cloud-config files in a specific order. Their order in the list influences when they are applied.

- `cloud-config-jsonp`: This content type allows you to write **JSON with Padding** (**JSONP**) responses. JSONP is commonly used to bypass web browser cross-domain policies. You might use this content type if you're writing a web app that needs to interact with a server on a different domain and uses JSONP to circumvent the same-origin policy.

The full capabilities of cloud config are beyond the scope of this book, but I encourage you to explore them in more detail through online documentation. The following configuration demonstrates how we can use `cloud init` to generate a user, a group, assign the user to the group, and set up permissions and settings for the machine:

```
#cloud-config
groups:
  - bar
users:
  - name: foo
    groups: sudo, bar
    shell: /bin/bash
    sudo: ['ALL=(ALL) NOPASSWD:ALL']
    ssh_authorized_keys:
      - ssh-rsa your-public-key
```

We can embed this in a `cloudinit_config` data source to generate the user data we pass to a newly created virtual machine:

```
data "cloudinit_config" "foo" {
  gzip          = false
  base64_encode = false

  part {
    content_type = "text/cloud-config"
    content      = file("${path.module}/users.yaml")
  }
}
```

Configuring DNS records

Managing **Domain Name System (DNS)** using automation is critical to specific release strategies such as blue-green deployment. Terraform provides an extensible framework that can easily handle such essential configurations.

While most cloud providers offer their own DNS services, from Amazon's Route 53 to Azure's Private DNS zones, there is usually a first-party solution for managing DNS on the cloud of your choice. Several third-party providers for public DNS registrars have DNS service offerings such as Cloudflare, Akamai, GoDaddy, and DynDNS.

However, because Terraform offers such an extensible foundation, managing DNS is not limited to public cloud platforms through their respective providers. You can also manage your on-premises DNS servers or any custom DNS infrastructure built using infrastructure as a service in your chosen public or private clouds.

You can use the DNS provider with any DNS server that supports either the secret key (RFC 2845) or GSS-TSIG (RFC 3645) authentication method.

Summary

In this chapter, we looked in depth at the utility providers that HashiCorp has built to help us augment our IaC solutions. We learned how to integrate with external systems, work with assets stored on the filesystem, and randomize and fill in whitespace within Terraform. These Terraform providers are incredibly versatile, and as you explore them more, you will find them more and more valuable.

As you would when using other providers, always reference the provider in your `required_providers` block with an explicit version number. Do not implicitly take the latest. Other than that, resources from these providers can be embedded in any Terraform module. Take special care when designing reusable modules to ensure you have minimal provider requirements on upstream client modules, as this can add additional complexity to users who hope to reuse your module when it requires a dozen different providers to be declared!

In the next chapter, we will establish some architectural concepts we can apply to our IaC, no matter the cloud platform we target. After all, our IaC is only as good as the architecture that it defines. Therefore, we must have a sound understanding of the typical elements of cloud service anatomy and the mechanics of different computational paradigms such as virtual machines and containers. So, next, we'll look at virtual machine architecture through a multi-cloud lens.

Part 2:
Concepts of Cloud Architecture and Automation

Without a solid foundation in cloud architecture and software development processes, the journey into Infrastructure as Code would be a futile one. Luckily, many of these concepts transcend cloud platforms, and once you understand the key concepts, you'll be ready to apply that knowledge within the cloud of your choice—be it AWS, Azure, or GCP.

This part has the following chapters:

- *Chapter 4, Foundations of Cloud Architecture – Virtual Machines and Infrastructure-as-a-Service*

- *Chapter 5, Beyond VMs – Core Concepts of Containers and Kubernetes*

- *Chapter 6, Connecting It All Together – GitFlow, GitOps, and CI/CD*

4

Foundations of Cloud Architecture – Virtual Machines and Infrastructure-as-a-Services

This book aims to help you master Terraform, but what does it take to be a true master? Terraform is an **Infrastructure-as-Code** (**IaC**) tool that enables you to describe your cloud architecture using code. Without a solid understanding of the underlying architecture, you can never become a true master of Terraform. Therefore, I've included the next few chapters to provide the groundwork for ubiquitous architectural concepts across cloud platforms to lay the foundation for later chapters, when we will build sophisticated cloud architectures in three distinct cloud computing paradigms:

- Virtual machines
- Containers
- Serverless

With this foundation, you will understand the necessary concepts to follow along with the solution architectures we will build in later chapters.

In this chapter, we will focus on the key concepts that are critical for understanding, architecting, and automating virtual machine-based solutions. First, we will lay a foundation for fundamental networking concepts such as subnets, routing, perimeter-based security, peering, **Virtual Private Networks** (**VPNs**), and dedicated network connections.

Next, we'll delve into the basic anatomy of virtual machines, including disks and network interfaces. We will then be considering the subtle nuances between Windows and Linux virtual machines. Next, we will cover auto-scaling.

Finally, we'll round it out by discussing how virtual machines are provisioned, covering both mutable and immutable infrastructure practices and their corresponding IaC practices and tools.

This chapter covers the following topics:

- Understanding the key concepts of networking
- Understanding the key concepts of compute
- Understanding the role of virtual machine images

Understanding the key concepts of networking

Depending on how you and your organization plan on leveraging the cloud, you will likely work with one or more of the three paradigms for provisioning infrastructure: virtual machines, containers, or serverless. Each paradigm has different benefits and detractors that you must consider when selecting them for your solution architecture. Still, it is crucial to recognize that each paradigm has its own time and place that makes it worthwhile. In this book, I hope to help you learn how to leverage Terraform to deploy sophisticated solutions in these paradigms on the three significant hyperscalers (at the time of writing).

Each of these paradigms has specific concepts that transcend cloud platforms that you—as a practitioner and architect—need to understand to design and implement solutions using Terraform.

Virtual machines are a standard service on every cloud platform because most organizations would like to leverage the cloud with their existing applications with minimal change. Virtual machines enable these organizations to have complete control of the configuration of their environment from the operating system up. With this low level of control, organizations can move applications to cloud infrastructure with minimal change, yet ultimate control.

This approach is practical because virtual machines are a concept and architecture that is well-known by most IT organizations. Organizations looking to migrate to the cloud probably already use virtual machines in their on-premises data centers.

That means that as you automate that infrastructure in the cloud, you'll need to understand the core concepts and common architectural patterns.

With virtual machines, the good news is that most of the anatomy is relatively similar across cloud platforms, so if you know what you're looking for, there is a good chance you will find the corresponding service—or Terraform resource—that implements that particular aspect of the solution. There may be subtle differences between cloud platforms that you must learn through conducting detailed analysis and optimizing your solutions. Still, if you understand the basic concepts, it'll be pretty easy to map them across the cloud platforms and get productive using Terraform relatively quickly.

In this book, we will build an end-to-end solution using virtual machines on AWS, Azure, and Google Cloud Platform. To do so, you must understand some critical concepts that transcend cloud platforms to help you navigate the architecture and relevant Terraform resources within the respective cloud platform's Terraform provider.

Networking

All virtual machines live on a network and each cloud platform has a corresponding service that handles this aspect of the solution. A network itself is relatively simple to create. It only needs one primary piece of information: the network address space, a block of IP addresses that fall within a contiguous range.

An IP address is made up of 32 bits. These bits are grouped into octets and translated into integers between 0 and 255. IPv4 has four octets in a single IP address, resulting in over 4 billion addressable IP addresses. In IPv6, there are 16 octets and many more IP addresses.

CIDR notation is a method for representing IP address ranges as contiguous blocks. A CIDR block comprises an IP address starting the range and a prefix length separated by a forward slash. For example, 10.0.1.0/24 represents a range of IP addresses starting with 10.0.1.0 and extending through to 10.0.1.255—256 IP addresses. 10.0.1.0 is the starting IP address, and 24 is the number of bits that should be in common. Since an IP address is composed of 32 bits and each decimal within the IP address represents 8 bits, 24 bits would mean that three of the four octets are shared within the range and only the last digit changes. Since the last digit ranges from 0 to 255, that gives us 256 IP addresses starting with 10.0.1.0 and going through to 10.0.1.255.

Several reserved IP address ranges exist for private networks. 10.0.0.0/8 and 172.0.0.0/12 are the most common ranges in enterprises, while I'm sure you've encountered 192.168.0.0/16 at home.

Getting familiar with CIDR notation and understanding the impact of selecting different-sized prefixes is essential. Usually, /16 is the largest (65,536 IP addresses) and /28 the smallest (16 IP addresses) prefix supported by cloud platforms—but it does vary, so you should check your cloud platform's documentation. More importantly, consider your requirements and if you have an in-house networking team at your organization, by all means, consult them when settling on a range that fits for your solution.

Usually, organizations maintain a list of IP address ranges that have been allocated to different teams or applications to prevent IP address conflicts. This practice is critical when starting in the cloud for the first time at your organization if you already have an on-premise network. If you use a default—such as 10.0.0.0/16—or always use the same address range, you could be hurt if you ever want to connect your project to other networks within your organization.

Although it can vary by cloud platform, you would usually provision a virtual network within a specific region, as on AWS and Azure. However, with Google Cloud Platform, virtual networks are global and span all regions.

Subnets

Once you have settled on an IP address space for your network, you will be carving it into subnets. Subnets allow you to segment your network for various reasons, including improved security or organizational and operational efficiencies.

From a security standpoint, subnets are very important to isolate components of your architecture to reduce the blast radius if a problem occurs in one subnet. By creating routing rules to control network traffic between subnets, you can increase security by cutting down the surface area for an attack.

Depending on the cloud platform, subnets might also influence the physical location of resources provisioned within such as an availability zone. This is the case on AWS. However, Azure and GCP do not have this limitation, as their subnets can contain resources that span the entire region.

Routing

Once you have segmented your virtual network using subnets, it's crucial to establish the traffic patterns of network traffic using **route tables**.

Route tables allow you to direct network traffic to the correct endpoint based on different rules for different types of traffic. For example, there may be a delineation between internet traffic routed to an internet gateway or a NAT gateway. Similar network routing rules can route traffic to on-premise networks through VPN or Direct Connect connections, peered virtual networks, transit gateways, or service endpoints.

Network security

Once you have a virtual network and a set of subnets, each with its own purpose and resources, you will likely need to apply security controls to ensure that only the expected network traffic can pass between resources within the various subnets.

Most cloud platforms have some manifestation of this concept, but they may have different names. They may have other mechanisms for attachment—either on a subnet, virtual machine, or virtual **Network Interface Card** (**NIC**). They include inbound and outbound rules. They can also come in stateless and stateful forms and sometimes support both `Allow` and `Deny` rules, while other times they only support `Allow` rules.

Azure and AWS provide a lower-level mechanism focusing primarily on the physical network layer and a higher level focusing on more of the logical application layer. Google Cloud Platform wraps both concepts into one structure and calls them firewall rules.

AWS has **Network Access Control Lists** (**NACLs**), which attach to subnets and control the flow of network traffic between subnets. As a result, they only work on network address ranges—not AWS resources such as network gateways or service endpoints. They are stateless, which means that, in most cases, you need the inbound and outbound rules to match for connectivity to succeed.

In contrast, AWS also has security groups, which are stateful, only support `Allow` rules, and allow you to route traffic between different network address ranges and AWS resources using their unique identifiers. Security groups can be logically attached to a subnet or directly onto virtual machines (EC2 instances), but AWS evaluates them at the virtual machine level. Attaching a security group to a subnet only results in an implicit cascading attachment of that security group to all virtual machines within that subnet.

Azure similarly has two constructs for constraining network traffic: **Network Security Groups (NSGs)** and **Application Security Groups (ASGs)**. NSGs are in many ways a combination of AWS's NACLs and security groups but shed some logical attachment capabilities with a focus on the physical network layer. ASGs are logical and can be associated with a virtual machine through NICs. Just like AWS NACLs, you can think of NSGs as controlling the flow of traffic between networks, while AWS's security groups and Azure's ASGs both focus on controlling traffic at a finer grain—with an application-centric lens—between resources within the network.

Google Cloud Platform has one construct: firewall rules. This construct is stateful but also supports `Allow` and `Deny` rules. It can be attached to a virtual network or a region, or it can be attached globally.

Network peering

Virtual network peering is a networking feature offered by most cloud platforms that allows you to connect virtual networks within the same cloud platform without additional VPN-based connectivity.

To create a peering connection between two virtual networks, they must be in the same cloud platform, and there should not be any conflicts within their network address space. This potential quagmire is one reason why it's essential to think through and apply proper governance around allocated network address ranges.

Peering is a capability that eliminates the need for more complex private site-to-site connections using VPN connections and is the preferred method for connecting networks within the cloud.

Service endpoints

Most cloud platforms provide services that are primarily accessed directly via the internet. In situations where security is paramount, avoiding transmitting data across the internet is essential. Service endpoints are a feature provided by cloud platforms that enable private network communication between virtual networks and specific services within the cloud environment without traversing the public internet.

While this concept and goal exists and remains the same across all cloud providers we will cover in this book, it goes by different names, has varying support across each platform's service offerings, and may have other attachment and routing mechanisms to set service endpoints up.

VPN and Direct Connect

When virtual network peering isn't an option, you can always leverage traditional site-to-site VPN connectivity options to connect networks from your on-premises networks or across cloud providers.

When setting up a VPN connection, most cloud platforms require you to provide a resource representing the source network and destination network configuration.

The destination network is where you host the entry point for your VPN and where the VPN traffic traverses to gain connectivity to cloud-hosted resources. The source network is where you have devices that need to connect to the destination network. The source network is often on-premise, but it doesn't have to be. After that, the most common use case is connecting networks on two different cloud platforms.

In this section, we learned the critical concepts of cloud networking that you will encounter whenever you provision virtual machines, no matter your target cloud platform. There might be some subtle changes on each platform that affect how you'll use each and how they will affect the availability and structure of your architecture, but their function is essentially the same.

Next, we'll look at the critical concepts of virtual machines, including basic anatomy. This includes disks, NICs, and the virtual machine itself, as well as operating system-specific differences between Windows and Linux and cloud-specific capabilities such as auto-scaling.

Understanding the key concepts of compute

A virtual machine is a software emulation of a physical computer. Just like a regular computer, it runs an operating system and whatever applications you install on it. Ultimately, it does run on physical hardware. However, in the cloud, the cloud platform abstracts the physical hardware and the hypervisor that manages the virtual machines from the user.

Virtual machines are most commonly available on cloud platforms in two flavors: Linux and Windows, with various current and historical versions supported through marketplace offerings on the cloud platform itself.

The primary configuration attributes of a virtual machine are its size, the virtual machine image to use as its operating system disk, additional data disks, and network configuration.

Cloud platforms use a **Stock-Keeping Unit** (**SKU**) to create a standard configuration that dictates the size and hardware profile of the virtual machine. This pattern is typical across cloud platforms, but the SKU names follow different naming conventions. Cloud platforms do have a similar organization system with sub-categories such as general purpose, compute-optimized, and memory-optimized. There are also those with particular hardware components such as **Graphics Processing Units** (**GPUs**).

The virtual machine image is a disk image of a pre-configured operating system, which can include additional software pre-installed depending on the image's purpose. The virtual machine image is an essential component in the automation of virtual machines. We'll go into further depth on this later.

Disks

Virtual machines can attach additional data disks to add extra storage. Like virtual machines, the disks can have varying sizes and performance characteristics. Unlike virtual machine sizes, which vary using categorical SKUs that indicate a fixed configuration type, disks use a continuous metric for sizing: **Gigabytes** (**GB**).

In addition to the disk size, you can also choose from several different performance classes optimized for different workload scenarios, such as general purpose, throughput optimized, and provisioned IOPS, which seeks to guarantee a reliable level of performance.

The SKU you select influences the number and class of disks you can attach to your virtual machine, with larger virtual machines supporting a larger quantity of disks.

Network Interface Cards (NICs)

Virtual machines can attach NICs that logically represent a physical network interface card. As with disks, the size of a virtual machine can impact the number of NICs you can add and the features you can enable.

Through NIC configuration, you can either team the network interfaces together to create higher bandwidth or attach them to different subnets to connect a virtual machine. The latter option lets you straddle the line between two separate networks.

Linux versus Windows

Linux and Windows virtual machines are identical anatomically in terms of virtual machine sizes, disks, and NICs. Still, there are a few key differences to be aware of when using Terraform and other tools to manage them.

Authentication and remote access

Windows virtual machines usually require an administrator username and password. In contrast, Linux virtual machines usually require an SSH key. After the initial setup, you can configure Windows to support SSH access, but password-based credentials are needed initially.

This caveat also manifests in remotely accessing virtual machines using Windows and Linux. Windows uses **Remote Desktop Protocol** (**RDP**), which requires a password-based login. Linux uses SSH, which can support either password or key-based login.

Configuration scripts

Windows supports several different types of scripting by default. However, the most common are batch scripting, which uses the Windows **Command-Line Interpreter** (**CMD**), and **PowerShell**. While Microsoft initially developed PowerShell specifically for automating administration tasks on Windows, support for PowerShell has since been added on Linux, although community adoption has not hit critical mass.

While Linux distributions vary, **Bourne Again SHell** (**Bash**) is the default for most distributions. There are others—for example, `ksh`, `csh`, and `tsch`—and while their capabilities are similar to Bash, their popularity varies.

Windows has even joined the party by introducing **Windows Subsystem for Linux** (**WSL**), which, when installed, can execute Bash scripts natively on Windows.

Auto-scaling

One of the quintessential advantages of leveraging the cloud is the ability to add elasticity to your solutions at scale. That is to increase capacity when there is heavy usage of your application and decrease capacity when your application's use goes down.

Cloud platforms provide mechanisms that make achieving this very easy. Although they may have different names for this capability, the anatomy of the solution remains the same. You simply give details on the virtual machine image that you want, how large the virtual machine should be, any hard range constraints in terms of the number of instances (such as a minimum and a maximum), and finally, you provide several parameters to control when and how fast to scale up or scale down.

This section has taught us some of the basics of how we provision virtual machines. These concepts manifest across different cloud platforms. While there may be small subtleties between the various cloud platforms, they operate similarly.

Next, we'll look at the role that the virtual machine image plays in how we can automate virtual machines.

Understanding the role of virtual machine images

Virtual machines need an operating system and other applications installed to serve their purpose. A virtual machine image is a single file containing a virtual disk with a bootable operating system installed on it. It's a snapshot of a virtual machine at a particular point in time. This snapshot contains the state of the virtual machine, including the operating system, installed applications, and other settings.

Static virtual machines

When setting up a single virtual machine, or even a group of them with different roles and responsibilities within a solution's architecture, there is a process of configuration that needs to happen to get each virtual machine into the state required to perform its duties as part of the solution.

This configuration includes the following steps:

1. Installing the operating system
2. Configuring the operating system
3. Installing software updates and security patches
4. Installing third-party software
5. Configuring third-party software

Of course, each of these steps may change depending on the role of the virtual machine within the solution. The further down the order a step is, the more likely it becomes that the configuration will change, with operating system installation being the most stable and third-party software configuration having the most diversity depending on the virtual machine's role.

For example, a simple two-tier architecture requiring a Java web application to talk to a PostgreSQL database would have two roles. One role installs the Java Web Application server, while another installs the PostgreSQL database. Both virtual machines might share the exact same operating system, configuration, and security patches in this scenario. Still, when it comes to third-party software, one might need Java Web Application server software, while the other might need PostgreSQL database server software.

Each role requires different configuration steps to configure the server to fulfill its purpose. For example, these steps might include steps such as installing software packages, setting environment variables, updating configuration files, creating user accounts, setting up permissions, running custom scripts, or any other action required to set up the machine.

When working with the cloud, you pass this configuration to the virtual machine by specifying an operating system disk image. The disk image that is used will determine whether the virtual machine will spin up with nothing but a clean install of Ubuntu 22.04—ready to be manually configured—or a fully working Java Web Application server that requires no manual intervention whatsoever.

Each cloud platform provides a large set of disk images that you can use to start virtual machines for various purposes. The most common ones are baseline images with a specific version of an operating system installed, such as Windows Server 2019, Ubuntu 22.04, or RedHat Enterprise Linux.

With so many marketplace images providing a baseline operating system install, you can spin up a virtual machine with Ubuntu 22.04, install the Java Web Application software, configure it precisely to your specifications, and create a new virtual machine image. This new virtual machine image will boot up as a Java Web Application server rather than a brand new installation of Ubuntu 22.04, which means that you are that much closer to using this virtual machine to host your web application.

You can use automation technologies that manage this configuration to perform the actions you might perform manually, assuming you were starting from a clean operating system installation. Several automation tools focus on this problem—you might be surprised to learn that Terraform is not one of them. While Terraform can provide this configuration through several different techniques, that's not its primary focus. Usually, Terraform should work together with another tool with this focus. The two of these tools should make a joint decision on how to share the responsibility of deploying this configuration.

Using configuration manager

One popular approach is to leverage Terraform to provision the virtual machines required in your solution and rely on the configuration management tool to handle the rest of the configuration on each virtual machine from the operating system.

This approach has the benefit of isolating the responsibility of configuration management entirely to a tool that is fit to handle this task. Some examples of popular tools include **Chef** or **Puppet**, which use agents to apply configuration onto virtual machines—or it could be a tool such as **Ansible** that requires no agent and uses SSH as the primary method to apply configuration.

Due to Ansible's heavy reliance on SSH and Windows's limited support for this remote access method, Ansible has not historically been an ideal candidate for managing Windows-based virtual machines in this manner. Tools such as Chef and Puppet have seen more robust adoption in enterprise IT environments where Windows Server was the dominant server operating system. However, this does appear to be changing, with additional support from Ansible and newer versions of Windows making it easier to manage with this approach.

Custom virtual machine images

After you have configured your virtual machine to the point that it is ready to take on its role within the system with only some minor final configuration changes, you can capture a snapshot of the operating system disk and create a virtual machine image from it that you can use to spin up additional virtual machines. When you use this image, these virtual machines will already have the configuration you have set up previously, with no need to set everything up again.

This approach has the benefit of increased startup speed. Since you already did most of the work when you built the image, that work doesn't have to happen every time you spin up a new virtual machine. Instead, you will only need to wait for the cloud platform to launch the virtual machine. It will have everything you need installed and ready to go without waiting for the configuration manager to set everything up.

The most common tool used to do this is called **Packer**. It's an open source product published by **HashiCorp**.

You can write Packer templates in JSON or HCL. However, you should use the latter, as it makes managing and organizing your code much easier. A Packer template consists of three parts:

- Builders that establish connectivity to a target platform to build a virtual machine

- Provisioners that provide instructions that must be executed on the virtual machine before creating an image

- Post-processors that execute after the builders and provisioners and perform any last-minute operations before creating the artifact

Packer's provisioners include three main types:

- **Script execution**: Execute scripts in various shell environments supporting Windows and Linux

- **File**: Upload files or directories from the local environment to the virtual machine

- **Flow control**: Pause execution or trigger a Windows restart to let settings take effect

Build versus bake

Taking a clean installation of the operating system and using a configuration management tool to apply the desired state on it is what I call the *build* approach. Its converse, the *bake* approach, uses an automation tool—such as Packer—that will launch a temporary virtual machine, set everything up, and then snap a new virtual machine image.

The build option is ideal for Day 2 Operations because it allows you to easily apply patches and manage the environment over time. With configuration management tools in charge, you have a live connection to your virtual machines and can update them quickly without disruption. In contrast, when using the bake approach, you will first need to bake a new image, then upgrade all the virtual machines to use the latest image. This results in downtime while you tear down the machine using the old image and spin up the machine using the new image. It can also be a slow process to develop the virtual machine image, as each bake can take a considerable amount of time, while the configuration management tool provides relatively near real-time feedback if there is an issue.

The bake approach truly shines when there is time sensitivity in how fast you need to spin up additional virtual machines and you don't want to wait for the configuration manager to do a clean install of your entire solution stack on the virtual machine, as this uses up valuable time that you could use to service end user requests. Situations that can benefit from this include the following:

- **Failover and recovery**: When you have identified that a previously healthy virtual machine has become unhealthy and needs to be replaced rapidly, this situation could be due to an outage or transient hardware failure.

- **Auto-scaling**: When you need to scale up to meet spikes in traffic for your service, it's ideal for your new virtual machine to pick up the load as quickly as possible when a scale-up event is triggered. If it does not, you may need to build in additional buffer times by reducing the threshold for scaling up and increasing the threshold for scaling down. This approach allows the system to spin up resources earlier and spin them down more slowly, ensuring that the inherent time delay doesn't impact your end users.

Build versus bake is not a mutually exclusive endeavor. There is usually a split between the two. In most situations, there are pieces of configuration that you can never bake into the images. These fall into the following categories:

- **Frequency**: You should bake configurations that change into the image at a very low frequency. Conversely, you should include configurations that you may need to adjust at runtime in the build.

- **Post-provisioning values**: You should bake configurations that require values that are only available after provisioning. These values might include private IP addresses, DNS hostnames, or other metadata generated during provisioning that is only known at the end.

With that, we've come to the end of this chapter.

Summary

This chapter looked at the core concepts required to understand virtual machines across multiple cloud platforms. In this book, we will build an end-to-end solution using virtual machine architecture for each of the three hyperscalers: AWS, Azure, and Google Cloud Platform. The providers for each will manifest and exercise these concepts slightly differently. The resources will change, but the concepts as they manifest in our architecture will be relatively consistent.

In this chapter, I have gone over common concepts across cloud platforms that are necessary to understand in order to automate solutions. These include cloud networking concepts like virtual networks, subnets, peering, and service endpoints, which are essential for creating and managing isolated network environments and ensuring efficient communication between resources. We also explored computing concepts such as virtual NICs for network connectivity and virtual disks for scalable storage solutions.

Another critical topic discussed is the build vs. bake dilemma, addressing how much operating system configuration should be built into a machine image versus how much should be added after the machine has been provisioned. This involves understanding the trade-offs between pre-configuring images (baking) to streamline deployment processes and configuring them post-deployment (building) to enhance flexibility and reduce image management complexity. By understanding these concepts, you will be better equipped to design and automate robust, scalable solutions across different cloud platforms.

In the next chapter, we will explore the core concepts needed for a new cloud computing paradigm: **containers**.

5

Beyond VMs – Core Concepts of Containers and Kubernetes

In the previous chapter, we familiarized ourselves with **virtual machine** (**VM**) architecture and the core concepts and mechanics needed to automate VM-based solutions. In this book, we will build end-to-end solutions covering the three significant hyperscalars—**Amazon Web Services** (**AWS**), Azure, and **Google Cloud Platform** (**GCP**)—and covering three cloud computing paradigms: VMs, containers, and serverless. In this chapter, we will look at the core concepts needed to tackle container-based architecture solutions using the managed Kubernetes offerings from each cloud platform.

To accomplish this, we must understand the basics of containers, Kubernetes, and how they fit within the Terraform ecosystem. As with VMs and the surrounding toolchains used for configuration management and the **build-versus-bake** dilemma, with container-based architecture, we need to make some decisions about where the boundary between Terraform and other tools will exist and how best to integrate configuration management of our containers and container orchestrators with the cloud infrastructure that we provision to host them.

The chapter covers the following topics:

- Understanding key concepts of container architecture
- Leveraging Docker to build container images
- Working with container registries
- Understanding key concepts of container orchestration and Kubernetes
- Understanding Kubernetes manifests
- Leveraging the Kubernetes provider to provision Kubernetes resources
- Leveraging the Helm provider to provision Kubernetes resources

Understanding key concepts of container architecture

VMs are great when you want minimal changes to operate your applications and software in the cloud, but they also have drawbacks. With the maximum control you get from having a full VM—of whatever size you happened to provision—you are free to use as many (or as few) of the VM's resources as you can. However, many organizations have found that their fleet of VMs is plagued by low utilization even when best practices in workload isolation or the **single responsibility principle** (**SRP**) are followed.

Inversely, when maximum utilization is the objective, organizations load up a single VM with so many disparate services and components that each VM—while highly utilized—becomes a bit of a quagmire to manage and maintain. The VM will have a myriad of dependency conflicts, with resource contention cropping up between the horde of independent but cohabitating processes within the same VM.

This dilemma between workload isolation and resource utilization is the problem that container technology aims to solve and where container orchestrators, such as Kubernetes, help by bringing resiliency and scalability.

In this book, we will build an end-to-end solution using Kubernetes-based container technology on AWS, Azure, and GCP. To do so, you must understand some critical concepts that transcend cloud platforms to help you navigate the architecture and relevant Terraform resources within the respective cloud platform's Terraform provider.

Containers

Containers allow you to package your applications into an isolated environment logically separated from other applications without the overhead incurred by virtualizing the underlying physical hardware and the resource consumption of a full-on operating system. Whether it is Windows or Linux, the operating system consumes resources that take away from your capacity.

Containers use two Linux kernel primitives: *namespaces* and *control groups*. These constructs allow the container runtime to set up an isolated environment within the Linux operating system. Namespaces are all about isolation, which allows us to split the operating system into multiple virtual operating systems with their own process tree, root filesystem, user, and so on. Each container might feel like a regular operating system, but it's not. Control groups police the allocation of the host system's resources—including CPU, memory, and disk I/O—to ensure that the actual physical server is not overwhelmed by resources consumed by the containers.

The last component that enables containers is a layered filesystem. This is similar to how we used to build VM images—only with better isolation between layers. When we build a VM layer, when we apply changes to and create a new VM image, we can no longer sort out the base layer from the top layer. Containers can apply filesystem layers that contain only the differences between the lower layers. This approach creates an extremely compact and highly efficient way of layering changes onto each container image to compose the final filesystem that the container operates on—with the topmost layer being writable by the container itself.

One of the key benefits of containers is their efficiency. Unlike VMs, which require separate operating systems and resource allocations for each instance, containers directly leverage the host system's kernel. This approach means they consume fewer resources and start up much faster than their VM counterparts. Multiple containers can run simultaneously on a single host, thus using system resources more efficiently. This allows us to create higher-density workloads—thus reducing the waste of valuable system resources such as CPU and memory to idleness, and when working in the cloud, this waste is like pouring money down the drain!

Now that we have a solid understanding of what a container is and how it differs from a VM, let's look at the de facto tool for managing the configuration of an individual container: **Docker**. While this book isn't about Docker per se, if you are going to be a master of Terraform and work with container-based architectures, you will inevitably come into contact with this tool either directly or need to integrate it into the **continuous integration/continuous deployment (CI/CD)** process.

Leveraging Docker to build container images

The Docker engine makes the process of setting up containers much simpler. It provides a consistent meta-language for describing containers and command-line tools for building, interrogating, and running container images.

Writing a Dockerfile

Docker uses a simple syntax that you can use to define basic information about your container. This basic structure includes what base image to build onto (FROM), who the author is (MAINTAINER), files to copy and commands to execute (COPY and RUN), and what the entry point process should be (CMD).

Much of this is similar to the structure of a Packer template, except for the entry point process. With Packer, it's just a VM; whatever processes are running, based on how you configure, it will be running. With Docker, you need to explicitly state what process to start because containers run a single process in isolation.

You can also configure the runtime further by setting the working directory, adding environment variables, and exposing network ports.

A simple Dockerfile looks like this:

```
# Use an official Python runtime as a parent image
FROM python:3.7-slim

# Set the working directory in the container to /app
WORKDIR /app

# Copy the current directory contents into the container at /app
```

```
COPY . /app

# Install any needed packages specified in requirements.txt
RUN pip install --no-cache-dir -r requirements.txt

# Make port 80 available to the world outside this container
EXPOSE 80

# Run app.py when the container launches
CMD \["python", "app.py"]
```

Notice that we are building from a base image called `python:3-7slim` and copying the current folder's contents to the container's `/app` directory. This step will copy the `app.py` script into the container so that it is available when we set it as the execution point at the bottom of the file. This Python script sets up a web server and exposes it to port `80`.

Building a Docker image

Just as with Terraform, Docker uses the current working directory to derive its context. Therefore, when building a Docker image, you need to execute the `docker build` command from the same directory where your Dockerfile resides. However, you can override this by specifying a different path:

```
docker build -t your-image-name .
```

The `-t` flag lets you tag your image with a memorable name. The `.` instance may seem out of place, but it tells Docker to look for the Dockerfile in the current directory.

After the build completes, you can see your image listed by running the following command:

```
docker images
```

Running Docker images

Docker images are like the VM images we built using Packer, which represent a VM we have yet to start. They have potential energy but need to be launched as the operating system disk of a VM to achieve kinetic energy and become a running VM. Docker images are the same for containers. We need to start a container using the image and specify the runtime configuration:

```
docker run -p 4000:80 your-image-name
```

In this case, because we exposed port `80` in the container, we need to map a port to the container's port `80`. The `-p` flag maps a network port inside the container to a port on the host machine. This setting will route traffic from port `4000` on the host to port `80` on the container.

You can run as many containers as your host machine can handle. You are constrained only by the technical resources of the host machine. Sometimes, the cloud platform imposes constraints depending on what SKU of VM your host machine is running.

To see which containers are running, you can execute the following Docker command:

```
docker ps
```

This section should help you understand the basic principles of working with Docker images. While there are many more commands and flags you can use with Docker to manage your images and containers, this is out of the scope of this book. I'm providing you with enough theory and practice to be productive in building container-based architectures using Terraform.

In this section, we familiarized ourselves with the command-line tool used to create container images: Docker.

In the next section, we'll look at how to publish these container images that we create with Docker to container registries so that we can deploy containers with them.

Working with container registries

A **container registry** is just a server-side application that acts as central storage and allows you to distribute container images to the host machines that need to run them. This approach is advantageous when leveraging a CI/CD pipeline where you need a central location to pull down your container images.

They often provide versioning, labeling, and sharing mechanisms that let you keep track of different versions of your container images, maintain stable releases, and share images with others—either within your organization or publicly.

Just as with `git`, anybody can set up a container registry on their own, but several managed services provide best-in-class service offerings on each of the respective clouds. There is also a cloud-agnostic and community-oriented solution: Docker Hub. Docker Hub is the default registry where Docker looks for images, and you can use it for both images you want to share publicly or keep private for internal purposes. It offers a free tier and paid plans with more storage and features.

Docker Hub

The mechanics of interacting with a container registry are broadly similar depending on the service—with only slight variations. As an example, because it is the default container registry that Docker uses, I'll show you how to use **Docker Hub** to authenticate, tag, push, and pull your images.

First, you need to authenticate. Depending on your registry service, this step might require additional tools. However, you won't need to install any other tools for Docker Hub but, naturally, you will need to register an account on Docker Hub:

```
docker login
```

The preceding command will initiate an interactive login process where you must supply your Docker Hub username and password.

Before you can push your image to a registry, you must tag it with the registry's address:

```
docker tag foo:1.0 markti/foo:1.0
```

The preceding command first specifies the `my-image` source image of a specific version, `1.0`. Then, it specifies a target image under my `markti` Docker Hub account for the same image and version. It's crucial to synchronize the image name and version between your local and remote environments to maintain consistency between the environments. After your image is tagged, you can push it to the registry:

```
docker push markti/foo:1.0
```

The preceding command pushes the image to the remote container registry. Now, you can pull the image with the appropriate permissions using your Docker Hub username as the registry name, the container image name, and the tag:

```
docker pull markti/foo:1.0
```

Remember that container registries might have slightly different naming conventions and authentication processes.

In this section, we looked at how to work with container registries, which serve as a critical infrastructure for our container-based architecture. In the next section, we're ready to look at Kubernetes—both from an architectural standpoint and at its practical usage as a developer, operator, and within CI/CD pipelines.

Understanding key concepts of container orchestration and Kubernetes

Kubernetes is a platform that expands on the responsibilities of the container runtime, which operates at an individual host level. Kubernetes' job is to perform this across multiple nodes. As we learned in the first section of this chapter, the container runtime uses a Linux operating system construct—control groups—to protect the health of the operating system by ensuring that the physical (or virtual) host that the containers are running on remains healthy. Kubernetes essentially does the same thing but across many, many servers.

Most applications or systems will naturally be organized into different components, layers, or microservices—each with its own responsibilities and corresponding application code and technology stack that implements its functionality. Each component within such a system will have its own container that has this software installed.

When we deploy systems using VMs, we do so in such a way that the same component is deployed to two more VMs, and we ensure that these VMs do not share the same underlying physical equipment. This separation could be as simple as a different physical host in the same rack, all the way up to a different physical host in an entirely different data center—sometimes separated by many tens, if not hundreds, of miles. This allows us to achieve **high availability** (**HA**) and resiliency during an outage or an issue affecting some underlying component of the physical hardware.

Unlike when using VMs, our application components don't sit on isolated VMs; they sit on the cluster nodes, oftentimes with pods from other applications.

Kubernetes tries to make sure that our application containers don't sit on the same node. That way, if one of the cluster's nodes fails, our application will not go down. Kubernetes also takes it a step further by intelligently reorganizing the containers on other health nodes. In order to do this, Kubernetes maintains a divide between its own internal **logical layer** and the underlying **physical layer** and maps the device by assigning logical deployments, or pods, to physical deployments and nodes. This separation between the logical and the physical layers is one of Kubernetes' huge advantages and what makes it so effective at managing applications and services on top of a potentially unlimited underlying physical infrastructure:

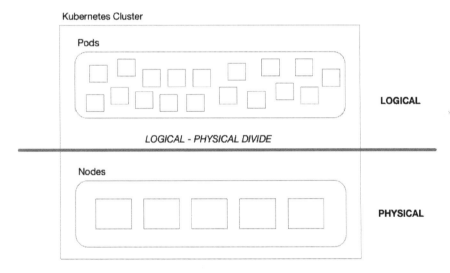

Figure 5.1 – Logical-physical divide

That's pretty much it, but there are a lot of ways we can customize how our application's components are deployed to Kubernetes to meet the specific needs of our application.

Kubernetes is flexible enough to run on a fleet of VMs on a cloud provider or physical bare-metal servers down to running on a single computer—such as your laptop. This flexibility makes it an ideal choice for hybrid cloud scenarios. It streamlines the problematic task of integration testing by allowing developers to run a copy of the entire solution on their laptop that closely mimics a production environment.

Kubernetes offers a rich set of features that fulfill most of the needs for running workloads at scale, such as service discovery, secrets management, horizontal scaling, automated rollouts and rollbacks, and self-healing capabilities—making it an ideal candidate to run both stateless and stateful applications at scale while avoiding vendor lock-in.

Kubernetes architecture is a set of loosely coupled and extensible components. This modularity allows adaptations for different cloud providers to integrate with their specific solutions for networking, storage, service mesh, and so on.

As with Terraform, Google designed Kubernetes to encourage the adoption of **infrastructure as code (IaC)** by leveraging a declarative approach for defining your application's runtime environment. Due to the extensibility of both Terraform and Kubernetes, several integration options exist. In this chapter, we'll discuss a few of those approaches and trade-offs that come along with each—but before we do that, we need to introduce some critical concepts of Kubernetes' internal architecture and operating model. Only with this foundation can we maximize the potential of leveraging Terraform and Kubernetes together.

Kubernetes architecture

Kubernetes is a distributed software system, and its design is relatively similar to that of other such systems. Because its responsibility spans a cluster of interconnected computer systems that can scale from just a few to literally thousands, it is organized like an army. There are officers, soldiers, and a central command. The soldiers are organized into smaller sub-groups, and each needs to maintain continuous contact with the central command in order to operate effectively by receiving new orders and providing the status of the current situation. The central commands receive status reports from the various officers that oversee their soldiers and operating orders and determine whether different areas of the battlefield need more troops or fewer troops, issuing orders to reallocate different sub-groups of the soldiers to different locations across the battlefield. Let's dive into each component and their roles.

Master node

The **master node** is the central command of the Kubernetes cluster—it's essentially where the generals of the army operate. For smaller skirmishes, there is typically only one central command, but for truly epic entanglement, you might need more than one for each theatre of war. It oversees the entire system and makes high-level decisions. As with any good central command, it must perform several functions:

- **API server**: Any army must take input from its civilian government, which provides objectives to complete and defines what success looks like. In many ways, this is very much like the role of the API server. Instead of taking input from politicians via that red telephone, it takes input from the end user (usually a system administrator or software developer) over a REST-based interface. The definition of success looks a bit different as well, which is the definition of how the end user's applications and services should be deployed and how to tell if they are healthy.

- **Controller manager**: Napoleon Bonaparte famously said, "*An army marches on its stomach*," which highlights the importance of sound logistics when waging war. An army is more than just boots and guns. You need food and water, uniforms and tents, and fuel for your trucks and trains. The controller manager performs a similar function as it is responsible for monitoring inventories and distributing resources so that the desired state of the army is maintained and they are empowered to accomplish their mission.

- **Scheduler**: Our very own George Washington famously said "*Discipline is the soul of an army*"— and to enforce that discipline, an army must have an officer corps that efficiently executes orders across the field of battle, assigning soldiers across the battlefield to where they are most needed. In this sense, it assigns pods to appropriate nodes based on resource availability and the objective to be accomplished.

- **etcd**: Any army is made up of soldiers and organizational units; to keep track of all this complexity, there must be a sophisticated personnel management office that keeps records of assignments, deployments, career progression, and so on. They keep track of what everyone is doing and what they are doing in their military roles. `etcd` plays this role in Kubernetes by maintaining configuration data, the state of the cluster, and creating a **single source of truth** (**SSOT**).

Worker nodes

Worker nodes are the battlefields where the soldiers of this army do what must be done to achieve the objective. They are the physical (or virtual) machines where your containers run. On any battlefield, there must be a sergeant who commands a squad of soldiers. The sergeant of Kubernetes is called the **Kubelet**. As with a sergeant, the Kubelet is autonomous within its area of the battlefield, executing orders received from central command and commanding the troops within their squad—the pods—and it maintains the chain of command with its superiors at central command—or the master node—that might delegate new orders.

The containers running within the node, being monitored by their attentive sergeant, the Kubelet, need a container runtime in order to operate. There are several different container runtimes, such as `containerd`, **CRI-O**, or Docker, which we learned about in the first section of this chapter. Although there are many container runtimes, we still use the same tooling—Docker—to build images. The runtime is really only responsible for running the containers. There are some other details to it, and it's definitely a rabbit hole, but this is what we need to know within the context of this book.

With soldiers distributed across an expansive battlefield, there needs to be a way for messages to be sent back and forth between the soldiers, their officers, and the central command. On the battlefield, this has changed throughout history from flags, banners, smoke signals, drums, horns, and bugles to modern times with telegraph, radio, and satellite communication. For the pods, this is the network traffic that is being routed to the node. The **kube-proxy**, as with the Kubelet, runs on every node and is responsible for routing network traffic to the correct destination.

Pods

That's enough about the big hats. It's time to talk soldiers. A soldier is the smallest participant on the battlefield, and soldiers, collectively, are the primary force in military operations. The same is true for pods within the context of Kubernetes. **Pods** are where all the work actually happens. Everything else going on inside a Kubernetes cluster is to facilitate the effectiveness of pods in achieving their individual objectives, much like the myriad of characters that support our frontline troopers on the battlefield by making sound strategic decisions, allocating resources, organizing soldiers into units, and assigning orders.

A pod is not a container but a Kubernetes-specific construct and, as with the soldier, the smallest unit of deployment within a cluster. A pod can have one or more containers inside of it that share resources and configurations to perform a common objective.

Instead of directly deploying individual containers, you create a pod and place containers within it. When you declare more than one container within the same pod, you are tightly coupling them together—in that they share the same network namespace, **inter-process communication (IPC)**, namespace, and filesystem.

The following diagram illustrates these core components of Kubernetes architecture:

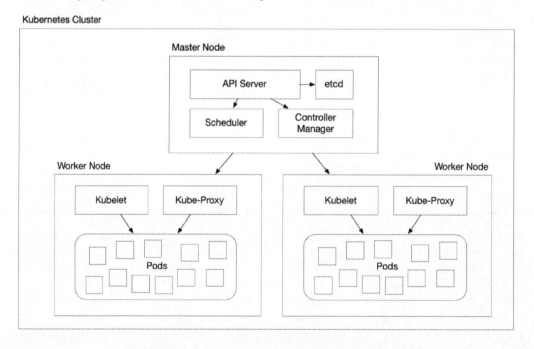

Figure 5.2 – Key Kubernetes architectural components

Now that we understand the core components of the architecture, we'll delve into a couple of other important topics. I do want to call out that this book is about mastering Terraform, and while part of that journey is understanding the architectures that you will be designing and provisioning with Terraform, this book does not intend to be an in-depth guide to Kubernetes. Hence, I am focusing on just the key concepts that you need to be aware of when building solutions with these technologies using Terraform.

Services

For more complex military operations, we may need to allocate a larger military unit to complete the mission successfully. This is where we have a lieutenant that would command multiple squads. The lieutenant delegates orders to the appropriate squads, with each deployed to a different area on the battlefield. This is similar to the role of a **service** in Kubernetes, which allows us to group pods together with a common purpose and distribute them across multiple nodes. The service is responsible for load balancing across pods, and any incoming requests intended for those pods would be addressed to the service to route accordingly—much like how orders from a captain or higher in the chain of command would be delegated down to a lieutenant, and they would take the necessary steps to dole them out to the squads under their command.

In this way, the service plays a crucial role in workloads that require a stable endpoint for communicating with pods, such as a web application or a REST API. This is because Kubernetes assigns a stable IP address and DNS name to the service, which remains unchanged even if the underlying pods change, enabling other applications or services within or outside the cluster to establish a reliable connection with the service.

Namespaces

Lastly, we need to cover an important concept of Kubernetes' logical model: the **namespace**. The namespace provides complete separation from all services and pods deployed within the cluster at the logical level. Namespaces do not apply to the physical resources of clusters, such as nodes or persistent volumes. They only apply within the logical realm of Kubernetes as it relates to pods and other related resources. You can think of it as branches within the military. Resources in different namespaces, as with soldiers in different branches of the army, share a central command, and they can communicate and coordinate with each other, but they are isolated in terms of chain of command and resource allocation. Therefore, pods in different namespaces can operate on the same nodes but can't coexist in the same service since that, too, has a namespace.

We've covered the key components of Kubernetes architecture. There is definitely a lot more that is out of the scope of this book, but this should give you enough of the conceptual overhead to understand Kubernetes architecture at a high level. Next, we'll delve a bit deeper into some of the resources that are used to configure pods and services.

Configuration and secrets

One of the key areas where Terraform and Kubernetes will likely interact is the area of configuration and secrets. This is because, quite often, Terraform is provisioning other resources that will supply endpoint URLs, authentication credentials, logging, or identity configuration. Therefore, it's important to understand which Kubernetes resources should be used to connect these configuration settings to the appropriate place in your Kubernetes deployments.

ConfigMaps

A **ConfigMap** is a special kind of Kubernetes resource that can be used to provide non-sensitive configuration to a pod. The configuration is stored as a set of key-value pairs, which can be used to configure either environment variables for containers or command-line arguments for an application that you want to run inside the container.

A pod can reference one or more ConfigMap objects, and then the application can reference the keys in the key-value pairs to obtain their values. This creates a separation of the application, which is running in the pod, from the configuration, which is stored in a ConfigMap. This means that the same ConfigMap can be used by more than one pod specification.

By default, only other pods within the same namespace can access ConfigMaps. If you want more granular security, you can apply for **role-based access control (RBAC)**.

Secrets

While Kubernetes does have an internal method for storing secrets and making them available to your pods, when you are deploying to the cloud, you will often use a cloud-specific secret provider instead. There are a number of advantages to leveraging an external secret store. First, with an external secret store, you would have more centralized management, which would make it easier for operators to manage the environment. Second, most external secret providers offer features and capabilities that the built-in secret storage in Kubernetes doesn't have, such as the ability to version and rotate secrets. Lastly, offloading secret storage reduces the burden on the etcd database on the cluster, thus freeing up more resources for workloads running in your pods.

When you leverage an external secret store, Terraform will likely be provisioning it along with the secrets that your pods will need. In order to take advantage of an external secret store, you will need to provision a SecretProviderClass resource that is specific to the external secret store you plan on using. It will provide a bridge between your pods and the secrets you store there. There are often platform-native configurations depending on the cloud platform you are using to configure this provider. Most managed Kubernetes service offerings provide built-in support for the corresponding secret storage service and streamline the authentication and authorization required for your pods to access secrets.

In this book, we will be working with the Managed Kubernetes offerings of three cloud platforms: Amazon **Elastic Kubernetes Service (EKS)**, **Azure Kubernetes Service (AKS)**, and **Google Kubernetes Engine (GKE)**.

Continuous deployment (CD)

Kubernetes has a multitude of ways to provision resources. It has both imperative and declarative covered with the `kubectl` command-line tool and Kubernetes YAML manifests (which also use the `kubectl` command-line tool) respectively. Because this is a book on Terraform, I think it's clear the approach we would prefer! Yes—declarative! And because Kubernetes also has its own REST API, it's possible to build a Terraform provider that communicates with it as well. All of these approaches, using `kubectl` either with imperative commands or YAML manifests or using `terraform` and the `kubernetes` Terraform provider, are examples of the traditional push model.

Push model

The **push model** is when your CI/CD pipeline is executing the configuration of the Kubernetes environment externally from the cluster. This could be done with any tool. The most common approach is to provision the cloud environment using Terraform as the first step of the CI/CD pipeline and then execute `kubectl` commands, either just plain old `bash` or YAML manifest files, using `kubectl apply -f foo.yaml`:

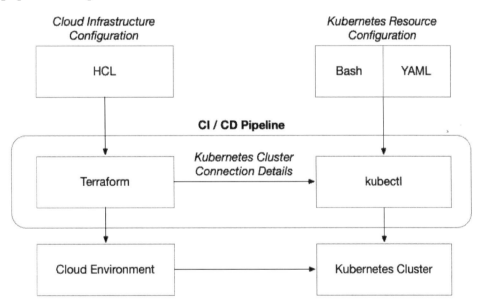

Figure 5.3 – CI/CD pipeline with Terraform and Kubernetes command-line interface

In this case, the cloud environment is defined in **HashiCorp Configuration Language** (HCL), which is executed as part of the first stage of the pipeline, and then the **Kubernetes cluster configuration** is output from this Terraform process to the next stage of the pipeline where `kubectl` is executed to create deployments on the newly created or existing Kubernetes cluster. The Kubernetes cluster's existence will depend on whether it was the first time `terraform apply` was executed or not.

The next method is to use Terraform for both of these stages, replacing the `kubectl` stage with a second Terraform stage, this time using a second Terraform root module that only uses the Kubernetes provider for Terraform. The Terraform root module that provisioned the cloud environment stays in its own folder and is completely isolated from this second Terraform code base:

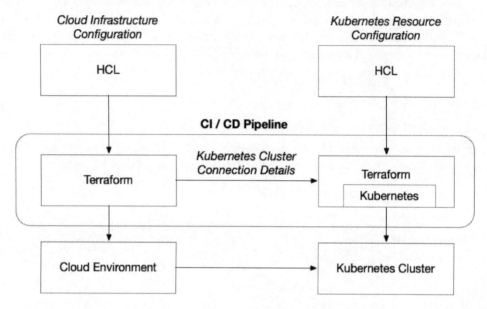

Figure 5.4 – CI/CD pipeline with Terraform using the Kubernetes provider for Terraform

The first Terraform stage still uses our target cloud platform's Terraform provider to provision the Kubernetes cluster and other required resources within our cloud environment. Likewise, the CI/CD pipeline still passes the Kubernetes cluster configuration that is output from this first Terraform stage to the second Terraform stage where we provision Kubernetes resources to our Kubernetes cluster using the Kubernetes provider for Terraform.

Pull model

An alternative to the push model is the **pull model**, which flips things upside down. Instead of the Kubernetes resources being provisioned by some actor outside of the Kubernetes cluster itself, the CI/CD pipeline installs a CD service on the cluster, and this service connects to a specified source code repository containing Kubernetes YAML manifests and provisions the resources on the Kubernetes cluster:

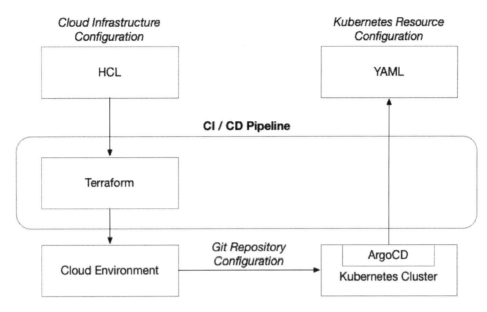

Figure 5.5 – CI/CD pipeline with Terraform and ArgoCD

This approach takes advantage of the immutable and declarative aspects of YAML-based Kubernetes deployments and creates an SSOT for a Kubernetes deployment within a Git source code repository. As a result, this approach has become more and more identified as a best practice when it comes to fully embracing GitOps, which we'll delve into more detail in the next chapter.

In this section, we took a high-level look at Kubernetes—what purpose it serves, how it works, and how it can interconnect our containers with the underlying infrastructure that we provision. These are all critical things to understand as we use Terraform to provision and manage the Kubernetes infrastructure that we'll use to run our containers. Next, let's look at how Kubernetes natively handles deployments before we contrast that with what we can do with Terraform's Kubernetes providers.

Understanding Kubernetes manifests

As we discussed in the previous section, `kubectl` is a command-line application that can be used to either imperatively or declaratively execute commands on a Kubernetes cluster. You can use `kubectl` to deploy resources and inspect and manage cluster resources, among other common operational activities.

Kubernetes manifests

When deploying resources to a Kubernetes cluster, you can either use `kubectl` commands directly to perform operations to provision resources or use YAML manifests to define the desired state of resources and use `kubectl` to execute against these manifests. These two different ways of using `kubectl` parallel the way there are imperative ways to provision resources to cloud platforms such as AWS and Azure through their respective command-line applications and the way Terraform provisions the desired state of resources during `terraform apply`.

When you're using `kubectl` commands directly, you're giving instructions right away in the command line. For example, if you want to create a deployment, you might issue a command such as this:

```
kubectl run nginx --image=nginx
```

In this case, `kubectl` will create a deployment for `nginx` with mostly default settings, and it will do so immediately.

This method can be useful for quick, one-off creations or when you need to make an immediate change.

When using YAML manifests, you're writing the desired state of your resources in a declarative manner. For example, a deployment might be written like this in a YAML file:

```yaml
apiVersion: apps/v1
kind: Deployment
metadata:
  name: nginx-deployment
spec:
  replicas: 3
  selector:
    matchLabels:
      app: nginx
  template:
    metadata:
      labels:
        app: nginx
    spec:
      containers:
      - name: nginx
        image: nginx:1.14.2
        ports:
        - containerPort: 80
```

You would then use `kubectl` to apply this file, like so:

```
kubectl apply -f my-deployment.yaml
```

This tells Kubernetes to make the cluster's actual state match the desired state described in the file.

The benefit of this approach is that the file serves as a **source of truth** (**SOT**) for the resource configuration. The files can be version-controlled, making it easy to track changes, roll back if needed, and reuse configurations.

Generally, it's considered a best practice to manage your Kubernetes resources using configuration files, especially in production environments. That being said, direct `kubectl` commands are useful for debugging and quick prototyping tasks, but you should consider using a declarative approach to manage resources in the long term.

Deployment manifest

When creating an application in Kubernetes, you use a deployment to specify how you want it to be configured. Kubernetes will then automatically adjust the current state of the application to match your desired configuration:

```
apiVersion: apps/v1
kind: Deployment
metadata:
  name: my-app
spec:
  replicas: 3
  selector:
    matchLabels:
      app: my-app
  template:
    metadata:
      labels:
        app: my-app
    spec:
      containers:
      - name: my-app
        image: my-app:1.0
        ports:
        - containerPort: 8080
```

This deployment manifest describes a desired state that includes running three instances (or replicas) of the my-app application.

Service manifest

A **service** is a method of grouping a collection of pods that form an application, allowing them to be presented as a network service:

```
apiVersion: v1
kind: Service
metadata:
  name: my-service
spec:
  selector:
    app: my-app
  ports:
    - protocol: TCP
      port: 80
      targetPort: 8080
```

This service manifest will create a network service that will route traffic to the `my-app` pods on port `8080`.

Configuration and secrets

Because Kubernetes is where we will host our applications and services, we need to have a way to provide runtime configuration settings, both non-sensitive and secret.

ConfigMaps

As we discussed in the previous section, a ConfigMap is how we pass non-sensitive data into our pods. The ConfigMap is a key area where Terraform and Kubernetes integration takes place because many of the configuration settings are likely generated by Terraform. This is an important consideration when designing how you provision to Kubernetes, as you want to minimize the manual steps required to provision to Kubernetes. We'll look at strategies on how to avoid this in future sections covering Kubernetes and Helm providers:

```
apiVersion: v1
kind: ConfigMap
metadata:
  name: my-config
data:
  my-value: "Hello, Kubernetes!"
```

This ConfigMap is named `my-config`, and it holds a key-value pair of `my-value: Hello, Kubernetes!`.

Now, when we want to reference this ConfigMap from one of our deployments, we simply use the `configMapRef` block to pull in the correct value from the ConfigMap and set an environment variable inside our container:

```
apiVersion: apps/v1
kind: Deployment
metadata:
  name: my-app
spec:
  replicas: 1
  selector:
    matchLabels:
      app: my-app
  template:
    metadata:
      labels:
        app: my-app
    spec:
      containers:
      - name: my-app
        image: my-app:1.0
        env:
        - name: MY_VALUE
          valueFrom:
            configMapKeyRef:
              name: my-config
              key: my-value
```

In this deployment, the `my-app` application has a `MY_VALUE` environment variable whose value is pulled from the `my-config` ConfigMap, and when the pod is running, it can get a `Hello, Kubernetes!` value from that environment variable.

Secrets

Just as with the non-sensitive configuration settings, many of our secrets will be provisioned by Terraform using the target cloud platform's secret management service. As a result, we won't be using the Kubernetes `Secret` resource but will be defining a `SecretProviderClass` resource that will enable integration with the cloud platform's secret management service and pull in the desired secrets. Because this is cloud platform-specific, we'll cover this in more detail in each of the solutions we build on AWS, Azure, and GCP, using their respective managed Kubernetes offerings.

In this section, we looked at how Kubernetes handles deployments natively—both using its own `kubectl` command-line utility and its own YAML-based deployment manifests, which allow us to describe Kubernetes resources we want to provision in a declarative way—similar to what Terraform allows us to do with the underlying cloud infrastructure. In the next section, we'll look at the Kubernetes provider, which gives us a way of managing Kubernetes natively using Terraform.

Using the Kubernetes provider to provision Kubernetes resources

The Kubernetes provider for Terraform is a plugin that allows Terraform to manage resources on a Kubernetes cluster. This includes creating, updating, and deleting resources such as deployments, services, and pods.

When using the Kubernetes Terraform provider, your infrastructure description is written in HCL instead of YAML. This is the language used by Terraform to describe infrastructure and service configurations.

The Kubernetes Terraform provider

As we discussed in the previous section, because Kubernetes has a REST API that acts as a uniform control plane for all management operations, it's possible to create a Terraform provider that we can use to automate it in the same fashion that we do with the AWS, Azure, and GCP cloud platforms.

Just as with other cloud platforms, we need to authenticate against the control plane. One big difference with Kubernetes is that the management control plane is hosted on the Kubernetes cluster itself—more specifically, as we discussed in the *Understanding key concepts of container orchestration and Kubernetes* section of this chapter, on the master node. This means we need to specify the endpoint address of the Kubernetes cluster. This is usually provided by the Terraform resource that provisions the Kubernetes cluster on the target cloud platform.

In order to authenticate with the Kubernetes cluster, we need to typically use a cluster certificate, but some cloud platforms support more sophisticated authentication methods that tie into your organization's directory systems such as Microsoft Entra ID.

Here is an example of what the provider configuration would typically look like when using certificate-based authentication:

```
provider "kubernetes" {
  host                    = var.cluster_endpoint

  client_certificate      = file(var.client_cert_path)
  client_key              = file(var.client_key_path)
  cluster_ca_certificate  = file(var.cluster_ca_cert_path)
}
```

Here's what each field is for:

- `host`: The hostname (in the form of URI) of the Kubernetes master. It can be sourced from the `KUBE_HOST` environment variable.
- `client_certificate`: This is used for client authentication against the Kubernetes REST API.
- `client_key`: This is paired with `client_certificate` and is used as part of the **Transport Layer Security** (**TLS**) handshake that happens between the Terraform provider and the Kubernetes REST API.
- `cluster_ca_certificate`: This is the **certificate authority** (**CA**) for the Kubernetes cluster and is used to verify the authenticity of the Kubernetes cluster's REST API.

Another common method for configuring the Kubernetes provider for Terraform is to use a `kube_config` file:

```
provider "kubernetes" {
  load_config_file = true
  config_path      = "~/.kube/config"
  context          = "foo"
}
```

In this situation, all of the details needed to connect and authenticate with the cluster are stored within the file. We just need to point the provider at the location where the file exists. By default, this location is `~/.kube/config`. Of course, this file can contain multiple cluster connections, each referred to as a *context*. Therefore, we may need to specify the context. However, if you are running in a CI/CD pipeline, this is very unlikely because you will likely use a custom path.

Kubernetes resources

When you use the Kubernetes provider for Terraform, we get the same declarative model that we get with Kubernetes' native YAML manifests, but we get all the features and capabilities of HCL. This allows us to pass input variables, generate dynamic local values, and use string interpolation—the works!

However, the downside of all this is that we have to use HCL to define Kubernetes resources. This goes against the grain of the Kubernetes ecosystem as most Kubernetes documentation and practitioners asking and answering questions online will be using YAML. If we can tolerate the translation from YAML into HCL, then it might be worth considering using the Kubernetes provider for Terraform:

```
resource "kubernetes_deployment" "my_app" {
  metadata {
    name = "my-app"
  }

  spec {
```

```
    replicas = 3

    selector {
      match_labels = {
        app = "my-app"
      }
    }

    template {
      metadata {
        labels = {
          app = "my-app"
        }
      }

      spec {
        container {
          image = "my-app:1.0"
          name  = "my-app"

          port {
            container_port = 8080
          }
        }
      }
    }
  }
}
```

The preceding example is of an HCL equivalent of the Kubernetes YAML that provisions a Kubernetes deployment resource. Notice the prolific use of curly braces, which can be rather jarring for somebody who is used to looking at YAML.

Evaluating the trade-offs

With this approach, your Kubernetes resources are defined in HCL, and you then use the `terraform apply` command to create or update those resources as opposed to using `kubectl` either imperatively or declaratively.

As with the native YAML approach for Kubernetes, this process is also declarative, meaning you describe what you want but leverage Terraform to figure out how to do it. This is similar to how Kubernetes itself works, but you're using the Terraform provider to generate the plan and do the work.

While it may seem like a great thing to use one language—HCL—to manage other parts of your infrastructure (such as cloud resources on AWS or GCP) and use it to manage your Kubernetes resources, however, because most Kubernetes documentation and samples are in YAML, you will be spending a significant amount of time mapping from YAML into HCL. This can make it difficult to learn and effectively manage Kubernetes at scale.

Therefore, it is usually better to let Terraform manage the underlying infrastructure that Kubernetes sits on while managing Kubernetes using its own declarative approach using YAML and `kubectl`. However, if you can overcome the translation from YAML into HCL—or an even better option that we'll address later: encapsulate your Kubernetes deployments into Helm charts—then it might be easier to use Terraform's Kubernetes provider to eliminate the additional integration with `kubectl` commands embedded in `bash` scripts that you'll have to do at the end of your `terraform apply` operation.

There might also be certain Kubernetes resources that are tightly coupled with your cloud platform and the configuration that Terraform manages for you. These might be individual or standalone resources that connect a Kubernetes Service account to a cloud platform identity or a ConfigMap that sources the bulk of its values from Terraform outputs.

In this section, we looked at how we can use Terraform to provision resources to Kubernetes and compared and contrasted this approach to the native Kubernetes options using `kubectl`—both imperatively and declaratively using YAML-based manifests. In the next section, we'll look at the Helm provider to see if it provides a better alternative to the options we've evaluated thus far.

Leveraging the Helm provider to provision Kubernetes resources

As we discussed previously, Kubernetes has a built-in declarative model based on YAML that allows you to provide resources to your cluster. However, as we saw, one of the challenges of using this model is that there is no way to use dynamic values inside your YAML-based specifications. That's where Helm comes in. In this section, we'll look at what Helm is exactly, its basic structure, how to use it, and how we can integrate it with our Terraform pipelines or use it directly with the Helm provider for Terraform.

What is Helm?

Helm is widely referred to as a package manager for Kubernetes, but I find this definition a bit perplexing as a software developer who is used to working with package managers for software libraries such as Maven, NuGet, or npm or operating system package managers such as `apt` or Chocolatey. I suppose at some levels, they share a similarity in aggregating multiple components into a single, versioned package and providing a convenient way to pull these packages into other projects for reuse.

However, I think a big difference and a unique part of Helm's architecture is the nature of the templating engine. At its core, Helm allows you to create templates containing one or more Kubernetes YAML manifests and allows you to infuse more dynamic customization within your Kubernetes resources, thus making your Kubernetes deployments much more reusable and easier to manage and maintain. These templates are referred to as **charts** or **Helm charts**.

In many ways, a Helm chart reminds me more of what a Terraform module is rather than a traditional package management software—whether it's apt or NuGet. The similarities abound when comparing a Terraform module with a Helm chart. They both operate within a folder and define a method for taking input variables and producing outputs:

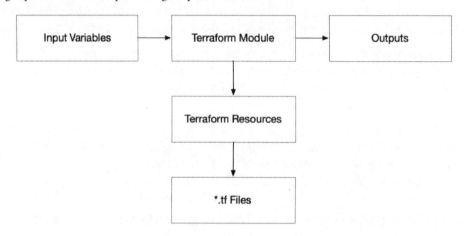

Figure 5.6 – Terraform module inputs, outputs, and resources

A Terraform module encapsulates an aggregation of several Terraform resources (or other modules) defined within .tf files, and HCL allows you to implement any number of dynamic configurations using built-in capabilities of the language:

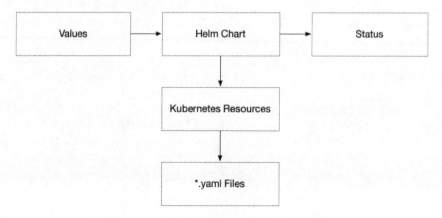

Figure 5.7 – Helm chart inputs, outputs, and resources

As mentioned, a Helm chart performs a similar aggregation but with Kubernetes resources that are defined within .yaml files and use Kubernetes YAML-based markup. Helm defines its own templating engine based on Go templates that offers a wide range of features that allow you to implement a similar level of dynamic configuration that you can achieve with HCL.

As you can see, the basic structure of a Helm chart is quite simple. It is not as simple as a Terraform module because we have nested folders that preclude users from being able to cleanly nest Helm charts within each other. Sub-charts need to be created in a special charts directory and can be completely encapsulated within this folder or simply reference an existing chart hosted elsewhere. This is similar to how Terraform modules work in that you can reference a local module or one hosted at any number of remote locations. A subtle difference is how Terraform modules can be declared in any .tf file, and their definition simply needs to be stored in another local folder or remote location:

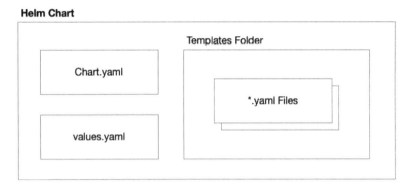

Figure 5.8 – Helm chart anatomy

The Chart.yaml file is a special file inside the Helm chart that acts as the main entry point file that contains key identification metadata and other dependencies such as other Helm charts defined either locally or in a remote location:

```
apiVersion: v2
name: my-webapp
version: 0.1.0
description: A basic web application Helm chart
```

The values.yaml file is a file that defines the input variables for a Helm chart. This is an example where in HCL we have no restriction on where we put input variables, by convention—and for our own sanity, we put input variables into a variables.tf file. In Helm, this convention of isolating input variable declarations is canonized into a well-known file that is recognized beyond a simple convention:

```
replicaCount: 1
image:
  repository: nginx
  tag: stable
```

```
  pullPolicy: IfNotPresent
service:
  type: ClusterIP
  port: 80
ingress:
  enabled: false
  annotations: {}
  path: /
  hosts:
    - my-webapp.local
  tls: []
```

The `templates` folder is where all our YAML-based manifests will go. However, the YAML is a bit different because it will most likely have many dynamic values injected into it using a Go templating convention ({ { and } }) to denote symbolic references that Helm will resolve using the Go templating engine:

```
apiVersion: apps/v1
kind: Deployment
metadata:
  name: {{ template "my-webapp.fullname" . }}
  labels:
    app: {{ template "my-webapp.name" . }}
spec:
  replicas: {{ .Values.replicaCount }}
  selector:
    matchLabels:
      app: {{ template "my-webapp.name" . }}
  template:
    metadata:
      labels:
        app: {{ template "my-webapp.name" . }}
    spec:
      containers:
        - name: {{ template "my-webapp.name" . }}
          image: "{{ .Values.image.repository }}:{{ .Values.image.tag }}"
          imagePullPolicy: {{ .Values.image.pullPolicy }}
          ports:
            - containerPort: 80
```

Helm charts can then be installed onto a Kubernetes cluster using a different command-line tool called `helm`. This tool performs a number of different functions, including autogenerating a basic chart structure, packaging charts for distribution, managing chart repositories, and installing charts onto the cluster.

Both `kubectl` and `helm` use the same method to authenticate with a Kubernetes cluster, but they are used for different purposes when managing the cluster, just as with `kubectl`, which can apply declarative Kubernetes configuration using the following command:

```
kubectl apply -f <file>.yaml
```

The `helm` command can be used to provision a Helm chart to a Kubernetes cluster using the following command:

```
helm install my-webapp ./my-webapp
```

In this regard, Helm could similarly be integrated into a Terraform CI/CD pipeline that first provisions the cloud environment using Terraform and the relevant cloud platform provider (for example, `aws`, `azurerm`, or `googlecloud`) and then uses the `helm` command-line tool to install Helm charts onto the Kubernetes cluster using connection and authentication information provided by the output of the Terraform stage of the pipeline;

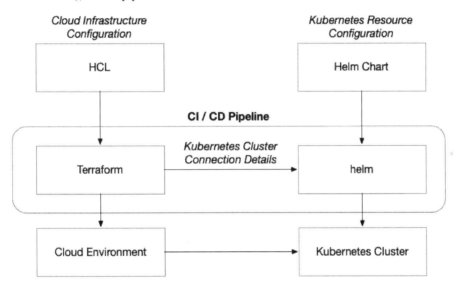

Figure 5.9 – Helm chart anatomy: Terraform and Helm integration in a CI/CD pipeline

In the next subsection, we'll look at how the same process could be streamlined using the Helm provider for Terraform, thus replacing the `bash` scripts executing `helm` commands imperatively and managing it with Terraform.

The Helm Terraform provider

In the previous section, we looked at how Helm works, the structure of a Helm chart, and how its structure and functionality compare and contrast to Terraform modules. Now, we'll look at how we can use Terraform to manage our Kubernetes environment using the Helm provider for Terraform. This provider is a close brother to the Kubernetes provider for Terraform because they both interact with the Kubernetes REST API as the control plan for managing Terraform resources.

The advantage of using Terraform with Helm is that it enables you to manage your Kubernetes applications alongside your other infrastructure, using the same configuration language and tooling. As we know, Helm allows us to create parameterized templates using Kubernetes' declarative YAML manifests and a templating language, but we still need to use `bash` scripts to execute `helm` commands and pass in parameters to the Helm chart. Some Helm charts can have very complicated configurations with dozens of parameters. So, using Terraform eliminates the additional integration with external `bash` scripts that execute `helm` commands.

At the same time, it also allows Kubernetes practitioners to develop Kubernetes templates in their native toolset. So, if you have Kubernetes specialists in your organization who want to build their own custom Helm charts, this allows them to keep doing their thing while plugging into a declarative deployment approach using Terraform. This also allows you to leverage the massive ecosystem that already exists for Helm and Kubernetes without any additional translation into HCL.

As with the Kubernetes provider, you need to initialize the provider first by declaring it as a required provider:

```
terraform {
    required_providers {
        helm = {
            source = "hashicorp/helm"
            version = "~> 2.0.0"
        }
    }
}
```

Then, in your root module, you need to create an instance of the provider. The provider configuration for the Helm provider closely resembles that of the Kubernetes provider:

```
provider "helm" {
    kubernetes {
        config_path = "~/.kube/config"
    }
}
```

In fact, both the Helm and Kubernetes providers can be used side by side in the same Terraform module in case some additional Kubernetes resources need to be provisioned to augment what's in the Helm chart itself.

The Helm provider can be used to create a two-stage Terraform CI/CD pipeline where the first stage provisions the cloud environment using Terraform and the corresponding cloud platform's provider. The second stage uses the cluster connection and authentication settings output by the first stage to configure the Helm provider and runs `terraform apply` again using a different Terraform code base containing the Helm configuration:

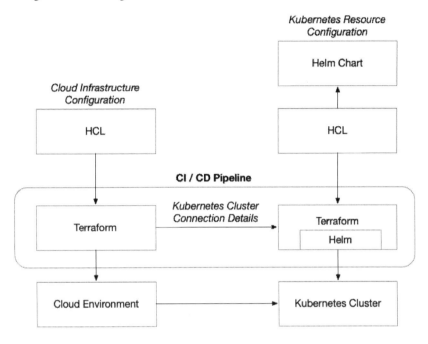

Figure 5.10 – Helm chart anatomy: Terraform and Helm integration in a CI/CD pipeline

The Terraform code base for the second stage is often quite small, only using a single resource. The `helm_release` resource is the only resource in the provider—which is quite different if you have ever used one of the cloud platform providers such as AWS, Azure, or GCP!

The `helm_release` resource simply takes the inputs that we would expect to pass to the `helm install` command by specifying the chart name and version and an external repository (if necessary):

```
resource "helm_release" "my_application" {
    name       = "my-application"
    repository = https://kubernetes-charts.storage.googleapis.com/
    chart      = "my-application-chart"
    version    = "1.0.0"
}
```

This concludes the section on the Helm provider.

Summary

In this chapter, we learned the basic concepts needed to understand containers, container orchestrators, and the ways you can provision and manage container-based infrastructure using both Kubernetes native tooling via `kubectl` and Helm and the corresponding Terraform providers for both Kubernetes and Helm.

This is the end of the cross-platform, cloud-agnostic knowledge that we need to build both VM- and container-based architectures across all three hyperscalars. Since serverless is inherently platform-specific and offers significant abstraction from the underlying infrastructure, I will cover each hyperscalar's offering in its respective chapter.

In the next chapter, we will move beyond cloud architecture paradigms and spend some time understanding how teams deliver IAC solutions using CI/CD pipelines that fuse the infrastructure provisioning, configuration management, and application deployment processes into a cohesive, end-to-end workflow.

6

Connecting It All Together – GitFlow, GitOps, and CI/CD

GitOps is a contemporary approach to software development and operations that strives to make the management of infrastructure and applications easier and more efficient. It achieves this by using **Git** as the primary source of truth and adopting a declarative approach wherever possible. This methodology integrates the principles of version control and continuous delivery to optimize the software development life cycle and facilitate better teamwork between development and operations teams—and sometimes a fusion of the two disciplines into a true **DevOps** team.

The chapter covers the following topics:

- Understanding key concepts of GitOps
- Leveraging GitHub for source control management
- Leveraging GitHub Actions for **continuous integration/continuous deployment** (**CI/CD**) pipelines

Understanding key concepts of GitOps

There are many ways of implementing GitOps, and we'll look at several in this chapter, but at its core, GitOps is about applying the software development life cycle to both application source code and infrastructure configuration—or **infrastructure as code** (**IaC**). The Git repository becomes the source of truth for what is in production, what *was* in production, and what *will* be in production soon. In order to do so, the Git repository will have to include configuration files, application code, infrastructure definitions, and deployment manifests—everything needed to reproduce a fully working version of the application.

Declarative representations are preferred over compiled artifacts, but when source code is compiled into artifacts, they need to be versioned and tied back to a commit within the Git repository itself. Tools such as Terraform, Docker, and Kubernetes interpret these declarative files and automatically apply changes to the system to conform to the desired state.

Any changes to the Git repository are automatically and continuously applied to the target environment, no matter where the environment sits in the life cycle—a development, staging, or production environment. This automated process ensures consistency and reduces the risk of manual errors.

This can be achieved through a **push** or a **pull** model, which we first saw in the previous chapter when looking at different CI/CD pipeline approaches for Kubernetes-based solutions. Due to Kubernetes's influence within the GitOps space, it is often a foregone conclusion that the goal is to establish a pull model. However, a pull model is not required to implement GitOps. There are many ways to implement GitOps, and each approach has distinct trade-offs that should be evaluated in your specific context.

Whether you use the push model or the pull model, one of the big advantages of using GitOps is that it provides transparency and visibility into the changes made to the system by keeping a log of all deployments and updates through the normal source control management process. The Git commit history is transformed into an audit trail that makes it easier to understand what changes were made when they occurred, and by whom. The combination of the complete configuration and code to produce an end-to-end working system and a versioned copy makes it relatively easy to roll back to a previous state in the event of issues. Of course, stateful portions of your systems will likely need additional engineering to ensure both new deployments and rollbacks are uneventful.

Using this approach can improve software delivery processes, resulting in greater efficiency, reliability, and scalability while simultaneously encouraging collaboration between development, operations, and other teams. This is the key reason why adopting this approach is critical to enabling a DevOps culture within an organization.

Due to the heavy reliance on Git—traditionally a software development tool—team members without an application development background can tend to struggle. Therefore, if you come from a non-developer background such as a system administrator, network or security engineer, or other infrastructure discipline, it's very important that you take the time to learn basic Git commands and a **Gitflow** process, as this knowledge will be critical for you to be effective on the team.

Terraform—and tools like it—are a critical component to a GitOps toolchain as the use of IaC is an important pillar of this approach, but it's important to remember that Terraform is often just one ingredient in the grand recipe with the source control and pipelining tool playing the key role in facilitating the process. That's why, in this book, we'll be setting up sophisticated architectures using Terraform and CI/CD pipelines to provision them. Before we can get to that, we need to firmly understand what a CI/CD pipeline is and how to build one, which is what we will look at in the next section.

Understanding CI/CD

A CI/CD pipeline is an automated set of steps and processes that help software development teams build, test, and deploy their applications quickly and reliably. It is a fundamental component when implementing a GitOps process as it takes on the critical role of facilitating the continuous flow of changes from development to production, ensuring that new code is automatically integrated, tested, and delivered to end users as a working system:

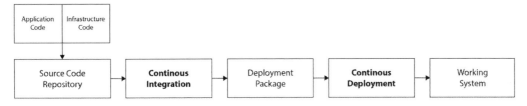

Figure 6.1 – Overview of the anatomy of a CI/CD pipeline

As its very name might suggest, a CI/CD pipeline actually consists of two processes that are stitched together. First, the **continuous integration** pipeline, which is responsible for building and ensuring the built-in quality of the application code of the system, and second, the **continuous deployment** pipeline, which is responsible for deploying that application code into its environment.

The CI/CD pipeline aggregates these two historically distinct processes: **integration testing** and **deployment**. However, by combining them, it provides a systematic and automated approach to continuously delivering new features and bug fixes to users, reducing the time and risk associated with manual deployments. This, in turn, fosters a culture of collaboration, frequent feedback, and rapid innovation within development teams.

A CI/CD pipeline that uses Terraform to provision infrastructure and deploys the latest code version to that infrastructure typically has two objectives. First, produce a version of the software that has been tested and verified to have satisfactory levels of built-in quality. Second, provision an environment—whatever that looks like—to host the application that is compatible and meets the software's requirements to function correctly and efficiently. The third and final step is to deploy the application to that environment.

The pipeline makes no judgments about how robust your cloud architecture might be. Depending on your needs, you may opt to sacrifice certain qualities of your solution architecture for expediency or cost. The pipeline's job is to provision whatever environment you tell it you need and to deploy the software to that environment, so once the pipeline has completed, your application is ready to accept incoming traffic from users.

In the next section, we'll dig deeper into the internal structure of a CI/CD pipeline and discuss the mechanics of what is going on along the way.

Anatomy of pipeline

In the previous sections, we learned about the fundamental principles of GitOps and that the CI/CD pipeline is grounded on a version control system such as Git, where developers commit their code changes. We can configure a CI/CD pipeline to trigger when certain key events take place within the code base, such as changes being pushed to a specific branch.

Once certain key events take place within the version control system, such as a developer pushing changes to a particular branch or path, the CI/CD pipeline is triggered. It will pull the latest code, build the application, and run a series of automated tests to verify the functionality and integrity of the application code:

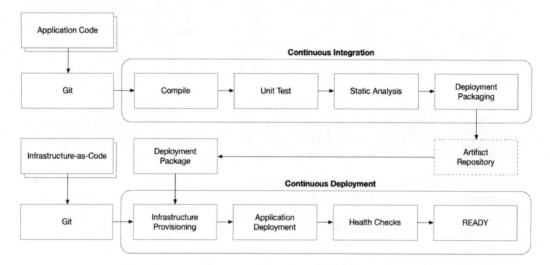

Figure 6.2 – Anatomy of a CI/CD pipeline

Various tests, including unit tests, integration tests, and sometimes even acceptance tests, can be conducted to ensure that the code meets quality standards and does not introduce regressions.

Unit tests operate on individual components and use mocks to isolate the tests' outcomes around a single component by injecting placeholders for the component's downstream dependencies:

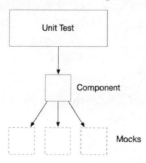

Figure 6.3 – Unit tests are isolated on a single component

Integration tests operate across two or more components. They can use mocks or not, and their focus is on the reliability of interactions between components. Sometimes, for very intricate or complex components, you might want integration tests that focus on the various use cases surrounding them while keeping other components' outputs predictable using mocks:

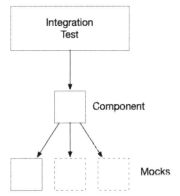

Figure 6.4 – Integration tests are focused on two or more components and how they interact

System tests introduce real-world dependencies, such as databases or messaging subsystems, into the mix and allow you to achieve much more realistic coverage across a system without fully deploying it:

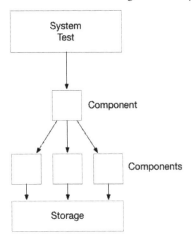

Figure 6.5 – System tests

System tests have a broader focus, often introducing real-world dependencies such as databases and external systems

An **end-to-end test** is one where you provide the entire host environment for the application—as it would be in production—and execute tests that mimic an actual client application or end user as closely as possible:

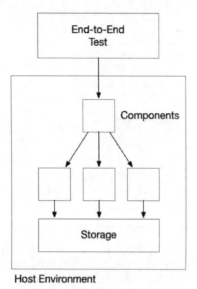

Figure 6.6 – End-to-end tests

End-to-end tests attempt to mimic, as closely as possible, actual end-user activity with the system fully operational, end to end.

It depends on the requirements of the particular application and organization, what kind of testing, and how much needs to be done on an application. Terraform can also play a crucial role in the continuous integration process by provisioning **just-in-time** (**JIT**) environments for system or end-to-end testing environments. Terraform allows you to dynamically create an environment fit for purpose, execute your tests, and then shut everything down.

Depending on the level of reliability that you want in your release process, you could opt for a deeper and more robust level of testing before the continuous deployment process is initiated.

After the continuous integration process is successfully completed, the application is packaged into a deployment package (e.g., a Docker container or a JAR file) that contains all the necessary dependencies and configurations and is ready to be deployed.

During the continuous deployment process, both the Git source code and this deployment package are used to provide the environment and deploy the package to the target environment. Terraform is crucial in provisioning or updating the required infrastructure, such as virtual machines, containers, or serverless resources. As we looked at in the previous chapters, Terraform can also optionally perform the application deployment through a pre-built virtual machine image or a Kubernetes deployment with pre-built container images.

After deployment, the CD pipeline can run additional verification tests to ensure that the application runs correctly in the target environment by utilizing health checks built into the application and infrastructure.

Regardless of the architecture, the outcome of the CD pipeline is that it applies environment-specific configurations—usually derived from Terraform outputs, which contain vital configuration details—to the artifact, thus, customizing it for the target environment. These configurations might include database connection strings, API endpoints, or other settings that differ between environments.

As you can see, Terraform plays an essential role in this process but is not the only player on the field. Each step in this process is equally important and plays a critical role in consistently releasing software with built-in quality. In this book, we will review three architectures and three corresponding techniques for deployment for each of the three paradigms of cloud hosting: virtual machines, containers, and serverless. These solutions will be built using GitHub as the source control repository and GitHub Actions as the tool we use to implement our CI/CD pipelines. Depending on the architecture of the software and how it is hosted within the environment, the deployment technique may vary.

In the next section, we'll look at the source control management aspects of GitOps, which include the developer workflows that add structure to our DevOps teams that are executing in this manner.

Leveraging GitHub for source control management

GitHub is just one option for source control management software. We'll be using it in this book, but it's important for you to understand that the concepts and patterns implemented using GitHub are consistent no matter what source control provider you end up using for your projects. There may be small differences between the syntax and mechanisms that implement and execute pipelines, but the source control management system is just `git` under the hood.

An important part of source control management is how to use it in a structured way on a team—large or small. These are conventions that your team can use so that you have consistent expectations across the team about how new features are shepherded through your development process and into production.

Gitflow is a common model that uses a combination of well-known, long-lived, and consistent naming conventions for short-lived branches. As we will see in the next subsection, it is highly customizable and a bit of a *Choose Your Own Adventure*, which is why it has become one of the most common operating models for development teams, no matter the size.

We'll also look at a miniature variant called GitHub flow, which is an example of trunk-based development. This model advocates for keeping the `main` branch always deployable and minimizing the use of long-lived branches. Instead of creating long-lived stable branches for various purposes and designs, developers work directly on the `main` branch using only short-lived `feature` branches that are quickly merged back into `main`.

In the next section, we'll take a closer look at Gitflow to see what the developer experience would look like and how it would integrate with the automation systems that we build using Terraform.

Gitflow

Gitflow is one of the most popular branching models and workflows used by development teams around the world. Its prolific nature has led to the development of different variations and adaptations to suit different development environments and teams' preferences. At its core, Gitflow leverages a `main` branch to indicate production quality code and a `develop` branch that grants development teams a safe place to merge and perform integration testing:

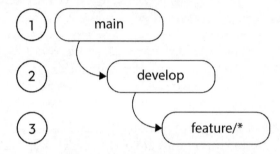

Figure 6.7 – Gitflow at its simplest

In Gitflow, `main` is the main branch representing the production-ready code. Only code that is ready for production should live in this branch. Features that are under development are created by individual developers on their own `feature/*` branch and then merged into a shared `develop` branch that acts a bit like a staging environment before being merged into `main`.

However, as mentioned before, Gitflow is highly customizable and there have been several extensions to this core model developed over the years with varying levels of adoption.

Sometimes, `release` branches are used for preparing and testing releases, starting from `develop` and merging back into both `develop` and `main`. This can give a team greater control over when and how they release a set of features into production.

The real world happens fast. As a result, sometimes critical changes need to be made rapidly to production to fix a specific issue. That's when `hotfix` branches are used by starting from `main` and merging back into both `develop` and then `main` once a hotfix has been fully tested:

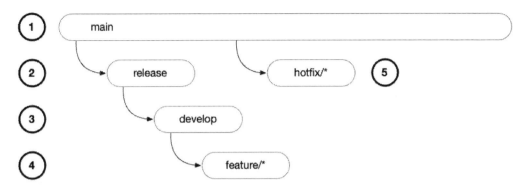

Figure 6.8 – Gitflow extended

Gitflow is highly customizable:

- `main`: Production only code (1)
- `release`: Release staging (2)
- `develop`: Integrating testing (3)
- `feature/*`: Feature development (4)
- `hotfix/*`: Critical patches to production (5)

Gitflow does not dictate a specific versioning scheme, but it is common to use semantic versioning (e.g., `{MAJOR}.{MINOR}.{PATCH}`) to indicate the significance of changes made in each release. Gitflow does provide a clear separation of tasks, making it suitable for larger teams and projects that require strict control over the development and release process. However, this structure can be overwhelming for smaller teams or experimental projects:

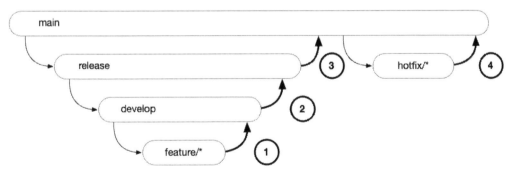

Figure 6.9 – Gitflow integration with CI/CD pipelines

The Gitflow process has several key events where automation might be triggered:

1. **Feature integration**: The developer submits a pull request from their `feature/*` branch into `develop`. This often triggers a CI/CD pipeline that includes application code with built-in quality, unit, and integration tests. The merge of this pull request initiates a release pipeline that is deployed to the development environment.

2. **Feature releases**: The team lead submits a pull request from the `develop` branch into `release`. This usually includes additional testing, such as system and even end-to-end tests. The merge of this pull request initiates a release pipeline that deploys to the staging or release environment.

3. **Production releases**: The release manager submits a pull request from `release` into `main`. This usually includes additional variations of end-to-end tests that check performance or load and may include upgrade or version testing. The merge of this pull request initiates a release pipeline that deploys to the production environment.

4. **Critical patch**: The developer submits a pull request from a `hotfix/*` branch into `main`. This would likely execute a smaller catalog of test suites but would likely include version or upgrade testing. The merge of this pull request initiates a release pipeline that deploys to the production environment.

It's important to point out that this is probably the most extensive configuration of Gitflow, but humans being humans, I'm sure somebody out there has come up with an even more complex incarnation of Gitflow. In the next section, let's look at something a little more simple and lightweight by going back and taking a look at Trunk-Based Development using GitHub flow.

GitHub flow

As we've discussed, GitHub flow is the little brother of Gitflow. It's much more simple and lightweight and perfect for small teams or experimentation. It focuses on only one branch—`main`—with new features being introduced for individual `feature/*` branches. Developers create `feature` branches from `main`, work on their changes, and then submit pull requests to merge them back into the `main` branch. Releases are often tagged from `main` after thorough testing:

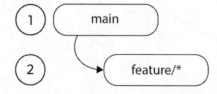

Figure 6.10 – GitHub flow for small teams or experiments

The main difference is that there is no official process around creating staging branches such as `develop` or `release` branches where integration testing is performed. The responsibility for integration testing resides on the individual developer of the feature within their own `feature` branch—in essence, taking individual responsibility for their changes working in production.

This also means that we have fewer key events which a CI/CD pipeline will trigger from. We only have a pull request from `feature/*` into `main` and then merge into `main` to trigger events. Additional testing can be performed on the `feature/*` branches themselves or teams can optionally introduce a manual trigger for a production release, which allows for more time to perform testing on `main`.

As mentioned previously, GitHub flow is great for smaller teams that don't have dedicated teams focused on integration testing!

Each variation of Gitflow has its strengths and weaknesses, and the choice of workflow depends on the project's specific needs, team size, development process, and the tools or platforms used for version control. It's essential to evaluate the requirements and preferences of the team and project to select the most suitable branching model. I'll go over a few of these options in this book in more detail, but for the most part, I will use GitHub Flow to keep things simple in my examples.

Using GitHub Actions for CI/CD pipelines

GitHub Actions is a CI/CD service offered by GitHub that provides a platform for you to implement automation around your source control management process no matter what workflow you choose.

In order to hook into GitHub Actions, you need to define YAML files that specify the tasks that you want to be automated. These files are called **workflows** and they are stored in the `.github/workflows` directory of your source code repository. The basic anatomy of a workflow consists of jobs. Jobs have steps. Steps can be a simple script that you execute or something more complex packaged together called an action:

```
jobs:
  build:
    runs-on: ubuntu-latest # The type of runner (virtual machine) that
the job will run on

    steps:
    - name: Checkout code # Name of the step
      uses: actions/checkout@v2 # Use a pre-built action to checkout
the current repo

    - name: Run a command
      run: echo "Hello, World!" # Commands to run

  test:
```

```
        needs: build # Specifies that this job depends on the 'build' job
        runs-on: ubuntu-latest

        steps:
        - name: Checkout code
          uses: actions/checkout@v2

        - name: Run tests
          run: |
            npm install
            npm test**
```

The preceding code has two jobs: build and test. The jobs are grouped under the jobs: section and each job has steps grouped under the steps: section. You can customize the image that your job runs on using the runs-on attribute. This allows you to specify a container image that is customized to your needs with the correct Linux distribution or software configuration.

By default, a step simply executes a bash script using the run attribute, but you can utilize an action by specifying the action type with the uses attribute.

To execute Terraform, you simply need it installed on your agent. This can be done easily using an action provided by HashiCorp called hashicorp\setup-terraform@v2. The following code snippet demonstrates how to do this while specifying the specific version of Terraform that you want to use:

```
  steps:
  - uses: hashicorp/setup-terraform@v2
    with:
      terraform_version: 1.5.5
```

There are additional attributes, but they are more for edge cases and are beyond the scope of this book. I recommend you check out the documentation for the action to check out all the different options available: https://github.com/hashicorp/setup-terraform.

You must always store sensitive data as secrets to ensure that the data is not exposed in the logs. This can easily be accomplished by leveraging GitHub environments or other secret management services.

Virtual machine workloads

When building automation pipelines that provision virtual-machine-hosted workloads, your toolchain should consist of something that can be used to set up the initial configuration of the virtual machine, provision the virtual machine, and make updates to the virtual machine's configuration over time. The tools that we will cover in this book for these purposes are Packer, Terraform, and Ansible, respectively.

Packer build pipeline

As we discussed when we looked at developing Packer templates, developers write and commit Packer configuration files using **HashiCorp Configuration Language** (**HCL**) to their Git repository.

An independent pipeline is triggered when changes are pushed to the version control system affecting the folder where the Packer configuration files are stored. Within that pipeline, Packer is utilized to build virtual machine images for each server role (e.g., frontend, backend, and database). Packer is configured with the latest configurations for each role within the application, including the necessary software and settings unique to each layer. After successfully building each image, Packer creates machine images optimized for the cloud provider of choice (e.g., **Amazon Machine Images** (**AMIs**) for **Amazon Web Services** (**AWS**) or Azure Managed Images for Azure).

Sometimes, Packer can fail due to transient issues with the virtual machine itself or just bugs within your script. You can use a **debug mode** within Packer that will allow you to pause the build process on the temporary virtual machine. This will allow you to connect to the machine, execute the command that failed manually, and troubleshoot the issues within the environment itself.

Depending on the target cloud platform, the generated machine images are stored in an artifact repository or directly in the cloud provider's image repository for later use by Terraform.

Terraform apply pipeline

Now that the virtual machine images are published to an image repository, Terraform simply needs to reference the correct image in order to provision a virtual machine with the right one. Similar to the Packer Build Pipeline, developers commit Terraform configuration files to their Git repository, and a separate pipeline is triggered whenever changes are pushed to the folder where the Terraform configuration is stored.

The Terraform configuration defines the network infrastructure, including subnets, security groups, and load balancers, needed for all the virtual machines within the solution. Terraform pulls the Packer-built machine images from the artifact repository or cloud provider's image repository and provisions the required number of virtual machines for each role, setting up any load balancers necessary to distribute the load across multiple servers to ensure high availability and fault tolerance.

Terraform can sometimes fail either for transient issues but also potential race conditions between resources that you are trying to provision that are implicitly dependent upon each other. We'll go into more advanced troubleshooting scenarios in *Chapter 17*, but for now, it's important to recognize that Terraform is idempotent, which means you can run it over and over again to reach a desired state—so, sometimes, just re-running the job can get you past the initial issue you faced.

Ansible apply pipeline

Finally, after Terraform applies the infrastructure changes and the virtual machines are set up using the Packer images, the environment is primed and ready. However, the environment is not yet fully operational as there will likely be certain configuration changes that need to be made specific to the environment that were not available during the Packer image build phase. This is what I call *last mile* configuration—where we put the last touches on the environment by applying any configuration settings only known after Terraform `apply` executes. There are different options for performing these last-mile configuration changes. You can use Terraform to dynamically configure user data to pass directly to the virtual machine, or you can use another tool to do the job.

Since most virtual machines also need some routine maintenance performed, it's good to consider a configuration management tool that can make updates to your environment without having to shut down or reboot virtual machines by changing the version of the Packer image used. That's where tools such as Ansible come in.

Ansible can be used as a configuration management tool to perform the last mile configuration on the virtual machines in addition to performing ongoing maintenance on the machines. Ansible scripts are applied to the deployed virtual machines to set environment-specific values, configure services, and perform other necessary tasks. In doing so, the environment is now ready for operators to perform routine maintenance using the already established Ansible configuration.

Like Terraform, Ansible is idempotent and can fall prey to similar transient errors. However, like Packer, Ansible is invoking change within the operating system itself. As a result, you just need to connect to one of these virtual machines and troubleshoot the commands that failed when Ansible executed its scripts.

By employing this approach, a virtual-machine-based solution can efficiently be provisioned and operated over the lifespan of the application. This allows for reproducible, scalable, and automated deployments and provides the necessary flexibility for different environments while ensuring consistent and reliable setups for each role within the solution.

Container workloads

When building automation pipelines that provision container-based workloads, your toolchain should consist of something that can be used to set the initial configuration of the various containers that need to be deployed, provision the Kubernetes cluster to host the containers and the underlying infrastructure that supports the Kubernetes cluster's operations, and then finally provision Kubernetes resources to the Kubernetes control pane using Kubernetes' REST API through a variety of different options.

Due to the immutability of the container images and their lightweight and speedy nature, it's easy to implement sophisticated rolling updates to roll out new versions of the container image across existing deployments. Therefore, the mechanics around provisioning and maintaining container-based workloads are really about building new container images and referencing the desired image within your Kubernetes configuration to invoke an update to the deployment.

Docker build pipeline

As we discussed when we looked at the principles around Docker and how it works, developers write and commit Docker files using their Git repository.

An independent pipeline is triggered when changes are pushed to the version control system, affecting the folder where the Docker configuration files are stored. Within that pipeline, Docker is utilized to build container images for each server role (e.g., frontend, backend, and database) within the application. Docker is configured with the latest configurations for each role within the application, including the necessary software and settings unique to each layer. The Docker image that is produced acts as our deployment package. As a result, it is versioned and stored in a Package repository called a container registry (which we discussed in *Chapter 5*). Once the new Docker image is there, we can reference it from the Kubernetes configuration and trigger a deployment in Kubernetes in a myriad of ways.

Kubernetes manifest update pipeline

In this pipeline, developers modify the manifests to reference the new version of the Docker image that was built and published in the previous step and submit a pull request to update the change. The trigger we use can be either a push model or a pull model. If you recall, in *Chapter 5*, *Container-Based Architectures*, we discussed several different methods for implementing a push model in this manner. Some options use `kubectl` and Kubernetes YAML manifests, and others use a Helm Chart with a set of YAML manifests that have been turned into a more dynamic template by using Helm.

Alternatively, using the pull model, we could use a continuous deployment agent hosted on the Kubernetes cluster itself, such as ArgoCD, that would pick up on changes within the Git repository and apply them to the cluster. Because ArgoCD is continuously monitoring the Git repository containing the Kubernetes manifests (or Helm Charts), whenever a new commit is made to the repository, it will automatically trigger a deployment process. ArgoCD isn't doing any magic; it is simply using `kubectl apply` to apply the latest version of the manifests to the Kubernetes cluster.

Terraform apply pipeline

As we have discussed in *Chapter 5*, due to Kubernetes architecture, the Kubernetes cluster is often a shared resource where multiple teams will deploy their own workloads by targeting their own namespace within the cluster. That's why it's often the case that this pipeline may be managed by a different team than the ones that own the Docker Build and Kubernetes Manifest pipelines. This pipeline is owned by the team responsible for provisioning and maintaining the Kubernetes cluster. Their responsibility is to ensure that the cluster is up and running and ready to accept deployments from ArgoCD.

Terraform could optionally be used to manage Kubernetes resources on the cluster, but as we addressed in *Chapter 5*, this may not be ideal in all situations due to team and organizational dynamics. It's best to consider your specific context and make the right decision for your team and organization.

In most cases, Terraform is simply used to provision the Kubernetes cluster and surrounding infrastructure on the cloud platform of choice. Developers will commit Terraform configuration files to their Git repository, and the pipeline is triggered whenever changes are pushed to the folder where the Terraform configuration is stored.

This approach allows developers to focus on code development and testing without worrying about the underlying infrastructure and deployment process. The development teams can rely on an isolated environment within the Kubernetes cluster that they deploy to and really only need to maintain their code base and the Docker file used to configure their application.

Serverless workloads

In serverless architecture, the deployment process can be greatly simplified. You typically have two main pipelines to manage the serverless framework and surrounding services and the actual function code themselves.

Terraform apply pipeline

This pipeline is responsible for provisioning the underlying infrastructure required to support the serverless workloads. It uses Terraform to define and manage the infrastructure components. The pipeline may create resources such as load balancers, API gateways, event triggers, and other logical components that serve as the foundation for serverless functions. These are often lightweight cloud services that are extremely quick to provision.

Serverless deployment pipeline

This pipeline is responsible for deploying individual serverless functions to the target platform (e.g., AWS Lambda or Azure Functions). Each serverless function typically has its own pipeline to handle its deployment, testing, and versioning. This maintains autonomy between the different components and allows teams to organize ownership that aligns with how they manage their code base. The pipeline really only involves packaging the function code, defining the configuration, and deploying it to the cloud platform of choice.

The serverless approach simplifies the deployment and management of code, and developers can focus more on writing the application logic while relying on automated deployment pipelines to handle infrastructure provisioning and serverless function deployments.

Terraform tools

There are a ton of tools out there to help improve Terraform code in terms of beauty, functionality, and maintainability. I won't boil the ocean here but I will mention some critical tools that are absolutely required for any Terraform continuous integration process.

Formatting

During development, you should install the HashiCorp Terraform plugin for Visual Studio Code. This will enable a ton of helpful productivity features within your editor but it will also automatically execute Terraform's built-in formatting function, `terraform fmt`, on saving each file. This will drastically help promote consistent formatting within your code base. This is a proactive approach that is dependent on the developer to take steps to configure their development environment properly.

In order to verify each developer is employing this technique to keep your project's Terraform code neat and tidy, you need to use a linter as part of your pull request process. Adding `tflint` to your pull request process will help prevent poorly formatted code from ever making it into your `main` branch!

Documentation

Now that the code is formatted properly, we should generate some documentation for our modules. This is useful whether you are writing root modules or reusable modules. The `terraform-docs` tool, when pointed at a Terraform module director, will generate a markdown README file that documents the key aspects of your Terraform module, including version requirements for both Terraform and the providers you employ, as well as details on the input and output variables. This tool is ideal to set up as a pre-commit operation to ensure that your documentation is automatically generated every time the code is merged. It reads annotations that are built-in to HCL, such as `description`, `type`, `required`, and any default values.

You can read more at `https://terraform-docs.io/user-guide/introduction/`.

Security scanning

Checkov is a static code analyzer that can scan your Terraform plan files to detect security and compliance violations. It has thousands of built-in policies spanning many platforms but most importantly including the cloud platforms that we explore in this book: AWS, Azure, and Google Cloud. However, at the time of writing, the policy coverage is most comprehensive for AWS, with both Azure and Google Cloud with significantly less coverage.

You can read more at `https://github.com/bridgecrewio/checkov`.

Summary

In this chapter, we learned the basic concepts of source control management, including detailed breakdowns of different branching and workflow strategies that are used by teams large and small. We looked at how our automation systems, namely our CI/CD pipelines, would integrate with these processes at key events.

In the next chapter, we will move conceptual knowledge and start working on our first solution, which is to leverage virtual machines on the first public cloud, AWS.

Part 3:
Building Solutions on AWS

Armed with the conceptual knowledge of Terraform and architectural concepts that transcend the implementation details of the major public cloud platforms, we'll explore building solutions on **Amazon Web Services** (**AWS**) with three cloud computing paradigms: virtual machines, containers with Kubernetes, and serverless with AWS Lambda.

This part has the following chapters:

- *Chapter 7, Getting Started on AWS – Building Solutions with AWS EC2*
- *Chapter 8, Containerize with AWS – Building Solutions with AWS EKS*
- *Chapter 9, Go Serverless with AWS – Building Solutions with AWS Lambda*

7
Getting Started on AWS – Building Solutions with AWS EC2

Now that we have a good foundation of the concepts needed to build real-world cloud solutions and automate them using **Infrastructure as Code** (**IaC**) with Terraform, we will start our journey with arguably the most popular cloud platform: **Amazon Web Services** (**AWS**).

In this chapter, we'll take a step-by-step approach to designing, building, and automating a solution using AWS's **virtual machine** (**VM**) service – **Elastic Cloud Compute** or EC2 for short. We'll also explore several other AWS services that are crucial for ensuring our solution's robustness and production readiness, such as secrets management, logging, and network security.

We have much to accomplish, but this is where the rubber hits the road. We'll begin to really apply the concepts we've been discussing and put them into practice on AWS.

This chapter covers the following topics:

- Laying the foundation
- Designing the solution
- Building the solution
- Automating the deployment

Laying the foundation

Cloud infrastructure is only as good as the applications and services deployed to it, so for this book, we will be building our sample architectures around a function use case for a fictional company called Söze Enterprises. Söze Enterprises was founded by a mysterious Turkish billionaire, Keyser Söze, who wants to take autonomous vehicles to the next level by building a platform that will allow both land and air vehicles – from any manufacturer – to coordinate their actions to improve safety and efficiency. Somehow, Keyser has already got Elon onboard, so it's only a matter of time before the other EV vendors follow suit.

We have inherited a team from one of Söze Enterprises' other divisions that has a strong core team of C# .NET developers, so we'll be building version 1.0 of the platform using .NET technologies. The elusive CEO, Keyser, was seen hobnobbing with Jeff Bezos in Monaco over the weekend, and word has come down from corporate that we will be using AWS to host the platform. Since the team doesn't have a ton of experience with containers and timelines are tight, we've decided to build a simple three-tier architecture and host on VMs using AWS's EC2 service. We've decided to use a Linux operating system to make it easier to convert containers in the future:

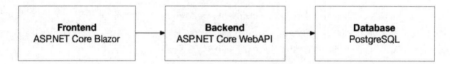

Figure 7.1 – Logical architecture for the autonomous vehicle platform

The platform will need a frontend, which will be a web UI built using ASP.NET Core Blazor. The frontend will be powered by a REST API backend, which will be built using ASP.NET Core Web API. Having our core functionality encapsulated into a REST API will allow autonomous vehicles to communicate directly with the platform and allow us to expand by adding client interfaces with additional frontend technologies such as native mobile apps and virtual or mixed reality in the future. The backend will use a PostgreSQL database for persistent storage since it's lightweight, industry-standard, and relatively inexpensive.

Designing the solution

Due to the tight timelines the team is facing, we want to keep the cloud architecture simple. Therefore, we'll be keeping it simple and using tried and tested services from AWS to implement the platform as opposed to trying to learn something new. The first decision we have to make is what AWS service each component of our logical architecture will be hosted on.

Our application architecture consists of three components: a frontend, a backend, and a database. The frontend and backend are application components and need to be hosted on a cloud service that provides general computing, while the database needs to be hosted on a cloud database service. There are many options for both types of services:

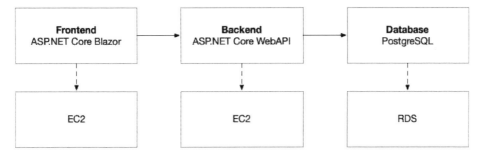

Figure 7.2 – Logical architecture for the autonomous vehicle platform

Since we've decided that we're going to use VMs to host our application, we have narrowed down the different services that we can use to host our application, and we have decided that AWS EC2 is the ideal choice for our current situation. There are other options, such as **Elastic Beanstalk**, that also use VMs, but we want to have total control over the solution and maintain as many cross-platform capabilities as possible in case we ever have to migrate to a different cloud platform:

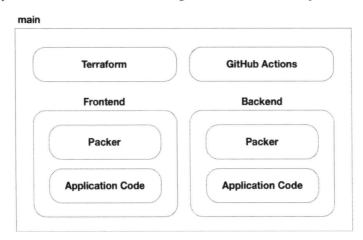

Figure 7.3 – Source control structure of our repository

This solution will consist of six parts. We still have the application code and Packer templates for both the frontend and backend. Then, we have GitHub Actions to implement our CI/CD process and Terraform to provision our AWS infrastructure and reference the Packer-built VM images for our EC2 instances.

Cloud architecture

The first part of our design is adapting our solution's architecture to the target cloud platform: AWS. This involves mapping application architecture components to AWS services and thinking through the configuration of those services so that they meet the requirements of our solution.

Virtual network

VMs must be deployed within a virtual network. On AWS, we use the AWS EC2 service to provide our VMs, and we use AWS **Virtual Private Cloud** (**VPC**) to provide our virtual network. When working on AWS, the term *EC2 instance* is used interchangeably with the term *virtual machine*. Likewise, the term *VPC* is used interchangeably with the term *virtual network*. In this book, I will try to use industry-standard terminology wherever possible. You should get in the habit of thinking this way as this will allow your knowledge and skills to better transition between the different cloud platforms:

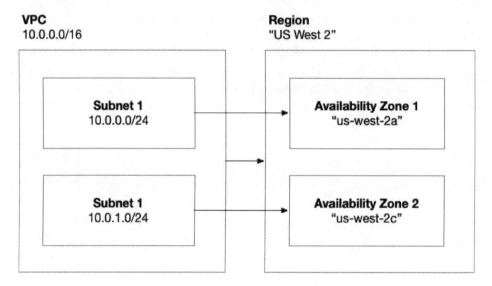

Figure 7.4 – AWS virtual network architecture

As we've discussed previously, a virtual network is divided into a set of subnets. On AWS, a virtual network is scoped to a specific region, and a subnet is scoped to an Availability Zone within that region. Therefore, to build highly available systems on AWS, we must distribute our workloads across multiple Availability Zones. Therefore, if one Availability Zone experiences an outage, our workload, when deployed into the other Availability Zone, will prevent disruption to the end users.

Our application's VMs need to be provisioned into subnets within a virtual network. The frontend of our application needs to be accessible over the internet, while the backend only needs to be accessible to the frontend. Therefore, we should provision separate subnets for the internet-accessible frontend and our private backend. This is a common pattern when it comes to creating *public* and *private* subnets:

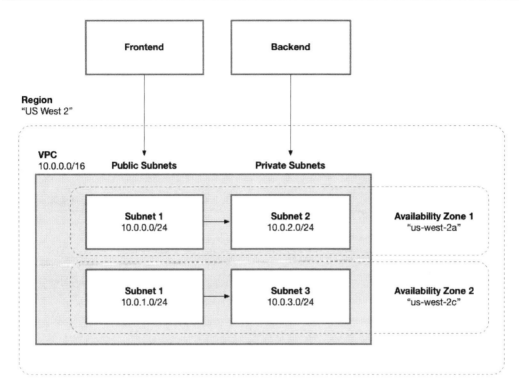

Figure 7.5 – Public and private subnets for the frontend and backend application components

In this pattern, two pairs of public and private subnets are created. Each pair is provisioned in the same Availability Zone. The reason why each pair shares the same Availability Zone is due to the dependency between the frontend and the backend. For example, if there is an outage affecting the Availability Zone of the backend, the frontend won't be able to operate. Likewise, if there is an outage affecting the Availability Zone of the frontend, no traffic will be routed to the backend. We can create as many pairs of these public/private subnets as there are Availability Zones within a region. Most regions have four to five Availability Zones, but usually, two to three Availability Zones are sufficient for most workloads. After that, you are more likely to benefit from setting up a multi-region deployment.

Network routing

There are a few other components that we need to set up within this virtual network to enable our VMs to function properly. In AWS, when you provision a VM in a virtual network, you won't have internet access! For most connected applications, internet access is required to allow connectivity to third-party services. Without this, operators would be inconvenienced as they would be unable to perform operating system upgrades and patches using internet-hosted package repositories:

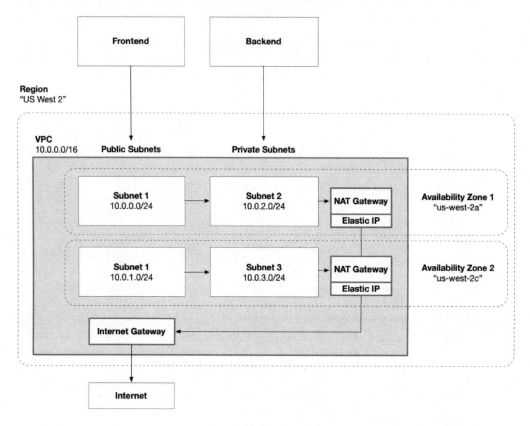

Figure 7.6 – Internet and NAT gateways enable internet access for VMs within the subnets

The internet gateway is attached to the virtual network at the region level, providing internet access to the entire VPC, while the NAT gateways are deployed into each public subnet at the Availability Zone level to allow EC2 instances in private subnets to access the internet without being directly accessible from the internet. Each NAT gateway also needs its own static public IP address to grant access. This can be achieved by using the Elastic IP service on AWS:

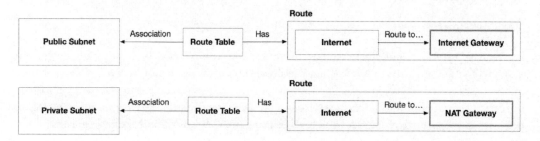

Figure 7.7 – Route tables associated with the subnets that direct traffic to the correct gateway

The final step in establishing internet access to our VMs in private subnets is routing internet-bound traffic to the correct NAT gateway for each subnet; VMs in public subnets can directly access the internet. This can be done using route tables. In the public subnet, we route internet traffic to the internet gateway. In the private subnet, we route internet traffic to the NAT gateway.

Load balancing

Now that our subnets have been set up and connected using proper routing tables, we can provision our VMs. To achieve high availability, we need at least one VM to be provisioned for each subnet for both the frontend and the backend of our solution. We can increase the number of VMs in each subnet to achieve even more reliability or scale:

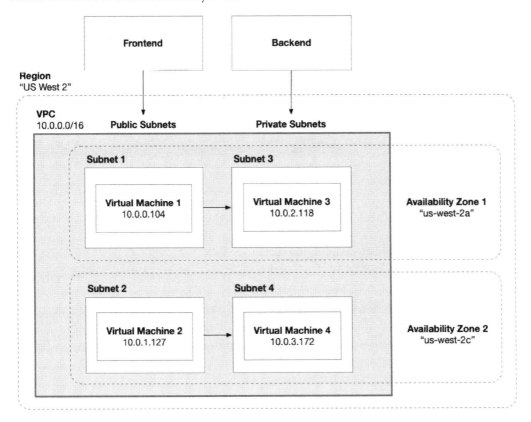

Figure 7.8 – VMs provisioned for our virtual network

The problem with the current design is that we need a way for our system to respond correctly to an outage affecting one of our Availability Zones. This is where a load balancer comes in. It allows us to get the double benefit of routing traffic to healthy endpoints and distributing the load evenly across our resources.

In AWS, the **Application Load Balancer** (**ALB**) service performs this function. The load balancer's job is to be the single point of contact for clients to send requests to. The load balancer then forwards that traffic to VMs and routes the corresponding responses back to the client from where the request originated:

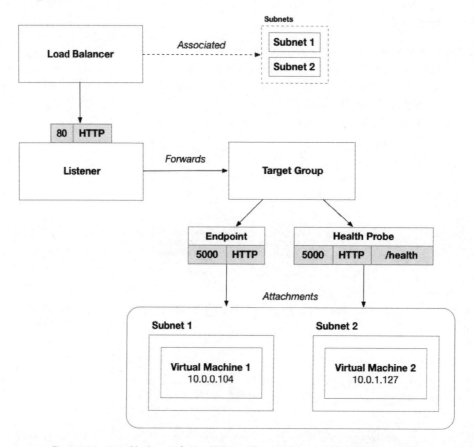

Figure 7.9 – Load balancer forwarding traffic to VMs across Availability Zones

In the AWS ALB, the first thing we need to set up is the listener. On this listener, you specify a port, a protocol, and one or more actions you want to perform when a request is received. The most basic type of action is to forward the request to a target group.

In our solution, the target group will consist of a set of VMs. The target group specifies what port and protocol the request should be sent to, as well as a health probe with a specific application path. The health probe can optionally be set up on a different port and protocol, where it provides several different settings to control how frequently it should be probed and how to evaluate whether the endpoint is healthy or unhealthy. Healthy is usually indicated by an HTTP status code of 200. Anything else is considered unhealthy.

For both our frontend and backend, we have a simple set of VMs for the target group with an endpoint configured for the HTTP protocol on port 5000 (the default port for ASP.NET Core).

The frontend is an **ASP.NET Core Blazor** application. As a result, it uses **SignalR** (which abstracts WebSocket communication) to provide real-time connectivity between the web browser and the server. As a result, we need to enable sticky sessions so that this can function properly. Sticky sessions will allow the client to continue to use the same VM, thus allowing the WebSocket to stay alive and not be disrupted by changing which web server it communicates with.

For the health probe, the frontend will use the root path of the web application, while the backend will use a special path that routes to a controller that's been configured to respond to the health probe.

Network security

Now that our virtual network has been fully configured and our VMs have been set up behind load balancers, we need to think about what network traffic we want to allow through the system. In AWS, this can be controlled by creating security groups, which allow traffic to be sent between components of your architecture on specific ports using specific protocols.

The first step in this process is to think through the logical stops for our network traffic as it makes its way through our solution:

Figure 7.10 – Logical components of our architecture

The application components, including the frontend and the backend, are on this list, followed by the database. However, these aren't the only places where our network traffic flows. Since we introduced load balancers in front of both the frontend and the backend, we have two additional stops for network traffic.

The next step is to think about how each component communicates with others. This includes both the port and protocol but also the direction of the traffic. To do this, we need to think about the network traffic from the perspective of each component:

Figure 7.11 – Frontend load balancer network traffic flow

From the perspective of the frontend load balancer, we'll be receiving traffic from the internet on port 80 using the HTTP protocol. This inbound traffic is called **ingress**. Due to the target group configuration, we'll be forwarding those requests to the frontend on port 5000 using the HTTP protocol. This outbound traffic is called **egress**:

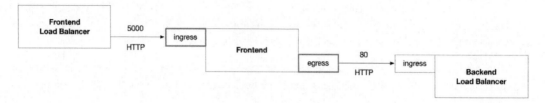

Figure 7.12 – Frontend network traffic flow

From the perspective of the frontend, we'll be receiving traffic from the frontend load balancer on port 5000 using the HTTP protocol. The C# application code will make requests to the REST web API hosted in the backend, but we'll be routing all our requests to the backend through the backend load balancer on port 80 using the HTTP protocol:

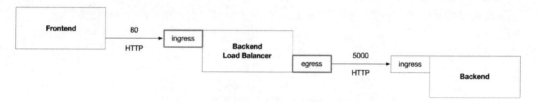

Figure 7.13 – Backend load balancer network traffic flow

From the perspective of the backend load balancer, we'll be receiving traffic from the frontend on port 80 using the HTTP protocol. Due to the target group configuration, we'll be forwarding those requests to the backend on port 5000 using the HTTP protocol:

Figure 7.14 – Backend network traffic flow

From the perspective of the backend, we'll be receiving traffic from the backend load balancer on port 5000 using the HTTP protocol. The C# application code will be making requests to the PostgreSQL database on port 5432 using the HTTPS protocol.

Secrets management

Secrets such as database credentials or service access keys need to be stored securely. Each cloud platform has a service that provides this functionality. On AWS, this service is called **AWS Secrets Manager**:

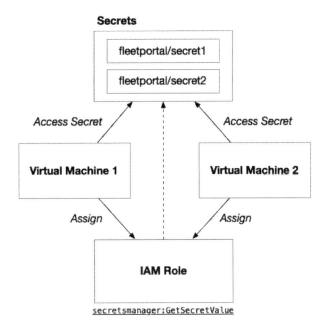

Figure 7.15 – Secrets stored in AWS Secrets Manager can be accessed
by VMs once they have the necessary IAM privileges

You simply create secrets on this service using a consistent naming convention, then construct an IAM role that has permission to access these secrets. The following IAM policy will grant permission to just secrets that start with `fleetportal/`:

```
{
    "Version": "2012-10-17",
    "Statement": [
        {
            "Effect": "Allow",
            "Action": "secretsmanager:GetSecretValue",
            "Resource":
"arn:aws:secretsmanager:region:account
id:secret:fleetportal/*"
        }
    ]
}
```

The values for `region` and `account-id` will need to be altered to reflect where the secrets were created. It's important to note that an AWS account is typically used as a security boundary for an application and an environment. So, we would likely have separate AWS accounts for our solution's development and production environments, as well as any other environments we may need. This will isolate our secrets manager secrets within the context of the AWS account and the region.

The two main attributes we use to grant permissions are `action` and `resource`. When implementing the principle of least privilege, it's important to be as specific as possible about the actions that are required for a particular identity. If access is not required, don't grant it. Likewise, we should ensure the resources we grant these permissions to are as narrow as possible. It's easy to be lazy and leave * in the resources or the actions. Still, we need to be aware that a malicious attacker could use overly generous permissions to move laterally within our environments.

VMs

Now that we have everything we need for our solution, we can finish by talking about where our application components will run: in VMs that have been provisioned using AWS EC2.

When provisioning VMs on AWS, you have two options. First, you can provide static VMs. In this approach, you need to specify key characteristics for every VM. Alternatively, you can use an **AWS Auto Scaling group** to dynamically provision and manage the VMs. In this approach, you provide the Auto Scaling group with some configuration and parameters on when to scale up and when to scale down, at which point the Auto Scaling group will take care of everything else.

When provisioning a static VM on AWS, you need to associate it with an **AWS key pair** to ensure that you can connect to its operating system. This will allow your operators to perform diagnostics and update or patch the software and operating system.

All VMs need to be connected to a virtual network, so when you set up a static VM, you need to specify the network configuration. This can be accomplished by creating a network interface and associating it with the VM. The network interface connects the VM to the appropriate subnet, which is the place where you attach one or more security groups.

The internal configuration of your VM is controlled by two critical attributes: the VM image and the user data. As we discussed in *Chapter 4*, the VM image can either be a vanilla installation of an operating system or it can be a fully configured version of your application. The decision of **build versus bake** is up to you.

User data allows you to run the *last mile* configuration when the VM starts up. This can be done using industry-standard `cloud-init` configuration to perform a wide variety of tasks such as setting up users/groups, setting up environment variables, or mounting disks:

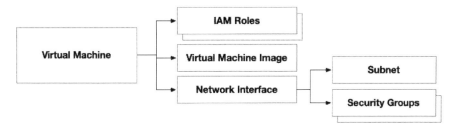

Figure 7.16 – Resource VMs created statically

AWS can dynamically manage your VMs based on the load that they incur. This is done using an Auto Scaling group. This Auto Scaling group is responsible for provisioning the VMs. Consequently, this means that the Auto Scaling group needs to have the key characteristics that define your VM set on its launch template. The Auto Scaling group uses this launch template to specify the configuration of each VM that it provisions:

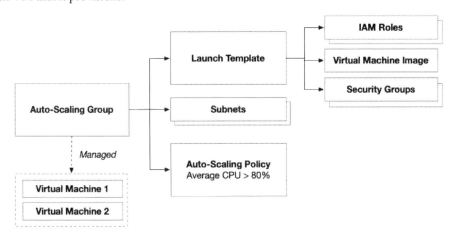

Figure 7.17 – VMs created and managed dynamically using an Auto-Scaling Group

Besides this launch template, the Auto Scaling group simply needs to be told what subnets the VMs should be provisioned into and under what circumstances it should provision or de-provision VMs from the set that it actively manages.

Monitoring

AWS has a cross-cutting service called **CloudWatch** that can capture logs and telemetry from various AWS services you consume within your solutions. We'll be using this as the primary logging mechanism within this book. Many services support CloudWatch out of the box with minimal to no configuration to get it working. At the same time, other services and scenarios require permissions to be granted to allow that service to log in to CloudWatch.

Deployment architecture

Now that we have a good idea of what our cloud architecture is going to look like for our solution on AWS, we need to come up with a plan for how to provision our environments and deploy our code.

VM configuration

In our solution, we have two VM roles: the frontend role, which is responsible for handling web page requests from the end user's web browser, and the backend role, which is responsible for handling REST API requests from the web application. Each of these roles has different code and a different configuration that needs to be set. Each will require its own Packer template to build a VM image that we can use to launch a VM on AWS:

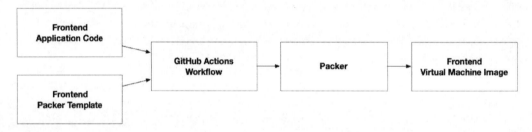

Figure 7.18 – Packer pipeline to build a VM image for the frontend

A GitHub Actions workflow that triggers off changes to the frontend application code and the frontend Packer template will execute `packer build` and create a new VM image for the solution's frontend.

Both the frontend and the backend will have an identical GitHub workflow that executes `packer build`. The key difference between the workflows is the code bases that they execute against. Both the frontend and the backend might have slightly different operating system configurations, and both will require different deployment packages for their respective application components:

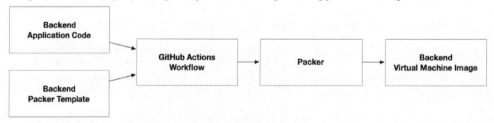

Figure 7.19 – Packer pipeline to build a VM image for the backend

It's important to note that the application code will be baked into the VM image rather than copied to an already running VM. This means that to update the software running on the VMs, each VM will need to be restarted so that it has a new VM image containing the latest copy of the code.

This approach makes the VM image an immutable deployment artifact that is versioned and updated each time there is a release of the application code that needs to be deployed.

Cloud environment configuration

Once the VM images have been built for both the frontend and the backend, we can execute the final workflow, which will both provision and deploy our solution to AWS:

Figure 7.20 – VM images are used as inputs to the Terraform
code, which provisions the environment on AWS

The Terraform code base will have two input variables for the version of the VM image for both the frontend and the backend. When new versions of the application software need to be deployed, the input parameters for these versions will be incremented to reflect the target version for deployment. When the workflow is executed, `terraform apply` will simply replace the existing VMs with VMs using the new VM image.

Now that we have a solid plan for how we will implement both the cloud architecture using AWS and the deployment architecture using GitHub Actions, let's start building! In the next section, we'll break down the HashiCorp configuration language code that we used to implement the Terraform and Packer solutions.

Building the solution

With our design in place, all we need to do is write the code that implements the design.

Packer

Our solution has a frontend and a backend application component. Although the application code is radically different, the way we build a VM image is not.

AWS plugin

As we discussed in *Chapter 4*, Packer – like Terraform – is an extensible command-line executable. Each cloud platform provides a plugin for Packer that encapsulates the integration with its services:

```
packer {
  required_plugins {
    amazon = {
      source  = "github.com/hashicorp/amazon"
      version = "~> 1.2.6"
    }
  }
}
```

Plugins need to be declared within a Packer solution. At the time of writing, the latest version of the AWS Packer plugin is `1.2.6`.

The AWS plugin for Packer provides an `amazon-ebs` builder that will generate an AMI by creating a new VM from a base image, executing the provisioners, taking an **Elastic Block Store** (**EBS**) disk image snapshot, and creating an **Amazon Machine Image** (**AMI**) from it. This behavior is controlled by the Amazon builder:

```
data "amazon-ami" "ubuntu2204" {
  filters = {
    architecture         = "x86_64"
    virtualization-type  = "hvm"
    root-device-type     = "ebs"
    name                 = "ubuntu/images/hvm-ssd/ubuntu-jammy-22.04-
amd64-server-*"
  }
  owners       = ["099720109477"]
  most_recent  = true
  region       = var.aws_primary_region
}
```

The first input to the Amazon `amazon-ebs` builder is the base image to use when creating the initial VM against which the Packer template's provisioners will be executed. The preceding code references the latest version of the Ubuntu `22.04` VM image within the target AWS region:

```
source "amazon-ebs" "vm" {
  region        = var.aws_primary_region
  ami_name      = "${var.image_name}-${var.image_version}"
  instance_type = var.aws_instance_type
  ssh_username  = "ubuntu"
  ssh_interface = "public_ip"
  communicator  = "ssh"
  source_ami    = data.amazon-ami.ubuntu2204.id
}
```

The `amazon-ebs` builder references the `amazon-ami` data source to ensure that the correct base image is used before the provisioners are executed. Here, `ami_name` is probably the most important attribute on this block as it dictates the version name that the VM image will be referenced by in `terraform apply` operations.

Operating system configuration

To avoid access control issues, it's a good idea to establish the context for the provisioners to be executed within:

```
locals {
  execute_command = "chmod +x {{ .Path }}; {{ .Vars }} sudo -E sh '{{
.Path }}'"
}
```

This is a standard `execute_command` parameter that can be used to set the context for all provisioners. It allows you to eliminate any unnecessary `sudo` commands within your installation scripts. The preceding `execution_command` parameter will allow your Packer template scripts to execute as a privileged user.

Our solution is built using ASP.NET Core. Therefore, we need to install .NET 6.0 SDK for our solution to work properly on the VMs. Ubuntu, like other Debian-based distributions of Linux, uses the `apt` command-line application to perform package management. By default, Ubuntu includes several public repositories that include most of the common software packages. However, sometimes, you need to set up additional package repositories when the default repositories don't work. Microsoft hosts a package repository for `apt`, that houses the correct software package we need to install .NET 6.0 on Ubuntu. Therefore, we need to add that repository before we can use `apt` to install .NET 6.0.

Our Packer template includes a file called `dotnet.pref` that has the following contents:

```
Package: *
Pin: origin "packages.microsoft.com"
Pin-Priority: 1001
```

We use the Packer `file` provisioner to copy this file to the correct location on the VM:

```
provisioner "shell" {
  execute_command = local.execute_command
  inline = [
    "cp /tmp/dotnet.pref /etc/apt/preferences.d/dotnet.pref"
  ]
}
```

Then, we execute the `install-dotnet6-prereq.sh` bash script, which downloads a `.deb` file and installs it using the `dpkg` tool. This registers the third-party repository hosted by Microsoft with the Debian package management tool.

Now, we can simply run `apt-get update -y` to get the latest version of the packages from all repositories, and we are ready to install .NET 6.0:

```
provisioner "shell" {
  execute_command = local.execute_command
  inline = [
    "apt-get install dotnet-sdk-6.0 -y"
  ]
}
```

If we don't include the `packages.microsoft.com` repository, then this `apt-get install` command will fail with an error message saying that the `dotnet-sdk-6.0` package could not be found.

Setting up a service in Linux

Most applications run as processes within Linux that run perpetually. This is often the case when the application needs to listen for network traffic – such as a web server. Another great benefit of setting up a service in Linux is that the operating system can auto-start the service every time the VM reboots. To do that, you need to set up a service definition file:

```
[Unit]
Description=Fleet Portal

[Service]
WorkingDirectory=/var/www/fleet-portal
ExecStart=/usr/bin/dotnet /var/www/fleet-portal/FleetPortal.dll

Restart=always
RestartSec=10  # Restart service after 10 seconds if the dotnet
service crashes

SyslogIdentifier=fleet-portal

User=fleet-portal-svc

Environment=ASPNETCORE_ENVIRONMENT=Production
Environment=DOTNET_PRINT_TELEMETRY_MESSAGE=false

[Install]
WantedBy=multi-user.target
```

This service file needs to be copied to the `/etc/systemd/system` folder. By running the `systemctl` command, it will be enabled so that the operating system will automatically start the service when the machine reboots. The `systemctl` command is also useful to `start`, `stop`, and check the `status` value of your service.

It's best practice to run services using their own identity. This allows you to grant the service access to only the resources on the VM that it needs:

```
provisioner "shell" {
    execute_command = local.execute_command
    inline = [
        "groupadd fleet-portal-svc",
        "useradd -g fleet-portal-svc fleet-portal-svc",
        "mkdir -p /var/www/fleet-portal",
        "chown -R fleet-portal-svc:fleet-portal-svc /var/www/fleet-
portal"
    ]
}
```

The preceding code sets up a local user and group for the service to run under and changes the ownership of the application's folder at `/var/www/fleet-portal` so that the service's user account has sufficient access to the application's executable and supporting files. Both the user and the application's working directory are specified in the service definition file.

Once the user is ready, we can install the service definition file and enable the service:

```
provisioner "shell" {
    execute_command = local.execute_command
    inline = [
        "cp /tmp/fleet-portal.service /etc/systemd/system/fleet-portal.
service",
        "systemctl enable fleet-portal.service"
    ]
}
```

This concludes the operating system configuration, which can be baked into the VM image. Any additional configuration steps require more information from the cloud environment that Terraform provisions.

Terraform

As we discussed in our design, our solution is made up of two application components: the frontend and the backend. Each has an application code base that needs to be deployed. Since this is the first time we will be using the `aws` provider, we'll look at the basic provider setup and how to configure the backend before we look at the nuts and bolts of each component of our architecture.

Provider setup

We need to specify all the providers that we intend to use in this solution within the `required_providers` block:

```
terraform {
  required_providers {
    aws = {
      source  = "hashicorp/aws"
      version = "~> 5.17"
    }
    cloudinit = {
      source  = "hashicorp/cloudinit"
      version = "~> 2.3.2"
    }
  }
}
```

We also need to configure the AWS provider to ensure that it uses the desired target region using the `primary_region` input variable:

```
provider "aws" {
  region = var.primary_region
}
```

Sometimes, you may want to add a secondary region in the future, so it's a good idea to establish the primary region when you start the project. Even if you only deploy to one region, you still have a *primary region*.

The AWS provider does require some additional parameters to specify the credentials to use to connect to AWS, but because these are sensitive values, we don't want to embed them into the code. We'll pass those values in later when we automate the deployment using the standard AWS `AWS_ACCESS_KEY_ID` and `AWS_SECRET_ACCESS_KEY` environment variables. It's important to note that there are many different ways to configure the AWS provider to authenticate with AWS. I recommend using environment variables as it is a consistent approach across cloud platforms and other Terraform providers, and it integrates easily with different pipeline tools, such as GitHub Actions, which we'll be using in the next section and future chapters.

Backend

Because we will be using a CI/CD pipeline to provision and maintain our environment in the long term, we need to set up a remote backend for our Terraform state. Because our solution will be hosted on AWS, we'll use the AWS **Simple Storage Service (S3)** backend to store our Terraform state.

Just like the AWS provider, we don't want to hard code the backend configuration in our code, so we'll simply set up a placeholder for the backend:

```
terraform {

  ...

  backend "s3" {
  }
}
```

We'll configure the backend's parameters using the `-backend-config` parameters when we run `terraform init` in our CI/CD pipeline.

It's important to ensure that the AWS IAM identity you use to authenticate with AWS has access to this S3 bucket. Otherwise, you will get authentication errors.

Input variables

It's good practice to pass in short names that identify the application's name and the application's environment. This allows you to embed consistent naming conventions across the resources that make up your solution, which makes it easier to identify and track resources from the AWS Console.

The `primary_region`, `vpc_cidr_block`, and `az_count` input variables drive key architectural characteristics of the deployment. They can't be hard-coded as it would limit the reusability of the Terraform code base.

The `vpc_cidr_block` input variable establishes the virtual network address space, which is often tightly regulated by an enterprise governance body. There is usually a process to ensure that teams across an organization do not use IP address ranges that conflict, thus making it impossible to allow those two applications to integrate or integrate with shared network resources within the enterprise in the future.

The `az_count` input variable allows us to configure how much redundancy we want within our solution. This will affect the high availability of the solution but also the cost of the deployment. As you can imagine, cost is also a tightly regulated characteristic of cloud infrastructure deployments.

Consistent naming and tagging

The AWS console is designed in such a way that it's rather difficult to get an application-centric view of your deployment. This is why it's extremely important to leave breadcrumbs within the resources that you deploy that indicate what application and environment they belong to. Almost all resources within the AWS provider have a map attribute called `tags`:

```
resource "aws_vpc" "main" {
  cidr_block = var.vpc_cidr_block
```

```
    tags = {
       Name         = "${var.application_name}-${var.environment_name}-
    network"
       application = var.application_name
       environment = var.environment_name
    }
}
```

You should make a habit of setting both the AWS console-recognized Name tag and a tagging scheme for your devices that establishes application and environment ownership of that resource. For our solution, we use two top-level input variables, application_name and environment_name, to set this context, and we'll embed these values on all the resources that we provision.

AWS can create an application-centric view within the AWS console using something called a resource group. Unlike on other platforms, a resource group on AWS is not a strong boundary around a set of resources but a loosely coupled relationship between resources derived from a common tagging scheme:

```
resource "aws_resourcegroups_group" "main" {
  name = "${var.application_name}-${var.environment_name}"

  resource_query {
    query = jsonencode(
      {
        ResourceTypeFilters = [
          "AWS::AllSupported"
        ]
        TagFilters = [
          {
            Key    = "application"
            Values = [var.application_name]
          },
          {
            Key    = "environment"
            Values = [var.environment_name]
          }
        ]
      }
    )
  }
}
```

The preceding code creates an AWS resource group that creates a central location where you can access all of your related resources from one place. Simply adding application and environment tags to all your resources will include them.

Virtual network

Because our solution is a standard three-tier architecture, we are configuring our virtual network into public and private subnets for the frontend and backend application components.

We want to distribute our VMs across the Availability Zones to ensure the high availability of our solution. Rather than hard-code the Availability Zones or just take the first two, we can randomly select the number of Availability Zones we want from the list of available ones for the given region using the `aws_availability_zones` data source and a `random_shuffle` resource from the `random` provider:

```
data "aws_availability_zones" "available" {
  state = "available"
}

resource "random_shuffle" "az" {
  input        = data.aws_availability_zones.available.names
  result_count = var.az_count
}
```

If the `az_count` input variable has a value of 2, then the preceding code will randomly select two Availability Zones from the region of the current AWS provider. Remember that the AWS provider is scoped to a particular region, and when we initialized the provider, we used the `primary_region` input variable to set that value.

Rather than hard-code the address space for our subnets, it would be nice if we could calculate our subnets' address space using HCL's built-in functions. The `cidrsubnet` function allows us to take an address space and split it into smaller address spaces:

```
locals {
  azs_random = random_shuffle.az.result

  public_subnets = { for k, v in local.azs_random :
    k => {
      cidr_block        = cidrsubnet(var.vpc_cidr_block, var.cidr_
split_bits, k)
      availability_zone = v
    }
  }
  private_subnets = { for k, v in local.azs_random :
    k => {
      cidr_block        = cidrsubnet(var.vpc_cidr_block, var.cidr_
split_bits, k + var.az_count)
      availability_zone = v
    }
```

```
    }
  }
```

The preceding code will generate two maps, one for the public subnets and another for the private subnets. It accomplishes this by taking the randomly selected Availability Zones and using `cidrsubnet` to grab the next available block of `/24` or `256` IP addresses for each (this is more than enough for our application to scale to a huge number of VMs in each Availability Zone in both the frontend and the backend):

```
public_subnets = {
  "0" = {
    "availability_zone" = "us-west-2c"
    "cidr_block" = "10.0.0.0/24"
  }
  "1" = {
    "availability_zone" = "us-west-2a"
    "cidr_block" = "10.0.1.0/24"
  }
}
private_subnets = {
  "0" = {
    "availability_zone" = "us-west-2c"
    "cidr_block" = "10.0.2.0/24"
  }
  "1" = {
    "availability_zone" = "us-west-2a"
    "cidr_block" = "10.0.3.0/24"
  }
}
```

The preceding code is the value that the `public_subnets` and `private_subnets` maps will have when evaluated with a `vpc_cidr_block` value of `10.0.0.0/16`, a `cidr_split_bits` value of 8 and an `az_count` value of 2.

By manipulating these input variables, we can reasonably size the virtual network and its corresponding subnets so that we don't monopolize available address spaces for other applications that we may want to provision within the broader organization. For example, setting `vpc_cidr_block` to `10.0.0.0/22` allocates a total IP address count of `1024` to our application. With an `az_count` value of 2 and a `cidr_split_bits` value of 2, we can allocate address space for our four subnets, each with `/24` and `256` IP addresses. This gives us sufficient room for our application to scale without over-allocating valuable IP address space:

```
resource "aws_subnet" "frontend" {

  for_each = local.public_subnets
```

```
  vpc_id             = aws_vpc.main.id
  availability_zone = each.value.availability_zone
  cidr_block         = each.value.cidr_block

}
```

We create each subnet by iterating over the corresponding map of subnet address spaces. The preceding code demonstrates how we can use this map to set the correct Availability Zone and address space for each subnet.

Network routing

As per our design, the public subnets route internet traffic to the internet gateway:

```
resource "aws_route_table" "frontend" {
  vpc_id = aws_vpc.main.id

  route {
    cidr_block = "0.0.0.0/0"
    gateway_id = aws_internet_gateway.main.id
  }
}

resource "aws_route_table_association" "frontend" {

  for_each = aws_subnet.frontend

  subnet_id        = each.value.id
  route_table_id = aws_route_table.frontend.id

}
```

We use the `aws_route_table` resource to define the route and then `aws_route_table_association` to link the route table to the corresponding subnet.

The private subnets route their internet traffic to a NAT gateway, which is provisioned in each private subnet:

```
resource "aws_eip" "nat" {

  for_each = local.private_subnets
```

```
}

resource "aws_nat_gateway" "nat" {

  for_each = local.private_subnets

  allocation_id = aws_eip.nat[each.key].id
  subnet_id     = aws_subnet.backend[each.key].id

  depends_on = [aws_internet_gateway.main]

}
```

Because each private subnet has its own NAT gateway, we need a route table for each subnet to route the traffic to the correct NAT gateway:

```
resource "aws_route_table" "backend" {

  for_each = local.private_subnets

  vpc_id = aws_vpc.main.id

  route {
    cidr_block     = "0.0.0.0/0"
    nat_gateway_id = aws_nat_gateway.nat[each.key].id
  }
}

resource "aws_route_table_association" "backend" {

  for_each = local.private_subnets

  subnet_id      = aws_subnet.backend[each.key].id
  route_table_id = aws_route_table.backend[each.key].id

}
```

Notice that, unlike the public subnets, which share the same route table, we need to iterate on the private_subnets map to create a different route table for each private subnet and associate it with the corresponding private subnet using the each symbol.

Load balancing

As per our design, we need two AWS ALB instances – one for the frontend and another for the backend. We'll use the `aws_lb` resource and related resources with the `aws_lb` prefix to provision the target group and listener configuration:

```
resource "aws_lb_target_group" "frontend_http" {

  name                          = "${var.application_name}-${var.
environment_name}-frontend-http"
  port                          = 5000
  protocol                      = "HTTP"
  vpc_id                        = aws_vpc.main.id
  slow_start                    = 0
  load_balancing_algorithm_type = "round_robin"

  stickiness {
    enabled = true
    type    = "lb_cookie"
  }

  health_check {
    enabled             = true
    port                = 5000
    interval            = 30
    protocol            = "HTTP"
    path                = "/"
    matcher             = 200
    healthy_threshold   = 3
    unhealthy_threshold = 3
  }

}
```

Notice that the sticky session configuration needed for the ASP.NET Core Blazor Web application's WebSocket configuration is implemented by a nested `stickiness` block. Likewise, the health probe is implemented by a nested `health_check` block. This structure will be identical for both the frontend and the backend, but the configuration will differ slightly, with the backend not requiring sticky sessions and having a different path for the health probe.

The VMs are explicitly included in the target group using the `aws_lb_target_group_attachment` resource:

```
resource "aws_lb_target_group_attachment" "frontend_http" {

  for_each = aws_instance.frontend

  target_group_arn = aws_lb_target_group.frontend_http.arn
  target_id        = each.value.id
  port             = 5000

}
```

Notice that we are iterating over the corresponding `aws_instance` resource map and referencing the AWS EC2 instance ID using `each.value.id`.

Finally, we must provision the AWS ALB itself:

```
resource "aws_lb" "frontend" {
  name                = "${var.application_name}
${var.environment_name}-frontend"
  internal            = false
  load_balancer_type  = "application"
  subnets             = [for subnet in values(aws_subnet.frontend) :
subnet.id]
  security_groups     = [aws_security_group.frontend_lb.id]

  tags = {
    Name        = "${var.application_name}-${var.environment_name}-
frontend-lb"
    application = var.application_name
    environment = var.environment_name
  }

}
```

Notice that we are dynamically constructing a list of subnets using the corresponding `aws_subnet` resource map. When a resource block is provisioned with a `count` value, that resource block becomes a list, while when it is provisioned with a `for_each` iterator, it becomes a map. This is an important detail to pay attention to when you want to reference it from other resources.

Lastly, we must connect our AWS ALB to the target group using the listener:

```
resource "aws_lb_listener" "frontend_http" {

  load_balancer_arn = aws_lb.frontend.arn
```

```
  port            = "80"
  protocol        = "HTTP"

  default_action {
    type              = "forward"
    target_group_arn =
aws_lb_target_group.frontend_http.arn
  }
}
```

Network security

As per our design, we have three logical components of our solution architecture through which network traffic will pass. Each needs its own security group and set of rules to allow ingress and egress traffic:

```
resource "aws_security_group" "frontend_lb" {
  name         = "${var.application_name}-${var.environment_name}-
frontend-lb-sg"
  description = "Security group for the load balancer"
  vpc_id       = aws_vpc.main.id
}
```

A security group is created using the `aws_security_group` resource and attached to a virtual network.

Not all components within the architecture will need both ingress and egress rules, but it's important to think about all the ways network traffic should be allowed to flow through the system:

```
resource "aws_security_group_rule" "frontend_lb_ingress_http" {
  type              = "ingress"
  from_port         = 80
  to_port           = 80
  protocol          = "tcp"
  security_group_id = aws_security_group.frontend_lb.id
  cidr_blocks       = ["0.0.0.0/0"]
}
resource "aws_security_group_rule" "frontend_lb_egress_http" {
  type                     = "egress"
  from_port                = 5000
  to_port                  = 5000
  protocol                 = "tcp"
  security_group_id        = aws_security_group.frontend_lb.id
  source_security_group_id = aws_security_group.frontend.id
}
```

The preceding code establishes the rules we designed for the frontend load balancer, which allows traffic in from the internet (for example, `0.0.0.0/0`) and allows traffic out to the frontend VMs (for example, `aws_security_group.frontend.id`).

Secrets management

To allow our VMs to access our AWS Secrets Manager resources, we need to define an IAM role and associate it with our VMs. This will allow our VMs to operate under the security context defined by the IAM policies attached to this IAM role:

```
resource "aws_iam_role" "backend" {
  name = "${var.application_name}-${var.environment_name}-backend"

  assume_role_policy = jsonencode({
    Version = "2012-10-17"
    Statement = [
      {
        Action = "sts:AssumeRole"
        Effect = "Allow"
        Sid    = ""
        Principal = {
          Service = "ec2.amazonaws.com"
        }
      },
    ]
  })
}
```

The preceding code creates the IAM role for the backend VMs, which need access to the PostgreSQL database's connection string that we will store in AWS Secrets Manager. The IAM role itself doesn't do anything unless there is a policy defined. We need to attach a policy definition to the role to grant specific privileges to the VMs:

```
resource "aws_iam_role_policy" "backend" {
  name = "${var.application_name}-${var.environment_name}-backend"
  role = aws_iam_role.backend.id

  policy = jsonencode({
    Version = "2012-10-17"
    Statement = [
      {
        Action = [
          "secretsmanager:GetSecretValue",
        ]
```

```
        Effect   = "Allow"
        Resource = "arn:aws:secretsmanager:secret:${var.application_
name}/${var.environment_name}/*"
      },
    ]
  })
}
```

The preceding code grants access to all VMs operating with this IAM role associated with accessing AWS Secrets Manager secrets that begin with the `fleet-ops/dev` prefix. We must build this prefix using our standard naming convention input variables, `application_name` and `environment_name`, which have `fleet-ops` and `dev` as values, respectively. When we provision the production version of the `fleet-ops` platform, the `environment_name` input variable will be set to `prod`, ensuring that the VMs in the `dev` environment don't have access to the secrets in the `prod` environment. Deploying the different environments of our application into isolated AWS accounts would also create a more secure security boundary.

VMs

When provisioning static VMs, we have much more control over the configuration of each machine. Some VMs have specific network and storage configurations to meet workload demands:

```
resource "aws_network_interface" "frontend" {

  for_each = aws_subnet.frontend

  subnet_id = each.value.id
}

resource "aws_network_interface_sg_attachment" "frontend" {

  for_each = aws_instance.frontend

  security_group_id    = aws_security_group.frontend.id
  network_interface_id = each.value.primary_network_interface_id

}
```

The preceding code creates a network interface that we can then attach to a VM. Notice that we are iterating over the frontend subnets. This will ensure we have exactly one VM in each subnet (and consequently each Availability Zone). This network interface is where we attach the security group for VMs in the frontend.

Finally, we provision the VM using the `aws_instance` resource, taking care to use the correct instance type, network interface, and AWS AMI:

```
resource "aws_instance" "frontend" {

  for_each = aws_subnet.frontend

  ami             = data.aws_ami.frontend.id
  instance_type   = var.frontend_instance_type
  key_name        = data.aws_key_pair.main.key_name
  user_data       = data.cloudinit_config.frontend.rendered
  monitoring      = true

  network_interface {
    network_interface_id = aws_network_interface.frontend[each.key].id
    device_index         = 0
  }

}
```

AWS has a cross-cutting service called CloudWatch that collects logs and telemetry across the various AWS services. To enable CloudWatch on your EC2 instances, you simply need to add the `monitoring` attribute and set it to `true`.

Monitoring

Depending on the service and its available configuration options within the Terraform resources used to provision it, to activate CloudWatch, you might need to go through the process of provisioning additional resources and setting up additional IAM permissions to grant the respective resource to write to CloudWatch.

The first thing we need to set up is an IAM policy that will allow the specific service access to assume an IAM role. In this case, we are granting VPC Flow Logs access to assume an IAM role:

```
data "aws_iam_policy_document" "vpc_assume_role" {
  statement {
    effect = "Allow"

    principals {
      type         = "Service"
      identifiers = ["vpc-flow-logs.amazonaws.com"]
    }
```

```
        actions = ["sts:AssumeRole"]
    }
}
```

We'll use this policy when we set up the IAM role to grant the VPC Flow Logs service access to this particular IAM role. This will be important later when we link everything together:

```
resource "aws_iam_role" "vpc" {
  name                = "${var.application_name}-${var.environment_
name}-network"
  assume_role_policy = data.aws_iam_policy_document.assume_role.json
}
```

The preceding code allows VPC Flow Logs to assume this role, eventually granting it access to writing logs to CloudWatch.

Next, we need to set up another IAM policy that will grant access to write to CloudWatch logs. You can further narrow the scope of an access policy by narrowing the allowed actions and the allowed resources the policy grants access to:

```
data "aws_iam_policy_document" "cloudwatch" {
  statement {
    effect = "Allow"

    actions = [
      "logs:CreateLogGroup",
      "logs:CreateLogStream",
      "logs:PutLogEvents",
      "logs:DescribeLogGroups",
      "logs:DescribeLogStreams",
    ]

    resources = ["*"]
  }
}
```

In the preceding code, we do a good job of being specific about the types of operations we want to grant access to by giving specific operations such as `logs:PutLogEvents`. However, the resources are set to `*`, a very wide access level. We should consider narrowing that down to just the resources that we need.

The next step is to attach the policy to the IAM role:

```
resource "aws_iam_role_policy" "cloudwatch" {
  name    = "${var.application_name}-${var.environment_name}-network-
cloudwatch"
```

```
    role   = aws_iam_role.vpc.id
    policy = data.aws_iam_policy_document.cloudwatch.json
}
```

At this point, we have an IAM role that is allowed to write to CloudWatch and we have allowed VPC Flow Logs to assume this role.

Next, we need to create a CloudWatch log group that will store the logs from VPC:

```
resource "aws_cloudwatch_log_group" "vpc" {
  name = "${var.application_name}-${var.environment_name}-network"
}
```

Finally, we'll connect VPC Flow Logs to the log group and assign the IAM role it should use to gain access to write to CloudWatch:

```
resource "aws_flow_log" "main" {
  iam_role_arn    = aws_iam_role.vpc.arn
  log_destination = aws_cloudwatch_log_group.vpc.arn
  traffic_type    = "ALL"
  vpc_id          = aws_vpc.main.id
}
```

The preceding code also links our VPC to the VPC Flow Logs service, thus completing the flow and placing the networking logs in the corresponding CloudWatch log group.

With that, we have implemented the Packer and Terraform solutions and have a working code base that will build VM images for both our frontend and backend application components while also provisioning our cloud environment into AWS. In the next section, we'll dive into YAML and Bash and implement GitHub Actions workflows.

Automating the deployment

As we discussed in our design, our solution is made up of two application components: the frontend and the backend. Each has a code base consisting of application code and an operating system configuration encapsulated within a Packer template. These two application components are then deployed into a cloud environment on AWS, which is defined within our Terraform code base.

There is an additional code base that we have yet to discuss: our automation pipelines. We will be implementing our automation pipelines using GitHub Actions:

main

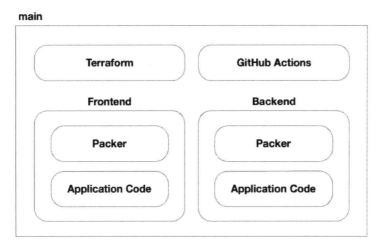

Figure 7.21 – Source code structure within our GitHub repository

In GitHub Actions, automation pipelines are called workflows and they are stored in a particular folder within the source code repository, namely `/.github/workflows`. Each of our code bases is stored in a separate folder. Our solutions source code repository's folder structure looks like this:

```
- .github
    - workflows
- dotnet
    - backend
    - frontend
- packer
    - backend
    - frontend
- terraform
```

As per our design, we will have GitHub Actions workflows that will execute Packer and build VM images for both the frontend (for example, `packer-frontend.yaml`) and the backend (for example, `packer-backend.yaml`). We'll also have workflows that will run `terraform plan` and `terraform apply`:

```
- .github
    - workflows
        - packer-backend.yaml
        - packer-frontend.yaml
        - terraform-apply.yaml
        - terraform-plan.yaml
```

Each folder path will allow us to control which GitHub Actions workflows should trigger so that we aren't unnecessarily running workflows when no applicable changes have been made.

Because we are following GitFlow, we'll have a main branch where the production version of all of our code will reside. Developers, whether they are working on updates to the application code (for example, C#), the operating system configuration (for example, the Packer template), or the cloud environment configuration (for example, the Terraform template), will create a branch off of `main` with the `feature/*` naming convention.

Once they've done this, they can submit a pull request. This indicates that the developer believes their code changes are ready to be merged back into the `main` branch – in other words, their code changes are ready for production!

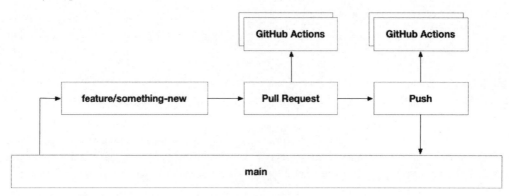

Figure 7.22 – GitFlow's pull request process

The pull request is a great time to perform some checks on our solution's code. For the application code, this could take the form of a build, static code analysis, and unit or integration tests. Each of these actions tests a different aspect of the application code. The build (that is, compiling the C# code base) is one of the most basic tests that we can perform. It simply tests whether the application code is valid C# and is devoid of inherent language syntax errors. Static code analysis can cover a wide range of code quality checks, including readability and maintainability or security and vulnerability assessments. The unit and integration tests check the functionality of the software components working individually and together to accomplish the underlying business purpose of the software. Executing these tests regularly is known as **continuous integration** (**CI**) and is half of the famous and often elusive **CI/CD pipeline**, where **CD** stands for **continuous delivery**.

The CI pipeline cuts down on routine work surrounding the built-in quality of the application code. Without it, these checks would need to be performed by humans through exhaustive code reviews and manual testing. We still need to do code reviews and manual testing, but a good CI pipeline will reduce the effort that humans need to perform.

Now that we've covered what built-in quality controls we can put on application code, what can we do with our operating system and our cloud environment configuration? Is there a way to test IaC without provisioning the infrastructure? There is, but there are limitations.

Packer

Because the VM image acts as an immutable artifact that contains a versioned copy of the application code and operating system configuration, we need to update this artifact any time something changes in either the application code or the operating system configuration:

```
on:
  push:
    branches:
    - main
    paths:
    - 'src/packer/frontend/**'
    - 'src/dotnet/frontend/**'
```

This means that we need a trigger on both code bases that affect the final artifact for Packer, which includes the application code and the operating system configuration within the Packer template itself. With GitHub Actions, we can add a list of `paths` that will trigger our workflow.

We should build a new VM image every time there is a pull request and every time there is a push onto `main`. When Packer is executed, it is essentially doing a pretty rigorous integration test. Therefore, it's useful to have it performed as part of our CI process. That means we need to have a VM image that is tested and verified to be production-ready before we push the code into the `main` branch:

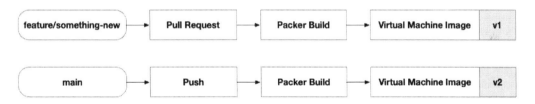

Figure 7.23 – VM image versioning

Our Packer workflow will generate a unique name and version for each VM image it produces. We can build tests into our Packer template to verify that the web server is running and listening on port `5000`. Using this version of the image, we can also launch a new VM and inspect the operating system's configuration ourselves to make sure everything is in order.

When we are confident that the code changes to either the application code or the operating system configuration are fully functional, we can approve the pull request and merge it into the `main` branch. This will trigger a new version of the VM image from the production-ready code in the `main` branch. We can use the new version of this production-ready VM image to update our cloud environment configuration when we are ready to deploy these changes to our environments.

The GitHub Actions workflow needs some ground rules to be established that control the specific versions of software and key locations within the code base. It's important to always be specific. This means using specific versions of software instead of relying on the internet Gods to decide which version you'll use. This might work well when you are running things locally on your machine and are there to solve the inevitable problems and conflicts that arise, but for an automation pipeline, there is no human there to correct things as they are happening; there are only assumptions – assumptions about what version of the software you're using.

We'll use two pieces of software: the .NET SDK and Packer. Likewise, we have two code bases: the C# .NET code base for the application and the HCL code base for Packer. As such, we must establish where these code bases are very clearly and upfront. Setting pipeline variables for them is a very useful way of accomplishing this as it ensures they are featured prominently in the YAML file and are stored in a reusable variable in case they will be repeated multiple times:

```
env:
  DOTNET_VERSION: '6.0.401' # The .NET SDK version to use
  PACKER_VERSION: '1.9.4' # The version of Packer to use
  WORKING_DIRECTORY: "./src/packer/frontend"
  DOTNET_WORKING_DIRECTORY: "./src/dotnet/frontend/FleetPortal"
```

Now that we have the triggers and some variables set for our workflow, we need to structure the jobs. For each Packer template, we will have two jobs: one that builds the C# .NET application code and produces a deployment package and another that runs `packer build` to produce the VM image:

```
jobs:

  build:
    runs-on: ubuntu-latest
    steps:

      ...

  packer:
    runs-on: ubuntu-latest
    steps:

      ...
```

The `build` job performs a pretty standard .NET build process, which includes restoring package dependencies from NuGet (the .NET package manager), building the code, running unit and integration tests, publishing a deployable artifact, and storing that artifact so that it can be used by future jobs within the pipeline:

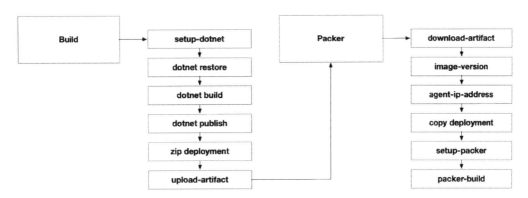

Figure 7.24 – Packer workflow

The `packer` job immediately downloads the `.zip` file containing the deployment artifact and puts it into a location where the Packer template's `file` provisioner expects it. Then, it generates a unique version of the name for the VM image that will be produced if successful:

```
- id: image-version
  name: Generate Version Number
  run: |
    echo "version=$(date +'%Y.%m').${{ github.run_number }}" >>
"$GITHUB_OUTPUT"
```

It does this by using Bash to generate the current year and month and appends `github.run_number` to ensure uniqueness if we happen to be running this pipeline more than once per day.

Next, it obtains the public IP address for the VM on which the GitHub Actions workflow is running:

```
- id: agent-ipaddress
  name: Check Path
  working-directory: ${{ env.WORKING_DIRECTORY }}
  run: |
    ipaddress=$(curl -s http://checkip.amazonaws.com)
    echo $ipaddress
    echo "ipaddress=$ipaddress" >> "$GITHUB_OUTPUT"
```

It does this so that when it runs `packer build`, it can configure Packer's plugin for AWS to poke a hole in the firewall to allow SSH traffic from the GitHub Actions machine to the temporary VM running on AWS where the Packer provisioners are executed.

Next, it installs a specific version of Packer:

```
- id: setup
  name: Setup `packer`
  uses: hashicorp/setup-packer@main
```

```
  with:
    version: ${{ env.PACKER_VERSION }}
```

Finally, it executes `packer build`, making sure to specify the `AWS_ACCESS_KEY_ID` and `AWS_SECRET_ACCESS_KEY` environment variables that the AWS plugin relies upon to authenticate to AWS's REST APIs:

```
- id: build
  name: Packer Build
  env:
    AWS_ACCESS_KEY_ID: ${{ vars.AWS_ACCESS_KEY_ID }}
    AWS_SECRET_ACCESS_KEY: ${{ secrets.AWS_SECRET_ACCESS_KEY }}
    PKR_VAR_image_version: ${{ steps.image-version.outputs.version }}
    PKR_VAR_agent_ipaddress: ${{ steps.agent-ipaddress.outputs.
ipaddress }}
  working-directory: ${{ env.WORKING_DIRECTORY }}
  run: |
    packer init ./
    packer build -var-file=variables.pkrvars.hcl ./
```

It also specifies two input variables to the Packer template using the `PKR_VAR_` prefixed environment variable technique so that it includes the image version and the build agent IP address, both of which were dynamically generated within the GitHub Actions workflow.

Terraform

With both of our VM images built and their versions input into our `tfvars` file, our Terraform automation pipeline is ready to take the reins and not only provision our environment but deploy our solution (although not technically). The deployment was technically done within the `packer build` process, with the physical deployment packages being copied to the home directory and the Linux service setup primed and ready. Terraform finishes the job by launching VMs using these images:

```
on:
  push:
    branches:
    - main
    paths:
    - 'src/terraform/**'
```

This means that we only need to trigger the Terraform automation pipeline when the Terraform code base changes. This could include configuration changes to the resources simply be an updated VM image version within the `tfvars` file:

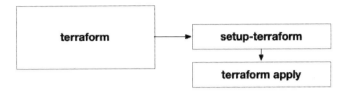

Figure 7.25 – The terraform apply workflow

As a result, the Terraform pipeline is quite simple. We simply need to execute either `terraform plan` or `terraform apply`, depending on whether we want to evaluate or execute the changes for our cloud environment.

In keeping with the *always be specific* mantra, we must dutifully designate the version of Terraform that we want to use and specify the location for the Terraform code base using pipeline variables:

```
env:
  TERRAFORM_VERSION: '1.5.7'
  WORKING_DIRECTORY: "./src/terraform"
```

Next, we must install the particular version of Terraform using the `setup-terraform` GitHub Action published by HashiCorp, which will handle the details of its installation for us:

```
- id: setup
  name: Setup `terraform`
  uses: hashicorp/setup-terraform@main
  with:
    version: ${{ env.TERRAFORM_VERSION }}
```

Finally, it executes `terraform apply` again, making sure to include the AWS credentials and the target backend location for the Terraform state:

```
- id: apply
  name: Terraform Apply
  env:
    AWS_ACCESS_KEY_ID: ${{ vars.AWS_ACCESS_KEY_ID }}
    AWS_SECRET_ACCESS_KEY: ${{ secrets.AWS_SECRET_ACCESS_KEY }}
    BACKEND_BUCKET_NAME: ${{ vars.BUCKET_NAME }}
    BACKEND_REGION: ${{ vars.BUCKET_REGION }}
  working-directory: ${{ env.WORKING_DIRECTORY }}
  run: |
    terraform init \
      -backend-config='bucket='$BACKEND_BUCKET_NAME \
      -backend-config='region='$BACKEND_REGION \
      -backend-config="key=aws-vm-sample"
```

```
terraform apply -target "random_shuffle.az" -auto-approve
terraform apply -auto-approve
```

The backend configuration is set using the `-backend-config` command-line argument, which frees us from having to hardcode these settings in our source code.

Notice that we execute `terraform apply` twice. First, we perform a targeted apply on the `random_shuffle.az` resource, after which we perform a general apply. The targeted apply ensures that the Availability Zones we are targeting have been selected before we calculate the IP address space for our networks. The need for this is driven by the dynamic nature of calculating the address space using the `cidrsubnet` function. If we wanted to avoid this targeted apply approach, we could opt for a more hard-coded approach of the Availability Zones and the corresponding address spaces.

That's it! With the completion of our Terraform GitHub Actions workflow, we have put the finishing touches on our end-to-end CI/CD pipeline. Our AWS-based solution will be up and running our VM cloud architecture in no time.

Summary

In this chapter, we built a multi-tier cloud architecture using AWS and VMs, a fully operational GitFlow process, and an end-to-end CI/CD pipeline using GitHub Actions.

In the next chapter, our fearless leader at Söze Enterprises will be throwing us into turmoil with some big new ideas, and we'll have to respond to his call to action. It turns out our CEO, Keyser, has been up late watching some YouTube videos about the next big thing – containers – and after talking with his pal Jeff on his superyacht, he has decided that we need to refactor our whole solution so that it can run on Docker and Kubernetes. Luckily, the good people at Amazon have a service that might help us out: AWS **Elastic Kubernetes Service** (**EKS**).

8
Containerize with AWS – Building Solutions with AWS EKS

In the previous chapter, we built and automated our solution on AWS while utilizing **Elastic Cloud Compute** (**EC2**). We built VM images with Packer and provisioned our VMs using Terraform. In this chapter, we'll follow a similar path, but instead of working with VMs, we'll look at hosting our application in containers within a Kubernetes cluster.

To achieve this, we'll need to alter our approach by ditching Packer and replacing it with Docker to create a deployable artifact for our application. Once again, we will be using the `aws` provider for Terraform, but this time, we'll be introducing something new: the `kubernetes` provider for Terraform, which will provision to the Kubernetes cluster after our AWS infrastructure has been provisioned using the `aws` provider for Terraform.

Again, with this approach, we will only focus on the new and different. I'll call out where we are building on previous chapters and when something is legitimately new.

This chapter covers the following topics:

- Laying the foundation
- Designing the solution
- Building the solution
- Automating the deployment

Laying the foundation

Our story continues through the lens of Söze Enterprises, founded by the enigmatic Turkish billionaire Keyser Söze. Our team has been hard at work building the next-generation autonomous vehicle orchestration platform. Previously, we had hoped to leapfrog the competition by leveraging Amazon's rock-solid platform, leveraging our team's existing skills, and focusing on feature development. The team was just getting into their groove when a curveball came down from above.

It turns out, over the weekend, our elusive executive was influenced by a rendezvous with Andy Jassy, the CEO of AWS, while scuba diving amid the rare and exotic marine life off the coast of the Galápagos. Keyser heard about the more efficient resource utilization leading to improved cost optimization and faster deployment and rollback times, and he was hooked. His new autonomous vehicle platform needed to harness the power of the cloud, and container-based architecture was the way to do it. So, he decided to accelerate his plans to adopt cloud-native architecture!

The news of transitioning to a container-based architecture means reevaluating their approach, diving into new technologies, and possibly even reshuffling team dynamics. For the team, containers were always the long-term plan, but now, things need to be sped up, which will require a significant investment in time, resources, and training.

As the team scrambles to adjust their plans, they can't help but feel a mix of excitement and apprehension. They know that they are part of something groundbreaking under Keyser's leadership. His vision for the future of autonomous vehicles is bold and transformative. And while his methods may be unconventional, they have learned that his instincts are often right. In this chapter, we'll explore this transformation from VMs to containers using AWS.

Designing the solution

As we saw in the previous chapter, where we built our solution using VMs using AWS EC2, we had full control over the operating system configuration through the VM images we provisioned with Packer. Now that we will be transitioning to hosting our solution on AWS **Elastic Kubernetes Service** (**EKS**), we'll need to introduce a new tool to replace VM images with container images – **Docker**:

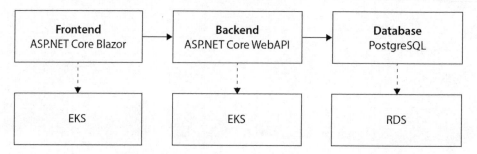

Figure 8.1 – Logical architecture for the autonomous vehicle platform

Our application architecture, comprising a frontend, a backend, and a database, will remain the same, but we will need to provision different resources with Terraform and harness new tools from Docker and Kubernetes to automate the deployment of our solution to this new infrastructure:

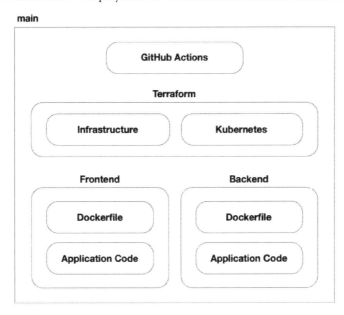

Figure 8.2 – Source control structure of our repository

In this solution, we'll have seven parts. We still have the application code and Dockerfiles (replacing the Packer-based VM images) for both the frontend and backend. We still have GitHub Actions to implement our CI/CD process, but now we have two Terraform code bases – one for provisioning the underlying infrastructure to AWS and another for provisioning our application to the Kubernetes cluster hosted on EKS. Then, we have the two code bases for our application's frontend and backend.

Cloud architecture

In the previous chapter, our cloud-hosting solution was a set of dedicated VMs. In this chapter, our objective is to leverage AWS EKS to use a shared pool of VMs that are managed by Kubernetes to host our application. To achieve this, we'll be using some new resources that are geared toward container-based workloads. However, much of the networking, load balancing, and other components will largely be the same.

Virtual network

Recalling our work in *Chapter 7* with EC2 instances and virtual networks, setting up a **virtual private cloud** (**VPC**) for AWS EKS follows a similar process. The core network is still there, with all the pomp and circumstance, from subnets – both public and private – to all the minutia of route tables, internet gateways, and NAT gateways, the virtual network we'll build for our EKS cluster will largely be the same as the one we created previously. The only difference will be how we use it:

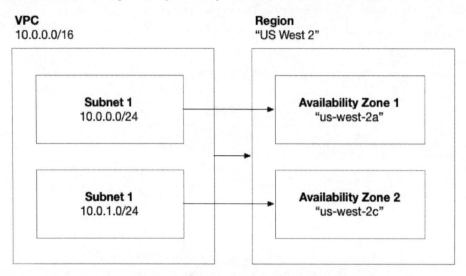

Figure 8.3 – AWS virtual network architecture

Previously, we used the public subnets for our frontend VMs and the private subnets for our backend. As we learned in *Chapter 5*, when we introduce Kubernetes into the mix, we'll be transitioning to a shared pool of VMs that host our application as pods. These VMs will be hosted in the private subnets and a load balancer will be hosted in the public subnets.

Container registry

Building on our exploration of container architecture in *Chapter 5*, we know that we need to build container images and we need to store them in a container registry. For that purpose, AWS offers **Elastic Container Registry** (**ECR**). This is a private container registry, unlike public registries such as Docker Hub, which we looked at in *Chapter 5*.

We'll need to utilize the Docker command-line utility to build and push images to ECR. To be able to do that, we need to grant an identity the necessary permissions. As we saw in the previous chapter, when we build VM images using Packer, we'll likely have a GitHub Actions workflow that builds and pushes the container images to ECR. The identity that the GitHub Actions workflow executes under will need permission to do that. Once these Docker images are in ECR, the final step is to grant our cluster access to pull images from the registry:

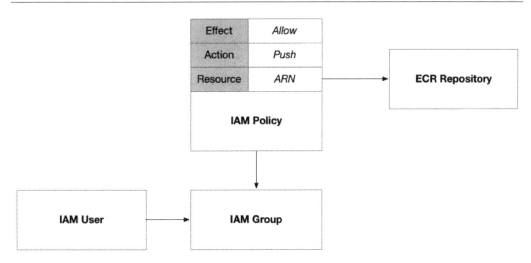

Figure 8.4 – IAM policy giving a group access to push container images to ECR

We'll set up an IAM group that we'll grant this permission to. This will allow us to add the user for the GitHub Action, as well as any other human users who want to push images directly from the command line. In AWS, IAM policies are extremely flexible; they can be declared independently or inline with the identity they are being attached to. This allows us to create reusable policies that can be attached to multiple identities. In this case, we'll define the policy that grants access to push images to this ECR and then attach it to the group. Then, membership in the group will grant users access to these permissions.

The final step is to grant access to the cluster such that it can pull images from our ECR when it schedules pods within the nodes. To do that, we can use a built-in AWS policy called `AmazonEC2ContainerRegistryReadOnly`. We'll need to reference it using its fully qualified ARN, which is `arn:aws:iam::aws:policy/AmazonEC2ContainerRegistryReadOnly`. Built-in policies have a common `arn:aws:iam::aws:policy` prefix that identifies them as published by AWS and not published by any specific user within their AWS account. When we publish our own policies, the fully qualified ARN will include our account number.

Load balancing

Unlike in the previous chapter, where we provisioned and configured our own AWS **Application Load Balancer (ALB)**, when using Amazon EKS, one of the advantages is that EKS takes on much of the responsibility of provisioning and configuring load balancers. We can direct and influence its actions using Kubernetes annotations but this is largely taken care of for us. In our solution, to keep things simple, we'll be using NGINX as our ingress controller and configuring it to set up an AWS **Network Load Balancer (NLB)** for us:

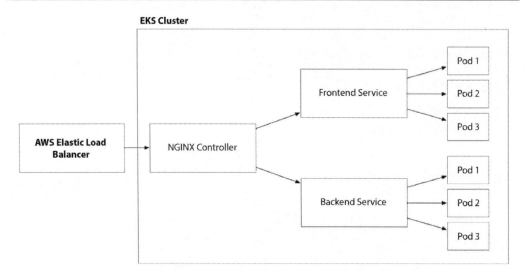

Figure 8.5 – Elastic load balancer working with an NGINX ingress
controller to route traffic to our application's pods

To delegate this responsibility to EKS, we need to grant it the necessary IAM permissions to provision and manage these resources. Therefore, we'll need to provision an IAM policy and attach it to the EKS cluster. We can do this using an IAM role that has been assigned to the cluster's node group:

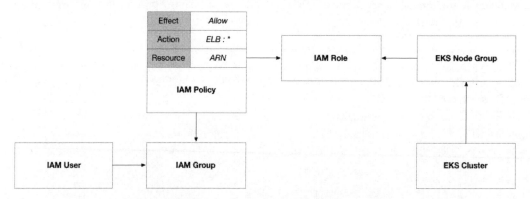

Figure 8.6 – IAM policy allowing EKS to provision and manage elastic load balancers

Then, we provision Kubernetes resources (for example, services and ingress controllers) and annotate them to inform the specific configuration of our elastic load balancers that we want EKS to enact on our behalf.

Network security

There are many ways to host services on Kubernetes and make them accessible outside of the cluster. In our solution, we'll be using an AWS elastic load balancer to allow external traffic into our cluster through our NGINX controller. There are other options, such as NodePort, which allow you to access a pod directly through an exposed port on the node. This would require public access to the cluster's nodes and is not the preferred method from both security and scalability perspectives.

If we want access to the cluster using `kubectl`, then we need to turn on public endpoint access. This is useful when you're developing something small on your own but not ideal when you're working in an enterprise context. You will most likely have the private network infrastructure in place so that you never have to enable the public endpoint.

Secrets management

Incorporating secrets into pods within an Amazon EKS cluster can be achieved through various methods, each with its advantages and disadvantages. As we did with VMs in the previous chapter, the method that we will explore is using AWS Secrets Manager secrets. Kubernetes has a built-in approach using Kubernetes Secrets. This method is straightforward and integrated directly into Kubernetes, but it has limitations in terms of security since secrets are encoded in Base64 and can be accessed by anyone with cluster access.

Integration with AWS Secrets Manager can help solve this problem but to access our secrets stored there, we need to enable our Kubernetes deployments to authenticate with AWS **Identity and Access Management (IAM)**. This is often referred to as Workload Identity and it is an approach that is relatively common across cloud platforms:

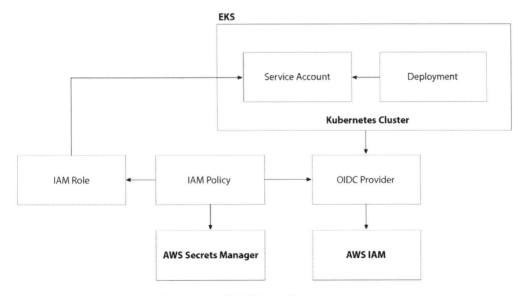

Figure 8.7 – AWS EKS with Workload Identity

To set up Workload Identity on EKS, we need to configure the cluster with an **OpenID Connect (OIDC)** provider. Then, we must set up an IAM role that has a policy that allows a Kubernetes service account to assume the role. This IAM role can then be granted access to any AWS permissions and resources that the Kubernetes deployment needs access to, including Secrets Manager secrets. The last thing we need to do is provision a Kubernetes service account by the same name within Kubernetes and give it a special annotation to connect it to the IAM role.

Once this is done, our Kubernetes deployments will be allowed to access our AWS Secrets Manager secrets but they won't be using that access. The final step is to configure the Kubernetes deployment to pull in the secrets and make them accessible to our application code running in the pods:

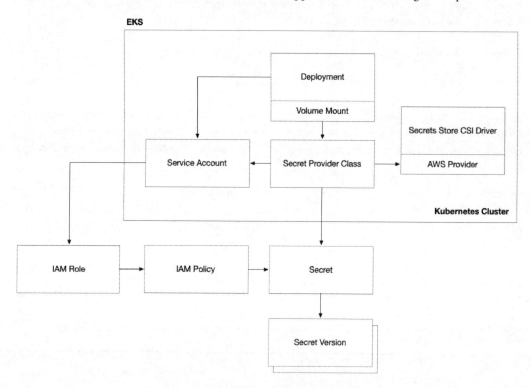

Figure 8.8 – AWS EKS Secrets Manager integration

Kubernetes has a common practice of doing this using volume mounts. As a result, there is a common Kubernetes provider known as the secrets store **Container Storage Interface** (**CSI**) provider. This is a cloud-agnostic technique that integrates Kubernetes with external secret stores, such as AWS Secrets Manager. This method offers enhanced security and scalability, but it requires more setup and maintenance.

To get this working, we need to deploy two components to our EKS cluster: the secrets store CSI driver and then the AWS provider for this driver that will allow it to interface with AWS Secrets Manager. Both of these components can be deployed to our EKS cluster with **Helm**. Once these important subsystems are in place, we can set up a special Kubernetes resource called `SecretProviderClass`. This is a type of resource that connects to AWS Secrets Manager through the CSI driver to access specific secrets. It connects to specific secrets in Secrets Manager using the service account that we granted access to via the IAM role and its permissions.

Kubernetes cluster

Amazon EKS offers a managed Kubernetes service that streamlines the deployment and management of containerized applications on AWS. The EKS cluster is the central figure of this architecture. EKS handles the heavy lifting of setting up, operating, and maintaining the Kubernetes control plane and nodes, which are essentially EC2 instances. When setting up an EKS cluster, users define node groups, which manifest as collections of EC2 instances that the EKS service is responsible for provisioning and managing.

There are several options for node groups that can host your workloads. The most common examples are AWS-managed and self-managed node groups. AWS-managed node groups are essentially on-demand EC2 instances that are allocated for the EKS cluster. AWS simplifies the management of these nodes but this imposes some restrictions on what AWS features can be used. Self-managed nodes are also essentially on-demand EC2 instances but they provide greater control over the features and configuration options available to them.

A great way to optimize for cost is to use a Fargate node group. This option takes advantage of AWS' serverless compute engine and removes the need to provision and manage EC2 instances. However, this is probably more suitable for unpredictable workloads rather than those that require a steady state. In those situations, you can take advantage of a combination of autoscaling and spot and reserved instances to reap significant discounts and cost reduction:

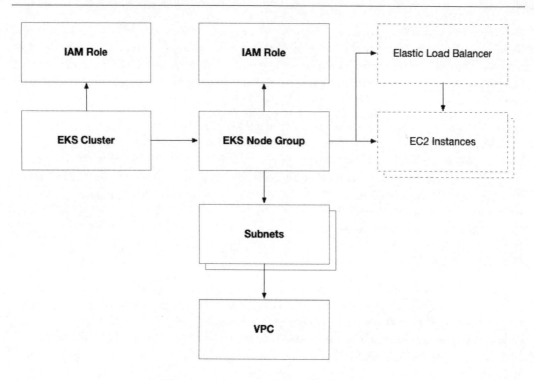

Figure 8.9 – Anatomy of an AWS EKS cluster

IAM policies are a major part of the configuration of EKS due to the nature of the service and how we delegate responsibility to it to manage AWS resources. This is similar to what we do with AWS Auto Scaling groups but even more so. IAM policies are attached to the cluster and individual node groups. Depending on the capabilities you want to enable within your cluster and your node groups, you might need additional policies.

The `AmazonEKSClusterPolicy` policy grants the cluster access to control the internal workings of the cluster itself, including node groups, CloudWatch logging, and access control within the cluster.

The `AmazonEKSVPCResourceController` policy grants the cluster access to manage network resources such as network interfaces, IP address assignment, and security group attachments to the VPC.

There are four policies (`AmazonEKSWorkerNodePolicy`, `AmazonEKS_CNI_Policy`, `AmazonEC2ContainerRegistryReadOnly`, and `CloudWatchAgentServerPolicy`) that are essential for the operation of EKS worker nodes. These policies absolutely must be attached to the IAM role that you assign to your EKS node group. They grant access to the EKS cluster's control plane and let nodes within the node group integrate with the core infrastructure provided by the cluster, including the network, container registries, and CloudWatch. As described previously, we also added an optional policy to allow the EKS cluster to manage elastic load balancers.

Deployment architecture

Now that we have a good idea of what our cloud architecture is going to look like for our solution on AWS, we need to come up with a plan on how to provision our environments and deploy our code.

Cloud environment configuration

Building upon the methodology we established in *Chapter 7* for provisioning EC2 instances, our approach to provisioning the AWS EKS environment will follow a similar pattern. The core of this process lies in utilizing GitHub Actions, which will remain unchanged in its fundamental setup and operation:

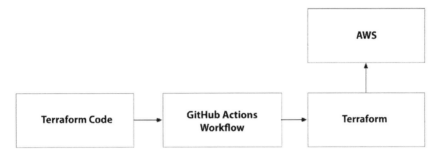

Figure 8.10 – The Terraform code provisions the environment on AWS

However, instead of provisioning EC2 instances as we did previously, the Terraform code will be tailored to set up the necessary components for an EKS environment. This includes the creation of an EKS cluster and an ECR. The GitHub Action will automate the execution of this Terraform code, following the same workflow pattern we used before.

By reusing the GitHub Actions workflow with different Terraform scripts, we maintain consistency in our deployment process while adapting to the different infrastructure requirements of the EKS environment. This step will need to be executed in a standalone mode to ensure certain prerequisites are there, such as the container registry. Only once the container registry is provisioned can we build and push container images to it for our frontend and backend application components.

This step will also provision the EKS cluster that hosts the Kubernetes control plane. We'll use this in the final step in conjunction with the container images to deploy our application.

Container configuration

Unlike Packer, which doesn't rely on any existing infrastructure to provision the application deployment artifacts (for example, the AMIs built by Packer), our container images need to have a container registry before they can be provisioned:

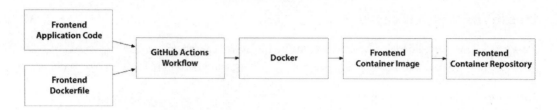

Figure 8.11 – Docker pipeline to build a container image for the frontend

The workflow is very similar to that of Packer in that we combine the application code and a template that stores the operating system configuration. In this case, it stores a Dockerfile rather than a Packer template.

Kubernetes configuration

Once we've published container images for both the frontend and backend, we're ready to complete the deployment by adding a final step that executes Terraform using the Kubernetes provider so that it will deploy our application to the EKS cluster:

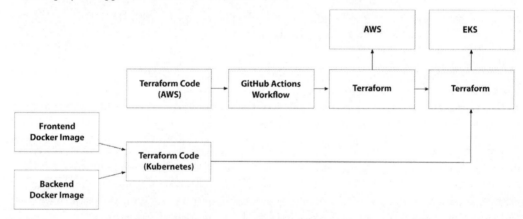

Figure 8.12 – Container images as inputs to terraform code, which
provisions the environment on EKS' Kubernetes control plane

We will output key pieces of information from the previous Terraform step that provisioned the AWS infrastructure. This will include details about the ECR repositories and the EKS cluster. We can use these as inputs for the final Terraform execution step where we use the Kubernetes provider. We have separated this step into separate Terraform workspaces to decouple it from the AWS infrastructure. This recognizes the hard dependency between the Kubernetes control plane layer and the underlying infrastructure. It allows us to independently manage the underlying infrastructure without making changes to the Kubernetes deployments, as well as make changes that are isolated within the Kubernetes control plane that will speed up the release process.

In this section, we reviewed the key changes in our architecture as we transitioned from VM-based architecture to container-based architecture. In the next section, we'll get tactical in building the solution, but we'll be careful to build on the foundations we built in the previous chapter when we first set up our solution on AWS using VMs powered by EC2.

Building the solution

In this section, we'll be taking our theoretical knowledge and applying it to a tangible, functioning solution while harnessing the power of Docker, Terraform, and Kubernetes on the AWS platform. Some parts of this process will require significant change, such as when we provision our AWS infrastructure using Terraform; other parts will have minor changes, such as the Kubernetes configuration that we use to deploy our application to our Kubernetes cluster; and some will be completely new, such as the process to build and push our Docker images to our container registry.

Docker

As we saw in the previous chapter, where we built VM images in Packer, there is a certain amount of operating system configuration that needs to be set up. With Docker, we are doing largely the same thing but we are doing it for a specific process. This means much of the work that we did in setting up the service in Linux is eliminated because the container runtime controls when the application is running or not. This is fundamentally different than configuring the Linux operating system to run an executable as a service. As a result, much of this boilerplate is eliminated.

Another major difference is that with the Packer image, we build the application outside of Packer and we drop a zipped artifact containing the application as part of the Packer build. With Docker, we'll build the application and produce the artifact within the container build process. After this process is complete, we'll follow a similar process where we drop the deployment package into a clean container image layer to eliminate any residual build artifacts:

```
FROM mcr.microsoft.com/dotnet/sdk:6.0 AS build-env
WORKDIR /app
```

The following line sets the base image for the build stage. It uses the official Microsoft .NET SDK image (version 6.0) from the **Microsoft Container Registry** (**MCR**):

```
COPY ./FleetPortal/FleetPortal.csproj ./FleetPortal/
RUN dotnet restore ./FleetPortal/FleetPortal.csproj
```

Before we build the project, we need to resolve its dependencies. The dotnet restore command will do this by pulling all the dependencies from NuGet (the .NET package manager):

```
COPY . ./
RUN dotnet publish ./FleetPortal/FleetPortal.csproj -c Release -o out
```

Here, we execute the `dotnet publish` command, which creates the binaries for the project. The `-c Release` option specifies that the build should be optimized for production. We drop the files into the `out` folder to be picked up by a future step:

```
FROM mcr.microsoft.com/dotnet/aspnet:6.0
WORKDIR /app
COPY --from=build-env /app/out .
```

We start a new build stage with the .NET runtime image as the base and we copy the binaries that we built from the previous stage to this new one. This will ensure that any intermediate build artifacts are not layered into the container image:

```
ENTRYPOINT ["dotnet", "FleetPortal.dll"]
```

Finally, we set the startup command for the container. When the container starts, it will run `dotnet FleetPortal.dll`, which starts our ASP.NET application. It will start listening for incoming web server traffic.

Terraform

As we discussed in our design, our solution is made up of two application components: the frontend and the backend. Each has a code base of application code that needs to be deployed. However, with a Kubernetes solution, the infrastructure is simplified in that we only need a Kubernetes cluster (and a few other things). The important piece is the configuration within the Kubernetes platform itself.

As a result, much of the Terraform setup is very similar to what we did in the previous chapter, so we will only focus on new resources needed for our solution. You can check the full source code for this book on GitHub if you want to work with the complete solution.

Container registry

First, we'll set up repositories for both the frontend and backend of our application using AWS ECR. To simplify the dynamic creation of our ECR repositories, we can set up a local variable called `repository_list` that has constants for the two container images we need repositories for:

```
locals {
  repository_list = ["frontend", "backend"]
  repositories    = { for name in local.repository_list : name => name
  }
}
```

Then, we'll use a `for` expression to generate a map from this list that we can then use to create a corresponding ECR repository using the `for_each` iterator:

```
resource "aws_ecr_repository" "main" {

  for_each = local.repositories

  name                    = "ecr-${var.application_name}-${var.
environment_name}-${each.key}"
  image_tag_mutability = "MUTABLE"


}
```

Next, we'll set up an IAM group that we can grant access to push container images to:

```
resource "aws_iam_group" "ecr_image_pushers" {
  name = "${var.application_name}-${var.environment_name}-ecr-image-
pushers"
}
```

Now, we need to generate an IAM policy that grants access to each of the ECR repositories and attach it to the IAM group we created previously:

```
resource "aws_iam_group_policy" "ecr_image_pushers" {

  for_each = local.repositories

  name    = "${var.application_name}-${var.environment_name}-${each.
key}-ecr-image-push-policy"
  group = aws_iam_group.ecr_image_pushers.name

  policy = jsonencode({
    Version = "2012-10-17",
    Statement = [
      {
        Effect = "Allow",
        Action = [
          "ecr:GetDownloadUrlForLayer",
          "ecr:BatchGetImage",
          "ecr:BatchCheckLayerAvailability",
          "ecr:PutImage",
          "ecr:InitiateLayerUpload",
          "ecr:UploadLayerPart",
          "ecr:CompleteLayerUpload"
        ],
```

```
        Resource = aws_ecr_repository.main[each.key].arn
      }
    ]
  })
}
```

Finally, we must grant access to this group. We'll be granting access to the identities of developers on our team or the GitHub Actions workflows that will be pushing new images as part of our CI/CD process:

```
resource "aws_iam_group_membership" "ecr_image_pushers" {
  name  = "${var.application_name}-${var.environment_name}-ecr-image-
push-membership"
  users = var.ecr_image_pushers
  group = aws_iam_group.ecr_image_pushers.name
}
```

Kubernetes cluster

Now that our container registry is all set up and we can push images to it, we need to set up our Kubernetes cluster. That's where AWS EKS comes in. The cluster's configuration is relatively simple but there's quite a bit of work we need to do with IAM to make it all work.

Before we provision our EKS cluster, we need to set up the IAM role that it will use to interact with the rest of the AWS platform. This is not a role that our nodes or Kubernetes deployments will use. It's the role that EKS will use to enact configuration changes made to the cluster across all the AWS resources that are being used:

```
data "aws_iam_policy_document" "container_cluster_assume_role" {
  statement {
    effect = "Allow"

    principals {
      type        = "Service"
      identifiers = ["eks.amazonaws.com"]
    }

    actions = ["sts:AssumeRole"]
  }
}
```

As a result, the EKS service will assume this role. Hence, the `assume` policy needs to allow a principal of the `Service` type with `eks.amazonaws.com` as its identifier:

```
resource "aws_iam_role" "container_cluster" {
  name                = "eks-${var.application_name}-${var.environment_
name}-cluster-role"
```

```
  assume_role_policy = data.aws_iam_policy_document.container_cluster_
assume_role.json
}
```

With this role, we are going to enable EKS to provision and manage the resources that it needs within our AWS account. As a result, we need to attach the built-in `AmazonEKSClusterPolicy` and `AmazonEKSVPCResourceController` policies:

```
resource "aws_iam_role_policy_attachment" "eks_cluster_policy" {
  policy_arn = "arn:aws:iam::aws:policy/AmazonEKSClusterPolicy"
  role       = aws_iam_role.container_cluster.name
}
```

The preceding code is an example of how to do this for one of the policies. You could create an `aws_iam_role_policy_attachment` resource for each of the policies or use an iterator over a collection of the policies that we need to attach.

Now that this IAM role is ready, we can set up our cluster using the `aws_eks_cluster` resource:

```
resource "aws_eks_cluster" "main" {
  name                        = local.cluster_name
  role_arn                    = aws_iam_role.container_cluster.arn

  vpc_config {

    security_group_ids = [
      aws_security_group.cluster.id,
      aws_security_group.cluster_nodes.id
    ]

    subnet_ids              = local.cluster_subnet_ids
    endpoint_public_access  = true
    endpoint_private_access = true
  }

  // Other configurations like logging, encryption, etc.
}
```

A significant portion of the configuration is done within the `vpc_config` block, which references many of the same structures that we provisioned in the previous chapter.

One thing that you might want to keep in mind is how important the IAM policies are for enabling this EKS cluster to be successfully provisioned. Since there is no direct relationship between the IAM role's policy attachments, you should ensure that IAM role permissions are created before we attempt to provision the EKS cluster. The following code demonstrates the use of the `depends_on` attribute, which allows us to define this relationship explicitly:

```
depends_on = [
  aws_iam_role_policy_attachment.eks_cluster_policy,
  aws_iam_role_policy_attachment.eks_vpc_controller_policy,
  aws_cloudwatch_log_group.container_cluster
]
```

The EKS cluster is just the control plane. For our cluster to have utility, we need to add worker nodes. We can do this by adding one or more node groups. These node groups will be composed of a collection of EC2 instances that will be enlisted as worker nodes. These nodes also need their own IAM role:

```
data "aws_iam_policy_document" "container_node_group" {

  statement {
    sid     = "EKSNodeAssumeRole"
    actions = ["sts:AssumeRole"]

    principals {
      type        = "Service"
      identifiers = ["ec2.amazonaws.com"]
    }
  }
}
```

A key difference is that because this role will be assumed by the worker nodes, which are EC2 instances, the IAM role's `assume` policy needs to align with this fact.

Just as before with our EKS cluster, which needed an IAM role to be set up as a prerequisite, the same is true for our node group. Now that the node group's IAM role is ready, we can use the following code to create an EKS node group associated with the previously defined cluster. It specifies the desired, minimum, and maximum sizes of the node group, along with other configurations, such as the AMI type and disk size:

```
resource "aws_eks_node_group" "main" {
  cluster_name    = aws_eks_cluster.main.name
  node_group_name = "ng-user"
  node_role_arn   = aws_iam_role.container_node_group.arn
  subnet_ids      = local.cluster_subnet_ids

  scaling_config {
```

```
      desired_size = 3
      min_size     = 1
      max_size     = 4
  }

  ami_type        = var.node_image_type
  instance_types  = [var.node_size]
}
```

Again, just like with the EKS cluster, the IAM role's policy attachments are critical to making the node group functional. Therefore, you need to make sure that all policy attachments are attached to the IAM role before you start provisioning our node group. As we discussed in the previous section, there are four policies (, AmazonEKSWorkerNodePolicy, AmazonEKS_CNI_Policy, AmazonEC2ContainerRegistryReadOnly, and CloudWatchAgentServerPolicy) that are essential for the operation of EKS worker nodes:

```
depends_on = [
  aws_iam_role_policy_attachment.eks_worker_node_policy,
  aws_iam_role_policy_attachment.eks_cni_policy,
  aws_iam_role_policy_attachment.eks_ecr_policy,
  aws_iam_role_policy_attachment.eks_cloudwatch_policy
]
```

As you add additional features to your EKS cluster, you may introduce additional IAM policies that grant the cluster and its worker nodes different permissions within AWS. When you do, don't forget to also include these policies in these depends_on attributes to ensure smooth operations.

Logging and monitoring

We can enable CloudWatch logging on the cluster by simply adding the enabled_cluster_log_types attribute to the aws_eks_cluster resource:

```
enabled_cluster_log_types = ["api", "audit"]
```

This attribute takes one or more different log types. I'd recommend checking the documentation for all the different options supported. Next, we need to provision a CloudWatch log group for the cluster:

```
resource "aws_cloudwatch_log_group" "container_cluster" {
  name             = "/aws/eks/${local.cluster_name}/cluster"
  retention_in_days = 7
}
```

This requires a specific naming convention and it needs to match the name you use for your cluster. Therefore, it's a good idea to extract the value you pass to the name attribute of the aws_eks_cluster resource as a local variable so that you can use it in two places.

Workload identity

With the cluster provisioned, we need to get the OIDC issuer certificate from the cluster so that we can use it to configure the OpenID Connect provider with AWS IAM. The following code uses the `tls_certificate` data source from the `tls` utility provider, which we covered in *Chapter 3*, to obtain additional metadata about the certificate:

```
data "tls_certificate" "container_cluster_oidc" {
  url = aws_eks_cluster.main.identity[0].oidc[0].issuer
}
```

With this additional metadata, we can use the `aws_iam_openid_connect_provider` resource to connect the cluster to the AWS IAM OIDC provider by referencing `sts.amazonaws.com`:

```
resource "aws_iam_openid_connect_provider" "container_cluster_oidc" {
  client_id_list   = ["sts.amazonaws.com"]
  thumbprint_list = [data.tls_certificate.container_cluster_oidc.
certificates[0].sha1_fingerprint]
  url              = data.tls_certificate.container_cluster_oidc.url
}
```

We've already set up several IAM roles, including one for the EKS cluster and another for the worker nodes of the cluster. Therefore, I won't reiterate the creation of the `aws_iam_role` resource for the workload identity. However, this new role does need to have a very distinct assumption policy. The workload identity IAM role needs to reference the OIDC provider and a yet-to-be-provisioned Kubernetes service account:

```
data "aws_iam_policy_document" "workload_identity_assume_role_policy"
{
  statement {
    actions = ["sts:AssumeRoleWithWebIdentity"]
    effect  = "Allow"

    condition {
      test     = "StringEquals"
      variable = "${replace(aws_iam_openid_connect_provider.container_
cluster_oidc.url, "https://", "")}:sub"
      values   = ["system:serviceaccount:${var.k8s_namespace}:${var.
k8s_service_account_name}"]
    }

    principals {
      identifiers = [aws_iam_openid_connect_provider.container_
cluster_oidc.arn]
      type        = "Federated"
    }
```

```
    }
  }
```

As you can see, in the preceding code, the service account follows a very specific naming convention: `system:serviceaccount:<namespace>:<service-account-name>`. We replace `<namespace>` with the name of the Kubernetes namespace and likewise, we replace `<service-account-name>` with the name of the service account. It's important to point out that we are referencing resources that do not exist yet. As such, the reference to them within the workload identity IAM role's assumption policy is a pointer or a placeholder to this yet-to-be-created resource. Both the Kubernetes namespace and the service account are resources that will need to be created within the Kubernetes control plane. We'll tackle that in the next section using the `kubernetes` Terraform provider.

Secrets management

Now that we have an IAM role for our workload identity, we simply need to grant it access to the AWS resources we want it to use. Therefore, we will use the `aws_iam_policy_document` data source once more to generate an IAM policy that we will attach to the workload identity's IAM role. This is where we have the opportunity to grant it access to any resource in AWS that our application code will need. For our solution, we'll start with access to AWS Secrets Manager secrets by granting it access to read secrets using the `secretsmanager:GetSecretValue` action:

```
data "aws_iam_policy_document" "workload_identity_policy" {
  statement {
    effect = "Allow"

    actions = [
      "secretsmanager:GetSecretValue",
      "secretsmanager:DescribeSecret",
    ]

    resources = [
      "arn:aws:secretsmanager:${var.primary_region}:${data.aws_caller_
identity.current.account_id}:secret:*",
    ]
  }
}
```

This policy will grant the IAM role access to the secrets within this account. We could further refine its access by enhancing the * wildcard path to ensure that it has access to only certain secrets. This can be done by implementing a naming convention that uses a unique prefix for your secrets. The `application_name` and `environment_name` variables are a perfect way to implement this naming convention and to tighten access to your Kubernetes workloads to AWS Secrets Manager.

Now, we just need to provision secrets to Secrets Manager with the right naming convention:

```
resource "aws_secretsmanager_secret" "database_connection_string" {
  name        = "${var.application_name}-${var.environment_name}-
connection-string"
  description = "Database connection string"
}
```

AWS Secrets Manager uses a parent resource called `aws_secretsmanager_secret` as a logical placeholder for the secret itself but recognizes that the secret's value might change over time:

```
resource "aws_secretsmanager_secret_version" "database_connection_
string" {
  secret_id     = aws_secretsmanager_secret.database_connection_
string.id
  secret_string = random_password.database_connection_string.result
}
```

Those different values for the secret are stored in `aws_secretsmanager_secret_version` resources. You can generate complex secrets using the `random` provider but it's probably more common to obtain `secret_string` from the outputs of other resources.

Kubernetes

In *Chapter 5*, we introduced Kubernetes architecture and automation techniques using YAML and **HashiCorp Configuration Language** (**HCL**). In our solutions in this book, we will be using the Terraform provider for Kubernetes to automate our application's deployment. This allows us to both parameterize the Kubernetes configurations that would otherwise be trapped in hard-coded YAML files and provision a combination of Kubernetes primitives and Helm charts with the same deployment process.

Provider setup

Ironically, the first thing we need to do to set up the `kubernetes` provider is initialize the `aws` provider so that we can get information about our EKS cluster. We can do that using the data sources provided and a single input variable: the cluster's name. Of course, the AWS region is also an implied parameter to this operation but it is part of the `aws` provider configuration rather than inputs to the data sources themselves:

```
data "aws_eks_cluster" "cluster" {
  name = var.eks_cluster_name
}
```

We'll use both the `aws_eks_cluster` and `aws_eks_cluster_auth` data sources to grab the data we need to initialize the `kubernetes` provider:

```
provider "kubernetes" {
  host                   = data.aws_eks_cluster.cluster.endpoint
  cluster_ca_certificate = base64decode(data.aws_eks_cluster.cluster.
certificate_authority[0].data)
  token                  = data.aws_eks_cluster_auth.cluster.token
  load_config_file       = false
}
```

Interestingly, the Helm provider setup is pretty much identical to the Kubernetes provider configuration. It seems a bit redundant, but it's relatively straightforward:

```
provider "helm" {
  kubernetes {
    host                   = data.aws_eks_cluster.main.endpoint
    cluster_ca_certificate = base64decode(data.aws_eks_cluster.main.
certificate_authority[0].data)
    token                  = data.aws_eks_cluster_auth.main.token
  }
}
```

Namespace

Creating the Kubernetes namespace is extremely simple:

```
resource "kubernetes_namespace" "main" {
  metadata {
    name = var.k8s_namespace
    labels = {
      name = var.k8s_namespace
    }
  }
}
```

This will act as the logical container for all of the Kubernetes resources that we provision for our application.

Service account

In the previous section, we built one-half of this bridge when we set up the OpenID Connect provider configuration within AWS and we specified the Kubernetes namespace and service account name ahead of time. Now, we'll finish constructing this bridge by provisioning `kubernetes_service_account` and ensuring that `namespace` and `name` match our AWS configuration:

```
resource "kubernetes_service_account" "workload_identity" {

  metadata {
    name      = var.k8s_service_account_name
    namespace = var.k8s_namespace
    annotations = {
      "eks.amazonaws.com/role-arn" = var.workload_identity_role
    }
  }
}
```

We also need to add an annotation that references the unique identifier (or ARN) for the workload identity's IAM role. We can set this up as an output variable in our Terraform workspace that provisions the AWS infrastructure and routes its value to an input variable on the Terraform workspace for our Kubernetes configuration. This is a great example of how the `kubernetes` provider for Terraform can be a useful way of configuring Kubernetes resources that require tight coupling with the cloud platform.

Secrets store CSI driver

With the service account set up, our application is one step closer to being able to access our secrets in AWS Secrets Manager. However, before we can do that, we need to set up the secrets store CSI driver. As we discussed previously, this is a common Kubernetes component that provides a standard mechanism for using volume mounts as a way to distribute remotely managed secrets to workloads running in Kubernetes. The driver is extremely flexible and can be extended through providers that act as adapters for different external secret management systems.

First, we need to install the secrets store CSI driver Helm chart:

```
resource "helm_release" "csi_secrets_store" {

  name       = "csi-secrets-store"
  repository = "https://kubernetes-sigs.github.io/secrets-store-csi-driver/charts"
  chart      = "secrets-store-csi-driver"
  namespace  = "kube-system"

  set {
    name = "syncSecret.enabled"
```

```
        value = "true"
    }

}
```

We can optionally enable secret synchronization by using the `syncSecret.enabled` attribute to make the secrets accessible from Kubernetes secrets. This makes it extremely convenient to inject the secrets into our application's pods without customized code to retrieve them from the mounted volume.

Next, we need to install the AWS provider for the CSI driver:

```
resource "helm_release" "aws_secrets_provider" {

    name        = "secrets-provider-aws"
    repository  = "https://aws.github.io/secrets-store-csi-driver-provider-aws"
    chart       = "secrets-store-csi-driver-provider-aws"
    namespace   = "kube-system"

}
```

Both of these Helm charts provision several different Kubernetes resources to your cluster under the `kube-system` namespace. If you encounter errors, interrogating the pods hosting these components is a good place for you to start debugging your configuration.

Secret provider class

Once we've installed both the CSI driver and its AWS provider, we are ready to connect to AWS Secrets Manager. So far, we have only enabled this ability; we haven't exercised it by accessing secrets.

That's what the `SecretProviderClass` resource is for. It connects to a specific set of secrets within AWS Secrets Manager. You'll notice that the way this type of resource is provisioned is different than other resources in Kubernetes. While other resource types have a corresponding Terraform resource, `SecretProviderClass` uses a `kubernetes_manifest` resource.

That's because this resource type is managed through a Kubernetes **custom resource definition (CRD)**; it's not a built-in type within Kubernetes:

```
resource "kubernetes_manifest" "secret_provider_class" {

  manifest = {
    apiVersion = "secrets-store.csi.x-k8s.io/v1"
    kind       = "SecretProviderClass"
    metadata = {
      name       = "${var.application_name}-${var.environment_name}-secret-provider-class"
```

```
      namespace = var.k8s_namespace
    }
    spec = {
      provider = "aws"
      parameters = {
        objects = yamlencode([ ... ])
      }
      secretObjects = [ ... ]
    }
  }
}
```

The structure of `SecretProviderClass` has two parts. First, `parameters` is where we declare what secrets we want to bring in:

```
{
    objectName         = "fleet-portal-dev-connection-string"
    objectType         = "secretsmanager"
    objectVersionLabel = "AWSCURRENT"
}
```

Here, `objectName` corresponds to either the relative name of the Secrets Manager secret or a fully qualified ARN for the secret. Next, `objectType` indicates what CSI driver provider should be used to access the secret, while `objectVersionLabel` allows us to select a specific version of the secret within Secrets Manager. For AWS, to access the latest version (probably the most common use case), you need to specify `AWSCURRENT` as the value.

Next, there is a collection of `secretObjects` that's used to define corresponding Kubernetes secret objects:

```
{
  data = [
    {
      key        = "fleet-portal-dev-connection-string"
      objectName = "fleet-portal-dev-connection-string"
    }
  ]
  secretName = "fleet-portal-dev-connection-string"
  type       = "Opaque"
}
```

These `secretObjects` will later be used in the deployment specification of our application to create environment variables for each secret within the pods.

Deployment

The Kubernetes deployment is one of the most significant resources that we have to provision within Kubernetes. As a result, it can be rather intimidating as there are several rather complex nested sections. The most important thing going on in the deployment is the container specification. This sets up the actual runtime environment for our pods.

The most important piece of information is the container image we want to use in our pods. To configure this, we need to construct the fully qualified path to the container image stored in our ECR. To do that, we need two pieces of information. First, we need the AWS account number and second, we need the AWS region name where our ECR repository is provisioned to:

```
locals {
  account_id          = data.aws_caller_identity.current.account_id
  container_registry = "${local.account_id}.dkr.ecr.${var.primary_
region}.amazonaws.com/"
}
```

The AWS account number can easily be obtained from the `aws_caller_identity` data source. This is an extremely simple data source that provides contextual information about the AWS account and IAM identity that Terraform is using with the `aws` provider. As a result, to create this data source, you simply create it without any parameters:

```
data "aws_caller_identity" "current" {}
```

This is a common pattern for accessing Terraform provider authentication context and cloud platform provisioning scope – in this case, what AWS account and what region we are provisioning to.

Here is the version of the same YAML code converted into HCL using an input variable to set different attributes on the entity:

```
resource "kubernetes_deployment" "web_app" {
  metadata {
    name      = local.web_app_name
    namespace = var.k8s_namespace
  }

  spec {
    replicas = 3

    selector {
      match_labels = {
        app = local.web_app_name
      }
    }
```

```
    template {
      metadata {
        labels = {
          app = local.web_app_name
        }
      }

      spec {
        service_account_name = kubernetes_service_account.workload_
identity.metadata[0].name

        container {
          image = local.web_app_image_name
          name  = local.web_app_name
          port {
            container_port = 5000
          }
          env_from {
            config_map_ref {
              name = kubernetes_config_map.web_app.metadata.0.name
            }
          }
        }
      }
    }
  }

}
```

The local variable we use for the container image name is the fully qualified path to our container image within ECR. It follows the `<account>.dkr.ecr.<region>.amazonaws.com/<repository>:<tag>` structure. Here, `<account>` is the AWS account number, which can be accessed using the `aws_caller_identity` data source. Then, `<region>` is the AWS region, which is accessible from the input variables. Finally, `<repository>` is the ECR repository name and `<version>` is the tag for the specific version of the container image.

We can set `service_account_name` by referencing other Kubernetes resources provisioned within this Terraform workspace. This is a key difference between using YAML and the `kubernetes` provider for Terraform. If we were using YAML this, would have to be hard-coded, whereas with HCL, we can reference other resources within the Terraform workspace.

To reference an AWS Secrets Manager secret, we need to modify the `container` block so that it includes another `env` block:

```
env {
  name = "DB_CONNECTION_STRING"
  value_from {
    secret_key_ref {
      name = "fleet-portal-dev-connection-string"
      key  = "fleet-portal-dev-connection-string"
    }
  }
}
```

This allows us to reference one of the `secretObjects` objects we declared within `SecretProviderClass` and give it an environment variable name that our application code can reference to access the secret.

Service

The Kubernetes service is primarily a network routing mechanism. It defines the port on which the service should be exposed to external clients and what port the network traffic should be forwarded to on the pods:

```
resource "kubernetes_service" "web_app" {
  metadata {
    name      = "${local.web_app_name}-service"
    namespace = var.k8s_namespace

  }
  spec {
    type = "ClusterIP"
    port {
      port        = 80
      target_port = 5000
    }
    selector = {
      app = local.web_app_name
    }
  }
}
```

Here, `selector` specifies which pods traffic should be forwarded to and it should match the corresponding pods, with the `app` label set to the same value as the service's selector.

ConfigMap

As we know from *Chapter 5*, the ConfigMap resource is a great way to pass non-sensitive configuration settings to your pods:

```
resource "kubernetes_config_map" "web_app" {
  metadata {
    name      = "${local.web_app_name}-config"
    namespace = var.k8s_namespace
  }

  data = {
    BackendEndpoint = ""
  }
}
```

Often, the Terraform workspace that provisions the infrastructure will output several different values that need to be included in a Kubernetes ConfigMap (URIs, AWS ARNs, DNS, and so on).

Ingress

The ingress controller is a component of Kubernetes that routes external network traffic into the cluster. It works in conjunction with a Kubernetes ingress, which defines specific rules that route traffic for specific services. This is very similar to the structure of the CSI driver and `SecretProviderClass`. One provides the foundational subsystem, thus enabling the capability, while the other implements a specific configuration using that underlying subsystem.

One of the most popular ingress controllers is a load balancer called NGINX. We can set up the NGINX ingress controller using a Helm chart. The components that are deployed by this Helm chart are why we needed an additional IAM policy that allows our EKS cluster to configure AWS ELB resources. That's because the Kubernetes configurations of the ingress controller and ingress resources will be interpreted by EKS and manifested as the provisioning and configuration of AWS ELB resources. This means that instead of explicitly configuring ELB resources using the `aws` Terraform provider, you will be annotating Kubernetes deployments and the necessary ELB resources will be provisioned and configured on your behalf.

The first thing we need to do is install the NGINX ingress controller using a Helm chart:

```
resource "helm_release" "ingress" {
  name       = "ingress"
  repository = "https://charts.bitnami.com/bitnami"
  chart      = "nginx-ingress-controller"

  create_namespace = true
  namespace        = "ingress-nginx"
```

```
  set {
    name  = "service.type"
    value = "LoadBalancer"
  }
  set {
    name  = "service.annotations"
    value = "service.beta.kubernetes.io/aws-load-balancer-type: nlb"
  }


}
```

This will install NGINX and deploy a Kubernetes service for NGINX running under the namespace we specified. The next step is to configure an ingress for our application:

```
resource "kubernetes_ingress_v1" "ingress" {
  metadata {
    name        = "${local.web_app_name}-ingress"
    namespace = var.k8s_namespace
    annotations = {
      "kubernetes.io/ingress.class" = "nginx"
    }
  }
  spec {
    rule {
      http { ... }
    }
  }
}
```

An ingress resource is pretty simple. You need to set the namespace and specify what ingress controller you want to use. Then, you need to specify paths so that you can route network traffic to the correct Kubernetes services:

```
  path {
    path      = "/"
    path_type = "Prefix"

    backend {
      service {
        name = kubernetes_service.web_app.metadata[0].name
        port {
          number = 80
        }
      }
```

```
    }
  }
```

It's also pretty important to establish explicit `depends_on` statements for the Kubernetes services for the frontend and backend application deployments as well as the ingress controller since we don't reference it directly within the HCL configuration:

```
depends_on = [
  kubernetes_service.web_app,
  kubernetes_service.web_api,
  helm_release.ingress
]
```

Now that we've built out the three components of our architecture, in the next section, we'll move on to how we can automate the deployment using Docker to build and publish the container images and then Terraform to provision our infrastructure and deploy our solution to Kubernetes.

Automating the deployment

In this section, we'll shift our focus from building our application and its environment to implementing deployment automations to efficiently provision our solution to AWS. Container-based architectures involve three core deployment motions. First, we must create and publish container images to a container registry. Next, we must provision the Kubernetes cluster environment where containers will be hosted. Finally, we must deploy the Kubernetes resources that will create the containers within Kubernetes pods and reference the container images we published.

Docker

Like the VM image that we built with Packer in the previous chapter, the container image acts as an immutable artifact that contains a versioned copy of the application code and operating system configuration. We need to update this artifact every time something changes in either the application code or the operating system configuration:

```
on:
  push:
    branches:
    - main
    paths:
    - 'src/dotnet/frontend/**'
```

Just like with Packer, we need to trigger a new container image to be built every time the application code and the operating system are configured within the Dockerfile itself. With GitHub Actions, we can add a list of `paths` that will trigger our workflow:

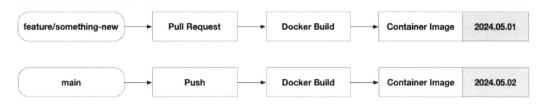

Figure 8.13 – VM image versioning

Now that we have the triggers and some variables set for our workflow, we need to structure `jobs`. For each Packer template, we will have two jobs: one that builds the C# .NET application code and produces a deployment package and another that runs `packer build` to produce the VM image:

```
jobs:

  build:
    runs-on: ubuntu-latest
    steps:


      . . .

  packer:
    runs-on: ubuntu-latest
    steps:


      . . .
```

The `build` job performs a pretty standard .NET build process, which includes restoring package dependencies from NuGet (the .NET package manager), building the code, running unit and integration tests, publishing a deployable artifact, and storing that artifact so that it can be used by future jobs within the pipeline:

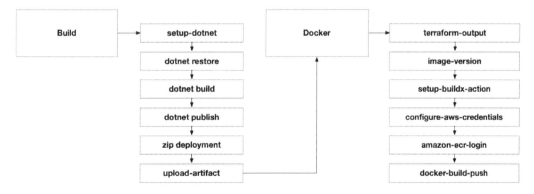

Figure 8.14 – Docker workflow

The `docker` job immediately runs Terraform to obtain outputs of the ECR container repository that we want to target. We don't have to run Terraform here but we could explicitly specify the ECR repository's fully qualified path.

Then, it generates a unique version of the name for the container image that will be produced if successful. We'll generate this image version based on the current date and the GitHub Action's run number. This will guarantee that the image version is unique so that we don't have to manually set it or worry about conflicts when pushing to the repository:

```
- id: image-version
  name: Generate Version Number
  run: |
    echo "version=$(date +'%Y.%m').${{ github.run_number }}" >>
"$GITHUB_OUTPUT"
```

Next, we need to set up Docker:

```
- name: Set up Docker Buildx
  uses: docker/setup-buildx-action@v1
```

Now, we must configure our AWS credentials using an official AWS GitHub Action. We'll use an AWS access key and secret access key specified by the GitHub environment settings:

```
- name: Configure AWS Credentials
  uses: aws-actions/configure-aws-credentials@v4
  with:
    aws-access-key-id: ${{ vars.AWS_ACCESS_KEY_ID }}
    aws-secret-access-key: ${{ secrets.AWS_SECRET_ACCESS_KEY }}
    aws-region: ${{ vars.PRIMARY_REGION }}
```

Once the credential has been configured, we can use the `amazon-ecr-login` action to connect to ECR:

```
- name: Log in to Amazon ECR
  id: login-ecr
  uses: aws-actions/amazon-ecr-login@v2
```

Finally, we'll build and push the image using an official Docker GitHub Action. It's important to note that this action is not specific to AWS. It uses standard container registry protocols to communicate with ECR using the fully qualified path to the ECR repository that we specify in the `tags` parameter:

```
- name: Build and push Docker image to ACR
  uses: docker/build-push-action@v5
  with:
    context: ${{ env.DOCKER_WORKING_DIRECTORY }}
    push: true
```

```
        tags: ${{ steps.terraform.outputs.registry_endpoint }}:${{
  steps.image-version.outputs.version }}
```

Both of our application components (the frontend and the backend) will have a repository, so the registry endpoint will be different depending on which container image we're pushing.

Terraform

In *Chapter 7*, we comprehensively covered the process of creating a Terraform GitHub Action that authenticates with AWS. Therefore, we won't be delving into it any further. I encourage you to refer back to *Chapter 7* to review the process.

Kubernetes

When we automate Kubernetes with Terraform, we are just running `terraform apply` again with a different root module. This time, the root module will configure the `kubernetes` and `helm` providers in addition to the `aws` provider. However, we won't create new resources with the `aws` provider; we will only obtain data sources from existing resources we provisioned in the previous `terraform apply` command that provisioned the infrastructure to AWS.

As a result, the GitHub Action that executes this process will look strikingly similar to how we executed Terraform with AWS. Some of the variables might change to include things such as the container image details and cluster information.

Summary

In this chapter, we designed, built, and automated the deployment of a complete and end-to-end solution using container-based architecture. We built onto the foundations from *Chapter 7*, where we worked with the foundational infrastructure of AWS VPCs but layered on AWS EKS to host our application in containers. In the next and final step in our AWS journey, we'll be looking at serverless architecture, moving beyond the underlying infrastructure, and letting the platform itself take our solution to new heights.

9

Go Serverless with AWS – Building Solutions with AWS Lambda

In this chapter, we will turn the page to the final installment of our three-part series on **Amazon Web Services** (**AWS**). Having previously built solutions on AWS using **Virtual Machines** (**VMs**) in *Chapter 7* and then in containers in *Chapter 8*, our journey now leads us to an exploration of what building a truly serverless solution looks like on AWS.

While the foundational concepts and practices from the preceding chapters will help us, some aspects of the solution are completely absent here. Namely, we don't need to worry about any operating system configuration, whether it be in Packer or Docker.

Our attention now turns to adapting our application code to **Lambda**'s application model. While this necessitates changes to our application code to align with Lambda's approach, it also presents opportunities to enhance scalability and efficiency without the burden of managing servers. This shift in focus promises a more streamlined and efficient process. We'll spend a bit more time adjusting our application code to conform than provisioning new services using Terraform.

This chapter covers the following topics:

- Laying the foundation
- Designing the solution
- Building the solution
- Automating the deployment

Laying the foundation

Our story continues through the lens of Söze Enterprises, founded by the enigmatic Turkish billionaire Keyser Söze. Our team has been hard at work building the next-generation autonomous vehicle orchestration platform. Our initial strategy involved minimizing change to allow the team to focus on driving features into our product. However, our elusive CEO had other ideas and pushed us to adopt container technology to make our product more flexible and scalable going forward. Working with Keyser, there is never a dull moment, but managing such radical change so quickly can be frustrating.

Meanwhile, in Davos, Switzerland, with the World Economic Forum in full swing, Keyser has a chance encounter at the espresso bar with Werner Vogels, with whom he immediately hits it off. When Werner gets a glimpse of Keyser's immense vision for the autonomous vehicle platform, he casually suggests that maybe Keyser shouldn't concern himself with infrastructure at all and that leveraging AWS's serverless offerings could free him from the shackles of infrastructure management to allow him to focus on his grand vision.

Thanks to Werner's insights and Keyser's whimsical decision-making, our team veers deeper into AWS, explicitly transitioning from Amazon **Elastic Kubernetes Service (EKS)** to AWS Lambda for serverless computing. This might require a complete re-think of our application architecture, but it could free us from the significant operational overhead of managing low-level infrastructure.

Designing the solution

In this section, we will look at the overall design of our solution, given the shift from VM- and container-based architectures toward serverless architectures. Serverless has the quintessential objective of eliminating heavy infrastructure from the stack at its core. Therefore, we will look for ways to shed any AWS services requiring significant fixed costs, such as EC2 instances or EKS clusters, and replace them with serverless options. This change in our operational context and technology landscape will require us to rethink our solution's design, implementation, and deployment strategy:

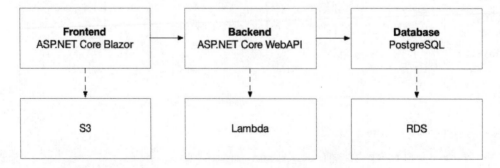

Figure 9.1 – Logical architecture for the autonomous vehicle platform

Our application's architecture doesn't change significantly, but we will be using different Azure services to host it. In this case, we'll be using Azure Storage to host the application's frontend and Azure Functions to host the application's backend:

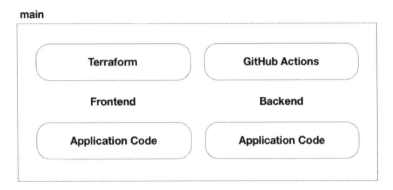

Figure 9.2 – Source control structure of our repository

In this solution, we'll have four parts of our code base. The first two are the Terraform code that provisions the environment and the GitHub Actions code that executes the deployment process. Then we have the two code bases for our application's frontend and backend.

Cloud architecture

In *Chapter 7*, our cloud-hosting solution was a set of dedicated EC2 instances. In *Chapter 8*, it was a set of shared EC2 instances managed by our Kubernetes cluster's node pool. Using VMs, whether standalone VMs or ones that are part of a Kubernetes node pool, has the most sunk cost.

In *Chapter 8*, our entire solution was executed on containers that allowed the front- and backends to coexist as a set of containers on the same VMs. This saved some money, but we still needed servers to host the workload. In this chapter, we will have a new objective: to take advantage of the power of the cloud by leveraging cloud-native services that abstract the underlying infrastructure from us and allow us to truly only pay for what we use. AWS's serverless offerings will be crucial to us in this endeavor.

Frontend

In previous chapters, we hosted our frontend on public-facing servers that returned the HTML and JavaScript that composed our web application. However, we still require a cloud-hosted solution to host the files and respond to requests in both solutions.

However, due to the nature of the web application running within the end user's browser, we don't need to use cloud-hosted VMs to host what are essentially flat files. We can use simple cloud storage to host the frontend as a static website and rely on the cloud platform to shoulder the burden of returning the web content.

On AWS, we can use **Simple Storage Service (S3)**. This service allows us to host static web content that is internet-accessible. S3 handles all the load balancing, SSL termination, and scaling up to meet huge spikes in demand:

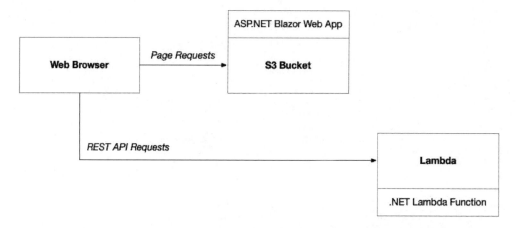

Figure 9.3 – S3 handles web page requests, Lambda handles REST API requests

In order to do this, we'll need an S3 bucket. We will need to enable public internet access to its contents. This will require a combination of S3 and IAM configuration. All S3 buckets have an internet-accessible public domain. When we activate the static websites feature of S3, internet traffic gets routed to content hosted in our bucket.

This will give us a huge advantage because S3 has no sunk costs. Creating an S3 bucket costs you absolutely zero dollars per month. Like other serverless offerings, it uses a set of micro-transactions to measure your activity and charge you for precisely what you use. In S3, this can be a bit complicated, as several measurements incur costs:

Metric	Unit	Scale	Price
Storage	GB	1,000	$0.023
Read transactions	Transactions	10,000	$0.0004
Write transactions	Transactions	10,000	$0.005
Other operations	Transactions	10,000	$0.01

Table 9.1 – AWS S3's micro-transactional pricing

The preceding table shows all the costs you will run into when using AWS to host your static websites. The prices listed are accurate for AWS's US West (Oregon) region at the time of writing. Prices may have changed by the time you read this, so it's best to check the latest prices for the most accurate cost estimation.

I included these prices to make a point. We can host a static website on a three-node Kubernetes cluster for approximately $300 a month, or on AWS S3 for less than $0.01 a month. Which approach would you choose?

Backend

Like our frontend, in previous chapters, our backend was also hosted on VMs in two different ways: dedicated VMs and shared VMs within the node pool on our Kubernetes cluster.

Unlike the frontend, our backend doesn't have the option of running entirely client-side inside the end user's web browser. In the backend, we have custom code that needs to run on a server. Therefore, we need to find a solution to host these components without all the overhead of a fleet of VMs.

We can use Lambda Functions on AWS to accomplish this. AWS Lambda is a managed service that allows you to deploy your code without paying the sunk costs for any of the underlying VMs. Like S3, it has its micro-transactional pricing model that charges you for precisely what you use:

Metric	Unit	Scale	Price ($)
Execution time	GB/s	1	$0.0000166667
Total executions	Transactions	1,000,000	$0.020

Table 9.2 – AWS Lambda's micro-transactional pricing

The preceding table shows the costs associated with deploying your code to Lambda Functions. The first thing you'll probably notice is that, like S3, these prices are extremely low and measure a very small amount of activity on the platform.

For example, the execution time metric has a unit of GB/s, which is the amount of memory that your Lambda Function uses per second in GB. Given that it measures at a per-second interval, you don't have to run your Lambda Functions very long to rack up quite a few of these. The execution time cost can be adjusted based on how much memory you allocate. You can choose to allocate any amount of memory between 128 MB and 10 GB.

While straightforward, the total executions metric is subject to AWS Lambda's built-in constraints, including execution time limits. For example, each of these executions is limited to 15 minutes. Suppose you are trying to respond to requests from a web application. In that case, you probably won't want to design your Lambda Function to take 15 minutes anyway, as this would be a poor experience for the end users of the web browser. In this scenario, you would want your Lambda Function to return in no more than a few seconds. However, Lambda Functions can be employed for many different tasks besides responding to HTTP requests from a browser. In these situations, you must carefully design your Lambda solution to stay within this execution time limitation. This may require you to think about how to split up the work so that it can be processed more parallelly by hundreds, if not thousands, of instances of your Lambda Function:

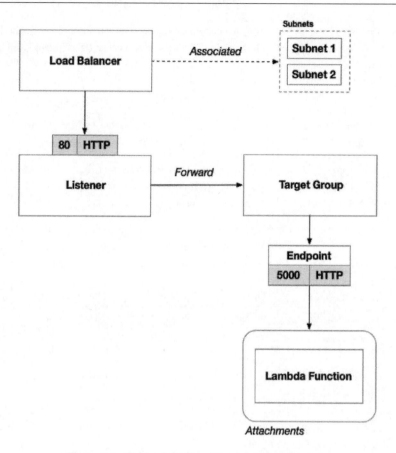

Figure 9.4 – The backend's architecture using Lambda

Previously, our ASP.NET REST API was set up using a traditional ASP.NET project that used controllers to implement the REST API endpoints. However, when transitioning to Lambda Functions, we would expect the code base to be structured much differently. To host our REST API as Lambda Functions, we need to conform to the framework that Lambda dictates. As a result, the ASP.NET controller classes must be refactored to conform to this standard. In the next section, we'll delve into the code that makes this possible.

Deployment architecture

Now that we have a good idea of what our cloud architecture for our solution on AWS will look like, we need to devise a plan for provisioning our environments and deploying our code.

In *Chapter 7*, when we deployed our application to VMs, we baked our compiled application code into a VM image using Packer. Similarly, in *Chapter 8*, when we deployed our application to containers on our Kubernetes cluster, we baked our application code into container images using Docker. With serverless, this completely changes because AWS's serverless offerings completely abstract away the operating system. This means that all we are responsible for is producing a compatible deployment package.

Creating the deployment package

As we discussed in the previous section, our application has two components: the frontend and the backend. Each has a different deployment target. For the frontend, we are going to be deploying as a static website to AWS S3, while the backend is going to be deployed as an AWS Lambda Function. Since both are .NET projects, we will be using both .NET and AWS platform-specific tools in order to create deployment packages and deploy them to their target AWS services. The following diagram shows the process we will go through in order to provision our environment, package our application code, and deploy it to the target environment out in AWS:

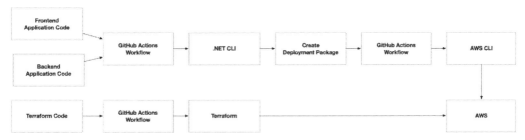

Figure 9.5 – The resource deployment pipeline to build our .NET application code for deployment to AWS

For the frontend, this means enabling the feature to deploy our ASP.NET Blazor web application as a web assembly. This will allow the frontend to be hosted as a static website running completely client-side without server-side rendering. This is only possible because of the way we have designed our front-end web application, which uses HTML, CSS, and JavaScript to interact with server-side REST APIs. It's important to note that ASP.NET Blazor supports both hosting options. Still, we chose to go down the client-side-only path and eliminate any dependency on server-side page rendering. As a result, when we use the .NET CLI to publish our ASP.NET Blazor project, it will emit a folder containing static web content. Then, using the AWS CLI, we can upload the contents of this folder to our S3 bucket to complete the deployment.

Using the .NET CLI, we will publish our project for the backend, which emits all the files necessary for the AWS Lambda service to recognize and execute our Lambda Function.

Once this is done, we must zip this folder into a ZIP archive. Finally, we can use the AWS CLI to deploy this ZIP archive to our Lambda Function.

Now that we have a solid plan for how we will implement both the cloud architecture using AWS and the deployment architecture using GitHub Actions, let's start building! In the next section, we'll break down the HashiCorp Configuration Language code we use to implement the Terraform and modify the application code to conform to AWS Lambda's framework.

Building the solution

Now that we have a solid design for our solution, we can begin building it. As discussed in the previous section, since we'll be using AWS serverless offerings such as AWS S3 and Lambda Functions to host our application, we will need to make some changes to our application code. We never had to do this in *Chapters 7* and *8*, as we were able to deploy our application to the cloud by packaging it in either a VM image (using Packer) or a container image (using Docker). Therefore, we need to write some Terraform code and update our application code in C# to build our solution.

Terraform

As we discussed in our design, our solution consists of two application components: the frontend and the backend. Each has its own code base of application code that needs to be deployed. In previous chapters, we also had the operating system configuration. Now that we are using serverless offerings, this is no longer our responsibility, as the platform will take care of it for us.

Much of the Terraform setup is very similar to what we have done in previous chapters, so we will only focus on new resources needed for our solution. If you want to work with the complete solution, you can check the full source code for this book, which is available on GitHub.

Frontend

First, we need to provision an AWS S3 bucket to which we can deploy our frontend. The S3 bucket is one of the most common Terraform resources to be provisioned, as many other AWS services use S3 buckets for different purposes:

```
resource "aws_s3_bucket" "frontend" {
  bucket          = "${var.application_name}-${var.environment_name}-
frontend"

  tags = {
    Name          = "${var.application_name}-${var.environment_name}-
frontend"
    application = var.application_name
    environment = var.environment_name
  }
}
```

However, we need to configure our S3 bucket a bit differently by using a couple of additional resources. First, we need to configure public access using the `aws_s3_bucket_public_access_block` resource. Then we need to configure our static website using the `aws_s3_bucket_website_configuration` resource:

```
resource "aws_s3_bucket_public_access_block" "frontend" {
  bucket = aws_s3_bucket.frontend.id

  block_public_acls       = false
  block_public_policy     = false
  ignore_public_acls      = false
  restrict_public_buckets = false
}
```

The configuration is pretty simple, but it is critical for enabling our S3 bucket to be accessible over the internet. By altering our configuration here, we could also opt to host static websites that are not accessible over the internet. This might be ideal for intranet websites that we only want accessible when on a private network:

```
resource "aws_s3_bucket_website_configuration" "frontend" {
  bucket = aws_s3_bucket.frontend.id

  index_document {
    suffix = "index.html"
  }

  error_document {
    key = "error.html"
  }

}
```

This configures the S3 bucket to specify the default web page when it redirects web traffic to the content stored within our bucket. The `index.html` page aligns with what our ASP.NET Blazor web application uses by default.

Lastly, we need to configure **Identity and Access Management** (**IAM**) to allow access to our S3 bucket. A common technique within the `aws` provider is to use a Data Source resource to generate IAM policy documents that can then be attached to other provisioned resources:

```
data "aws_iam_policy_document" "frontend" {
  statement {
    actions   = ["s3:GetObject"]
    resources = ["${aws_s3_bucket.frontend.arn}/*"]
```

```
    principals {
      type        = "*"
      identifiers = ["*"]
    }
  }
}
```

The preceding data source emits the correct policy document, which we can use when configuring the S3 bucket's policy using an `aws_s3_bucket_policy` resource:

```
resource "aws_s3_bucket_policy" "frontend" {
  bucket = aws_s3_bucket.frontend.id
  policy = data.aws_iam_policy_document.frontend.json

  depends_on = [aws_s3_bucket_public_access_block.frontend]
}
```

Backend

Lambda Functions are deployed to an `aws_lambda_function` resource, but the most important thing to set up first is the IAM role you will use for your Lambda Function. This will be how we allow our Lambda Function access to other resources on AWS, such as secrets and logging. It is also how we allow it to communicate with databases and other services our application code needs to communicate with:

```
data "aws_iam_policy_document" "lambda" {
  statement {
    effect = "Allow"

    principals {
      type        = "Service"
      identifiers = ["lambda.amazonaws.com"]
    }

    actions = ["sts:AssumeRole"]
  }
}
```

We will start with an IAM policy document for the `sts:AssumeRole` permissions and scope it to Lambda Functions. Then we define the IAM role and use this as the `assume_role_policy`:

```
resource "aws_iam_role" "lambda" {
  name                 = "${var.application_name}-${var.environment_
name}-lambda"
```

```
    assume_role_policy = data.aws_iam_policy_document.lambda.json
}
```

We can grant more permissions later by defining additional policies and attaching them to this IAM role; more on that later. Now, it's time to provision our Lambda Function:

```
resource "aws_lambda_function" "main" {
  function_name = "${var.application_name}-${var.environment_name}"
  role          = aws_iam_role.lambda.arn
  runtime       = "dotnet6"
  filename      = "deployment.zip"
  handler       = "FleetAPI::FleetAPI.Function::FunctionHandler"

  tags = {
    Name        = "${var.application_name}-${var.environment_name} lambda"
    application = var.application_name
    environment = var.environment_name
  }
}
```

As in the previous two chapters, we must consistently tag our AWS resources with the `application` and `environment` tags. These tags organize our deployment into an AWS resource group for easier centralized management.

A key attribute here is `runtime`, which in our case is .NET 6. Depending on your technology stack, this will, of course, vary. However, perhaps the most important attribute is `handler`. This is also the trickiest one to set, as it needs to be carefully aligned with our application code. The `handler` is a path to a component in our application code. In .NET, this path is made up of three parts: the namespace, the fully qualified class name, and the method name.

We can also use an optional nested block to set additional environment variables to help configure the Lambda Function:

```
environment {
  variables = {
    SECRET_SAUCE = random_string.secret_sauce.result
  }
}
```

This can be a useful way to pass in configuration to Lambda, which is output by other Terraform resources.

Logging

As we've seen, AWS uses IAM policies to grant access to other foundational services on the platform. This is necessary for even things such as logging:

```
resource "aws_iam_policy" "lambda_logging" {
  name        = "${var.application_name}-${var.environment_name}-
lambda-logging-policy"
  description = "Allow Lambda to log to CloudWatch"

  policy = jsonencode({
    Version = "2012-10-17"
    Statement = [
      {
        Action = [
          "logs:CreateLogGroup",
          "logs:CreateLogStream",
          "logs:PutLogEvents"
        ]
        Effect   = "Allow"
        Resource = "arn:aws:logs:*:*:*"
      }
    ]
  })
}
```

In the preceding code, we are creating a policy that allows our Lambda Function to write to CloudWatch.

Finally, we must attach this policy to the IAM role that we created for our Lambda Function:

```
resource "aws_iam_role_policy_attachment" "lambda_logging" {
  role       = aws_iam_role.lambda.name
  policy_arn = aws_iam_policy.lambda_logging.arn
}
```

This is what it looks like:

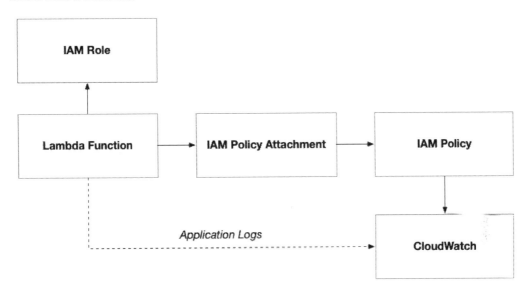

Figure 9.6 – IAM policy to grant access to CloudWatch logging

This will allow us to use CloudWatch to see what's happening inside our application code every time our Lambda Function is executed, which is critical for troubleshooting and debugging.

Secrets management

We saw that we could set environment variables on our Lambda Function. Still, if we want better control over our secrets, we may want to use AWS Secrets Manager to manage them and then configure our Lambda Function to access them from there.

For example, we'll set up a password using the `random_password` resource from the `random` utility provider that we reviewed in *Chapter 3*. Sometimes AWS services generate secrets on your behalf and sometimes they allow you to specify your own. In that situation, the `random_password` resource can be very useful:

```
resource "random_password" "secret_sauce" {
  length  = 8
  lower   = false
  special = false
}
```

The preceding code declares a password that we will use as our secret. Then we need to create a Secrets Manager `secret` to hold this secret:

```
resource "aws_secretsmanager_secret" "secret_sauce" {
  name = "secret-sauce"

  tags = {
    application = var.application_name
    environment = var.environment_name
  }
}
```

The preceding code generates the secret, but you must store secret values in the `aws_secretsmanager_secret_version` sub-resource:

```
resource "aws_secretsmanager_secret_version" "secret_sauce" {
  secret_id     = aws_secretsmanager_secret.secret_sauce.id
  secret_string = random_string.secret_sauce.result
}
```

There are additional features that can be enabled to handle automatic rotation and custom encryption that you could also consider.

Now that our secret has been created and stored in Secrets Manager, we must create an IAM policy to grant our Lambda Function access:

```
resource "aws_iam_policy" "lambda_secrets" {
  name        = "${var.application_name}-${var.environment_name}-
secrets-policy"
  description = "Policy to allow Lambda function to access secrets."

  policy = jsonencode({
    Version = "2012-10-17",
    Statement = [
      {
        Action = ["secretsmanager:GetSecretValue"],
        Effect = "Allow",
        Resource = [
          aws_secretsmanager_secret.secret_sauce.arn
        ]
      }
    ]
  })
}
```

We will use `aws_iam_role_policy_attachment` to attach the policy to the Lambda Function's IAM role just as we did for the permissions to log to CloudWatch. If you need to use additional secrets, you can continue to add them to the resource array where `secret_sauce` has been added.

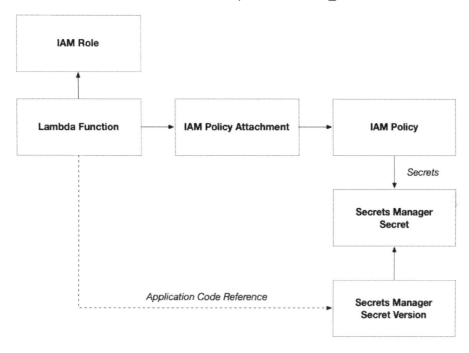

Figure 9.7 – Resource IAM policy to grant access to Secrets Manager secrets

As you can see, the Lambda Function has a much simpler deployment. We don't need a virtual network or any other surrounding resources we provisioned in previous chapters to get off the ground. For most applications, the built-in security of Lambda Functions and Secrets Manager is sufficient. If we wanted to enable private networking because our application has to follow some regulatory compliance, we could do that. However, it is not required.

Application code

AWS Lambda is inherently event-based. Each Lambda Function is triggered by a different type of event. The AWS Lambda service provides many different event types to trigger your Lambda Function from a wide variety of other AWS services. This makes it easy to design Lambda Functions that can respond to all sorts of activities within your AWS environment. For the purposes of this book, we'll focus on the Application Load Balancer only. If you are interested in this topic, I'd recommend that you check out all the other options that AWS Lambda has—they are quite extensive.

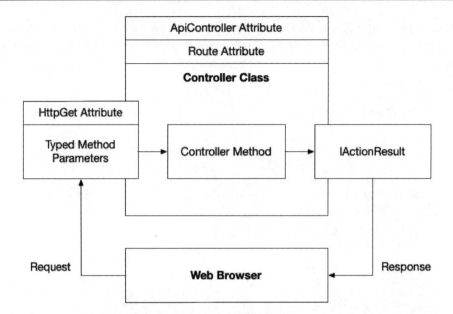

Figure 9.8 – Resource ASP.NET MVC Controller class anatomy

In a traditional ASP.NET REST API solution, you have Controller classes embodying a specific route and methods that implement different operations at that route. The Controller class must be decorated with an `ApiController` attribute that informs the ASP.NET runtime that this class should be used to process incoming web requests at the route specified in the `Route` attribute.

Each method is decorated with an attribute that denotes which HTTP verb the method should respond to. In the preceding example, we used `HttpGet`, but there are corresponding attributes for each supported HTTP verb. The method can take strongly typed parameters that can be part of the route, query string, or request body. The method returns an `IActionResult` by default, which allows us to return different data structures depending on the outcome of the request.

To implement a REST API using Lambda Functions, we need to implement a class using the SDK Lambda function. This requires us to slightly adjust how we implement both our class and our method. We will employ different class and method attributes to achieve a similar outcome: defining an endpoint that responds to web requests at a specific route.

The Lambda Function class is not decorated with any attributes. A method should take in a request object and an `ILambdaContext` object. This method should also return a corresponding response object. Depending on the type of event you are designing your Lambda Function to respond to, you will need to use different classes for the request and response objects. AWS has published some libraries to encapsulate common structures of these various types to make them easier to build:

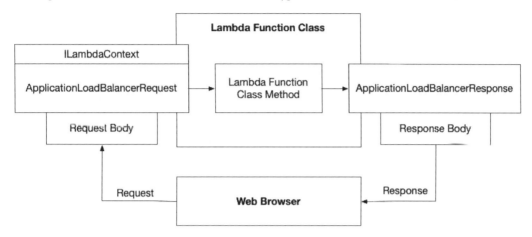

Figure 9.9 – Resource AWS Lambda Function class anatomy

In this book, we are using the Application Load Balancer; therefore, we used the `Amazon.Lambda.ApplicationLoadBalancerEvents` library to provide a standard implementation of our request and response objects. As you can see, we are taking in an `ApplicationLoadBalancerRequest` and returning an `ApplicationLoadBalancerResponse`.

If we want to implement a more complex Lambda Function that supports different functionalities or operations, we can implement our routing logic around the `ApplicationLoadBalancerRequest` object's `Path` and `HttpMethod` properties. These correspond to the ASP.NET framework's route and HTTP verb attributes that decorate each controller class and its methods.

As we can see, the cloud architecture radically simplifies. However, one trade-off is that our backend code needs to be adapted to the AWS Lambda framework. This will require development and testing efforts to transform our code base into this new hosting model. This starkly contrasts with what we explored in previous chapters, where we hosted on VMs or containerized and hosted on a Kubernetes cluster. While conforming to the AWS Lambda application model does take work, its benefits are twofold. First, it allows us to take advantage of a close-to-zero sunk cost. Second, it allows us to fully abstract the underlying infrastructure from us and let the AWS platform take care of scalability and high availability. This allows us to focus more on the functionality of our solutions than on the plumbing required to keep the lights on.

Now that we have implemented Terraform to provision our solution and made changes to our application code to conform it to the AWS Lambda framework, in the next section, we'll dive into YAML and Bash. We will also implement GitHub Actions workflows.

Automating the deployment

As discussed in the previous section, serverless offerings such as AWS Lambda and S3 abstract the operating system configuration away. Therefore, when we deploy, we simply need an application package that is compatible with the target platform. In this section, we'll create an automation pipeline using GitHub Actions to provision our application to its new serverless home in AWS.

Terraform

The first thing that we need to do is to provision our environment to AWS. This is going to be extremely similar to the way we did this in the previous chapters. In *Chapter 7*, we needed to ensure that our VM images were built and available before we executed Terraform because the Terraform code base referenced the VM images when it provisioned the VMs. With our VM architecture, application deployment happens before Terraform provisions the environment:

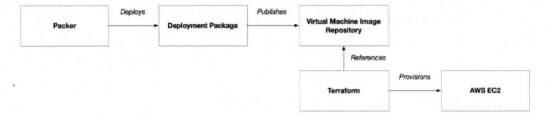

Figure 9.10 – Packer-produced VM images are a prerequisite for Terraform

In *Chapter 8*, we provisioned our Kubernetes cluster using AWS EKS without such a prerequisite. In fact, the application deployment occurred after the Kubernetes cluster was online. This means that with container-based architecture, application deployment happens after Terraform provisions the environment:

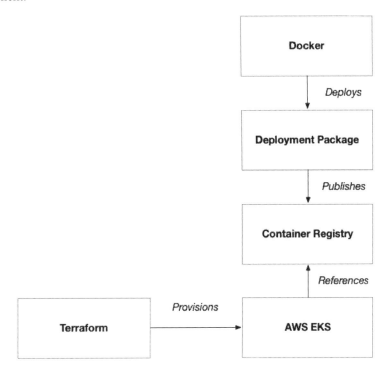

Figure 9.11 – Docker-produced container images are provisioned to Kubernetes after Terraform executes

When using AWS's serverless offerings, the deployment process mirrors what we saw when deploying our application as containers to Kubernetes. Just like with this approach, we need to build a deployment artifact for AWS's serverless offerings. For the frontend, that means simply generating the static web content. For the backend, that means generating a Lambda Functions ZIP archive. These artifacts share a similar purpose to the Docker images in that they are a target service-compatible way of packaging our application for deployment:

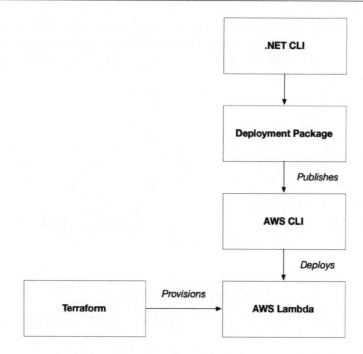

Figure 9.12 – The .NET CLI produces deployment artifacts that
are provisioned to AWS after Terraform executes

As you can see, the serverless deployment looks very similar to the approach used with the container-based architecture. That's because AWS is fulfilling the role that Kubernetes played when using a serverless approach. AWS just has custom tools to facilitate the deployment of the application.

Deployment

Now that Terraform has provisioned the AWS infrastructure that we need for our serverless solution, we need to take the final step of deploying both the deployment artifacts to the appropriate locations in AWS.

We will use .NET and AWS custom tools to produce and deploy the artifacts to these target locations.

Frontend

As we saw in other chapters, our .NET application code needs to follow a continuous integration process, whereby the code is built and tested using automated unit testing and other built-in quality controls. Nothing changes there except that we need to add some special handling to the deployment artifact that these processes produce in order to make sure it is available to our GitHub Action's job that deploys the workload to the appropriate location.

The `dotnet publish` command outputs the deployment artifact of the .NET application code. This output for the ASP.NET Blazor web application is a folder container: a collection of loose files with HTML, JavaScript, and CSS in it. In order to pass all of these files efficiently from one GitHub Actions job to another, we need to zip them up into a single file:

```
- name: Generate the Deployment Package
  run: |
    zip -r ../deployment.zip ./
  working-directory: ${{ env.DOTNET_WORKING_DIRECTORY }}/publish
```

Now that the static web content has been zipped into a ZIP archive, we will use the `upload-artifact` GitHub action to save this file to GitHub Actions. This will make the file available for future jobs that are executed within the pipeline:

```
- name: Upload Deployment Package
  uses: actions/upload-artifact@v2
  with:
    name: dotnet-deployment
    path: ${{ env.DOTNET_WORKING_DIRECTORY }}/deployment.zip
```

Future jobs can simply download the artifact using a corresponding `download-artifact` GitHub action and the same name that was used to upload it:

```
- uses: actions/download-artifact@v3
  with:
    name: dotnet-deployment
```

Since the ASP.NET Blazor web application will be hosted as static web content on our AWS S3 bucket, we need to ensure that we unzip it before uploading the contents. If we were to upload the ZIP archive to S3, the web application wouldn't work correctly because all the web content would be trapped inside the archive file:

```
- name: Unzip Deployment Package
  run: |
    mkdir -p ${{ env.DOTNET_WORKING_DIRECTORY }}/upload-staging
    unzip ./deployment.zip -d ${{ env.DOTNET_WORKING_DIRECTORY }}/
upload-staging
```

Now that the static web content has been unzipped to the staging directory, we can use the `aws s3 sync` command to deploy all of the files in the folder to the S3 bucket:

```
      - id: deploy
        name: Upload to S3 Bucket
        env:
          AWS_ACCESS_KEY_ID: ${{ vars.AWS_ACCESS_KEY_ID }}
          AWS_SECRET_ACCESS_KEY: ${{ secrets.AWS_SECRET_ACCESS_KEY }}
          AWS_REGION: ${{ vars.BACKEND_REGION }}
        working-directory: ${{ env.DOTNET_WORKING_DIRECTORY }}/upload-
staging
        run: |
          aws s3 sync . s3://${{ needs.terraform.outputs.frontend_
bucket_name }}
```

Backend

To deploy the Lambda Function, the exact same process is followed to pass the artifact from the GitHub Actions job that builds the deployment artifact to the job that actually deploys it.

The only difference is that we will use the `aws lambda update-function-code` command to provision a ZIP archive to the Lambda Function:

```
      - name: Deploy
        env:
          AWS_ACCESS_KEY_ID: ${{ vars.AWS_ACCESS_KEY_ID }}
          AWS_SECRET_ACCESS_KEY: ${{ secrets.AWS_SECRET_ACCESS_KEY }}
          AWS_REGION: ${{ vars.BACKEND_REGION }}
          FUNCTION_NAME: ${{needs.terraform.outputs.lambda_function_
name}}
        run: |
          aws lambda update-function-code --function-name $FUNCTION_
NAME --zip-file fileb://deployment.zip
```

Unlike how we provisioned the frontend, we don't need to unzip the deployment package for the Lambda Function. AWS Lambda expects our application code to be bundled into a ZIP archive.

That's it! Now our application has been fully deployed to AWS S3 and Lambda!

Summary

In this chapter, we embarked on an ambitious journey, transitioning from a .NET solution that was previously architected on VMs and Kubernetes using Amazon EKS to a fully serverless architecture utilizing AWS Lambda Functions. This transformative step involved converting our traditional .NET REST API into a suite of Lambda Functions and hosting the frontend as a static website on Amazon S3, marking a significant evolution in our cloud-native development journey for our fictional company's autonomous vehicle fleet operations platform.

As we conclude this chapter, we have built three distinct solutions on AWS, spanning VMs, Kubernetes, and now serverless architectures. We've also demonstrated our ability to navigate and leverage AWS's diverse capabilities to meet our evolving needs.

Looking ahead, we are poised to embark on a new chapter of our cloud journey with Microsoft Azure. Under the guidance of our elusive and visionary CEO, Keyser Söze, who has now forged a partnership with Microsoft, we stand at the threshold of exploring similar architectures in the Azure ecosystem. With our sights now set on Azure, I invite you to continue our journey as we enter this alternate universe, ready to tackle new challenges and uncover new possibilities on a completely different cloud platform.

Part 4:
Building Solutions on Azure

Armed with the conceptual knowledge of Terraform and architectural concepts that transcend the implementation details of the major public cloud platforms, we'll explore building solutions on Microsoft Azure with three cloud computing paradigms: virtual machines, containers with Kubernetes, and serverless with Azure Functions.

This part has the following chapters:

- *Chapter 10, Getting Started on Azure – Building Solutions with Azure Virtual Machines*
- *Chapter 11, Containerize on Azure – Building Solutions with Azure Kubernetes Service*
- *Chapter 12, Go Serverless on Azure – Building Solutions with Azure Functions*

10

Getting Started on Azure – Building Solutions with Azure Virtual Machines

Now that we've built our solution end-to-end on the AWS platforms and followed our team's journey from their initial VM architecture to Kubernetes and then finally culminating with serverless, we're ready to switch gears and enter an alternate reality where Keyser has saddled up to his dear friends at Microsoft. In this next set of chapters, we will follow a similar path as in *Chapters 7* through *9*, but in this alternate version, we'll work with Microsoft Azure.

This chapter will pick up where we started our journey on AWS; in *Chapter 7*, where we built a doppelgänger solution using AWS. In that chapter, we went into great detail about elements of the solution that are 100% cloud agnostic. This included a detailed explanation of exactly how we use Packer to provision our .NET-based application code to a Linux VM and a detailed explanation of how to set up GitHub Actions for a VM-based CI/CD pipeline.

Since an overwhelming majority of this remains the same when we move to Azure, we won't be revisiting these topics in this chapter at the same length. However, I would encourage you to put a bookmark in *Chapter 7* and reference it frequently.

This chapter covers the following topics:

- Laying the foundation
- Designing the solution
- Building the solution
- Automating the deployment

Laying the foundation

Our team at Söze Enterprises applauds their achievement of responding to the whimsical technical course correction of their fearless leader, Keyser Söze, and marvels at their success and fortune in launching their product successfully on AWS. Here, they used VMs, Kubernetes, and serverless technology. The comforting orange complexion of the AWS console begins to melt away when suddenly, the air fills with an eerie yet familiar sound: doodle-oo doodle-oo doodle-oo. An unexpected duo appears – one with shoulder-length brown hair under a black baseball cap and a simple black T-shirt; the other with a nerdy charm with tousled blond hair, thick black-rimmed glasses, and a red and blue plaid flannel over a white Aerosmith T-shirt. They start the familiar chant: doodle-oo doodle-oo doodle-oo. Suddenly, we're transported to another world – another universe, perhaps, where Azure's deep blue replaces AWS's bright orange. Söze Enterprises has partnered with Microsoft for their next-generation autonomous vehicle platform.

Just as before, we have inherited a team from one of Söze Enterprises' other divisions that has a strong core team of C# .NET developers, so we'll be building version 1.0 of the platform using .NET technologies. The elusive CEO, Keyser, was seen hobnobbing with Satya Nadella during the glitz and glamor of the Met Gala in New York City over the weekend, and word has come down from corporate that we will be using Microsoft Azure to host the platform. Since the team doesn't have a ton of experience with containers and timelines are tight, we've decided to build a simple three-tier architecture and host on Azure VMs:

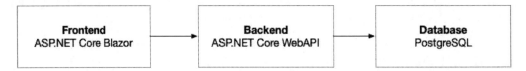

Figure 10.1 – Logical architecture for the autonomous vehicle platform

The platform will need a frontend, which will be a web UI built using ASP.NET Core Blazor. The frontend will be powered by a REST API backend, which will be built using ASP.NET Core Web API. Having our core functionality encapsulated into a REST API will allow autonomous vehicles to communicate directly with the platform and allow us to expand by adding client interfaces with additional frontend technologies such as native mobile apps and virtual or mixed reality in the future. The backend will use a PostgreSQL database for persistent storage since it's lightweight, industry-standard, and relatively inexpensive.

Designing the solution

Due to the tight timelines the team is facing, we want to keep the cloud architecture simple. Therefore, we'll keep it simple and use the tried and tested services of Microsoft Azure to implement the platform instead of trying to learn something new. The first decision we must make is what Azure service each component of our logical architecture will be hosted on.

Our application architecture consists of three components: a frontend, a backend, and a database. The frontend and backend are application components and need to be hosted on a cloud service that provides general computing, while the database needs to be hosted on a cloud database service. There are many options for both types of services:

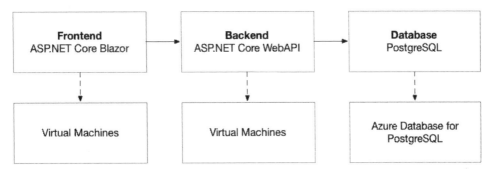

Figure 10.2 – Logical architecture for the autonomous vehicle platform

Since we have decided we're going to use VMs to host our application, we have narrowed down the different services that we can use to host our application, and we have decided that the Azure VM service is the ideal choice for our current situation. Other options, such as Azure App Service, also use VMs but we want to have total control over the solution and maintain as many cross-platform capabilities as we can in case we ever have to migrate to a different cloud platform:

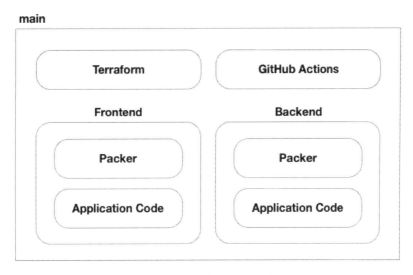

Figure 10.3 – Source control structure of our repository

In this solution, we'll have six parts. We still have the application code and Packer templates for both the frontend and backend. Then, we have GitHub Actions to implement our CI/CD process and Terraform to provision our Azure infrastructure and reference the Packer-built VM images for our Azure VMs.

Cloud architecture

In *Chapter 7*, we developed a similar solution using AWS and its equivalent offerings concerning VMs. As a result, our design for Azure will look rather similar. Many of the cloud services we use on AWS have equivalents to Microsoft Azure. This is largely because VMs, networks, and network security have stabilized in terms of how the industry views them. Don't expect to see radical differences in naming conventions and how things work. When working with this cloud computing paradigm, the differences between platforms are usually very subtle. Throughout this book, I will attempt to highlight synonymous terms across clouds to help you better translate your conceptual knowledge from one cloud to another.

Virtual network

VMs must be deployed within a virtual network. As you may recall from *Chapter 7* when we provisioned this solution on AWS, we needed to set up multiple subnets for our solution to span Availability Zones. That's because of the structure of virtual networks on AWS, how the virtual network is scoped to an AWS region, and how a subnet is scoped to an AWS Availability Zone. Azure is different.

On Azure, the virtual network and the subnets are scoped to a region. Zonal resiliency is built into the virtual network. Azure has two resiliency modes: one based on fault domains or *regional* and another based on Availability Zones or *zonal*. VMs can be provisioned in either of these two modes.

To provision a regional VM solution, you need to provision an availability set and specify how many fault domains you want to distribute your VMs across. When VMs are provisioned within this availability set, the Azure platform takes care to ensure that they are provisioned to hardware that does not share a common source of power and network switch, thus making it less likely that the entire workload will fail in the case of an outage isolated to a single fault domain. If you don't use an availability set, Azure will allocate your VMs based on available capacity and make no guarantee that your VMs won't be in the same fault domain.

To provision a zonal VM solution, you simply need to specify which Availability Zone to use to provision your VMs and ensure that you have more than one VM spread across multiple Availability Zones. An Availability Zone offers much more resiliency than a fault domain as instead of the Azure platform guaranteeing your VM doesn't share the same power source and network switch, it guarantees your VM is in a different physical data center within the region. In this book, we will focus on ensuring that our solution achieves zonal resiliency:

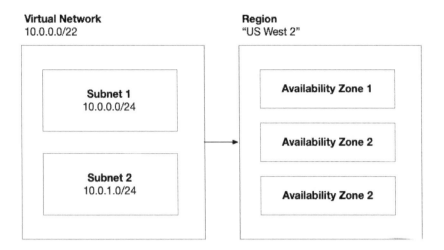

Figure 10.4 – Resource Azure virtual network architecture

In the preceding diagram, you can see that our virtual network and both its subnets can support VMs across all Availability Zones within the region:

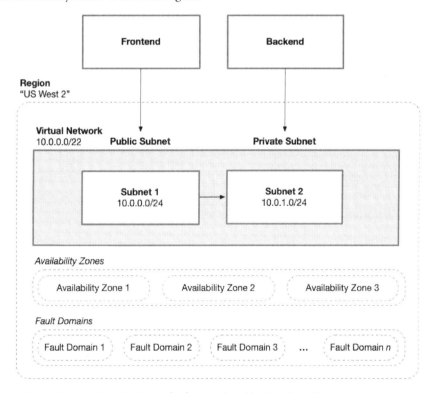

Figure 10.5 – Isolated subnets for frontend and backend application components

This means that we don't need to design our subnets based on the constraints of the cloud platform's resiliency boundaries as we do on AWS; we can design our subnets to match our workload's needs. In this case, we need a subnet for our solution's frontend, which hosts the ASP.NET Core Blazor web application, and we need a subnet for our solution's backend, which hosts the ASP.NET Core Web API. Whether we choose to provision VMs regionally, taking advantage of Azure's fault domains, or zonally, taking advantage of Azure's Availability Zones, does not affect the network design. Both options are available to us when we decide to provision VMs.

Network routing

In *Chapter 7*, when we set up this solution on AWS, we needed to configure an internet gateway, NAT gateways, and route tables for our VMs to have outbound access to the internet. On Azure, we don't need to configure equivalent components because Azure provides a default gateway and automatically configures VMs to use it. If we wanted to block internet access or route internet traffic another way, we would need to configure additional resources.

Load balancing

When discussing **load balancers** as a component of our architecture, we will inevitably use some well-established and familiar terms, but we will be using them in a different context. This can be confusing. Therefore, I hope to tackle the elephant in the room. Our solution has a frontend – the web application that serves up web pages for the end user's web browser. Our solution also has a backend – the REST Web API that our web application calls to talk to the database and perform stateful operations. Our solution will also leverage two load balancers: one to distribute load across our frontend web servers running the web application and another to distribute load across our backend web servers running the Web API:

Our Solution

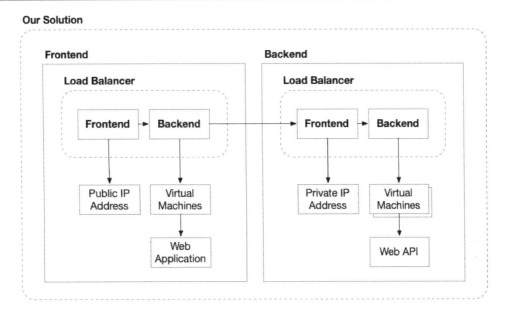

Figure 10.6 – Too many frontends and backends

Within the context of each load balancer, each load balancer will have a frontend and backend. It's important to note the context when using these terms as the frontend of our solution refers to a different architectural component at an altogether different architectural granularity. We need to understand that when we refer to the frontend of our solution, we are talking about all of the components that make up the frontend of our solution function properly, and when we are talking about the frontend of the *frontend* load balancer, we are talking about the networking endpoint that accepts traffic for the *frontend* of our solution.

In *Chapter 7*, when we set up this solution on AWS, we used the AWS **Application Load Balancer** (**ALB**) service. On Azure, we'll use the Azure Load Balancer service. Both services function very similarly but they are structured a little differently and use different terminology to describe similar concepts:

AWS	Azure	Description
ALB	Azure Load Balancer	Load balancer
Listener	Frontend IP Configuration	The singular endpoint that accepts incoming traffic on a load balancer
Target Group	Backend Address Pool	A collection of VMs that incoming traffic is forwarded to
Health Check	Health Probe	An endpoint published by each of the backend VMs that indicates it is healthy and ready to handle traffic

Table 10.1 – Mapping of synonymous load balancer components between AWS and Azure

As we discussed in *Chapter 4*, a load balancer provides a singular frontend endpoint and distributes network traffic across a multitude of backend VMs. On AWS, while they call this frontend endpoint a **listener**, on Azure, it is called the **frontend IP configuration**. Likewise, the backend VMs are called the **target group** in AWS, while they are called the **backend address pool** on Azure:

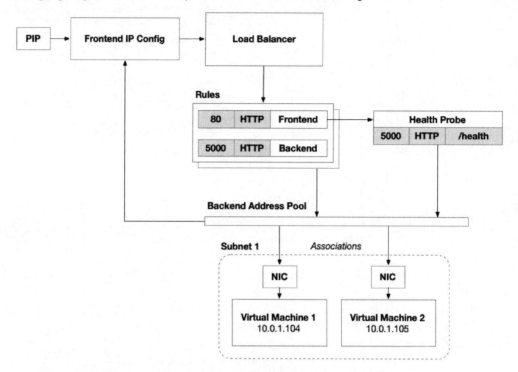

Figure 10.7 – Resource-isolated subnets for frontend and backend application components

Azure Load Balancer uses rules to determine how incoming traffic is routed to backend pools.

Azure Load Balancer organizes how it routes incoming traffic using rules. Each rule has a protocol, a frontend component, and a backend component. The rule's frontend component configures where and how the network traffic should come into the load balancer. This includes a port to expose, which frontend IP configuration to expose the port on, and what health probe it should use to determine which backend nodes are healthy and ready to receive traffic. The backend component of the rule specifies which backend address pool to route traffic to and what port to use.

The **health probe** is configured with its own protocol, port, and request path. This endpoint is hit regularly by the load balancer on each of the VMs within the backend address pool to verify they are healthy and ready to receive traffic. Because our application doesn't change, regardless of whether we deploy to AWS or Azure, the frontend of our solution – the web application – will continue to use the root path (/) and the backend – the REST Web API – will continue to use the custom health check endpoint we setup at /health.

Network security

In *Chapter 7* we set up four security groups in AWS for each logical stop that network traffic makes within our solution architecture. In Azure, we only need two security groups because Azure Load Balancer is automatically granted access to our VMs using the rules that we configured in it:

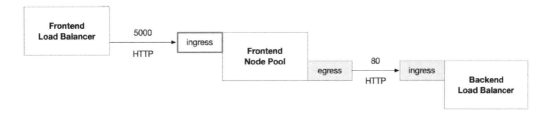

Figure 10.8 – Frontend node pool network traffic flow

From the perspective of VMs handling traffic within the frontend, they will receive traffic on port 5000 using the HTTP protocol. The C# application will make requests to the REST Web API hosted in the backend, but we'll be routing all our requests to the backend through the backend load balancer on port 80 using the HTTP protocol. On Azure, we don't need to explicitly allow this egress traffic within the network:

Figure 10.9 – Backend node pool network traffic flow

From the perspective of the VMs handling traffic within the backend, they will be receiving traffic on port 5000 using the HTTP protocol. The C# application code will be making requests to the PostgreSQL database on port 5432 using the HTTPS protocol. On Azure, we don't need to explicitly allow this egress traffic within the network.

Secrets management

Secrets such as database credentials or service access keys need to be stored securely. Each cloud platform has a service that provides this functionality. On Azure, this service is called **Azure Key Vault**:

AWS	Azure	Description
IAM	Microsoft Entra	Identity provider
Secrets Manager	Key Vault	Secure secret storage
IAM role	User-assigned managed identity	Identity for machine-to-machine interaction
IAM policy	Role-based access control (RBAC)	Provides permission to perform specific operations on specific services or resources
IAM role policy	Role assignment	Associates specific permissions with specific identities

Table 10.2 – Mapping synonymous identity and access management
components between AWS and Azure

Secrets stored in Azure Key Vault can be accessed by VMs once they have the necessary RBAC granted. In *Chapter 7*, we used an AWS IAM role assignment to allow a VM to do this. Azure works similarly by attaching one or more user-assigned managed identities to the VMs and then creating role assignments for the managed identities so that they have specific roles that grant the necessary permissions:

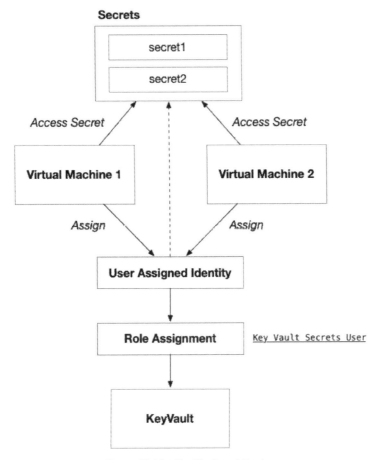

Figure 10.10 – Key Vault architecture

Granting the managed identity that is attached to the VMs access to the **Key Vault Secrets User** role will allow the VMs to read the secret values from Key Vault. This does not put the secrets on the machine. The VM will need to use the Azure CLI to access the Key Vault secrets.

VMs

Now that we have everything we need for our solution, we can finish by talking about where our application components will run: VMs provisioned on Azure's VM service. When provisioning VMs on Azure, you have two options. First, you can provision static VMs. In this approach, you need to specify key characteristics for every VM. The second option is to provision a **Virtual Machine Scale Set** (**VMSS**). This will allow you to dynamically scale up and down based on demand as well as auto-heal VMs that fail:

AWS	Azure	Description
EC2	VMs	VM service
AMI	VM image	VM image either from Marketplace or custom build (e.g., using tools such as Packer)
IAM role	User-assigned managed identity	Identity for machine-to-machine interaction
Auto Scaling group (ASG)	VMSS	Set of dynamically provisioned VMs that can be scaled up/down using a VM configuration template
Launch template	VM profile	Configuration template used to create new VMs

Table 10.3 – Mapping synonymous VM service components between AWS and Azure

In *Chapter 7*, we provisioned our solution using AWS **Elastic Cloud Compute** (**EC2**). Azure VMs share a similar structure to EC2 instances. Like on AWS, Azure VMs are connected to their corresponding subnet by way of a virtual network interface. However, on Azure, we have two types of network security rules: **network security groups** (**NSGs**) and **application security groups** (**ASGs**). While both are used to control traffic on Azure, NSGs focus on specifying lower-level network rules such as port and protocol filtering for network-level resources defined as IP address ranges. AGSs, on the other hand, provide a higher level of abstraction that allows you to group resources based on the role they play within the application:

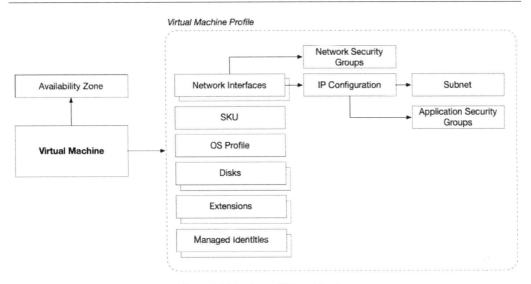

Figure 10.11 – Azure VM architecture

Alternatively, you can use an Azure VMSS to dynamically provision and manage the VMs. In this approach, you provide the VMSS with some configuration and parameters on when to scale up and when to scale down, and the VMSS will take care of everything else:

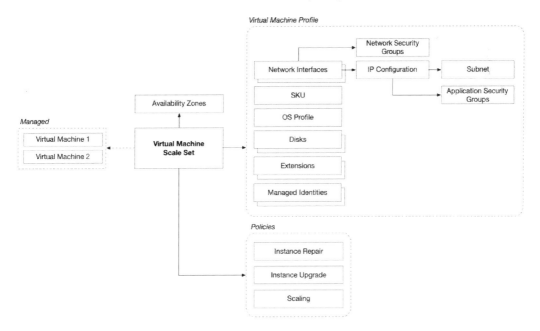

Figure 10.12 – Azure VMSS architecture

Azure VMSS allows you to provide fine-grained configuration for each of the VMs that it will spin up on your behalf. It also provides a set of policies that allow you to control the behavior of the VMSS relating to when instances fail unexpectedly, when Azure needs to update them, or whether to scale up or down the number of VMs.

Deployment architecture

Now that we have a good idea of what our cloud architecture is going to look like for our solution on Azure, we need to come up with a plan for how to provision our environments and deploy our code.

VM configuration

In our solution, we have two VM roles: the frontend role, which is responsible for handling web page requests from the end user's web browser, and the backend role, which is responsible for handling REST API requests from the web application. Each of these roles has a different code and different configuration that needs to be set. Each will require its own Packer template to build a VM image that we can use to launch a VM on Azure:

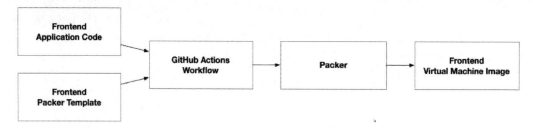

Figure 10.13 – Packer pipeline to build a VM image for the frontend

A GitHub Actions workflow that triggers off changes to the frontend application code and the frontend packer template will execute `packer build` and create a new VM image for the solution's frontend.

Both the frontend and the backend will have identical GitHub Actions workflows that execute `packer build`. The key difference between the workflows is the code bases that they execute against. Both the frontend and the backend might have slightly different operating system configurations, and both require different deployment packages for their respective application components:

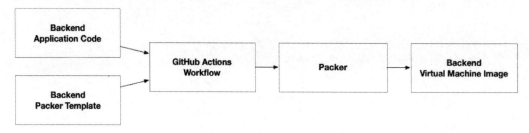

Figure 10.14 – Packer pipeline to build a VM image for the backend

It's important to note that the application code will be baked into the VM image rather than copied to an already running VM. This means that to update the software running on the VMs, each VM will need to be restarted so that it can be restarted with a new VM image containing the latest copy of the code.

This approach makes the VM image itself an immutable deployment artifact that is versioned and updated each time there is a release of the application code that needs to be deployed.

Cloud environment configuration

Once the VM images have been built for both the frontend and the backend, we can execute the final workflow that will both provision and deploy our solution to Azure:

Figure 10.15 – VM images as inputs to the Terraform code, which provisions the environment on Azure

The Terraform code base will have two input variables for the version of the VM image for both the frontend and the backend. When new versions of the application software need to be deployed, the input parameters for these versions will be incremented to reflect the target version for deployment. When the workflow is executed, `terraform apply` will simply replace the existing VMs with VMs using the new VM image.

Now that we have a solid plan for how we will implement both the cloud architecture using Azure and the deployment architecture using GitHub Actions, let's start building! In the next section, we'll break down the HCL code that we'll use to implement the Terraform and Packer solutions.

Building the solution

Now that we have a solid design for our solution, we can begin building it. As discussed in the previous section, we'll be using an Azure VM. As we did with AWS in *Chapter 7*, we'll need to package our application into VM images using Packer and then provision an environment that provisions an environment using these VM images.

Packer

In this section, we'll learn how to implement our Packer template provisioners so that we can install our .NET application code on a Linux VM. If you skipped *Chapters 7* through *9* due to a lack of interest in AWS, I can't hold that against you – particularly if your primary interest in reading this book is working on the Microsoft Azure cloud platform. However, I would encourage you to review the corresponding section within *Chapter 7* to see how we use Packer's provisioners to configure a Debian-based Linux VM with our .NET application code.

Azure plugin

As we discussed in *Chapter 4*, Packer – like Terraform – is an extensible command-line executable. Each cloud platform provides a plugin for Packer that encapsulates the integration with its services:

```
packer {
  required_plugins {
    azure = {
      source  = "github.com/hashicorp/azure"
      version = "~> 2.0.0"
    }
  }
}
```

In *Chapter 7*, we saw how to declare the Packer plugin for AWS as a required plugin. The preceding code demonstrates how to declare Azure's plugin instead – at the time of writing, the latest version is 2.0.0.

The Azure plugin for Packer provides an `azure-arm` builder that will generate Azure VM images by creating a new VM from a base image, executing the provisioners, taking a snapshot of the Azure managed disk, and creating an Azure managed image from it. Like the AWS plugin, this behavior is encapsulated within the Azure builder.

Just as the plugin for AWS encapsulated the logic to build VMs on AWS and its configuration was in AWS-centric terminology, so does the Azure plugin encapsulate all the logic to build VMs on Azure, and its configuration is in Azure-centric terminology. Packer does not try to create a standard builder interface across cloud platforms – rather, it isolates the cloud-specific configuration within the builders. This keeps things simple for users who know the target platform well and allows the builder to take advantage of any platform-specific features without additional layers of complexity by trying to rationalize the syntax across every platform.

As a result, the structure of the AWS and Azure builders is radically different in almost every way – from how they authenticate to how they look at marketplace images. There are some common fields and similarities, but they are very different animals.

The first big difference is how they pass authentication credentials. As we saw in *Chapter 7*, the AWS plugin allows us to use environment variables to pass in the AWS access key and secret key to authenticate with AWS. The Azure provider does not support this method and requires you to pass in all four attributes to authenticate using a Microsoft Entra (formerly Azure Active Directory) service principal. Those four attributes are as follows:

- **Tenant ID**: Unique identifier for the Microsoft Entra tenant

- **Subscription ID**: Unique identifier for the Microsoft Azure subscription

- **Client ID**: Unique identifier for the Microsoft Entra service principal that we will use as the identity of Terraform

- **Client secret**: Secret key for the Microsoft Entra service principal

The following code shows how the four Microsoft Azure credential attributes are passed into the Azure builder using input variables:

```
source "azure-arm" "vm" {
client_id        = var.arm\_client\_id
client\_secret    = var.arm\_client\_secret
subscription\_id = var.arm\_subscription\_id
tenant\_id        = var.arm\_tenant\_id


...
}
```

The following code shows how we reference the Azure marketplace version of the Ubuntu 22.04 Virtual Machine:

```
source "azure-arm" "vm" {

  ...


  image_offer     = "0001-com-ubuntu-server-jammy"
  image_publisher = "canonical"
  image_sku       = "22_04-lts"


  ...


}
```

Notice how, unlike in the AWS version, where we used a data source of `amazon-ami` to look up the same image in a specific AWS region, we don't need to do this on Microsoft Azure. Because of the way Azure structures marketplace images, there's no need to look up the region-specific unique identifier for the VM image.

The final part of the Azure builder should look very familiar to the AWS version:

```
source "azure-arm" "vm" {

  ...

  location                    = var.azure_primary_location
  communicator                = "ssh"
  os_type                     = "Linux"
  vm_size                     = var.vm_size
  allowed_inbound_ip_addresses = [var.agent_ipaddress]

}
```

In the preceding code, we see the same `communicator` attribute set to `ssh`, a `vm_size` attribute that corresponds to the AWS equivalent, `instance_type`, and an `allowed_inbound_ip_addresses` attribute that corresponds to the AWS equivalent, `temporary_security_group_source_cidrs`, which pokes a hole in the security group to allow the machine that GitHub Actions is executing on access to the temporary VM that Packer provisions.

Operating system configuration

To configure the operating system, we must install software dependencies (such as .NET 6.0), copy and deploy our application code's deployment package to the correct location in the local filesystem, configure a Linux service that runs on boot, and set up a local user and group with necessary access for the service to run as.

I expanded on these steps in detail in the corresponding section in *Chapter 7*, so I encourage you to review this section if you want to refresh your memory.

Platform-specific build tasks

Packer provides a way for you to execute provisioners only on particular builders. This allows you to accommodate platform-specific differences even within the operating system configuration.

In Microsoft Azure, we need to execute a platform-specific command as the last and final step before Packer shuts down the VM and creates the image. Those of you with experience setting up Microsoft Windows VM images will be familiar with a utility called `sysprep`. This tool is used to prepare a VM so that we can have an image created from its disk. Although we are not using a Windows operating system, Microsoft Azure needs us to execute a similar command so that we can prepare our Linux VM to have an image made:

```
provisioner "shell" {
  execute_command = local.execute_command
  inline = ["/usr/sbin/waagent -force -deprovision+user && export
HISTSIZE=0 && sync"]
  only = ["azure-arm"]
}
```

The archaic `waagent` command is of little importance. You just need to know that this command needs to be executed last for the VM image that Packer builds to be bootable when you launch a new VM from the image. However, do take notice of the `only` attribute, which takes a `list` value of `string`. The only value we have set in this `list` is `azure-arm`. This indicates to Packer that this provisioner only needs to be executed when we're building images using that plugin. As we know, the same Packer template can be used to do multi-targeting, which means you can build multiple images in the same template while targeting multiple different cloud platforms or regions. This means you can build the same VM image simultaneously on AWS, Azure, and Google Cloud. You could even build the same VM image on AWS in all 30+ regions. This isn't exactly practical as there are much better ways to replicate VM images across regions, but it can be done.

Terraform

As we discussed in our design, our solution is made up of two application components: the frontend and the backend. Each has an application code base that needs to be deployed. Since this is the first time we will be using the `azurerm` provider, we'll look at the basic provider setup and the configuration of the backend before we cover the nuts and bolts of each component of our architecture.

Provider setup

We need to specify all the providers that we intend to use in this solution within the `required_providers` block:

```
terraform {
  required_providers {
    azurerm = {
      source  = "hashicorp/azurerm"
      version = "~> 3.75.0"
    }
```

```
    cloudinit = {
      source  = "hashicorp/cloudinit"
      version = "~> 2.3.2"
    }
  }
  backend "azurerm" {
  }
}
```

We must also configure the Azure provider. Unlike the AWS provider, the Azure provider is not scoped to a particular region. This means you can provision resources across all Azure regions without declaring different Azure provider blocks:

```
provider "azurerm" {
  features {}
}
```

The Azure provider requires some additional parameters to specify the credentials to use to connect to Azure, but because these are sensitive values, we don't want to embed them in the code. We'll pass those values in later when we automate the deployment using the standard Azure credentials environment variables:

- **Tenant ID**: ARM_TENANT_ID

- **Subscription ID**: ARM_SUBSCRIPTION_ID

- **Client ID**: ARM_CLIENT_ID

- **Client secret**: ARM_CLIENT_SECRET

Backend

Because we will be using a CI/CD pipeline to provision and maintain our environment in the long term, we need to set up a remote backend for our Terraform state. Because our solution will be hosted on Azure, we'll use the Azure Blob storage backend to store our Terraform state.

Just like the Azure provider, we don't want to hard code the backend configuration in our code, so we'll simply set up a placeholder for the backend:

```
terraform {

  ...

  backend "azurerm" {
  }
}
```

We'll configure the backend's parameters using the `-backend-config` parameters when we run `terraform init` in our CI/CD pipeline.

Input variables

It's good practice to pass in short names that identify the application's name and the application's environment. This allows you to embed consistent naming conventions across the resources that make up your solution. This makes it easier to identify and track resources from the Azure portal.

The `primary_region`, `vnet_cidr_block`, and `az_count` input variables drive key architectural characteristics of the deployment. They can't be hard-coded as it would limit the reusability of the Terraform code base.

The `vnet_cidr_block` input variable establishes the virtual network address space, which is often tightly regulated by an enterprise governance body. There is usually a process to ensure that teams across an organization do not use IP address ranges that conflict, thus making it impossible in the future to allow those two applications to integrate or integrate with shared network resources within the enterprise.

The `az_count` input variable allows us to configure how much redundancy we want within our solution. This will affect the high availability of the solution but also the cost of the deployment. As you can imagine, cost is also a tightly regulated characteristic of cloud infrastructure deployments.

Consistent naming and tagging

Unlike the AWS console, Azure is designed in such a way that it is extremely easy to get an application-centric view of your deployment. For this, you can use resource groups:

```
resource "aws_vpc" "main" {
  cidr_block = var.vpc_cidr_block

  tags = {
    Name        = "${var.application_name}-${var.environment_name}-
network"
    application = var.application_name
    environment = var.environment_name
  }
}
resource "azurerm_virtual_network" "main" {

  ...

  tags = {
    application = var.application_name
    environment = var.environment_name
```

```
    }

}
```

It's still important to tag the resources that you deploy that indicate what application and what environment they belong to. This helps with other reporting needs, such as budgets and compliance. Almost all resources within the Azure provider have a map attribute called tags. Unlike AWS, each resource has a name value as a required attribute.

Virtual network

Just as we did in *Chapter 7*, we need to construct a virtual network and keep its address space as tight as possible to avoid gobbling up unnecessary address space for the broader organization in the future:

```
resource "azurerm_virtual_network" "main" {

  name                = "vnet-${var.application_name}-${var.
environment_name}"
  location            = azurerm_resource_group.main.location
  resource_group_name = azurerm_resource_group.main.name
  address_space       = [var.vnet_cidr_block]

}
```

Network creation in Azure is simpler than what we did with AWS because we don't have to segment our subnets based on Availability Zone:

```
resource "azurerm_subnet" "frontend" {

  name                 = "snet-frontend"
  resource_group_name  = azurerm_resource_group.main.name
  virtual_network_name = azurerm_virtual_network.main.name
  address_prefixes     = [cidrsubnet(var.vnet_cidr_block, 2, 1)]

}
```

Load balancing

As we discussed in the design, the Azure Load Balancer service is structured quite a bit differently than AWS's equivalent offering:

```
resource "azurerm_public_ip" "frontend" {
  name                = "pip-lb-${var.application_name}-${var.
environment_name}-frontend"
  location            = azurerm_resource_group.main.location
  resource_group_name = azurerm_resource_group.main.name
```

```
  allocation_method   = "Static"
  sku                 = "Standard"
  zones               = [1, 2, 3]
}


resource "azurerm_lb" "frontend" {
  name                = "lb-${var.application_name}-${var.environment_
name}-frontend"
  location            = azurerm_resource_group.main.location
  resource_group_name = azurerm_resource_group.main.name
  sku                 = "Standard"

  frontend_ip_configuration {
    name                 = "PublicIPAddress"
    public_ip_address_id = azurerm_public_ip.frontend.id
    zones                = [1, 2, 3]
  }
}
```

It's important to call out that to achieve zonal resiliency, we need to ensure that all components of our architecture are deployed in a zone-resilient way. This often requires setting the zones attribute and specifying which Availability Zones we want to provision into.

The backend configuration of Azure Load Balancer is a simple logical container for the backend address pool:

```
resource "azurerm_lb_backend_address_pool" "frontend" {
  loadbalancer_id = azurerm_lb.frontend.id
  name            = "frontend-pool"
}
```

This logical container must be linked to either static VMs or a VMSS:

```
resource "azurerm_network_interface_backend_address_pool_association"
"frontend" {

  count = var.az_count

  network_interface_id   = azurerm_network_interface.frontend[count.
index].id
  ip_configuration_name  = "internal"
  backend_address_pool_id = azurerm_lb_backend_address_pool.frontend.
id

}
```

In the preceding backend address pool association resource, we are iterating over `var.az_count`. This is the same number that we iterate over the VMs, which allows us to put a single VM into each Availability Zone. Unlike AWS, where the load balancer rules are split between a listener and a target group configuration, an Azure load balancer rule combines the two and then links them to a corresponding health probe:

```
resource "azurerm_lb_probe" "frontend_probe_http" {
  loadbalancer_id = azurerm_lb.frontend.id
  name            = "http"
  protocol        = "Http"
  port            = 5000
  request_path    = "/"
}


resource "azurerm_lb_rule" "frontend_http" {
  loadbalancer_id                = azurerm_lb.frontend.id
  name                           = "HTTP"
  protocol                       = "Tcp"
  frontend_port                  = 80
  backend_port                   = 5000
  frontend_ip_configuration_name = "PublicIPAddress"
  probe_id                       = azurerm_lb_probe.frontend_probe_
http.id
  backend_address_pool_ids       = [azurerm_lb_backend_address_pool.
frontend.id]
  disable_outbound_snat          = true
}
```

Notice how the load balancer rule connects many of the components, including the frontend IP configuration, the listener on AWS, the health probe, and the backend address pool – the target group on AWS.

Network security

First, we need to set up the logical ASG for each application architectural component. We'll have one for the frontend and one for the backend:

```
resource "azurerm_application_security_group" "frontend" {

  name                = "asg-${var.application_name}-${var.
environment_name}-frontend"
  resource_group_name = azurerm_resource_group.main.name
  location            = azurerm_resource_group.main.location

}
```

Next, we need to create NSGs that allow the necessary traffic into each of the ASGs:

```
resource "azurerm_network_security_group" "frontend" {

  name                  = "nsg-${var.application_name}-${var.
environment_name}-frontend"
  resource_group_name = azurerm_resource_group.main.name
  location            = azurerm_resource_group.main.location

}

resource "azurerm_network_security_rule" "frontend_http" {

  resource_group_name                          = azurerm_resource_group.
main.name
  network_security_group_name                  = azurerm_network_
security_group.frontend.name
  name                                         = "allow-http"
  priority                                     = "2001"
  access                                       = "Allow"
  direction                                    = "Inbound"
  protocol                                     = "Tcp"
  source_port_range                            = "*"
  destination_port_range                       = "5000"
  source_address_prefix                        = "*"
  destination_address_prefix                   = "*"
  destination_application_security_group_ids = [azurerm_application_
security_group.frontend.id]

}
```

Secrets management

First, we'll set up Key Vault:

```
resource "azurerm_key_vault" "main" {
  name                  = "kv-${var.application_name}-${var.
environment_name}"
  location            = azurerm_resource_group.main.location
  resource_group_name = azurerm_resource_group.main.name
  tenant_id           = data.azurerm_client_config.current.
tenant_id
  soft_delete_retention_days = 7
  purge_protection_enabled  = false
  sku_name                  = "standard"
  enable_rbac_authorization = true
}
```

Then, we'll set up a managed identity for each application architectural component:

```
resource "azurerm_user_assigned_identity" "frontend" {

    name                = "${var.application_name}-${var.environment_
name}-frontend"
    location            = azurerm_resource_group.main.location
    resource_group_name = azurerm_resource_group.main.name

}
```

Next, we'll grant the managed identity the necessary privileges using Azure role assignments:

```
resource "azurerm_role_assignment" "frontend_keyvault" {
    scope                = azurerm_key_vault.main.id
    role_definition_name = "Key Vault Secrets User"
    principal_id         = azurerm_user_assigned_identity.frontend.
principal_id
}
```

VMs

First, we'll obtain the VM image from our input variables. We built this VM image with Packer and provisioned it into a different Azure resource group:

```
data "azurerm_image" "frontend" {
    name                = var.frontend_image.name
    resource_group_name = var.frontend_image.resource_group_name
}
```

Then, we'll create the network interface for each VM by iterating over the var.az_count input variable:

```
resource "azurerm_network_interface" "frontend" {

    count = var.az_count

    name                = "nic-${var.application_name}-${var.
environment_name}-frontend${count.index}"
    location            = azurerm_resource_group.main.location
    resource_group_name = azurerm_resource_group.main.name

    ip_configuration {
        name                          = "internal"
        subnet_id                     = azurerm_subnet.frontend.id
        private_ip_address_allocation = "Dynamic"
    }
}
```

Finally, we'll set up the VM with all the necessary attributes and link it to the network interface, the VM image, and the managed identity:

```
resource "azurerm_linux_virtual_machine" "frontend" {

  count = var.az_count

  name                 = "vm-${var.application_name}-${var.environment_
name}-frontend${count.index}"
  resource_group_name = azurerm_resource_group.main.name
  location            = azurerm_resource_group.main.location
  size                = "Standard_F2"
  admin_username      = var.admin_username
  zone                = count.index + 1

  network_interface_ids = [
    azurerm_network_interface.frontend[count.index].id
  ]

  admin_ssh_key {
    username   = var.admin_username
    public_key = tls_private_key.ssh.public_key_openssh
  }

  os_disk {
    caching              = "ReadWrite"
    storage_account_type = "Standard_LRS"
  }

  source_image_id = data.azurerm_image.frontend.id
  user_data       = data.cloudinit_config.frontend.rendered

}
```

With that, we've implemented the Packer and Terraform solutions and have a working code base that will build VM images for both our frontend and backend application components and provision our cloud environment into Azure. In the next section, we'll dive into the YAML and Bash and implement the GitHub Actions workflows.

Automating the deployment

As we discussed in our design, our solution is made up of two application components: the frontend and the backend. Each has a code base consisting of application code and operating system configuration encapsulated within a Packer template. These two application components are then deployed into a cloud environment on Azure that's defined within our Terraform code base.

Just as we did in *Chapter 7* with the AWS solution, there is an additional code base that we have to discuss: our automation pipelines on GitHub Actions.

In *Chapter 7*, we went over the folder structure for our code base and where our GitHub Actions fit in so that we know that our automation pipelines are called workflows, and they're stored in `/.github/workflows`. Each of our code bases is stored in its respective folder. Our solutions source code repository's folder structure will look like this:

- `.github`
  - `workflows`
  - `dotnet`
    - `backend`
    - `frontend`
  - `packer`
    - `backend`
    - `frontend`
  - `terraform`

As per our design, we will have GitHub Actions workflows that will execute Packer and build VM images for both the frontend (for example, `packer-frontend.yaml`) and the backend (for example, `packer-backend.yaml`). We'll also have workflows that will run `terraform plan` and `terraform apply`:

- `.github`
  - `workflows`
    - `packer-backend.yaml`
    - `packer-frontend.yaml`
    - `terraform-apply.yaml`
    - `terraform-plan.yaml`

In *Chapter 7*, we went into greater detail on the GitFlow process and how it interacts with our GitHub Actions workflows, so for now, let's dig into how these pipelines will differ when targeting the Azure platform.

Packer

In *Chapter 7*, we went into great detail about each step of the GitHub Actions workflow that executes Packer to build VM images. Thanks to the nature of Packer's cloud-agnostic architecture, this overwhelmingly stays the same. The only thing that changes is the final step where we execute Packer.

Because Packer needs to be configured to build a VM on Microsoft Azure, we need to pass in different input variables that are Azure-specific. This includes the Microsoft Azure credential attributes, an Azure region, and an Azure resource group name.

Just as we did with the input variables for the Packer template for AWS, we must ensure that all Azure input variables are prefixed with `azure_`. This will help if we ever want to introduce multi-targeting as many cloud platforms will have similar required inputs, such as target region and VM size. While most clouds will have similar required inputs, the input values are not interchangeable.

For example, both Azure and AWS require you to specify the region that you want Packer to provide the temporary VM into and the resulting VM image to be stored. On Azure, the region has a value of `westus2`, while on AWS, it has a value of `us-west-2`. They may seem very similar, but they are miles apart (pun intended). Azure West US 2 region is completely different than AWS's West US 2 region – in fact, besides just being on different cloud platforms, they are physically different locations, with Azure's West US 2 region being located in Washington State and AWS's West US 2 region being located in Oregon. Neighbors, yes, the same thing – hardly.

This goes back to Packer's strategy of isolating platform-specific configuration within the builders. Therefore, if we are going to do multi-targeting, the AWS plugin is going to need input variables that are AWS-specific and the Azure plugin is going to need input variables that are Azure-specific. Hence, when we merge these plugins into one Packer template, we'll need input variables for both.

As a result, our `aws_primary_region`, which has a value of `us-west-2`, can sit right next to our `azure_primary_region`, which has a value of `westus2`, without any conflicts or confusion. Likewise, our `aws_instance_type` with a value of `t2.small` can sit right next to our `azure_vm_size` with a value of `Standard_DS2_v2`. The differences can get even more radical as you take advantage of more platform-specific capabilities within the builders.

The GitHub Actions workflow YAML files are identical to Azure, except for the additional input variables that need to be specified:

```
- id: build
  name: Packer Build
  env:
    PKR_VAR_arm_subscription_id: ${{ vars.ARM_SUBSCRIPTION_ID }}
    PKR_VAR_arm_tenant_id: ${{ vars.ARM_TENANT_ID }}
    PKR_VAR_arm_client_id: ${{ vars.PACKER_ARM_CLIENT_ID }}
    PKR_VAR_arm_client_secret: ${{ secrets.PACKER_ARM_CLIENT_SECRET }}
    PKR_VAR_image_version: ${{ steps.image-version.outputs.version }}
```

```
    PKR_VAR_agent_ipaddress: ${{ steps.agent-ipaddress.outputs.
ipaddress }}
  working-directory: ${{ env.WORKING_DIRECTORY }}
  run: |
    packer init ./
    packer build -var-file=variables.pkrvars.hcl ./
```

The preceding code references the four Azure credential attributes, which are stored as GitHub Actions variables and secrets, and transfers them to Packer using environment variables with the `PKR_VAR_` prefix.

Terraform

With both of our VM images built and their versions input into our `tfvars` file, our Terraform automation pipeline is ready to take the reigns and not only provision our environment but deploy our solution as well (although not technically). The deployment was technically done within the `packer build` process, with the physical deployment packages being copied to the home directory and the Linux service setup primed and ready. Terraform is finishing the job by actually launching VMs using these images.

In *Chapter 7*, we went into great detail about each step of the GitHub Actions workflow that executes Terraform to provision the cloud environment and deploy the application code. Thanks to the nature of Terraform's cloud-agnostic architecture, this overwhelmingly stays the same. The only thing that changes is the final step where we execute Terraform.

Just like we did in *Chapter 7* with the AWS provider, we can set the authentication context using environment variables that are specific to the `azurerm` provider. In this case, the four Azure credentials attributes are passed in with the following environment variables:

- **Tenant ID**: `ARM_TENANT_ID`
- **Subscription ID**: `ARM_SUBSCRIPTION_ID`
- **Client ID**: `ARM_CLIENT_ID`
- **Client secret**: `ARM_CLIENT_SECRET`

Just like we did in *Chapter 7* with the AWS provider, we need to configure the Azure-specific backend that stores the Terraform state using the `-backend-config` command-line arguments to the `terraform init` command. Unlike AWS, which only specifies an S3 bucket name to configure the backend to save the Terraform state to S3, to configure the Azure backend, we need to specify three fields to triangulate a location in Azure Blob storage to save the Terraform state – a resource group, storage account, and Blob storage container.

The hierarchy of Azure resources looks like this:

- Resource group

  - Storage account

    - Blob storage container

      - Terraform state files

Like with the AWS provider, the backend uses a *key* and the Terraform workspace name to uniquely identify the location to store state files:

```
- id: apply
  name: Terraform Apply
  env:
    ARM_SUBSCRIPTION_ID: ${{ vars.ARM_SUBSCRIPTION_ID }}
    ARM_TENANT_ID: ${{ vars.ARM_TENANT_ID }}
    ARM_CLIENT_ID: ${{ vars.TERRAFORM_ARM_CLIENT_ID }}
    ARM_CLIENT_SECRET: ${{ secrets.TERRAFORM_ARM_CLIENT_SECRET }}
    BACKEND_RESOURCE_GROUP_NAME: ${{ vars.BACKEND_RESOURCE_GROUP_NAME
}}
    BACKEND_STORAGE_ACCOUNT_NAME: ${{ vars.BACKEND_STORAGE_ACCOUNT_
NAME }}
    BACKEND_STORAGE_CONTAINER_NAME: ${{ vars.BACKEND_STORAGE_
CONTAINER_NAME }}
    TF_BACKEND_KEY: ${{ env.APPLICATION_NAME }}-${{ env.ENVIRONMENT_
NAME }}
  working-directory: ${{ env.WORKING_DIRECTORY }}
  run: |
    terraform init \
      -backend-config="resource_group_name=$BACKEND_RESOURCE_GROUP_
NAME" \
      -backend-config="storage_account_name=$BACKEND_STORAGE_ACCOUNT_
NAME" \
      -backend-config="container_name=$BACKEND_STORAGE_CONTAINER_NAME"
\
      -backend-config="key=$TF_BACKEND_KEY"

    terraform apply -auto-approve
```

Notice how, unlike with the AWS solution, we don't need to perform a targeted `terraform apply`. This is because we don't need to do dynamic calculations based on the number of Availability Zones in the region to configure our virtual network. This is due to Azure Virtual Network and its subnets spanning all Availability Zones within the region whereas, on AWS, a subnet is constrained to a specific Availability Zone within the parent virtual network's region.

These subtle architectural differences between the cloud platforms can create radical structural changes even when deploying the same solution using the same technologies. It is a sobering reminder that while knowledge of the core concepts we looked at in *Chapters 4* through *6* will help us transcend to a multi-cloud point of view, to implement practical solutions, we need to understand the subtle nuances of each platform.

Summary

In this chapter, we built a multi-tier cloud architecture using Azure VMs with a fully operation GitFlow process and an end-to-end CI/CD pipeline using GitHub Actions.

In the next chapter, our fearless leader at Söze Enterprises will be throwing us into turmoil with some big new ideas, and we'll have to respond to his call to action. It turns out our CEO, Keyser, has been up late watching some YouTube videos about the next big thing – containers – and after talking with his pal Satya on his superyacht, he has decided that we need to refactor our whole solution to run on Docker and Kubernetes. Luckily, the good people at Microsoft have a service that might help us out: **Azure Kubernetes Service (AKS)**.

11

Containerize on Azure – Building Solutions with Azure Kubernetes Service

In the previous chapter, we built and automated our solution on Azure utilizing Azure VMs. We built VM images with Packer and provisioned our VMs using Terraform. In this chapter, we'll follow a similar path, but instead of working with VMs, we'll look at hosting our application in containers within a Kubernetes cluster.

To achieve this, we'll need to alter our approach by ditching Packer and replacing it with Docker to create a deployable artifact for our application. Once again, we'll be using the `azurerm` provider for Terraform and revisiting the `kubernetes` provider for Terraform that we saw when we took the same step while on our journey with AWS.

Since an overwhelming majority of this remains the same when we move to Azure, we won't revisit these topics at the same length in this chapter. However, I would encourage you to put a bookmark in *Chapter 8* and reference it frequently.

This chapter covers the following topics:

- Laying the foundation
- Designing the solution
- Building the solution
- Automating the deployment

Laying the foundation

Our story continues through the lens of Söze Enterprises, founded by the enigmatic Turkish billionaire Keyser Söze. Our team has been hard at work building the next-generation autonomous vehicle orchestration platform. Previously, we had hoped to leapfrog the competition by leveraging Azure's rock-solid platform, leveraging our team's existing skills, and focusing on feature development. The team was just getting into their groove when a curveball came out of nowhere.

Over the weekend, our elusive executive was influenced by a rendezvous with Scott Guthrie, the President of Microsoft's Cloud + AI Division, in Abu Dhabi. The Yas Marina Circuit was buzzing with energy. The sun was setting, casting a golden glow over the track as fans and celebrities gathered for the season-ending Abu Dhabi Grand Prix. While in the exclusive Paddock Club, Keyser spotted Scott "Gu" in his iconic red polo near the hors d'oeuvres. Scott excitedly shared news about some recent improvements to **Azure Kubernetes Service (AKS)**. Keyser was enchanted by the prospect of more efficient resource utilization, leading to improved cost optimization and faster deployment and rollback times, and he was hooked. His new autonomous vehicle platform needed to harness the power of the cloud, and container-based architecture was the way to do it. So, he decided to accelerate his plans to adopt cloud-native architecture!

The news of transitioning to a container-based architecture means reevaluating their approach, diving into new technologies, and possibly even reshuffling team dynamics. For the team, containers were always the long-term plan, but now, things need to be sped up, which will require a significant investment in time, resources, and training.

As the team scrambles to adjust their plans, they can't help but feel a mix of excitement and apprehension. They know that they are part of something groundbreaking under Keyser's leadership. His vision for the future of autonomous vehicles is bold and transformative. And while his methods may be unconventional, they have learned that his instincts are often right. In this chapter, we'll explore this transformation from VMs to containers using Microsoft Azure.

Designing the solution

As we saw in the previous chapter, where we built our solution using VMs on Azure, we had full control over the operating system configuration through the VM images we provisioned with Packer. Just as we did when we went through the same process on our journey with AWS in *Chapter 8*, we'll need to introduce a new tool to replace VM images with container images – Docker:

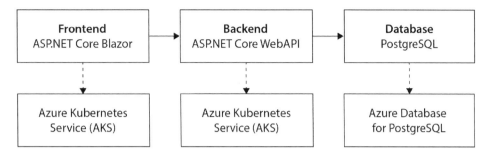

Figure 11.1 – Logical architecture for the autonomous vehicle platform

Our application architecture, comprising a frontend, a backend, and a database, will remain the same but we will need to provision different resources with Terraform and harness new tools from Docker and Kubernetes to automate the deployment of our solution to this new infrastructure:

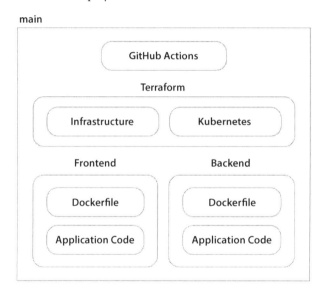

Figure 11.2 – Source control structure of our repository

In this solution, we'll have seven parts. We still have the application code and Dockerfiles (replacing the Packer-based VM images) for both the frontend and backend. We still have GitHub Actions to implement our CI/CD process, but now we have two Terraform code bases – one for provisioning the underlying infrastructure to Azure and another for provisioning our application to the Kubernetes cluster hosted on AKS. Then, we have the two code bases for our application's frontend and backend.

Cloud architecture

There will be many similarities between the work that we did in *Chapter 8* when we performed a similar transition from VMs to containers using AWS. We'll try and focus only on the key differences and avoid retreading the same ground. To obtain a complete and multi-cloud perspective, I'd encourage you to read *Chapter 8* (in case you skipped it) as well as the upcoming chapter, where we'll tackle the same problem on **Google Cloud Platform (GCP)**.

Virtual network

In the previous chapter, we set up a virtual network for two distinct groups of VMs, and then we connected our application to a database-managed service. When setting up a virtual network for a Kubernetes cluster, we'll use a similar approach. However, the considerations are slightly different. We no longer have distinct and loose VMs where we host different components of our application. However, depending on the configuration of our Kubernetes cluster, we may need to consider the placement of the different node pools that we configure and other services that we want to provision within that network to allow the workloads we host on Kubernetes to access them:

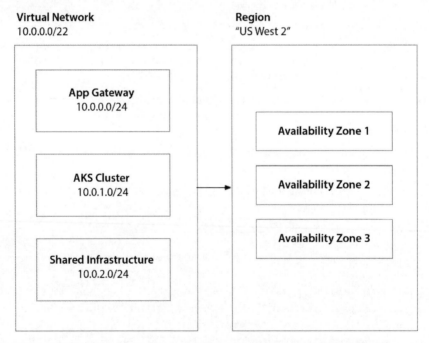

Figure 11.3 – With AKS, virtual network subnets are organized along
infrastructure boundaries rather than application boundaries

In its simplest form, a single subnet can be designated for all the node pools within an AKS cluster, but this can be very limiting as your workload needs to scale up over time. For more advanced scenarios, you should carefully consider the segmentation of your subnets based on your node pool design and scale considerations for each of your workloads. In doing so, you can provide better network isolation for the various workloads you host on the cluster.

As we saw when working with Amazon's Kubernetes offering in *Chapter 8*, Azure's Kubernetes offering also supports two networking modes: **Kubenet** and **CNI**. For this book, we'll be focusing on Kubenet as it's the most commonly used option.

Container registry

Just as we saw with AWS, Azure has a robust container registry service known as **Azure Container Registry** (**ACR**). It acts as a private registry for hosting and managing your container images and Helm charts. As we did in the expedition along the Amazon, we'll be using Docker to publish our container images to this repository so that we can reference them later from the Terraform code that provisions resources to our AKS cluster. We'll need to grant our cluster access using Azure managed identities and Azure **Role-Based Access Control** (**RBAC**), which is similar to how we granted access to Amazon EKS using AWS's IAM service policies.

Load balancing

One of the biggest advantages of hosting your container-based workloads using a Kubernetes-managed service is that much of the underlying infrastructure is automatically configured and maintained on your behalf. The service interprets your Kubernetes resource configuration and provisions the necessary resources within the cluster to properly configure Azure to support your workloads. Sometimes, this is handled transparently, and other times, there are special hooks that allow you more control over the configuration of the underlying resources on Azure.

In this manner, under the hood, AKS streamlines load balancing using either a basic Azure load balancer or a more feature-rich Azure application gateway. AKS manages the creation and configuration of these load balancers when services of the `LoadBalancer` type are created within the Kubernetes cluster. For more control, users can also utilize Ingress controllers such as NGINX or the Azure **Application Gateway Ingress Controller** (**AGIC**) for advanced routing, SSL termination, and other capabilities:

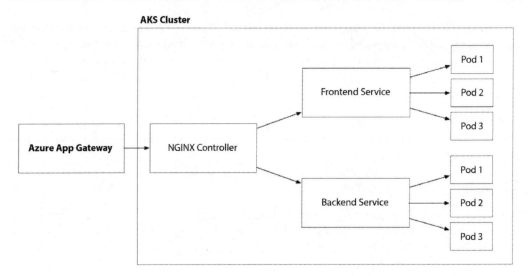

Figure 11.4 – Network traffic flow of an AKS cluster

As we saw in *Chapter 8* when working with AWS, we will be using the NGINX ingress controller but this time, we'll be provisioning an Azure Application Gateway service to route traffic to NGINX. This works a bit differently than on AWS, where the NGINX ingress controller automatically configures the ALB through Kubernetes annotation. With Azure, we need to set up the NGINX ingress controller and then provision Azure Application Gateway and configure it to forward traffic to NGINX.

Network security

In AKS, network security is managed in a manner akin to the practices described in *Chapter 10* for VMs as they are deployed within Azure virtual networks, thus allowing them to integrate seamlessly with existing Azure networking features. However, because Kubernetes has an overlay network called Kubenet, which is the network on which our workloads (or pods) live, we need to use Kubernetes Network policies to control network traffic between our workloads based on Kubernetes tags or namespaces. There are more advanced networking security capabilities when you are working with Azure CNI and other open source solutions such as Calico, but these are beyond the scope of this book.

Secrets management

Just as we saw on our tour down the Amazon, Azure's Kubernetes offering also integrates with other Azure services, such as Azure's secret management service, **Azure Key Vault**. This integration is done through a combination of an AKS extension being enabled on the cluster itself and Kubernetes resources that are provisioned within the cluster, creating Kubernetes resources that our pods can use as a conduit to the secrets hosted on Azure Key Vault. Again, nothing is stopping us from using native Kubernetes secrets, but Azure Key Vault provides a much more streamlined and secure mechanism for granting Azure secrets. It allows us to keep secrets up-to-date to avoid outages when secret rotations occur, and it allows us to use managed identities to access the secrets rather than storing them on the cluster itself.

Just as we saw in *Chapter 8* when building our solution with AWS EKS, we need to facilitate a bridge between Kubernetes and the cloud platform's identity management system. On AWS, that was IAM; on Azure, that's Entra ID. The process is largely the same but the terminology is different:

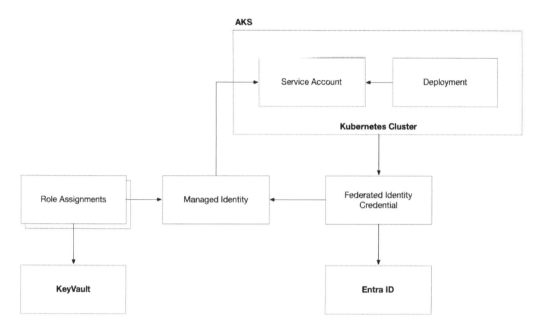

Figure 11.5 – AKS with Workload Identity

First, we need to create a managed identity that will represent the workload. This is an Azure resource that represents an Entra ID identity that is managed by the Azure platform. As we did with EKS, we need to federate between the Kubernetes cluster and Entra ID. On Azure, we do that by creating a federated identity credential that links the managed identity, the AKS cluster's internal Open ID Connect provider, and Entra ID. Like on AWS, we plant a seed for this managed identity so that it can linked to a Kubernetes service account resource that will be provisioned later within Kubernetes:

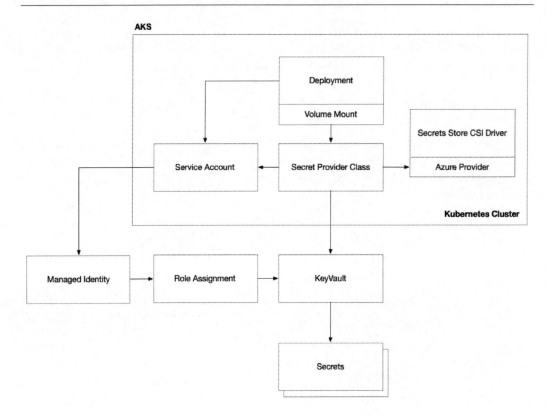

Figure 11.6 – AKS Secrets Manager integration

After Workload Identity has been established, we can grant access to Azure resources such as Key Vault and databases such as Azure Cosmos DB or Azure SQL Database. Just as we did in *Chapter 8* with EKS, we'll use the secrets store CSI driver and the Azure provider to integrate our Kubernetes deployments with Azure Key Vault.

Kubernetes cluster

Finally, creating a Kubernetes cluster using AKS involves a few critical components. As we've established, we need a virtual network, managed identities, and sufficient RBAC to access the resources our cluster needs, such as container registries and Azure Key Vault secrets. However, the main components of our Kubernetes cluster are the node pools, which provide compute resources to host our pods:

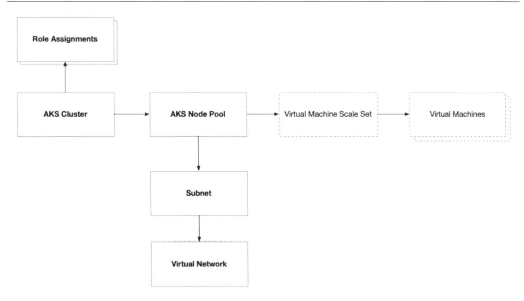

Figure 11.7 – Anatomy of an AKS cluster

By default, every AKS cluster comes with a default node pool, which is where Kubernetes' system services are hosted. However, we can add additional node pools either to isolate our application workloads or to grant access to different types of computing resources, such as different hardware profiles to meet the specific needs of different workloads.

Deployment architecture

As we saw with the cloud architecture, there were many similarities between the work that we did in *Chapter 8* with AWS. The deployment architecture will mirror what we saw in *Chapter 8* as well. We looked at the differences in the Terraform provider in the previous chapter when we configured the `azurerm` provider to provision our solution to Azure VMs.

Now, using container-based architecture, the only real differences from the way we deployed in *Chapter 8* with AWS will be the way we authenticate with the container registry and the Kubernetes cluster. I encourage you to review the deployment architectural approach outlined in the corresponding section of *Chapter 8*. In the next section, we'll go into the details of building the same solution on Azure, but again, we'll take care not to re-tread the same ground.

In this section, we reviewed the key changes in our architecture as we transitioned from VM-based architecture to container-based architecture. We were careful not to retread the ground we covered in *Chapter 8*, where we went through this transformation first on AWS. In the next section, we'll get tactical in building the solution, but again, we'll be careful to build on the foundations we built in the previous chapter when we first set up our solution on Microsoft Azure using VMs.

Building the solution

In this section, we'll be taking our theoretical knowledge and applying it to a tangible, functioning solution while harnessing the power of Docker, Terraform, and Kubernetes on the Microsoft Azure platform. Some parts of this process will require significant change, such as when we provision our Azure infrastructure using Terraform; other parts will have minor changes, such as the Kubernetes configuration that we use to deploy our application to our Kubernetes cluster; and some will have almost no change whatsoever, such as when we build and push our Docker images to our container registry.

Docker

In this section, we'll learn how to implement our Dockerfile, which installs our .NET application code and runs the service in a container. If you skipped *Chapters 7* through *9* due to a lack of interest in AWS, I can't hold that against you – particularly if your primary interest in reading this book is working on the Microsoft Azure cloud platform. However, I encourage you to review the corresponding section within *Chapter 8* to see how we use Docker to configure a container with our .NET application code.

Infrastructure

As we discussed in the previous section, much of the infrastructure is unchanged when using container-based architecture. Therefore, in this section, we'll be focusing on what's different when we use Azure's Kubernetes managed service.

Container registry

The first component we need to provision is our **container registry**. The container registry is often provisioned as part of a separate deployment that's reserved for shared infrastructure that is reused across multiple applications. This can help when you have a common set of custom-built images that multiple teams or projects need to use in their applications or services. However, you should keep in mind that the container registry does act as an important security boundary, so if you want to ensure that application teams can only access images built for their applications, you should provision an isolated container registry for each project team:

```
resource "azurerm_container_registry" "main" {

  name                      = replace("acr${var.application_name}${var.
environment_name}", "-", "")
  resource_group_name       = azurerm_resource_group.main.name
  location                  = azurerm_resource_group.main.location
  sku                       = "Premium"
  admin_enabled             = true
  zone_redundancy_enabled   = true


}
```

The preceding code provisions the Azure container registry. It's important to note that this resource has very specific requirements for the name:

```
resource "azurerm_role_assignment" "acr_push" {

  count = length(var.container_registry_pushers)

  scope                 = azurerm_container_registry.main.id
  role_definition_name  = "AcrPush"
  principal_id          = var.container_registry_pushers[count.index]


}
```

The preceding code creates a role assignment that will allow different users to push container images to this container registry. This is a critical requirement that allows our GitHub Action to publish the Docker image we build to our Azure container registry. Here, `principal_id` must be set to the identity of the service account that our GitHub Action impersonates. In this case, I passed in a collection of these and iterated over that collection using the `count` meta-argument. In the case of role assignments, because these resources are so lightweight, it doesn't matter much if we use `for_each` or `count` because the drop-create that will occur more frequently when using `count` has little impact on the deployment.

Kubernetes cluster

The next step is to provision a Kubernetes cluster using the `azurerm_kubernetes_cluster` resource. This resource will be the central figure in our AKS infrastructure:

```
resource "azurerm_kubernetes_cluster" "main" {

  name                 = "aks-${var.application_name}-${var.
environment_name}"
  location             = azurerm_resource_group.main.location
  resource_group_name  = azurerm_resource_group.main.name
  dns_prefix           = "${var.application_name}-${var.
environment_name}"
  node_resource_group  = "${azurerm_resource_group.main.name}-
cluster"
  sku_tier             = "Standard"


  ...


}
```

The preceding code configures some important top-level attributes that influence pricing, networking, and internally managed resource placement. AKS will provision resources to two resource groups. One is where the AKS resource exists, and the other is where AKS provisions the internal Azure resources that make up the internals of the cluster. This secondary resource group's name is controlled by the `node_resource_group` attribute. I would always recommend setting the `node_resource_group` name to something cohesive with the naming convention of the AKS cluster resource itself.

As we learned in *Chapter 5*, Kubernetes has several system services that need to be deployed and in good health for the cluster to function correctly. Our AKS cluster needs to have one or more node pools to host system and user workloads. The default node pool is a great place to host these system services:

```
resource "azurerm_kubernetes_cluster" "main" {

  ...

  default_node_pool {
    name                          = "systempool"
    vm_size                       = var.aks_system_pool.vm_size
    enable_auto_scaling           = true
    min_count                     = var.aks_system_pool.min_node_count
    max_count                     = var.aks_system_pool.max_node_count
    vnet_subnet_id                = azurerm_subnet.kubernetes.id
    os_disk_type                  = "Ephemeral"
    os_disk_size_gb               = 30
    orchestrator_version          = var.aks_orchestration_version
    temporary_name_for_rotation   = "workloadpool"

    zones = [1, 2, 3]

    upgrade_settings {
      max_surge = "33%"
    }

  ...

}
```

Additional node pools, such as the following one, can be created to allow us to isolate our custom deployments on dedicated computing resources so that they don't impact the day-to-day operations of the cluster:

```
resource "azurerm_kubernetes_cluster_node_pool" "workload" {

  name                    = "workloadpool"
```

```
    kubernetes_cluster_id = azurerm_kubernetes_cluster.main.id
    vm_size               = var.aks_workload_pool.vm_size
    enable_auto_scaling   = true
    min_count             = var.aks_workload_pool.min_node_count
    max_count             = var.aks_workload_pool.max_node_count
    vnet_subnet_id        = azurerm_subnet.kubernetes.id
    os_disk_type          = "Ephemeral"
    orchestrator_version  = var.aks_orchestration_version

    mode  = "User" # Define this node pool as a "user" aka workload node
pool
    zones = [1, 2, 3]

    upgrade_settings {
        max_surge = "33%"
    }

    node_labels = {
        "role" = "workload"
    }

    node_taints = [
        "workload=true:NoSchedule"
    ]

}
```

By setting a taint on the nodes within this node pool, we can ensure that only Kubernetes deployments that are explicitly targeted to this node pool will be scheduled here. By employing taints on your additional node pools, you can isolate Kubernetes system services from the default node pool and keep your workloads in their own space. This does have additional costs, but it will greatly improve the health and performance of the cluster. It is something you should do if you're planning on deploying production workloads to your cluster – but if you're just kicking the tires, feel free to skip it!

Identity and access management

Managed identities play an integral role in the configuration of AKS in several different ways. The first and most important is the managed identity that AKS will use to provision the internal resources:

```
resource "azurerm_kubernetes_cluster" "main" {

    ...

    identity {
```

```
    type          = "UserAssigned"
    identity_ids = [azurerm_user_assigned_identity.cluster.id]
  }

  ...


}
```

This identity needs to be assigned the `Managed Identity Operator` role to perform this function:

```
resource "azurerm_role_assignment" "cluster_identity_operator" {

  scope                 = azurerm_resource_group.main.id
  role_definition_name = "Managed Identity Operator"
  principal_id          = azurerm_user_assigned_identity.cluster.
principal_id

}
```

The preceding code creates this role assignment using a **user-assigned managed identity**. We explored this topic in the previous chapter, so we know that this is a special type of managed identity that we explicitly provision and assign role assignments to. This is in contrast to the system-assigned identity, which is a managed identity that is automatically provisioned and managed by the platform itself.

There is another important identity that needs to be set on the AKS cluster: the managed identity used by the kubelet system service that's deployed to each node within the cluster:

```
resource "azurerm_kubernetes_cluster" "main" {

  ...


  kubelet_identity {
    client_id                 = azurerm_user_assigned_identity.
cluster_kubelet.client_id
    object_id                 = azurerm_user_assigned_identity.
cluster_kubelet.principal_id
    user_assigned_identity_id = azurerm_user_assigned_identity.
cluster_kubelet.id
  }


}
```

The preceding code configures the cluster's kubelet identity. This is a little inconsistent than how managed identities are typically attached within the `azurerm` provider, so it's important to get the correct outputs from the user-assigned identity to the right attributes of the `kubelet_identity` block.

As we learned in *Chapter 5*, the kubelet system service processes orders from the scheduler. To do this, kubelet will need access to pull container images from our ACR. This will require the `AcrPull` role assignment to be added to the preceding managed identity:

```
resource "azurerm_role_assignment" "cluster_kubelet_acr" {

  principal_id           = azurerm_user_assigned_identity.cluster_
kubelet.principal_id
  role_definition_name = "AcrPull"
  scope                  = azurerm_container_registry.main.id


}
```

Secrets management

To integrate with Azure's secret management service, Key Vault, we need to take a couple of steps. The first is to simply enable the subsystem on the cluster itself. AKS has an extensible model for such features – including but not limited to enabling integrations with other Azure services and Kubernetes features such as **Kubernetes Event Driven Architecture (KEDA)**, **Azure Monitor**, and **Open Service Mesh**:

```
resource "azurerm_kubernetes_cluster" "main" {

  . . .

  key_vault_secrets_provider {
    secret_rotation_enabled  = true
    secret_rotation_interval = "5m"
  }

  . . .

}
```

The preceding code enables and configures secret rotation. This is just the first step in enabling AKS integration with Azure Key Vault; we also have to set up the CSI provider for pods to pull secrets from Key Vault. We'll look at that in the next section when we start provisioning things to the Kubernetes control plane.

Workload identity

To allow our pods to access other resources that are deployed to Azure, we need to allow them to impersonate a managed identity. Like the integration with Key Vault, we first need to enable this extension on the AKS cluster:

```
resource "azurerm_kubernetes_cluster" "main" {

  ...

  oidc_issuer_enabled      = true
  workload_identity_enabled = true

  ...

}
```

The preceding code activates an internal **OpenID Connect** (**OIDC**) endpoint that's used to sign and issue **JSON Web Tokens** (**JWTs**) for the service accounts within the cluster. After this is enabled, we'll also need Azure federated identity credential, which, once linked to the AKS cluster's OIDC issuer endpoint and the managed identity to be used by the workloads, creates federation between the cluster and Microsoft Entra ID. This allows the pods using the corresponding Kubernetes service account to interact with Azure services using the privileges of the managed identity:

```
resource "azurerm_federated_identity_credential" "main" {

  name                 = azurerm_user_assigned_identity.workload.name
  resource_group_name  = azurerm_resource_group.main.name
  audience             = ["api://AzureADTokenExchange"]
  issuer               = azurerm_kubernetes_cluster.main.oidc_issuer_
url
  parent_id            = azurerm_user_assigned_identity.workload.id
  subject              = "system:serviceaccount:${var.k8s_
namespace}:${var.k8s_service_account_name}"

}
```

Just as we did in *Chapter 8* when working with AWS, we'll link this to a Kubernetes service account in the next section when we provision resources to Kubernetes.

Kubernetes

As we saw in *Chapter 8*, we built out the Kubernetes deployments using the Terraform provider for Kubernetes. Like Packer and Docker, Kubernetes, in its own way, provides a control plane that operates consistently across cloud platforms. As a result, much of the Kubernetes deployment process is reusable, regardless of what cloud platform you choose. This is also one of the appeals of Kubernetes as a way to implement cloud agnostic or cloud portable workloads yet leverage the efficiency and elasticity that Kubernetes managed service offerings provide.

In this chapter, we won't retread the same topics. If you happened to skip *Chapters 7* through *9* due to a lack of interest in AWS, I highly recommend going back and reviewing the corresponding section in *Chapter 8* for more details about the implementation of the Kubernetes deployments.

Provider setup

As we saw in *Chapter 8*, when executing Terraform using the Kubernetes provider to provision resources to the Kubernetes control plane, we don't have to make many changes. We still authenticate against our target cloud platform, we still follow Terraform's core workflow, and we still pass in additional input parameters for platform-specific resources that we need to reference. Most notably, information about the cluster, other Azure services, such as ACR, Key Vault, and managed identities, and other details might need to be put into Kubernetes ConfigMaps that can be used by the pods to point themselves at the endpoint of their database:

```
data "azurerm_kubernetes_cluster" "main" {
    name                = var.kubernetes_cluster_name
    resource_group_name = var.resource_group_name
}
```

Here, we're using a layered approach to provision the infrastructure first and then provision to Kubernetes. As a result, we can reference the Kubernetes cluster using the data source for a resource that was provisioned by the Terraform workspace that's responsible for the Azure infrastructure. This allows users to access important connectivity details without exporting them outside of Terraform and passing them around during the deployment process.

The preceding code is a reference to the AKS cluster that was provisioned in the previous deployment stage. Using this reference, we can initialize the `kubernetes` provider by using several pieces of data to authenticate with the cluster:

```
provider "kubernetes" {
    host                  = data.azurerm_kubernetes_cluster.main.
kube_admin_config[0].host
    client_key            = base64decode(data.azurerm_kubernetes_
cluster.main.kube_admin_config[0].client_key)
    client_certificate    = base64decode(data.azurerm_kubernetes_
cluster.main.kube_admin_config[0].client_certificate)
    cluster_ca_certificate = base64decode(data.azurerm_kubernetes_
cluster.main.kube_admin_config[0].cluster_ca_certificate)
}
```

The client key is the private key that's used for authentication, the client certificate is the certificate that's paired with the private key to perform authentication, and the cluster's CA certificate is the certificate of the certificate authority that's used to verify the Kubernetes API server.

In addition, the `helm` provider can be configured using the same parameters. This can help provide pre-packaged templates of Kubernetes resources via Helm charts:

```
provider "helm" {
  kubernetes {
    ...
  }
}
```

Secrets

In the previous section, we enabled the Key Vault extension on the cluster itself. Now, we need to provide a way for the pods to connect to Azure Key Vault. This requires us to use the Kubernetes secrets store **Container Storage Interface (CSI)** driver. This configuration acts as a conduit, granting Workload Identity the necessary permissions to read specific secrets from the designated Key Vault:

```
resource "kubernetes_manifest" "secret_provider_class" {
  manifest = {
    apiVersion = "secrets-store.csi.x-k8s.io/v1"
    kind       = "SecretProviderClass"
    metadata = {
      name       = "web-app-secrets"
      namespace = var.namespace
    }
    spec = {
      provider = "azure"
        secretObjects = [
          {
            data = [
              {
                key         = "db-admin-password"
                objectName = "db-admin-password"
              }
            ]
            secretName = "db-admin-password"
            type       = "Opaque"
          }
        ]
        parameters = {
```

```
      usePodIdentity = "false"
      clientID       = var.service_account_client_id
      keyvaultName   = var.keyvault_name
      cloudName      = ""
      objects = yamlencode([
        {
          objectName    = "db-admin-password"
          objectType    = "secret"
          objectVersion = ""
        }
      ])
      tenantId = var.tenant_id
    }
  }
}
```

In the preceding code, we need to provision this Kubernetes resource into the namespace we plan on deploying our pods and specify the Key Vault, the managed identity that we configured with the Azure federated identity credential, and the Kubernetes service account.

Workload identity

To ensure that our pods use the managed identity, we need to take a few actions that use both Azure-specific schema and standard Kubernetes schema by provisioning resources within Kubernetes and configurations within the deployment specifications of our pods.

The first thing we need to do is create a Kubernetes service account. This is a standard resource within Kubernetes but we use Azure-specific schema to associate it with the Azure federated identity credential:

```
resource "kubernetes_service_account" "main" {
  metadata {
    namespace = var.namespace
    name      = var.service_account_name
    annotations = {
      "azure.workload.identity/client-id" = var.service_account_
client_id
    }
  }
}
```

Using Terraform allows us to substitute dynamic values that are created during the earlier stage of the provisioning process. Kubernetes has its own way of doing things but it involves using Helm and has additional implementation overhead.

Now that the service account exists in Kubernetes and is linked to the appropriate Azure managed identity credential, the next step is to enable Azure Workload Identity within the deployment. To do this, we need to specify a special label, `azure.workload.identity/use`, and set its value to `true`:

```
labels = {
    "azure.workload.identity/use" = "true"
}
```

This will inform AKS to connect the pods within this deployment to the managed identity linked through the Azure federated identity credential.

The next step is to specify the corresponding Kubernetes service account that we already linked to the Azure federated identity credential in the previous section. This service account is set on the pod's specification within the deployment:

```
spec {

    ...

    service_account_name = "workload"

    ...

}
```

Now that we have built out the three components of our architecture, in the next section, we'll learn how to automate the deployment using Docker so that we can build and publish the container images. Then, we'll use Terraform to provision our infrastructure and deploy our solution to Kubernetes.

Automating the deployment

In this section, we'll learn how to automate the deployment process for container-based architectures. We'll be employing similar techniques that we saw in *Chapter 8* when we took this same journey down the Amazon. As a result, we'll focus on what changes we need to make when we want to deploy to Microsoft Azure and AKS.

Docker

In *Chapter 8*, we covered each step of the GitHub Actions workflow that executes Docker to build, tag, and push our Docker container images. Thanks to the nature of Docker's cloud-agnostic architecture, this overwhelmingly stays the same. The only thing that changes is the way we must configure Docker so that it targets our Azure container registry.

Like in *Chapter 8*, we need to connect to the container registry that we provisioned with Terraform. On Azure, that means we'll need the Entra ID service principal's client ID and client secret:

```
- name: Login to Azure Container Registry
    uses: docker/login-action@v3
    with:
    registry: ${{ steps.terraform.outputs.registry_endpoint }}
    username: ${{ vars.DOCKER_ARM_CLIENT_ID }}
    password: ${{ secrets.DOCKER_ARM_CLIENT_SECRET }}
```

This service principal is the same identity that we configured as inputs in Terraform that provision the infrastructure. As part of that process, the `AcrPush` role assignment was associated with this identity. This grants it permission to publish images to ACR:

```
- name: Build and push Docker image to ACR
    uses: docker/build-push-action@v5
    with:
    context: ${{ env.DOCKER_WORKING_DIRECTORY }}
    push: true
    tags: ${{ steps.terraform.outputs.registry_endpoint }}/${{ env.
DOCKER_IMAGE_NAME }}:${{ steps.image-version.outputs.version }}
```

The preceding code uses `docker\build-push-action` to push the container image that we built in this GitHub Action to our Azure container registry. As we did in AWS, we reference the outputs from the Terraform infrastructure stage to obtain the ACR endpoint.

Terraform

In *Chapter 10*, we comprehensively covered the process of creating a Terraform GitHub Action that authenticates with Azure using a Microsoft Entra ID service principal. Therefore, we won't be delving into it any further. I encourage you to refer back to *Chapter 10* to review the process.

Kubernetes

When we automate Kubernetes with Terraform, we are just running `terraform apply` again with a different root module. This time, the root module will configure the `kubernetes` and `helm` providers in addition to the `azurerm` provider. However, we won't create new resources with the `azurerm` provider; we will only obtain data sources to existing resources we provisioned in the previous `terraform apply` command that provisioned the infrastructure to Azure.

As a result, the GitHub Action that executes this process will look strikingly similar to how we executed Terraform with Azure. Some of the variables might change to include things such as the container image details and cluster information.

Summary

In this chapter, we designed, built, and automated the deployment of a complete and end-to-end solution using container-based architecture. We built onto the foundations from *Chapter 10*, where we worked with the foundational infrastructure of Azure virtual networks but layered on AKS to host our application in containers. In the next and final step in our Azure journey, we'll be looking at serverless architecture, moving beyond the underlying infrastructure, and letting the platform itself take our solution to new heights.

12

Go Serverless on Azure – Building Solutions with Azure Functions

Are you ready? We are about to turn the page on Microsoft Azure – but only after we take the final step of transitioning our application to Serverless architecture. Like we did on the **Amazon Web Services** (**AWS**) platform, in the last two chapters, we worked hard to implement our solution on Microsoft Azure using **virtual machines** (**VMs**) and then containers.

We've taken time to do some comparisons between how things work on AWS and Microsoft Azure to help us understand the subtle and sometimes not-so-subtle differences between the cloud platforms.

We've noticed that while our Terraform code has been changing pretty consistently between cloud platforms, our application code and the operating system configuration – either in Packer or Docker – haven't. As we take our final step with Microsoft Azure, we'll be going through a similar process to what we went through when we transitioned our application to **AWS Lambda**. We'll have to completely refactor the application code.

This chapter covers the following topics:

- Laying the foundation
- Designing the solution
- Building the solution
- Automating the deployment

Laying the foundation

Our story continues through the lens of Söze Enterprises, founded by the enigmatic Turkish billionaire Keyser Söze. Our team has been hard at work building the next-generation autonomous vehicle orchestration platform. Our initial strategy involved minimizing change to allow the team to focus on driving features into our product. However, our elusive CEO had other ideas and pushed us to adopt container technology to make our product more flexible and scalable going forward. Working with Keyser, there is never a dull moment, but managing such radical change so quickly can be frustrating.

Meanwhile, in St. Barts, with the sun setting over the Caribbean and the cocktail party in full swing, Keyser has a chance encounter at the bar with Mark Russinovich, the CTO of Microsoft Azure. They immediately hit it off, chatting over mojitos. When Mark gets a glimpse of Keyser's immense vision for the autonomous vehicle platform, he casually suggests that maybe Keyser shouldn't concern himself with infrastructure at all. Mark explains how leveraging Azure Functions and other serverless offerings could free him from the shackles of infrastructure management, allowing him to focus entirely on his grand vision.

Thanks to Mark's insights and Keyser's whimsical decision-making, our team veers deeper into Microsoft Azure, explicitly transitioning from **Azure Kubernetes Service (AKS)** to **Azure Functions** for serverless computing. This might require a complete re-think of our application architecture, but it could free us from the significant operational overhead of managing low-level infrastructure.

Designing the solution

In this section, we will be taking a look at the overall design of our solution, given the shift from VM and container-based architectures toward serverless architectures. As we saw in *Chapter 9*, at its core, serverless has a quintessential objective of eliminating heavy infrastructure from the stack. Therefore, we will be looking for ways to shed any Azure services that require significant fixed costs, such as VMs or Kubernetes clusters, and replace them with serverless options. This change in our operational context and technology landscape will likely require us to rethink some things about our solution, both in terms of its design, implementation, and deployment strategy:

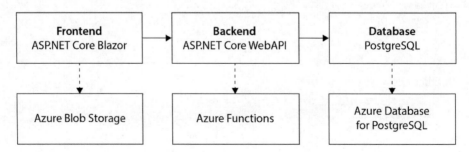

Figure 12.1 – Logical architecture for the autonomous vehicle platform

Our application's architecture doesn't change significantly, but we will be using different Azure services to host it. In this case, we'll be using Azure Storage to host the application's frontend, and we'll be using Azure Functions to host the application's backend:

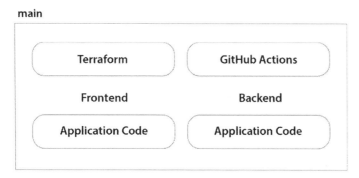

Figure 12.2 – Source control structure of our repository

In this solution, our code base will consist of four parts. First, we'll have the Terraform code that provisions the environment and the GitHub Actions code that executes the deployment process. Then, we'll have the two code bases for our application's frontend and backend.

Cloud architecture

In *Chapter 10*, our cloud-hosting solution was a set of dedicated VMs, and in *Chapter 11*, it was a set of shared VMs within our Kubernetes cluster's node pool. Using VMs has the most sunk cost, whether they are standalone VMs or part of a Kubernetes node pool.

In *Chapter 11*, our entire solution was executed on containers that allowed the frontend and the backend to coexist as a set of containers on the same VMs. This saved us some money, but we still needed servers to host the workload. In this chapter, we have a new objective: to take advantage of the power of the cloud by leveraging cloud-native services that abstract the underlying infrastructure from us and allow us to truly pay for only what we use. Azure's serverless offerings will be crucial to us in this endeavor.

Frontend

In previous chapters, we hosted our frontend on public-facing servers that returned the HTML and JavaScript that composed our web application. There, we still required a cloud-hosted solution to host the files and respond to requests.

However, due to the nature of the web application running within the end user's browser, we don't need to use cloud-hosted VMs to host what are essentially flat files. We can use simple cloud storage to host the frontend as a static website and rely on the cloud platform to shoulder the burden of returning the web content.

For this, we can use Azure Storage. This service has several different storage capabilities built into it, but for our static website, we'll be using Azure Blob storage. Blob storage allows us to host static web content that is internet accessible, and Azure Storage handles all the load balancing, SSL termination, and scaling up to meet huge spikes in demand:

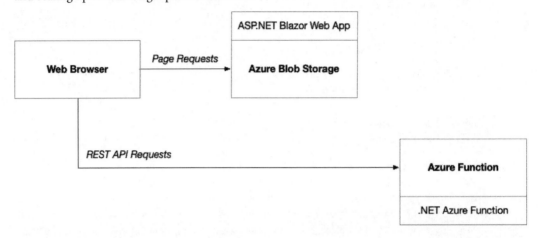

Figure 12.3 – Azure Storage handles web page requests, while Azure Functions handles REST API requests

To do this, we'll need to have an **Azure Storage** account and enable the static websites feature. This will create a special storage container called $web to where we can publish the web content. All Azure Storage accounts have an internet-accessible public domain. When we activate the static websites feature of Azure Storage, internet traffic gets routed to content hosted in the $web storage container.

This will give us a huge advantage because Azure Storage has absolutely no sunk costs. When you create an Azure Storage account, it costs you absolutely zero dollars ($0) per month. Like other serverless offerings, it uses a set of micro-transactions to measure your activity and charge you for precisely what you use. In **Azure Blob storage**, this can be a bit complicated as several measurements incur costs.

The following table shows all the costs you will run into when using Azure Storage to host your static websites:

Metric	Unit	Scale	Price
Storage	GBs	1,000	$0.0518
Read transactions	Transactions	10,000	$0.004
Write transactions	Transactions	10,000	$0.1125
Other operations	Transactions	10,000	$0.004

Table 12.1 – Azure Storage micro-transactional pricing

The pricing I chose is the most expensive option with geo-redundant, zone-redundant storage with additional read-only access in an alternate region. The prices that are listed here are for Azure's West US 2 region, though the prices may have changed by the time you are reading this, so it's best to check the latest prices for the most accurate cost estimation.

I included these prices to make a point. We can host a static website on a three-node Kubernetes cluster for approximately $300 a month or we can host a static website on Azure Storage for less than $0.01 a month on the most rock-solid storage tier that Azure has to offer. Which approach would you choose?

Backend

Like our frontend, in previous chapters, our backend was also hosted on VMs in two different ways: dedicated VMs and shared VMs within the node pool on our Kubernetes cluster.

Unlike the frontend, our backend doesn't have the option of running entirely client-side inside the end user's web browser. In the backend, we have custom code that needs to run on a server. Therefore, we need to find a solution to host these components without all the overhead of a fleet of VMs.

On Azure, we can use Azure Functions to accomplish this. Azure Functions is a managed service that allows you to deploy your code without paying the sunk costs for any of the underlying VMs. Like Azure Storage, it has a micro-transactional pricing model that charges you for precisely what you use.

The following table shows the costs that you will incur when deploying your code to Azure Functions:

Metric	Unit	Scale	Price
Execution time	GB/s	1	$0.000016
Total executions	Transactions	1,000,000	$0.020

Table 12.2 – Azure Functions micro-transactional pricing

The first thing that you'll probably notice is that, like Azure Storage, these prices are extremely small but they measure a very small amount of activity on the platform.

For example, the execution time metric has a unit of GB/s, which is the amount of memory, in gigabytes, your Azure Function uses per second. Given that it measures at a *per-second* interval, you don't have to be running Azure Functions very long to rack up quite a few of these.

The total executions is a rather simple metric that seemingly has no constraints, but Azure Functions have natural constraints built into them. For example, each of these executions is limited to 10 minutes. Now, if you are trying to respond to requests from a web application, you probably won't want to design your Azure Function to take 10 minutes anyway, as this would be a pretty poor experience for the end user using the web browser. In this scenario, you want your Azure Function to return in no more than a few seconds. However, Azure Functions can be employed for many different tasks besides responding to HTTP requests from a browser, and sometimes, it makes sense to run long-running activities. For those situations, you can opt to host your Azure Functions on a Premium Azure Functions service plan. This removes the execution length duration because rather than paying per transaction, you are essentially reserving capacity.

Azure Functions have multiple hosting options. There is the **Premium service plan** that we discussed previously, which allows you to reserve capacity, connect to private networks, remove the 10-minute cap on Azure Function execution duration, and allow your Azure Functions to run up to 60 minutes. These Premium plans have sunk cost as you are pre-allocating Azure resources to ensure your Azure Functions operate at maximum performance. You can even select different hardware configurations (CPU and memory) to better fit your workload's needs:

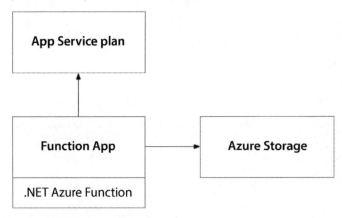

Figure 12.4 – Azure Functions are deployed to Function Apps, which are hosted on App Service plans

In stark contrast, there is the **Consumption service plan**, which has no sunk cost but more constraints on usage and no control over scaling and resource configuration of the host environment. The Consumption service plan is a good place to do development and testing, but if you're going to run production workloads, I'd highly recommend sticking with a Premium service plan.

Previously, our ASP.NET REST API was set up using a traditional ASP.NET project that used controllers to implement the REST API endpoints. However, when transitioning to Azure Functions, this solution structure is incompatible with the Azure Functions framework. To be able to host our REST API as Azure Functions, we need to conform to the framework that Azure Functions dictates. This means that the ASP.NET controller classes will need to be refactored so that they conform to this standard. In the next section, we'll delve into the code that makes this possible.

Deployment architecture

Now that we have a good idea of what our cloud architecture is going to look like for our solution on Azure, we need to come up with a plan for how to provision our environments and deploy our code.

In *Chapter 10*, when we deployed our application to VMs, we baked our compiled application code into a VM image using Packer. Similarly, in *Chapter 11*, when we deployed our application to containers on our Kubernetes cluster, we baked our application code into container images using Docker. With serverless, this completely changes because Azure's serverless offerings completely abstract away the operating system. This means that all we are responsible for is producing a compatible deployment package.

Creating the deployment package

As we discussed in the previous section, we have two components of our application: the frontend and the backend. Each has a different deployment target. We are going to deploy the frontend as a static website, while the backend is going to be deployed as an Azure Function. Since both are .NET projects, we will be using both .NET and Azure platform-specific tools to create deployment packages and deploy them to their target Azure services. The following diagram shows the process we'll go through to provision our environment, package our application code, and deploy it to the target environment out in Azure:

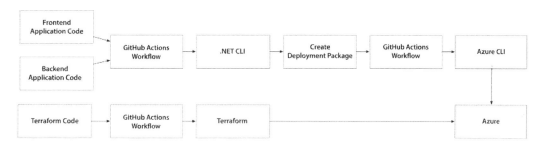

Figure 12.5 – Deployment pipeline to build our .NET application code for deployment to Azure

For the frontend, this means enabling the feature to deploy our ASP.NET Blazor web application as a WebAssembly. This will allow the frontend to be hosted as a static website that can run completely client-side without any server-side rendering. This is only possible because of the way we have designed our frontend web application, which uses HTML, CSS, and JavaScript to interact with server-side REST APIs. It's important to note that ASP.NET Blazor supports both hosting options, but we specifically chose to go down the client-side-only path and eliminate any dependency on server-side page rendering. As a result, when we use the .NET CLI to publish our ASP.NET Blazor project, it will emit a folder containing static web content. Then, using the Azure CLI, we can upload the contents of this folder to our Azure Blob storage account's $web container to complete the deployment.

For the backend, again using the .NET CLI, we need to publish our project. This will emit all the files needed to properly inform the Azure Functions service about our little Azure Function. Once this is done, we need to zip this folder up into a zip archive. Finally, we can use the Azure CLI to deploy this zip archive to our Azure Function.

Now that we have a solid plan for how we will implement both the cloud architecture using Azure and the deployment architecture using GitHub Actions, let's start building! In the next section, we'll break down the **HashiCorp Configuration Language** (**HCL**) code we can use to implement the Terraform code and modify the application code so that it conforms to the Azure Functions framework.

Building the solution

Now that we have a solid design for our solution, we can begin building it. As we discussed in the previous section, because we'll be using Azure serverless offerings such as Azure Storage and Azure Functions to host our application, we will need to make some changes to our application code. This is something that we never had to do in *Chapters 10* and *11* as we were able to deploy our application to the cloud by packaging it in either a VM image (using Packer) or in a container image (using Docker). Therefore, to build our solution, we need to write some Terraform code and update our application code in C#.

Terraform

As we discussed in our design, our solution is made up of two application components: the frontend and the backend. Each has a code base of application code that needs to be deployed. Unlike previous chapters, where we had operating system configuration as well, now that we are using serverless offerings, this is no longer our responsibility as the platform takes care of it for us.

Much of the Terraform setup is very similar to what we have done in previous chapters, so we will only focus on new resources needed for our solution. You can check the full source code for this book, which is available in this book's GitHub repository, if you want to work with the complete solution.

Frontend

First, we need to provision a storage account where we can deploy our frontend to. The Azure Storage account is one of the most common Terraform resources to be provisioned as many other Azure services use storage accounts for different purposes. However, we need to configure our storage account differently by using an optional block called `static_website`. This block will enable the static website feature and will place the `$web` container in our storage account by default:

```
resource "azurerm_storage_account" "frontend" {
  name                     = "st${var.application_name}${var.
environment_name}${random_string.main.result}"
  resource_group_name      = azurerm_resource_group.main.name
  location                 = azurerm_resource_group.main.location
```

```
  account_tier              = "Standard"
  account_replication_type = "LRS"

  static_website {
    index_document      = "index.html"
    error_404_document  = "404.html"
  }
}
```

Backend

Azure Functions are deployed to a resource called a function app. They come in two varieties – one for Windows and another for Linux. This can be quite perplexing – isn't the whole purpose of using a serverless offering so that you don't have to think about the operating system? However, the underlying operating system can impact the types of runtimes that are supported for your Azure Function.

To provide a function app, we need to have a service plan. As we mentioned in the previous section, there are multiple types of service plans. The two main types are Consumption and Premium. To use a Consumption service plan, you need to use Y1 as the SKU name, and to use a Premium service plan, you need to use either EP1, EP2, or EP3. Each of the Premium service plan SKUs has a different set of compute and memory resources:

```
resource "azurerm_service_plan" "consumption" {
  name                = "asp-${var.application_name}-${var.
environment_name}-${random_string.main.result}"
  resource_group_name = azurerm_resource_group.main.name
  location            = azurerm_resource_group.main.location
  os_type             = var.function_app_os_type
  sku_name            = var.function_app_sku
}
```

Now that we have a service plan, we can provision one or more function apps for it. The function apps do not need to share the same resource group, so you could have a central team manage the service plans and have each team manage its own function apps that are hosted within the service plan:

```
resource "azurerm_windows_function_app" "main" {
  name                       = "func-${var.application_name}-${var.
environment_name}-${random_string.main.result}"
  resource_group_name        = azurerm_resource_group.main.name
  location                   = azurerm_resource_group.main.location
  service_plan_id            = azurerm_service_plan.consumption.id
  storage_account_name       = azurerm_storage_account.function.name
  storage_account_access_key = azurerm_storage_account.function.
primary_access_key
```

```
  site_config {
    application_stack {
      dotnet_version = "v6.0"
    }
    cors {
      allowed_origins      = ["https://portal.azure.com"]
      support_credentials = true
    }
  }

}
```

The important thing is that the operating system of the service plan should match the function app's Terraform resource type. Only `azurerm_windows_function_app` resources should be provisioned to service plans with an `os_type` value of `Windows`, and likewise, only `azurerm_linux_function_app` resources should be provisioned to service plans with an `os_type` value of `Linux`.

The function app also needs a storage account to be provisioned. This should be different than the storage account that's used to provision the frontend. While it's a common practice to provision a dedicated storage account for the function app, it's technically possible to use the same storage account for both the function app and the frontend. However, given that there is no additional cost for an additional storage account, you only pay for the storage. I recommend provisioning a dedicated storage account to keep the separation between the two components of your architecture.

Secrets management

An important block for a function app is the `app_settings` block. This is where we can pass secrets to our Azure Functions, as well as other parameters that affect our deployment strategy and other runtime configurations:

```
  app_settings = {
    "SCM_DO_BUILD_DURING_DEPLOYMENT" = "false"
    "WEBSITE_RUN_FROM_PACKAGE"        = "1"
    "STORAGE_CONNECTION_STRING"       = azurerm_storage_account.
function.primary_connection_string
    "QUEUE_CONNECTION_STRING"         = azurerm_storage_account.
function.primary_connection_string
  }
```

Here, we are setting the connection string for the Azure Storage account that we will use to connect to blob and queue storage within the application. We can also use Key Vault to store these secrets using special syntax:

```
@Microsoft.KeyVault(VaultName=kv-fleetops-dev;SecretName=QUEUE_
CONNECTION_STRING)
```

If we replace the previous setting with the new one, we will no longer store the secret in the Azure Function app. The secret is only in Key Vault:

```
app_settings = {
    "QUEUE_CONNECTION_STRING" = "@Microsoft.
KeyVault(VaultName=${azurerm_keyvault.main.name};SecretName=${azurerm_
keyvault_secret.queue_connection_string.name})"
}
```

This also requires us to set up a role assignment to grant the Azure Function's user-assigned identity the necessary permissions to access the secrets stored in Key Vault. Without this necessary role assignment, even if we use the special syntax to refer to the Key Vault secret correctly, Azure Functions will not be able to access the secrets:

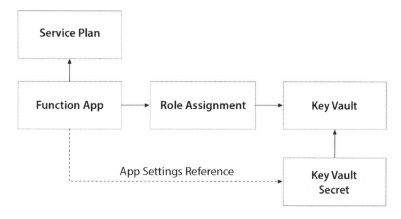

Figure 12.6 – The structure of Azure Functions resources

As you can see, the Azure function is a much more simple deployment. We don't need a virtual network or any of the other surrounding resources that we provisioned in previous chapters just to get off the ground. For most applications, the built-in security of Azure Functions and Key Vault is sufficient. However, if we wanted to enable private networking because our application has to follow some regulatory compliance, we can do that, but otherwise, it is not required.

Application code

Azure Functions are inherently event-based. Each Azure Function is triggered by a different type of event, and the Azure Functions SDK provides an extensible framework for triggering based on different types of events. Azure Functions has implemented several different triggers for all sorts of different Azure services, which makes it easy to design Azure Functions that can respond to all sorts of different activities taking place within your Azure environment. For this book, we'll only focus on the HTTP trigger, but if you are interested, I recommend checking out all the other options that Azure Functions has – it's quite extensive.tt

In a traditional ASP.NET REST API solution, you have controller classes that embody a specific route and then methods that implement different operations at that route:

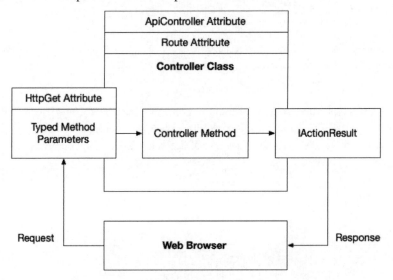

Figure 12.7 – ASP.NET MVC controller class anatomy

The controller class needs to be decorated with an ApiController attribute that informs the ASP. NET runtime that this class should be used to process incoming web requests at the route specified in the Route attribute.

Each method is decorated with an attribute that denotes which HTTP verb the method should respond to. In the preceding example, we use HttpGet, but there are corresponding attributes for each of the supported HTTP verbs. The method can take strongly typed parameters that can either be part of the route, the query string, or the request body. The method returns IActionResult by default, which allows us to return different data structures, depending on the outcome of the request.

To implement a REST API using Azure Functions, we need to implement a class using the Azure Function SDK. This requires us to slightly adjust how we implement both our class and our method. We will employ different class and method attributes to achieve a similar outcome: defining an endpoint that responds to web requests at a specific route.

The Azure Function class is not decorated with any attributes:

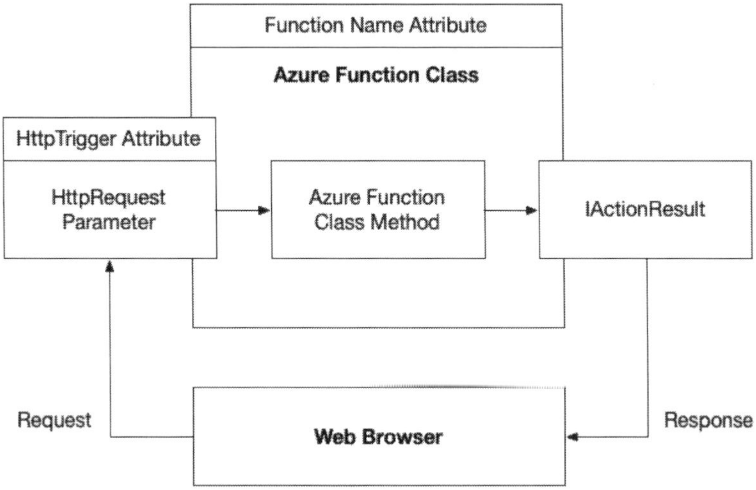

Figure 12.8 – Azure Function class anatomy

Only the methods should be decorated with a `FunctionName` attribute, which will correlate them with a named scope for the Azure Function framework. This attribute is similar to the `Route` attribute as it informs the base route of all of the methods implemented within this named context of Azure Functions. Azure Function classes can be implemented as static or non-static classes. I recommend using non-static classes as they allow you to use dependency injection to greatly improve the testability of your Azure Functions.

The methods in an Azure Functions class are where we tie into the event-triggering framework of Azure Functions. When responding to a web request, we need the first parameter of our method to be of the `HttpRequest` type, and we need to use the `HttpTrigger` attribute on this method parameter. Since we decorated the method with the `FunctionName` attribute already, the Azure Functions framework knows to interrogate this method for any available event triggers. Hence, supplying `HttpRequest` with the `HttpTrigger` attribute attached will meet the match criteria, and Azure Functions will wire up this method so that it responds to incoming web traffic accordingly.

This pattern is very similar to the traditional ASP.NET implementation using controller classes. However, it takes on a slightly different structure. All the same anatomical elements are there but just in different places: HTTP verb, route to the endpoint, input parameters (either a query string or on the request body), and the response body.

Unlike in a traditional ASP.NET project, the HTTP verb is not a method-level attribute. It's a parameter of the `HttpTrigger` attribute. The method does allow us to add additional input parameters as either query string or part of the route but not part of the request body itself.

As we can see, the cloud architecture radically simplifies things, but one trade-off is that our backend code needs to be adapted to the Azure Functions framework. This will require development and testing efforts to transform our code base into this new hosting model. This stands in stark contrast to what we explored in previous chapters, where we hosted on VMs or containerized and hosted on a Kubernetes cluster. While conforming to the Azure Functions model does take work, its benefits are two-fold: first, it allows us to take advantage of close to zero sunk cost, and second, it allows us to fully abstract the underlying infrastructure from us and let the Azure platform take care of scalability and high availability. This allows us to focus more on the functionality of our solutions rather than the plumbing required to keep the lights on.

Now that we have implemented Terraform to provision our solution and made changes to our application code so that it conforms to the Azure Functions framework, in the next section, we'll dive into YAML and Bash and implement the necessary GitHub Actions workflows.

Automating the deployment

As we discussed in the previous section, serverless offerings such as Azure Functions and Azure Storage abstract away the operating system configuration. Therefore, when we deploy, we just need an application package that's compatible with the target platform. In this section, we'll create an automation pipeline using GitHub Actions that will provision our application to its new serverless home in Azure.

Terraform

The first thing that we need to do is provision our environment to Azure. This is going to be extremely similar to the way we did this in the previous chapters. In *Chapter 10*, we needed to ensure that our VM images were built and available before we executed Terraform because the Terraform code base referenced the VM images when it provisioned the VMs. This means that with our VM architecture, application deployment happens before Terraform provisions the environment:

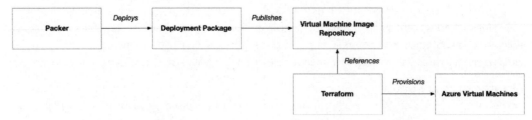

Figure 12.9 – Packer-produced VM images are a prerequisite for Terraform

In *Chapter 11*, when we provisioned our Kubernetes cluster using Azure Kubernetes, we had no such prerequisite. The application deployment occurred after the Kubernetes cluster was online. This means that with container-based architecture, application deployment happens after Terraform provisions the environment:

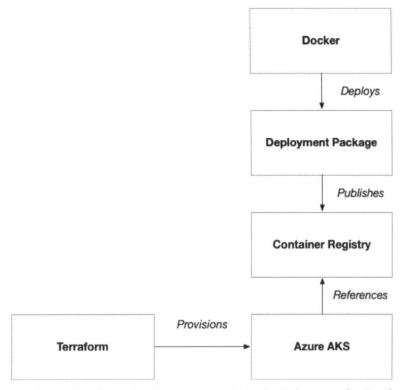

Figure 12.10 – Docker-produced container images are provisioned to Kubernetes after Terraform executes

When using Azure's serverless offerings, the deployment process mirrors that of what we saw when deploying our application as containers to Kubernetes. Just like with this approach, we need to build a deployment artifact for Azure's serverless offerings. For the frontend, that means simply generating the static web content, and for the backend, that means generating an Azure Functions ZIP archive. These artifacts share a similar purpose to the Docker images in that they are a target service-compatible way of packaging our application for deployment.

As shown in the following figure, the serverless deployment looks very similar to the approach we used with the container-based architecture:

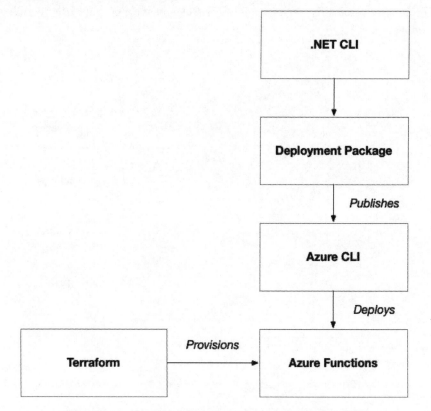

Figure 12.11 – The .NET CLI produces deployment artifacts that
are provisioned to Azure after Terraform executes

That's because Azure is fulfilling the role that Kubernetes played when using a serverless approach. Azure just has custom tools to facilitate the deployment of the application.

Deployment

Now that Terraform has provisioned the Azure infrastructure that we need for our serverless solution, we need to take the final step of deploying both deployment artifacts to the appropriate locations in Azure.

We will use .NET and Azure custom tools to produce the artifacts and deploy them to these target locations.

Frontend

As we saw in other chapters, our .NET application code needs to follow a continuous integration process where the code is built and tested using automated unit testing and other built-in quality controls. Nothing changes here, except that we need to add some special handling to the deployment artifact that these processes produce to make sure it is available to our GitHub Action's job that deploys the workload to the appropriate location.

The `dotnet publish` command is used to output the deployment artifact of the .NET application code. For the ASP.NET Blazor web application, this output is a folder container, a collection of loose files containing HTML, JavaScript, and CSS. To pass all these files efficiently from one GitHub Actions job to another, we need to zip them up into a single file:

```
- name: Generate the Deployment Package
  run: |
    zip -r ../deployment.zip ./
  working-directory: ${{ env.DOTNET_WORKING_DIRECTORY }}/publish
```

Now that the static web content has been zipped into a ZIP archive, we can use the `upload-artifact` GitHub Action to save this file to GitHub Actions. This will make the file available for future jobs that are executed within the pipeline:

```
- name: Upload Deployment Package
  uses: actions/upload-artifact@v2
  with:
    name: dotnet-deployment
    path: ${{ env.DOTNET_WORKING_DIRECTORY }}/deployment.zip
```

Future jobs can simply download the artifact using a corresponding `download-artifact` GitHub Action and the same name that was used to upload it:

```
- uses: actions/download-artifact@v3
  with:
    name: dotnet-deployment
```

Because the ASP.NET Blazor web application is going to be hosted as static web content on our Azure Storage account, we need to ensure that we unzip it to upload the contents to Azure Blob storage. If we were to upload the zip archive to Blob storage, the web application wouldn't work correctly because all of the web content would be trapped inside the archive file:

```
- name: Unzip Deployment Package
  run: |
    mkdir -p ${{ env.DOTNET_WORKING_DIRECTORY }}/upload-staging
    unzip ./deployment.zip -d ${{ env.DOTNET_WORKING_DIRECTORY }}/
upload-staging
```

Now that the static web content has been unzipped to the staging directory, we can use the `az storage blob upload-batch` command to deploy all of the files to the $web container:

```
- id: deploy
  name: Upload to Blob
  env:
    ARM_SUBSCRIPTION_ID: ${{ vars.ARM_SUBSCRIPTION_ID }}
    ARM_TENANT_ID: ${{ vars.ARM_TENANT_ID }}
    ARM_CLIENT_ID: ${{ vars.TERRAFORM_ARM_CLIENT_ID }}
    ARM_CLIENT_SECRET: ${{ secrets.TERRAFORM_ARM_CLIENT_SECRET }}
  working-directory: ${{ env.DOTNET_WORKING_DIRECTORY }}
  run: |
    az login --service-principal -u $ARM_CLIENT_ID -p $ARM_CLIENT_
SECRET --tenant $ARM_TENANT_ID
    az account set --subscription $ARM_SUBSCRIPTION_ID
    az storage blob upload-batch -s ./upload-staging/wwwroot -d
\$web --account-name ${{ steps.terraform.outputs.frontend_storage_
account_name }}
```

We need to make sure that we authenticate with Azure and that we are targeting the right Azure subscription that has the Azure Storage account that we want to target. Therefore, we need to execute the `az login` command to authenticate and then use `az account set` to ensure we are working on the right subscription. Once we've done that, we can execute `az storage blob upload-batch` to recursively upload all the files within the staging directory.

Azure Function

To deploy the Azure Function, the same process must be followed to pass the artifact from the GitHub Actions job that builds the deployment artifact to the job that deploys the artifact.

Like the az storage blob upload-batch command, we also need to authenticate and set the right Azure subscription. The only difference is that we are using the az functionapp deployment source config-zip command to provision a ZIP archive to the Azure Function:

```
    - name: Deploy
      env:
        ARM_SUBSCRIPTION_ID: ${{ vars.ARM_SUBSCRIPTION_ID }}
        ARM_TENANT_ID: ${{ vars.ARM_TENANT_ID }}
        ARM_CLIENT_ID: ${{ vars.TERRAFORM_ARM_CLIENT_ID }}
        ARM_CLIENT_SECRET: ${{ secrets.TERRAFORM_ARM_CLIENT_SECRET
}}
        RESOURCE_GROUP_NAME: ${{needs.terraform.outputs.resource_
group_name}}
        FUNCTION_NAME: ${{needs.terraform.outputs.function_name}}
      run: |
        az login --service-principal -u $ARM_CLIENT_ID -p $ARM_
CLIENT_SECRET --tenant $ARM_TENANT_ID --output none
        az account set -s $ARM_SUBSCRIPTION_ID --output none
        az functionapp deployment source config-zip -g $RESOURCE_
GROUP_NAME -n $FUNCTION_NAME --src ./deployment.zip
```

Unlike how we provisioned the frontend, we don't need to unzip the deployment package for the Azure Function. Azure Functions is expecting our application code to be bundled into a ZIP archive:

```
app_settings = {
  "SCM_DO_BUILD_DURING_DEPLOYMENT" = "false"
  "WEBSITE_RUN_FROM_PACKAGE"       = "1"
}
```

You might remember from the previous section where we set app_settings on the Azure Function that we set two settings – SCM_DO_BUILD_DURING_DEPLOYMENT and WEBSITE_RUN_FROM_PACKAGE. These two settings tell Azure Functions that our application code is already pre-compiled and bundled into a ZIP archive.

That's it! With that, our application has been fully deployed to Azure Storage and Azure Functions!

Summary

In this chapter, we designed, built, and automated the deployment of a complete end-to-end solution using serverless architecture using Azure Functions. To accomplish this, we finally had to make some major changes to our application code so that it conformed to the requirements of the serverless runtime. When adopting serverless offerings, you must make this distinct and considerable decision as it tightly couples your application code with the target cloud platform.

Throughout this journey, we have meticulously constructed three distinct solutions on the Azure platform by utilizing VMs, Kubernetes through **Azure Kubernetes Service** (**AKS**), and now, serverless with Azure Functions.

As we conclude this Azure-centric narrative, we stand on the brink of a thrilling new alternate reality. Guided by the enigmatic vision of our CEO, Keyser Söze, we are poised to embark on an adventurous collaboration with Google. This partnership is set to unfold in a realm of endless possibilities, mirroring our Azure achievements on Google Cloud. Our narrative will transition to exploring similar architectures on Google Cloud, so stay tuned as we venture into this *alternate universe* with Keyser Söze, delving into Google Cloud's offerings and continuing to innovate our solutions in cloud computing.

Part 5:
Building Solutions
on Google Cloud

Armed with the conceptual knowledge of Terraform and architectural concepts that transcend the implementation details of the major public cloud platforms, we'll explore building solutions on Google Cloud with three cloud computing paradigms: virtual machines, containers with Kubernetes, and serverless with Google Cloud Functions.

This part has the following chapters:

- *Chapter 13, Getting Started on Google Cloud – Building Solutions with GCE*
- *Chapter 14, Containerize on Google Cloud – Building Solutions with GKE*
- *Chapter 15, Go Serverless on Google Cloud – Building Solutions with Google Cloud Functions*

13

Getting Started on Google Cloud – Building Solutions with GCE

You've made it. After the previous six chapters, where we used two different cloud platforms and three different cloud computing paradigms to build six distinct solutions, we are finally ready to take our final journey by adapting our solution to **Google Cloud Platform** (**GCP**).

Like the last two adventures, in this alternate universe, we will be starting our journey by building our solution with a **virtual machine** (**VM**) architecture on Google Cloud. As we saw when we transitioned between AWS and Azure when we compared how the same solution architecture was built on the two different cloud platforms, some things changed a lot, while many things changed only a tiny bit – or not at all. We observed that our Terraform code changed pretty consistently across all chapters. However, other things, such as Packer, Docker, and GitHub Actions workflows, only changed slightly. Our .NET-based application code didn't change at all, whether being hosted in VMs or containers, but when we got to serverless, the application code went through radical refactoring.

The same is true as we move the solution to GCP. As a result, we won't be revisiting these topics at the same length in this chapter. However, I would encourage you to bookmark *Chapters 7* and *8* and refer to them frequently. This chapter will only focus on the changes we must make to deploy our solution on GCP.

This chapter covers the following topics:

- Laying the foundation
- Designing the solution
- Building the solution
- Automating the deployment

Laying the foundation

Our team at Söze Enterprises applauds their achievement of responding to the whimsical technical course correction of their fearless leader, Keyser Söze, and marvels at their success and fortune in launching their product successfully on Microsoft Azure. They utilized VMs, Kubernetes, and, finally, serverless technology. The comforting deep blue of the Azure portal begins to fade away when suddenly, the air fills with an eerie yet familiar sound: doodle-oo doodle-oo doodle-oo. The familiar duo appears – sitting in a cozy wood-paneled basement, a look typical of suburban basements from the late '80s and early '90s. The walls are adorned with posters and memorabilia, including a prominent Chicago Bears pennant, highlighting Wayne's love for rock music and sports. They start the familiar chant: doodle-oo doodle-oo doodle-oo. Suddenly, we're transported to another world – another universe, perhaps, where Google Cloud's sleek multicolored logo replaces Azure's deep blue. Söze Enterprises has now partnered with Google Cloud for their next-generation autonomous vehicle platform.

As before, we inherited a team from one of Söze Enterprises' other divisions with a strong core team of C# .NET developers, so we'll build version 1.0 of the platform using .NET technologies. The elusive CEO, Keyser, was rumored to have joined Google co-founder Sergey Brin aboard his super yacht, the Dragonfly, off the Amalfi Coast, and word has come down from corporate that we will be using Google Cloud to host the platform. Since the team doesn't have much experience with containers and timelines are tight, we've decided to build a simple three-tier architecture and host on Azure VMs:

Figure 13.1 – Logical architecture for the autonomous vehicle platform

The platform will need a frontend, which will be a web UI built using ASP.NET Core Blazor. The frontend will be powered by a REST API backend, which will be built using ASP.NET Core Web API. Having our core functionality encapsulated into a REST API will allow autonomous vehicles to communicate directly with the platform and allow us to expand by adding client interfaces with additional frontend technologies such as native mobile apps and virtual or mixed reality in the future. The backend will use a PostgreSQL database for persistent storage since it's lightweight, industry-standard, and relatively inexpensive.

Designing the solution

Due to the tight timelines the team is facing, we want to keep the cloud architecture simple. Therefore, we'll be keeping it simple and using Google Cloud services that will allow us to provision using familiar VM technologies as opposed to trying to learn something new. The first decision we have to make is what Google Cloud service each component of our logical architecture will be hosted on.

Our application architecture consists of three components: a frontend, a backend, and a database. The frontend and backend are application components and need to be hosted on a cloud service that provides general computing, while the database needs to be hosted on a cloud database service. There are many options for both types of services:

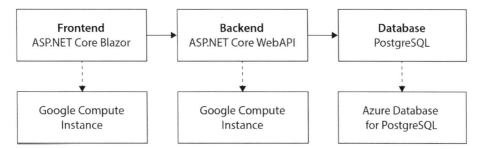

Figure 13.2 – Logical architecture for the autonomous vehicle platform and the hosts

Since we have decided we're going to use VMs to host our application, we have narrowed down the different services that we can use to host our application. We have decided **Google Compute Engine (GCE)** is the ideal choice for our current situation:

Figure 13.3 – Source control structure of our repository

This solution will have six parts. We still have the application code and Packer templates for both the frontend and backend. Then, we have GitHub Actions to implement our CI/CD process and Terraform to provision our Google Cloud infrastructure and reference the Packer-built VM images for our GCE instances.

Cloud architecture

The first part of our design is adapting our solution's architecture to the target cloud platform: Google Cloud. This involves mapping application architecture components to GCP services and thinking through the configuration of those services so that they meet the requirements of our solution.

Projects and API access

Before we get started, we need a project within the organization where a service account can be created for Terraform to use. This service account needs to be granted access to the `roles/resourcemanager.projectCreator` organizational role. This will allow you to create projects with Terraform, which will allow you to keep a complete solution together and avoid additional boilerplate prerequisites that are executed outside of Terraform using the command-line interface.

Once this has been done, you need to enable the **Cloud Resource Manager API** within the project where the Terraform service account resides. This API is required within the context of the Google Cloud project because of the way Google Cloud grants access to different features of the platform at the project level. It creates another gate for the Google Cloud identity to be able to access resources on GCP.

Your Terraform service account will also need access to Cloud Storage, which you plan on using to store Terraform state. When using the AWS and Azure providers, you can use different credentials to access the Terraform backend than you use to provision your environment. On Google Cloud, this can be accomplished by setting `GOOGLE_BACKEND_CREDENTIALS` with credentials for the identity you wish to use to communicate with the Google Cloud Storage bucket and `GOOGLE_APPLICATION_CREDENTIALS` with credentials for the identity you wish to use to communicate with Google Cloud to provision your environment.

Virtual network

VMs must be deployed within a virtual network. As you may recall from *Chapter 7*, when we provisioned this solution on AWS, we needed to set up multiple Subnets for our solution to span Availability Zones. In *Chapter 8*, when deploying the solution to Azure, we only needed two subnets – one for the frontend and one for the backend. That's because Azure's virtual network architecture is structured differently than AWS's and subnets on Azure span multiple Availability Zones.

Google Cloud's virtual network service is also structured differently. Unlike both AWS and Azure, which have virtual networks scoped to a particular region, virtual networks on GCP span multiple regions by default. Subnets are scoped to the region, which means, like Azure, a subnet on GCP can host VMs from multiple Availability Zones.

The following diagram shows that the Google compute network is not tied to the region like it is on AWS and Azure:

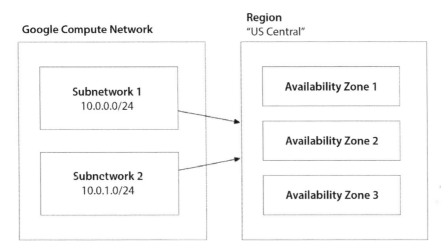

Figure 13.4 – Google Cloud network architecture

Although this seems like a significant difference at the root of the deployment hierarchy, it doesn't materially impact the design as the subnets (or *subnetworks*) are still tied to a region:

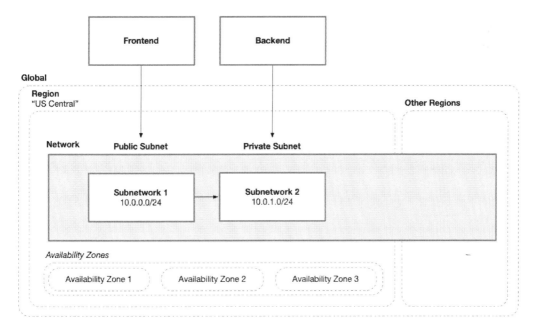

Figure 13.5 – Isolated subnets for the frontend and backend application components

When building a single-region solution, the multi-region capability of Google Cloud might seem like overkill. However, automatic spanning does simplify infrastructure management as businesses don't have to manually set up and maintain inter-regional connections. This not only reduces administrative overhead but also allows for more agile and scalable deployments in response to changing demands by making active-active multi-region deployments easier to build and maintain.

Network routing

Inside Google Cloud networks, the default setup is designed to provide straightforward and secure connectivity. As we know, by default, Google Cloud networks are global resources, meaning all the subnets (or *subnetworks*) within a single network can communicate with each other, regardless of their regional location, without the need for explicit routes or VPNs. This inter-subnet communication uses the system-generated routes in the network.

For routing configurations, Google Cloud has **routes**, which perform a role similar to AWS's route tables, directing traffic based on IP ranges. For situations where instances need to initiate outbound connections to the internet without revealing their IP, Google Cloud provides Cloud NAT, which is analogous to AWS's **NAT gateways**.

Like Azure, Google Cloud does not have a direct equivalent named **internet gateway**. Instead, internet connectivity in GCP is managed using a combination of system-generated routes and firewall rules.

Load balancing

Google Cloud has two options when it comes to load balancers: global and regional. Global load balancers distribute traffic across multiple regions, ensuring users are served from the nearest or most suitable region, while regional load balancers distribute traffic within a single region. The choice between them typically depends on the application's user distribution and the need for low-latency access. However, sometimes, other limitations force your hand:

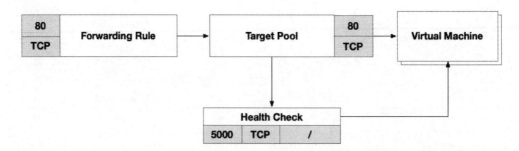

Figure 13.6 – Google Cloud regional load balancer

Unfortunately, the regional load balancer's target pool does not allow you to specify a different port for the backend instances. This means the target pool will forward traffic to the same port where it received traffic. For instance, if the forwarding rule is listening on port 80, the target pool will send traffic to port 80 of the backend instances.

To achieve your goal of forwarding from port 80 to port 5000, you would need to use the global load balancer instead of the regional load balancer:

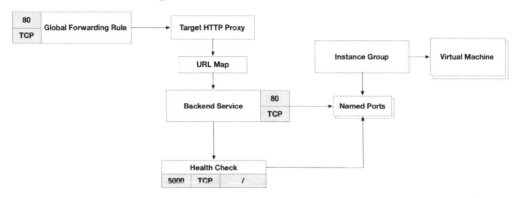

Figure 13.7 – Google Cloud global load balancer

The global load balancer requires that you set up instance groups to organize the VMs that the load will be distributed across. Google Cloud instance groups are similar to AWS Auto Scaling groups and Azure's **Virtual Machine Scale Sets** (**VMSS**), but they have a bit more flexibility in that you can either provide a VM template and allow GCP to *manage* the instances or you can provision the instances explicitly and add them later to the instance group. This dual-mode capability is similar to Azure's VMSS rather than AWS's Auto Scaling group, which can only operate in a *managed* mode.

As we saw when comparing AWS and Azure, all the anatomical parts of a load balancer are present and accounted for – they just might go by different names and connect in slightly different ways. The following table extends the mapping that we did between AWS and Azure and includes the GCP equivalents:

AWS	Azure	GCP	Description
Application Load Balancer (ALB)	Azure Load Balancer	URL map	Load balancer
Listener	Frontend IP configuration	Global forwarding rule	The singular endpoint that accepts incoming traffic on a load balancer
Target Group	Backend Address pool	Backend Service	A collection of VMs that incoming traffic is forwarded to
Health check	Health probe	Health check	An endpoint published by each of the backend VMs that indicates it is healthy and ready to handle traffic

Table 13.1 – Mapping of synonymous load balancer components between AWS, Azure, and GCP

The URL map and the Target HTTP proxy compose the global load balancer, which attaches to the forwarding rule, which acts as the singular endpoint, and the backend service, which represents the collection of VMs to distribute load across.

Network security

To control network traffic, Google Cloud offers firewall rules that allow users to specify which packets are allowed into and out of instances. While Google Cloud's firewall rules share some similarities with AWS's **network access control lists** (**NACLs**), it's crucial to note that GCP firewall rules are stateful, while AWS NACLs are stateless.

Secrets management

Secrets such as database credentials or service access keys need to be stored securely. Each cloud platform has a service that provides this functionality. On GCP, this service is called Google Cloud Secret Manager.

Again, we will see slight naming convention differences but all the anatomical parts are there. The following table extends the mapping that we did between AWS and Azure and includes the GCP equivalents:

AWS	Azure	GCP	Description
IAM	Microsoft Entra	Cloud Identity	Identity provider
Secrets Manager	Key Vault	Secret Manager	Secure secret storage
IAM role	User-assigned managed identity	Service account	Identity for machine-to-machine interaction
IAM policy	Role-based access control (RBAC)	IAM member	Permission to perform specific operations on specific services or resources
IAM role policy	Role assignment	IAM member	Associates specific permissions to specific identities

Table 13.2 – Mapping of synonymous IAM components between AWS, Azure, and GCP

Secrets stored in Google Cloud Secret Manager can be accessed by VMs once they have the necessary access granted. In *Chapter 7*, we used an AWS IAM role assignment to allow a VM to do this, and with Azure, we used user-assigned managed identities and ole assignments. On GCP, we need to use a service account and grant it permissions to the specific secrets:

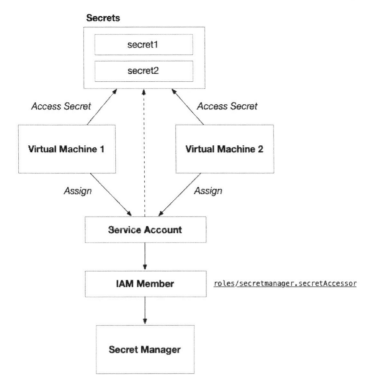

Figure 13.8 – Key Vault architecture

Granting the managed identity that is attached to the VMs access to the **Key Vault Secrets User** role will allow the VMs to read the secret values from Key Vault. This does not put the secrets on the machine. The VM will need to use the Azure CLI to access the Key Vault secrets.

VMs

Now that we have everything we need for our solution, we can finish by talking about where our application components will run: VMs provisioned on Google Cloud's Compute Engine service. When provisioning VMs on GCP, you have two options. First, you can provide static VMs. In this approach, you need to specify key characteristics for every VM. You can organize these VMs into an instance group to better manage the health and life cycle of the VMs. The second option is to provision an instance group manager. This will allow you to dynamically scale up and down based on demand, as well as auto-heal VMs that fail:

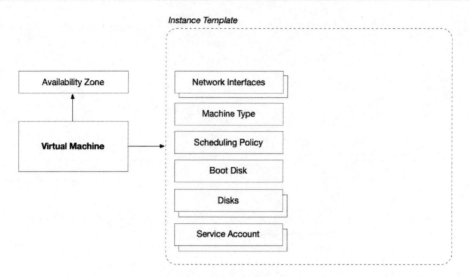

Figure 13.9 – Google Cloud Compute Engine instance architecture

Similar to Azure, Google Cloud separates the concept of grouping VMs that are tied together through the application life cycle from the management of their health and dynamic provisioning. In Azure, an availability set is a logical group that can be used to place individual VMs into a relationship so that their relationship is taken into consideration by the underlying platform:

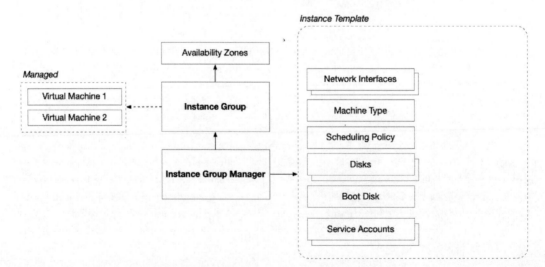

Figure 13.10 – Instance group manager architecture

On Google Cloud, that is an instance group. Both allow you to easily attach a pool of VMs to other services relevant to multiple VMs working a problem together, such as load balancers and health monitoring. To add dynamic provisioning and management, on Azure, you would need a VMSS. On Google Cloud, this is called an instance group manager.

Again, just as we saw previously, the names have been changed to protect the innocent, but make no mistake, they work the same way. The following table extends the mapping that we did between AWS and Azure and includes the GCP equivalents:

AWS	Azure	GCP	Description
EC2	VMs	Compute instance	VM service
AMI	VM image	Google compute image	VM image either from the marketplace or a custom build (for example, using tools such s Packer)
IAM role	User-assigned managed identity	Service account	Identity for machine-to-machine interaction
Auto Scaling group	VMSS	Instance group manager	Set of dynamically provisioned VMs that can be scaled up/down using a VM configuration template
Launch template	VM profile	Instance template	Configuration template used to create new VMs

Table 13.3 – Mapping of synonymous VM service components between AWS, Azure, and GCP

In *Chapter 7*, we provisioned our solution using AWS **Elastic Cloud Compute** (**EC2**) service and in *Chapter 8*, we did the same but with the Azure VM service. Like both of these platforms, on GCP, VMs are connected to virtual networks using network interfaces. Unlike AWS and Azure, these network interfaces cannot be provisioned independently of the VM and are then attached later.

We also discussed the subtle differences between how Azure and AWS handle network security, with AWS having low-level network security handled by NACLs that attach at the subnet and more logical security groups that attach at the instance and process network traffic in a stateful manner. Azure has similar constructs with network security groups, which focus more on network traffic between physical endpoints (IP address ranges and network gateways), and application security groups, which focus on network traffic between logical application endpoints. Google Cloud combines the two into Google Compute firewall resources that can control network traffic using physical network characteristics such as IP address ranges and logical constructs such as service accounts and tags.

This pattern of using tags to attach behavior or grant permissions is a common pattern on GCP and you should make note of it as other platforms do not regard tags as a method for establishing security boundaries.

Deployment architecture

Now that we have a good idea of what our cloud architecture is going to look like for our solution on Google Cloud, we need to come up with a plan on how to provision our environments and deploy our code.

VM configuration

In our solution, we have two VM roles: the frontend role, which is responsible for handling web page requests from the end user's web browser, and the backend role, which is responsible for handling REST API requests from the web application. Each of these roles has a different code and different configuration that needs to be set. Each will require its own Packer template to build a VM image that we can use to launch a VM on Google Cloud:

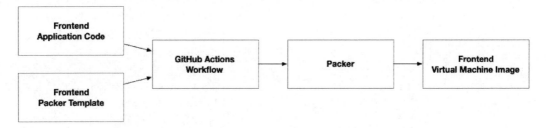

Figure 13.11 – Packer pipeline to build a VM image for the frontend

A GitHub Actions workflow that triggers off changes to the frontend application code and the frontend Packer template will execute `packer build` and create a new VM image for the solution's frontend.

Both the frontend and the backend will have identical GitHub workflows that execute `packer build`. The key difference between the workflows is the code bases that they execute against. Both the frontend and the backend might have slightly different operating system configurations, and both require different deployment packages for their respective application components:

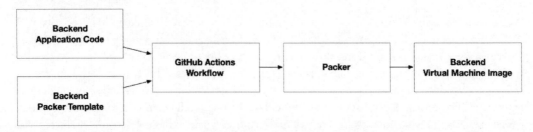

Figure 13.12 – Packer pipeline to build a VM image for the backend

It's important to note that the application code will be baked into the VM image rather than copied to an already running VM. This means that to update the software running on the VMs, each VM will need to be restarted so that it can be restarted with a new VM image containing the latest copy of the code.

This approach makes the VM image an immutable deployment artifact that is versioned and updated each time there is a release of the application code that needs to be deployed.

Cloud environment configuration

Once the VM images have been built for both the frontend and the backend, we can execute the final workflow that will both provision and deploy our solution to Google Cloud:

Figure 13.13 – VM images as inputs to the Terraform code, which
provisions the environment on Google Cloud

The Terraform code base will have two input variables for the version of the VM image for both the frontend and the backend. When new versions of the application software need to be deployed, the input parameters for these versions will be incremented to reflect the target version for deployment. When the workflow is executed, `terraform apply` will simply replace the existing VMs with VMs using the new VM image.

Now that we have a solid plan for how we will implement both the cloud architecture using Google Cloud and the deployment architecture using GitHub Actions, let's start building! In the next section, we'll break down the **HashiCorp Configuration Language** (**HCL**) code that we'll use to implement the Terraform and Packer solutions.

Building the solution

Now that we have a solid design for our solution, we can begin building it. As discussed in the previous section, we'll be using VMs powered by Google Cloud Compute Engine. As we did with AWS and Azure in *Chapters 7* and *10*, respectively, we'll need to package our application into VM images using Packer and then provision an environment that provisions an environment using these VM images.

Packer

In this section, we'll cover how to implement our Packer templates provisioners so that we can install our .NET application code on a Linux VM. If you skipped *Chapters 7* through *9* due to a lack of interest in (AWS, I can't hold that against you – particularly if your primary interest in reading this book is working on GCP. However, I would encourage you to review the corresponding section within *Chapter 7* to see how we use Packer's provisioners to configure a Debian-based Linux VM with our .NET application code.

Google Cloud plugin

As we discussed in *Chapter 4*, Packer – like Terraform – is an extensible command-line executable. Each cloud platform provides a plugin for Packer that encapsulates the integration with its services:

```
packer {
  required_plugins {
    googlecompute = {
      source  = "github.com/hashicorp/googlecompute"
      version = "~> 1.1.2"
    }
  }
}
```

In *Chapters 7* and *10*, we saw how to declare the Packer plugin for AWS and Azure (respectively) as a required plugin. The preceding code demonstrates how to declare Google Cloud's plugin – at the time of writing, the latest version is 1.1.2.

The Google Cloud plugin for Packer provides a `googlecompute` builder that will generate Google Cloud compute images by creating a new VM from a base image, executing the provisioners, taking a snapshot of the Google Cloud instance's boot disk, and creating a Google Cloud compute image from it. Like the AWS and Azure plugins, this behavior is encapsulated within Google Cloud's builder.

Just as the other plugins encapsulated the logic to build VMs on their respective platforms, its configuration was oriented using terminology specific to each platform. Packer does not try to create a standard builder interface across cloud platforms – rather, it isolates the cloud-specific configuration within the builders. This keeps things simple for users who know the target platform well and allows the builder to take advantage of any platform-specific features without additional layers of complexity by trying to rationalize the syntax across every platform.

As a result, the structure of the AWS, Azure, and Google Cloud builders is radically different in almost every way – from how they authenticate to how they look up marketplace images. There are some common fields and similarities, but they are very different animals:

```
source "googlecompute" "vm" {
```

```
project_id    = var.gcp_project_id
source_image  = "ubuntu-pro-2204-jammy-v20220923"
ssh_username  = "packer"
zone          = var.gcp_primary_region
image_name    = "${var.image_name}-${var.image_version}"


}
```

The preceding code shows how we reference the Google Cloud marketplace version of the Ubuntu 22.04 VM. Notice how, unlike the other providers, which have rather complex lookup mechanisms, Google Cloud simply has a single string to represent the desired image. Each approach produces the same outcome: we select a marketplace image hosted by the cloud platform to use as our boot disk, but we see different organizational philosophies manifesting in the three different clouds.

Operating system configuration

We must configure the operating system so that it installs software dependencies (such as .NET 6.0), copies and deploys our application code's deployment package to the correct location in the local filesystem, configures a Linux service that runs on boot, and sets a local user and group with necessary access for the service to run.

I expanded on these steps in detail in the corresponding section in *Chapter 7*, so I encourage you to review this section if you want to refresh your memory.

Terraform

As we discussed in our design, our solution is made up of two application components: the frontend and the backend. Each has a code base of application code that needs to be deployed. Since this is the first time we will be using the `google` provider, we'll look at basic provider setup and how to configure the backend before we consider the nuts and bolts of each component of our architecture.

Provider setup

First, we need to specify all the providers that we intend to use in this solution within the `required_providers` block:

```
terraform {
  required_providers {
    google = {
      source  = "hashicorp/google"
      version = "~> 5.1.0"
    }
    cloudinit = {
      source  = "hashicorp/cloudinit"
```

```
      version = "~> 2.3.2"
    }
    random = {
      source  = "hashicorp/random"
      version = "~> 3.5.1"
    }
  }
  backend "gcs" {
  }
}
```

We'll also configure the Google Cloud provider. The Google Cloud provider, like Azure but unlike AWS, is not scoped to a particular region. The Google Cloud provider doesn't even need to be scoped to a project. In this way, it is extremely flexible and can be used to provision cross-project and multi-region resources with the same provider declaration:

```
provider "google" {
  project = var.gcp_project
  region  = var.primary_region
}
```

One major difference between the Google provider and the AWS and Azure providers is how you authenticate. While Azure and AWS have environment variables that specify the identity, the Google Cloud provider relies on an authentication file, so this will alter how our pipeline tools integrate with Terraform to ensure a Google Cloud solution has the right identity. The GOOGLE_APPLICATION_CREDENTIALS environment variable specifies the path to this file. It is important to note that this file is a JSON file, but it contains secret information; therefore, it should be treated as a credential and protected as such.

Backend

Because we will be using a CI/CD pipeline to provision and maintain our environment in the long term, we need to set up a remote backend for our Terraform state. Because our solution will be hosted on Google Cloud, we'll use the Google Cloud Storage backend to store our Terraform state.

Just like the Google Cloud provider, we don't want to hard code the backend configuration in our code, so we'll simply set up a placeholder for the backend:

```
terraform {

  ...

  backend "gcs" {
  }
}
```

We'll configure the backend's parameters using the -backend-config parameters when we run terraform init in our CI/CD pipeline.

Input variables

It's good practice to pass in short names that identify the application's name and the application's environment. This allows you to embed consistent naming conventions across the resources that make up your solution, which makes it easier to identify and track resources from the Google Cloud Console.

The primary_region, network_cidr_block, and az_count input variables drive key architectural characteristics of the deployment. They mustn't be hard-coded as this will limit the reusability of the Terraform code base.

The network_cidr_block input variable establishes the virtual network address space, which is often tightly regulated by an enterprise governance body. There is usually a process to ensure that teams across an organization do not use IP address ranges that conflict, thus making it impossible to allow those two applications to integrate in the future or integrate with shared network resources within the enterprise.

The az_count input variable allows you to configure how much redundancy you want within our solution. This will affect the high availability of the solution but also the cost of the deployment. As you can imagine, cost is also a tightly regulated characteristic of cloud infrastructure deployments.

Consistent naming and tagging

Unlike the AWS console, and very similar to Azure, Google Cloud is designed in such a way that it is extremely easy to get an application-centric view of your deployment through projects. Therefore, it's not as important as an organizational strategy for your application to specify tags. By default, you will have a project-centric view of all the resources on Google Cloud:

```
resource "google_compute_network" "main" {

  ...

  tags = {
    application = var.application_name
    environment = var.environment_name
  }
}
```

It's still important to tag the resources that you deploy that indicate what application and what environment they belong to. This helps with other reporting needs, such as budgets and compliance. Almost all resources within the Google Cloud provider have a map attribute called tags. Like Azure, each resource usually has name as a required attribute.

Virtual network

Just as we did in *Chapters 7* and *8*, we need to construct a virtual network and keep its address space as tight as possible to avoid gobbling up unnecessary address space for the broader organization in the future:

```
resource "google_compute_network" "main" {
  name                       = "${var.application_name}-${var.
environment_name}"
  auto_create_subnetworks = false
}
```

The network creation in Google Cloud is simpler than what we did with AWS because we don't have to segment our subnets based on Availability Zone. This approach resembles how Azure structures subnets to span Availability Zones:

```
resource "google_compute_subnetwork" "frontend" {
  name          = "frontend"
  region        = var.primary_region
  network       = google_compute_network.main.self_link
  ip_cidr_range = cidrsubnet(var.network_cidr_block, 2, 1)
}
```

Load balancing

As we discussed in the design, the Google Cloud Load Balancing service is structured quite a bit differently than AWS and Azure's equivalent offerings.

The global forwarding rule acts as the main entry point for the global load balancer:

```
resource "google_compute_global_forwarding_rule" "frontend" { name =
"my-forwarding-rule" ip_protocol = "TCP" port_range = "80" target =
google_compute_target_http_proxy.http_proxy.self_link }
```

It then references a target HTTP proxy:

```
resource "google_compute_target_http_proxy" "http_proxy" {
  name    = "my-http-proxy"
  url_map = google_compute_url_map.url_map.self_link
}
```

Subsequently, this references a URL map:

```
resource "google_compute_url_map" "url_map" {
  name            = "my-url-map"
  default_service = google_compute_backend_service.backend_service.
self_link
}
```

The URL map points to a backend service, which ultimately defines which Google Cloud services will be handling the requests:

```
resource "google_compute_backend_service" "backend_service" {
  name          = "my-backend-service"
  port_name     = "http"
  protocol      = "HTTP"
  timeout_sec   = 10

  dynamic "backend" {
    for_each = google_compute_instance_group.frontend
    content {
      group = backend.value.self_link
    }
  }

  health_checks = [google_compute_http_health_check.frontend.self_
link]
}
```

In the preceding code, you can see that we are connecting the backend to both a health check and the instance group that contains the VMs that will ultimately be handling the incoming requests:

```
resource "google_compute_http_health_check" "frontend" {
  name = "${var.application_name}-${var.environment_name}-hc"

  port         = 5000
  request_path = "/"
}
```

The health check provides the configuration for the platform to determine if the backend service is healthy or not, with requests being sent to the health check endpoint on the corresponding backend service to determine if it is healthy enough to receive incoming traffic.

Network security

First, we need to set up the logical firewall for each application architectural component. We'll have one for the frontend and one for the backend:

```
resource "google_compute_firewall" "default-hc-fw" {

  name    = "${var.application_name}-${var.environment_name}-hc"
  network = google_compute_network.main.self_link

  allow {
```

```
    protocol = "tcp"
    ports    = [5000]
  }

  source_ranges = ["130.211.0.0/22", "35.191.0.0/16"]
  target_tags   = ["allow-lb-service"]
}
```

Google Cloud often has specific well-known IP addresses that need to be included in your firewall rules for them to grant the necessary permissions to communicate between services.

Secrets management

In *Chapter 7*, we set up secrets using AWS Secrets Manager and in *Chapter 8*, we did the same with Key Vault on Microsoft Azure. As you might remember from *Chapter 8*, Azure Key Vault is provisioned within a region. It's within this context that secrets can be created. Google Cloud's Secret Manager service works similarly to AWS in that there is no logical endpoint that needs to be provisioned where secrets are scoped within. The following code shows how to provision a secret within Google Cloud Secret Manager:

```
resource "google_secret_manager_secret" "db_password" {
  secret_id = "db-password-secret"

  replication {
    automatic = true
  }
}
```

This is a logical container for a secret that may have many different values over its life cycle as a result of regular secret rotation. The following code shows how we can define a specific version of the secret:

```
resource "google_secret_manager_secret_version" "db_password_version"
{
  secret       = google_secret_manager_secret.db_password.id
  secret_data = "abc1234"
}
```

This might be a value that we pull in from other Google Cloud resources that we provision. The following code grants a service account access to our secrets within Google Cloud Secret Manager:

```
resource "google_secret_manager_secret_iam_member" "secret_iam" {
  secret_id = "YOUR_SECRET_ID"
  role      = "roles/secretmanager.secretAccessor"

  member = "serviceAccount:YOUR_SERVICE_ACCOUNT_EMAIL"
}
```

VMs

When provisioning static VMs, we have much more control over the configuration of each machine. Some VMs have specific network and storage configurations to meet workload demands.

First, we'll obtain the VM image from our input variables. This is the VM image that we built with Packer and provisioned into a different Google Cloud project:

```
data "google_compute_image" "frontend" {
  name = var.frontend_image_name
}
```

Next, we'll create a VM using the Google Cloud instance. This resource will contain the network interface, disks, and service account configuration to set up our VM and connect it to the right subnetwork in our virtual network:

```
resource "google_compute_instance" "frontend" {

  count = var.frontend_instance_count

  name         = "vm${var.application_name}-${var.environment_name}-frontend-${count.index}"
  machine_type = var.frontend_machine_type
  zone         = local.azs_random[count.index % 2]

  boot_disk {
    initialize_params {
      image = data.google_compute_image.frontend.self_link
    }
  }

  // Local SSD disk
  scratch_disk {
    interface = "NVME"
  }

  network_interface {
    subnetwork = google_compute_subnetwork.frontend.self_link

    access_config {
      // Ephemeral public IP
    }
  }

  service_account {
    # Google recommends custom service accounts that have cloud-
platform scope and permissions granted via IAM Roles.
```

```
    email  = google_service_account.main.email
    scopes = ["cloud-platform"]
  }


  tags = ["ssh-access", "allow-lb-service"]


}
```

Then, we'll create the network interface for each VM by iterating over the `var.az_count` input variable:

```
locals {
  zone_instances = { for z in local.azs_random : z =>
    {
      instances = flatten([
        for i in google_compute_instance.frontend :
        i.zone == z ? [i.self_link] : []
      ])
    }
  }
}
```

At this point, we can set up instance groups for each zone:

```
resource "google_compute_instance_group" "frontend" {

  count = var.az_count

  named_port {
    name = "http"
    port = 5000
  }

  name      = "frontend-${count.index}"
  zone      = local.azs_random[count.index]
  instances = local.zone_instances[local.azs_random[count.index]].
instances
}
```

Finally, we'll set up the VM with all the necessary attributes before linking it to the network interface, the VM image, and the managed identity.

With that, we have implemented the Packer and Terraform solutions and have a working code base that will build VM images for both our frontend and backend application components and provision our cloud environment into Google Cloud. In the next section, we'll dive into the YAML and Bash and implement the necessary GitHub Actions workflows.

Automating the deployment

As we discussed in our design, our solution is made up of two application components: the frontend and the backend. Each has a code base of application code and operating system configuration encapsulated within a Packer template. These two application components are then deployed into a cloud environment on Azure that is defined within our Terraform code base.

Just as we did in *Chapters 7* and *8* with the AWS and Azure solutions, there is an additional code base that we have to discuss: our automation pipelines on GitHub Actions.

In *Chapter 7*, we went over the folder structure for our code base and where our GitHub Actions fit in so that we know that our automation pipelines are called workflows, and they're stored in `/.github/workflows`. Each of our code bases is stored in its respective folder. Our solutions source code repository's folder structure will look like this:

- `.github`
  - `workflows`
  - `dotnet`
    - `backend`
    - `frontend`
  - `packer`
    - `backend`
    - `frontend`
  - `terraform`

As per our design, we will have GitHub Actions workflows that will execute Packer and build VM images for both the frontend (for example, `packer-frontend.yaml`) and the backend (for example, `packer-backend.yaml`). We'll also have workflows that will run `terraform plan` and `terraform apply`:

- `.github`
  - `workflows`
    - `packer-backend.yaml`
    - `packer-frontend.yaml`
    - `terraform-apply.yaml`
    - `terraform-plan.yaml`

In *Chapter 7*, we covered the GitFlow process and how it interacts with our GitHub Actions workflows in greater detail. So, for now, let's dig into how these pipelines will differ when targeting the Azure platform.

Packer

In *Chapter 7*, we covered each step of the GitHub Actions workflow that executes Packer to build VM images. Thanks to the nature of Packer's cloud-agnostic architecture, this overwhelmingly stays the same. The only thing that changes is the final step where we execute Packer.

Because Packer needs to be configured to build a VM on Google Cloud, we need to pass in different input variables that are Google Cloud-specific. This includes the file path to the Google Cloud credential file, a Google Cloud region, and a Google Cloud project ID.

Just as we did with the input variables for the Packer template for AWS, we must ensure that all Google Cloud input variables are prefixed with `gcp_`. This will help if we ever want to introduce multi-targeting as many cloud platforms will have similar required inputs, such as target region and VM size. While most clouds will have similar required inputs, the input values are not interchangeable.

For example, each cloud platform will require you to specify the region that you want Packer to provide the temporary VM into and the resulting VM image to be stored. On Google Cloud, the region has a value of `us-west2-a`, as we saw with Azure and AWS, and each cloud platform will have infuriatingly similar and slightly different region names.

Google Cloud does have a major difference in the way credentials are usually specified. Whereas AWS and Azure usually have particular environment variables that will house context and credentials, Google Cloud uses a file. As a result, before we run Packer, we need to ensure that the Google Cloud secret file has been dropped at a well-known location so that our Packer action can pick it up:

```
- name: Create Secret File
  env:
    GOOGLE_APPLICATION_CREDENTIALS: ${{ secrets.GOOGLE_APPLICATION_
CREDENTIALS }}
  working-directory: ${{ env.WORKING_DIRECTORY }}
  run: |
    # Create a local file with the secret value
    echo -n "$GOOGLE_APPLICATION_CREDENTIALS" > gcp.json
```

The GitHub Actions workflow YAML files are identical for Google Cloud, except for the use of a single input variable that is needed to specify the path to the credential file – that is, `gcp.json`:

```
- id: build
  name: Packer Build
  env:
    GOOGLE_APPLICATION_CREDENTIALS: "gcp.json"
    PKR_VAR_gcp_project_id: ${{ vars.GOOGLE_PROJECT }}
```

```
    PKR_VAR_image_version: ${{ steps.image-version.outputs.version }}
    PKR_VAR_agent_ipaddress: ${{ steps.agent-ipaddress.outputs.
ipaddress }}
  working-directory: ${{ env.WORKING_DIRECTORY }}
  run: |
    packer init ./
    packer build -var-file=variables.pkrvars.hcl ./
```

The preceding code references the secret file we created from the GitHub Actions secret. The Google Cloud plugin for Packer will use the GOOGLE_APPLICATION_CREDENTIALS environment variable to load the secret file so that it can authenticate with Google Cloud.

Terraform

With both of our VM images built and their versions input into our .tfvars file, our Terraform automation pipeline is ready to take the reigns and not only provision our environment but deploy our solution as well (although not technically). The deployment was technically done within the packer build process, with the physical deployment packages being copied to the home directory and the Linux service setup primed and ready. Terraform is finishing the job by actually launching VMs using these images.

In *Chapter 7*, we covered each step of the GitHub Actions workflow that executes Terraform to provision the cloud environment and deploy the application code. Thanks to the nature of Terraform's cloud-agnostic architecture, this overwhelmingly stays the same. The only thing that changes is the final step where we execute Terraform.

Just like we did in *Chapters 7* and *8* with the AWS and Azure providers, we need to set the authentication context using environment variables that are specific to the google provider. In this case, the single GOOGLE_APPLICATION_CREDENTIALS attribute is passed to connect the provider with how it should authenticate with Terraform to provision the environment:

```
- name: Create Secret File for Terraform
  env:
    GOOGLE_APPLICATION_CREDENTIALS: ${{ secrets.GOOGLE_APPLICATION_
CREDENTIALS }}
  working-directory: ${{ env.WORKING_DIRECTORY }}
  run: |
    # Create a local file with the secret value
    echo -n "$GOOGLE_APPLICATION_CREDENTIALS" > gcp-terraform.json
```

The preceding code generates the necessary secret file for Terraform to authenticate with Google Cloud to provision the environment.

Just like we did in *Chapters 7* and *8* with the AWS and Azure providers, we need to configure the Google-Cloud-specific backend that stores the Terraform state by using the `-backend-config` command-line arguments alongside the `terraform init` command. The additional GOOGLE_ BACKEND_CREDENTIALS argument informs Terraform how to authenticate with the Google Cloud Storage backend that we are using to store the Terraform state:

```
- name: Create Secret File for Backend
  env:
    GOOGLE_BACKEND_CREDENTIALS: ${{ secrets.GOOGLE_BACKEND_CREDENTIALS
}}
  working-directory: ${{ env.WORKING_DIRECTORY }}
  run: |
    # Create a local file with the secret value
    echo -n "$GOOGLE_BACKEND_CREDENTIALS" > gcp-backend.json
```

The preceding code generates the necessary secret file for Terraform to authenticate with Google Cloud so that it can store and retrieve the Terraform state for the environment.

Unlike with the AWS and Azure providers – and highlighting how significantly the Terraform backend implementations can diverge – the backend uses a *prefix* and the Terraform workspace name to uniquely identify the location to store state files:

```
- id: plan
  name: Terraform Apply
  env:
    GOOGLE_BACKEND_CREDENTIALS: gcp-backend.json
    GOOGLE_APPLICATION_CREDENTIALS: gcp-terraform.json
    BACKEND_BUCKET_NAME: ${{ vars.BACKEND_BUCKET_NAME }}
    TF_VAR_gcp_project: ${{ vars.GOOGLE_PROJECT }}
  working-directory: ${{ env.WORKING_DIRECTORY }}
  run: |
    terraform init \
      -backend-config='bucket='$BACKEND_BUCKET_NAME \
      -backend-config="prefix=gcp-vm-sample"

    terraform apply -auto-approve
```

Notice how, like with the Azure solution, we don't need to perform a targeted `terraform apply` command. This is because we don't need to do dynamic calculations based on the number of Availability Zones in the region to configure our virtual network.

These subtle architectural differences between the cloud platforms can create radical structural changes, even when we're deploying the same solution using the same technologies. It is a sobering reminder that while knowledge of the core concepts we looked at in *Chapters 4* through 6 will help us transcend to a multi-cloud point of view, to implement practical solutions, we need to understand the subtle nuances of each platform.

Summary

In this chapter, we built a multi-tier cloud architecture using VMs powered by Google Cloud Compute Engine with a fully operation GitFlow process and an end-to-end CI/CD pipeline using GitHub Actions.

In the next chapter, our fearless leader at Söze Enterprises will be throwing us into turmoil with some big new ideas, and we'll have to respond to his call to action. It turns out our CEO, Keyser, has been up late watching some YouTube videos about the next big thing – containers – and after talking with his pal Sundar on his superyacht, he has decided that we need to refactor our whole solution so that it can run on Docker and Kubernetes. Luckily, the good people at Google have a service that might help us out: **Google Kubernetes Engine** (**GKE**).

14

Containerize on Google Cloud – Building Solutions with GKE

In the previous chapter, we built and automated our solution on Google Cloud by utilizing **Google Compute Engine** (**GCE**). We built **virtual machine** (**VM**) images with Packer and provisioned our VM using Terraform. In this chapter, we'll follow a similar path, but instead of working with VMs, we'll look at hosting our application in containers within a Kubernetes cluster.

To achieve this, we'll need to alter our approach by ditching Packer and replacing it with Docker to create a deployable artifact for our application. Once again, we'll be using the `google` provider for Terraform and revisiting the `kubernetes` provider for Terraform that we looked at when we took the same step while on our journey with AWS and Azure.

Since the overwhelming majority of this remains the same when we move to Google Cloud, we won't revisit these topics at the same length in this chapter. However, I would encourage you to bookmark *Chapter 8* and refer to it frequently.

This chapter covers the following topics:

- Laying the foundation
- Designing the solution
- Building the solution
- Automating the deployment

Laying the foundation

Our story continues through the lens of Söze Enterprises, founded by the enigmatic Turkish billionaire Keyser Söze. Our team has been hard at work building the next-generation autonomous vehicle orchestration platform. Previously, we had hoped to leapfrog the competition by leveraging Google Cloud's rock-solid platform, leveraging our team's existing skills, and focusing on feature development. The team was just getting into their groove when a curveball came out of nowhere.

Over the weekend, our elusive executive was influenced by a rendezvous with Sundar Pichai, the CEO of Alphabet and Google's parent company, in Singapore. Keyser was seen gobbling down street food with Sundar on Satay Street. During this brief but enjoyable encounter, Sundar extolled the virtues and prowess of Kubernetes and Google's unique position as the original developers of the open source technology. Keyser was enchanted by the prospect of more efficient resource utilization, leading to improved cost optimization and faster deployment and rollback times, and he was hooked. His new autonomous vehicle platform needed to harness the power of the cloud, and container-based architecture was the way to do it. So, he decided to accelerate his plans to adopt cloud-native architecture!

The news of transitioning to a container-based architecture means reevaluating their approach, diving into new technologies, and possibly even reshuffling team dynamics. For the team, containers were always the long-term plan, but now, things need to be sped up, which will require a significant investment in time, resources, and training.

As the team scrambles to adjust their plans, they can't help but feel a mix of excitement and apprehension. They know that they are part of something groundbreaking under Keyser's leadership. His vision for the future of autonomous vehicles is bold and transformative. And while his methods may be unconventional, they have learned that his instincts are often correct. In this chapter, we'll explore this transformation from VMs to containers using Google Cloud.

Designing the solution

As we saw in the previous chapter, where we built our solution using VMs on Google Cloud, we had full control over the operating system configuration through the VM images we provisioned with Packer. Just as we did when we went through the same process on our journey with AWS and Azure in *Chapters 8* and *11*, we'll need to introduce a new tool to replace VM images with container images – **Docker**:

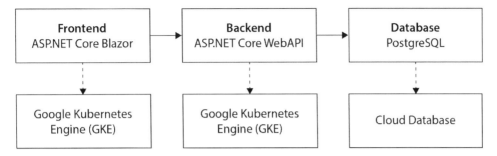

Figure 14.1 – Logical architecture for the autonomous vehicle platform

Our application architecture, comprising a frontend, a backend, and a database, will remain the same, but we will need to provision different resources with Terraform and harness new tools from Docker and Kubernetes to automate the deployment of our solution to this new infrastructure:

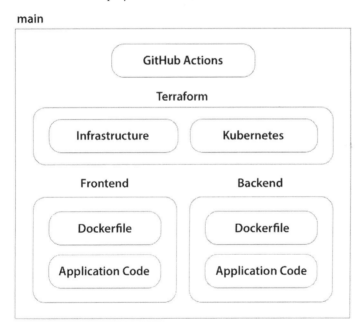

Figure 14.2 – Source control structure of our repository

This solution will have seven parts. We still have the application code and Dockerfiles (replacing the Packer-based VM images) for both the frontend and backend. We also still have GitHub Actions to implement our CI/CD process, but we now have two Terraform code bases – one for provisioning the underlying infrastructure to Google Cloud and another for provisioning our application to the Kubernetes cluster hosted on GKE. Then, we have the two code bases for our application's frontend and backend.

Cloud architecture

Google Kubernetes Engine (**GKE**) is a sophisticated offering that allows you to provision a managed Kubernetes cluster in a multitude of ways, depending on your objectives, whether that is to maximize simplicity of operations or highly customized configurations.

Autopilot

One of the simplest ways of operating a Kubernetes cluster on Google Cloud is using the Autopilot feature of GKE. Turning on the Autopilot feature abstracts much of the complexity of operating a Kubernetes cluster. This option changes the operating model radically, so much so that it is probably more akin to some of the container-based serverless options on other clouds than it does the managed Kubernetes offerings that we've delved into in previous chapters. As a result, it is outside the scope of this book. However, if this approach appeals to you, I suggest that you investigate further in Google's documentation (`https://cloud.google.com/kubernetes-engine/docs/concepts/autopilot-overview`). I'm pointing this out because, unlike AWS and Azure, which have separately branded services that abstract away container orchestration, **Google Cloud Platform** (**GCP**) has this capability coupled with its managed Kubernetes offering.

Regional versus zonal

GKE supports two primary cluster types: regional and zonal. The cluster type affects how the cluster's underlying physical infrastructure is provisioned across GCP, which subsequently affects the resiliency of the Kubernetes cluster:

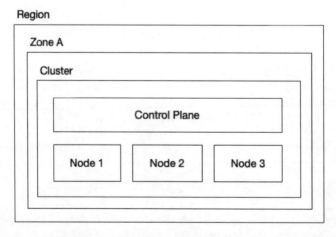

Figure 14.3 – The GKE zonal cluster hosts the control plane and all nodes within a single Availability Zone

A zonal cluster is deployed within a single Availability Zone within a given region. As we know, each region has a name, such as us-west1. To reference a specific zone, we append the zone number to the end of the region name. For example, to reference Availability Zone A in the West US 1 region, we can refer to it by its name – that is, us-west1-a:

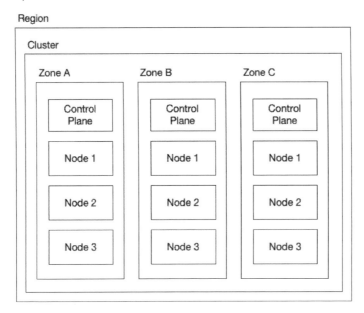

Figure 14.4 – The GKE regional cluster replicates the control plane
and nodes across all zones within the region

A regional cluster is deployed across Availability Zones within a given region. When you deploy a regional cluster, by default, your cluster is deployed across three Availability Zones within that region. This approach results in higher availability and resiliency in case of an Availability Zone outage.

Virtual network

As we discussed in the previous chapter, when we set up our VM-based solution on Google Cloud, we will need a virtual network to host our GKE cluster. This will allow us to configure a private GKE cluster so that the Kubernetes control plane and the node have private IP addresses and are not directly accessible from the internet.

In the previous chapter, where we set up our VM-based solution, we set up two subnets: one for the frontend and one for the backend. However, when using a Kubernetes cluster to host our solution, both the frontend and backend will be hosted on the same Kubernetes nodes.

This straightforward approach, where multiple node pools share one subnet, can suffice for less complex configurations. However, while this setup simplifies network management, it can potentially limit the scalability of individual node pools due to shared network resources and address space constraints.

For more scalable and flexible architectures, especially in larger or more dynamic environments, it's often advantageous to allocate separate subnets for different node pools. This method allows each node pool to scale independently and optimizes network organization, providing better resource allocation and isolation. This kind of structured subnetting becomes increasingly important as the complexity and scale of the Kubernetes deployments grow, making it a key consideration in GKE network planning and configuration.

Container registry

Like the other cloud platforms we've been delving into in this book, Google Cloud also offers a robust container registry service known as **Google Artifact Registry**, which is a private registry for hosting and managing container images and Helm charts. Artifact Registry supports many other formats besides container images but we'll only be using it in this capacity.

Google Artifact Registry is set up pretty similarly to other cloud providers. It resembles **Azure Container Registry** a bit more though because it can host multiple repositories, allowing you to host multiple container images in the same Artifact Registry.

Load balancing

GKE has a very similar experience to other managed Kubernetes offerings that we have looked at in this book. By default, when a Kubernetes service is provisioned to a private cluster, GKE will automatically provision an internal load balancer for this service. This will make the Kubernetes service available within the virtual network but not to the outside world.

This works well for our backend REST API but doesn't work for our public web application, which is intended to be accessible from the public Internet. Like on AWS and Azure, to make the frontend service accessible to the internet, we need to configure an ingress controller on the cluster and a public load balancer that has a public IP address and will route traffic to the ingress controller on the GKE cluster:

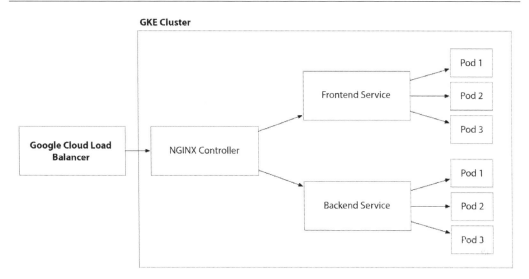

Figure 14.5 – The GKE cluster with an NGINX ingress controller automating a Google Cloud load balancer

As we did in previous chapters, we'll set up an NGINX ingress controller and configure it to automatically provision the necessary external load balancer.

Network security

When working with GKE, network security is managed in a manner akin to the practices described in *Chapter 13* for VMs, leveraging similar concepts and tools within the Google Cloud ecosystem. GKE clusters are typically deployed within a virtual network, allowing them to seamlessly integrate with other Google Cloud services.

Similar to the other managed Kubernetes offerings, the virtual network acts as the primary boundary for network security, within which GKE has its internal network where pods and services communicate. Google Cloud firewalls are used to define security rules at the subnet level, controlling inbound and outbound traffic similar to how they are employed with VMs.

Additionally, GKE takes advantage of native Kubernetes network policies for finer-grained control within the cluster, allowing administrators to define how Pods communicate with each other and with other resources in the virtual network. This dual-layered approach, combining the external security controls of the virtual network with the internal mechanisms of GKE, creates a comprehensive and robust network security environment for Kubernetes deployments.

Workload identity

As we did with AWS and Azure in previous chapters, we'll be setting up a workload identity to allow our application's pods to authenticate with other Google Cloud services using a Google Cloud identity provider. This will allow us to use the built-in role-based access control to grant access for Kubernetes service accounts to other Google Cloud resources.

Secrets management

GKE does not have direct integration with Google Secrets Manager like other cloud platforms. Instead, the options available to you are to leverage native Kubernetes secrets or to access Google Secrets Manager from your application code itself. This approach does have some security advantages but it is less ideal as it tightly couples your application to GCP SDKs.

Kubernetes cluster

Building a Kubernetes cluster using GKE involves a few key decisions that determine the modality of your cluster. As we've discussed in this book, we will omit the use of Autopilot to maintain congruency with the other managed Kubernetes offerings from the other cloud platforms we've looked at in this book. So, we will focus on building a private Kubernetes cluster with its own virtual network.

Like other managed Kubernetes offerings, GKE provides flexibility to configure node pools based on workload types, but unlike those offerings, you don't need to set up node pools for running core Kubernetes services. GKE handles all that on your behalf! This abstraction greatly simplifies cluster design. Overall, GKE's simplicity and robust feature set allow us to build highly scalable Kubernetes clusters with minimal effort.

Deployment architecture

As we saw with the cloud architecture, there were many similarities between our work in *Chapters 8* and *11* with AWS and Microsoft Azure. The deployment architecture will mirror what we saw in those chapters as well. In the previous chapter, we saw the differences in the Terraform provider when we configured the `google` provider to provision our solution to VMs using GCE.

In the context of container-based architecture, the only significant difference from our deployment in the previous chapters with AWS and Azure will be the way we authenticate with the container registry and the Kubernetes cluster. It's important to recall the deployment architectural approach outlined in the corresponding section of *Chapter 8*. In the next section, we'll build the same solution on GCP, ensuring we don't repeat the same information.

In this section, we reviewed the key changes in our architecture as we transitioned from VM-based architecture to container-based architecture. We were careful not to retread the ground we covered in *Chapter 8*, where we first went through this transformation on the AWS platform. In the next section, we'll get tactical in building the solution, but again, we'll be careful to build on the foundations we built in the previous chapter when we first set up our solution on GCP using VMs.

Building the solution

In this section, we'll be taking our theoretical knowledge and applying it to a tangible, functioning solution while harnessing the power of Docker, Terraform, and Kubernetes on GCP. Some parts of this process will require significant change, such as when we provision our Google Cloud infrastructure using Terraform; other parts will have minor changes, such as the Kubernetes configuration that we use to deploy our application to our Kubernetes cluster, and some will have almost no change whatsoever, such as when we build a push our Docker images to our container registry.

Docker

In this section, we'll go into great detail on how we can implement our Dockerfile, which installs our .NET application code and runs the service in a container. If you skipped *Chapters 7* through *9* due to a lack of interest in AWS, I can't hold that against you – particularly if your primary interest in reading this book is working on GCP. However, I would encourage you to review the corresponding section within *Chapter 8* to see how we can use Docker to configure a container with our .NET application code.

Infrastructure

As we know, Terraform is not a write-once, run-anywhere solution. It is a highly extensible **Infrastructure as Code** (**IaC**) tool that uses a well-defined strategy pattern to facilitate the management of multiple cloud platforms. This yields very similar conceptually structured solutions but with significant variations embedded within the differing implementation details and nomenclature of each corresponding cloud platform.

As we discussed in the previous section, the virtual network configuration will largely be identical and the load balancer will be automatically provisioned by GKE via the NGINX ingress controller. Therefore, in this section, we will only focus on the new resources that we need to replace our VMs with a Kubernetes cluster.

Container registry

The first thing we need is a Google Cloud Artifact Registry that we can push Docker images to. We'll use this as part of our Docker build process later when we build and push Docker images to be used by our GKE cluster:

```
resource "google_artifact_registry_repository" "main" {
  project       = google_project.main.project_id
  location      = var.primary_region
  repository_id = "${var.application_name}-${var.environment_name}"
  format        = "DOCKER"
}
```

Service account

To grant our applications and services the ability to implicitly authenticate with Google Cloud and access other services and resources hosted therein, we need to set up a service account that we can associate with the workloads running on our cluster. This is similar to the IAM role and managed identity we specified on AWS and Azure, respectively:

```
resource "google_service_account" "cluster" {
  project      = google_project.main.project_id
  account_id   = "sa-gke-${var.application_name}-${var.environment_
name}-${random_string.project_id.result}"
  display_name = "sa-gke-${var.application_name}-${var.environment_
name}-${random_string.project_id.result}"
}
```

Kubernetes cluster

This Terraform code creates a GKE cluster with a customized name – that is, Google Cloud Region. The `location` attribute is extremely critical as its value can determine if the cluster is regional or zonal. Simply making a tiny change from `us-west1` to `us-west1-a` has this effect:

```
resource "google_container_cluster" "main" {

  project = google_project.main.project_id
  name    = "gke-${var.application_name}-${var.environment_name}-
${random_string.project_id.result}"
  location = var.primary_region

  remove_default_node_pool = true
  initial_node_count       = 1


}
```

By default, GKE will automatically provision a default node pool. This is a common practice that, unfortunately, prioritizes the graphical user experience via the Google Cloud console over the IaC experience. This problem is not unique to Google Cloud; both AWS and Azure have similar areas of friction where automation is an afterthought. As a result, we are at least left with attributes that allow us to circumvent this behavior. By setting `remove_default_node_pool` to `true`, we can ensure that this default behavior is eliminated. Furthermore, setting `initial_node_count` to `1` can further speed up this process.

As we discussed previously, GKE abstracts the Kubernetes master services from us so that we don't need to worry about deploying a node pool for these Kubernetes system components. Therefore, we are left with defining our node pools for our applications and services to run on:

```
resource "google_container_node_pool" "primary" {

  project    = google_project.main.project_id
  name       = "gke-${var.application_name}-${var.environment_name}-
${random_string.project_id.result}-primary"
  location   = var.primary_region
  cluster    = google_container_cluster.main.name
  node_count = var.node_count

  node_config {

    ...

  }

}
```

The basic configuration of a node pool resource connects it to the corresponding cluster and specifies a node_count value. The node_config block is where we configure more details for the nodes within the pool. The node pool configuration should look similar to what we saw in *Chapters 8* and *11* when we configured the managed Kubernetes offerings of AWS and Azure. Node pools have a count that controls how many VMs we can spin up and a VM size that specifies how many CPU cores and memory each node gets. We also need to specify the service account under which the node pool will operate:

```
node_config {

  machine_type = var.node_size

  preemptible  = false
  spot         = false

  service_account = google_service_account.cluster.email

  oauth_scopes = [
    "https://www.googleapis.com/auth/cloud-platform",
    "https://www.googleapis.com/auth/logging.write",
    "https://www.googleapis.com/auth/monitoring"
  ]
}
```

Here, `oauth_scopes` is used to specify what permissions the nodes should have access to. To enable Google Cloud logging and monitoring, we need to add scopes to allow the nodes to tap into these existing Google Cloud services.

Workload identity

To enable a workload identity, we need to modify both our cluster and node pool configuration. The cluster needs to have the `workload_identity_config` block defined with `workload_pool` set with a specific magic string that will provision the GKE metadata service within the cluster:

```
resource "google_container_cluster" "main" {

  ...

  workload_identity_config {
    workload_pool = "${google_project.main.project_id}.svc.id.goog"
  }

}
```

Once the GKE metadata service is made available within the cluster, we need to configure our node pools so that they integrate with it using the `workload_metadata_config` block. We can do this by specifying `GKE_METADATA` as the mode:

```
node_config {

  ...

  workload_metadata_config {
    mode = "GKE_METADATA"
  }

}
```

Kubernetes

In *Chapters 8* and *11*, we built out the Kubernetes deployments using the Terraform provider for Kubernetes on AWS and Azure, respectively. We'll follow the same approach here, building on the infrastructure we provisioned in the previous section.

Provider setup

As we saw in *Chapter 11*, there is not much that changes when executing Terraform using the Kubernetes provider to provision resources to the Kubernetes control plane. We still authenticate against our target cloud platform, follow Terraform's core workflow, and pass in additional input parameters for platform-specific resources that we need to reference. Most notably, information about the cluster and other GCP services such as Secrets Manager and other details that might need to be put into Kubernetes ConfigMaps can be used by the pods to point them at the endpoint of their database.

As we saw in *Chapters 8* and *11*, when we accomplished the same task on AWS and Azure, I am using a layered approach to provision the infrastructure first and then provision to Kubernetes. As a result, we can reference the Kubernetes cluster using the data source from the Terraform workspace that provisions the Google Cloud infrastructure. This allows us to access important connectivity details without exporting them outside of Terraform and passing them around during deployment:

```
data "google_container_cluster" "main" {
  name     = var.cluster_name
  location = var.primary_region
}
```

As you can see, in the preceding code, when using the data source, we only need to specify the cluster name and its target region. Using this data source, we can then initialize the kubernetes provider:

```
provider "kubernetes" {

  token                    = data.google_client_config.current.access_
token
  host                     = data.google_container_cluster.main.endpoint
  client_certificate       = base64decode(data.google_container_cluster.
main.master_auth.0.client_certificate)
  client_key               = base64decode(data.google_container_cluster.
main.master_auth.0.client_key)
  cluster_ca_certificate = base64decode(data.google_container_cluster.
main.master_auth.0.cluster_ca_certificate)

}
```

This configuration varies slightly from the provider initialization techniques we used with AWS and Azure in previous chapters with the addition of token. Similar to how we initialized the helm provider on other cloud platforms, we can pass the same inputs to set up the Helm provider.

Workload identity

As we discussed in *Chapters 8* and *11*, where we implemented a workload identity on both AWS and Azure, we need a way for our Kubernetes workloads to be able to implicitly authenticate with Google Cloud services and resources. To do so, we need an identity provisioned within Google Cloud, which we saw in the previous section of this chapter, but we also need something provisioned within Kubernetes that will connect our pod specifications to the Google Cloud service account:

```
resource "kubernetes_service_account" "main" {
  metadata {
    namespace = var.namespace
    name      = var.service_account_name
    annotations = {
      "iam.gke.io/gcp-service-account" = var.service_account_email
    }
  }
  automount_service_account_token = var.service_account_token
}
```

The preceding code will provision the Kubernetes service account that will complete the linkage with the Google Cloud configuration that we provisioned in the previous section.

Now that we've built out the three components of our architecture, in the next section, we'll move on to how we can automate the deployment using Docker so that we can build and publish the container images. We'll also look at doing this using Terraform so that we can provision our infrastructure and deploy our solution to Kubernetes.

Automating the deployment

In this section, we'll look at how we can automate the deployment process for container-based architectures. We'll employ similar techniques we saw in *Chapter 8* when we took this same journey down the Amazon. As a result, we'll focus on what changes we need to make when we want to deploy to Microsoft Azure and the Azure Kubernetes Service.

Docker

In *Chapter 8*, we covered each step of the GitHub Actions workflow that causes Docker to build, tag, and push our Docker container images. Thanks to the nature of Docker's cloud-agnostic architecture, this overwhelmingly stays the same.

The only thing that changes is that Google Cloud encapsulates a service account's credentials into a JSON file that is downloaded from the Google Cloud console rather than a secret string like on AWS or Azure. As a result, much of the Google Cloud tooling is set up to look for this file at a specific path location.

Therefore, we need to use a special username `_json_key` and reference the value of the JSON file stored in a GitHub Actions secret:

```
    - name: Login to Google Container Registry
      uses: docker/login-action@v3
      with:
        registry: ${{ needs.terraform-apply.outputs.container_
registry_endpoint }}
        username: _json_key
        password: ${{ secrets.GOOGLE_APPLICATION_CREDENTIALS }}
```

The only thing that changes is the way we must configure Docker so that it targets Google Artifact Registry.

Terraform

In *Chapter 13*, we comprehensively covered the process of creating a Terraform GitHub Action that authenticates with GCP using a service account. Therefore, we won't be delving into it any further. I encourage you to refer back to *Chapter 10* to review the process.

Kubernetes

When we automate Kubernetes with Terraform, we are just running `terraform apply` again with a different root module. This time, the root module will configure the `kubernetes` and `helm` providers in addition to the `google` provider. However, we won't ever create new resources with the `google` provider; we will only obtain data sources to existing resources we provisioned in the previous `terraform apply` command that provisioned the infrastructure to Google Cloud.

As a result, the GitHub Action that executes this process will look strikingly similar to how we executed Terraform with Google Cloud. Some of the variables might change to include things such as the container image details and cluster information.

Summary

In this chapter, we designed, built, and automated the deployment of a complete and end-to-end solution using container-based architecture. We built onto the foundations from *Chapter 13*, where we worked with the foundational infrastructure of Google Cloud networking but layered on GKE to host our application in containers. In the next and final step in our GCP journey, we'll be looking at serverless architecture, thus moving beyond the underlying infrastructure and letting the platform itself take our solution to new heights.

15

Go Serverless on Google Cloud – Building Solutions with Google Cloud Functions

We are almost there! In this chapter, we will build the last of the nine solutions we'll build in this book. We are about to close the door on Google Cloud—but only after we take the final step of transitioning our application to serverless architecture as we did on AWS and Azure. In the previous two chapters, we worked hard to implement our solution on Google Cloud using virtual machines and then containers.

We've taken time to make some comparisons between how things work across all three cloud platforms to help us understand the subtle and sometimes not-so-subtle differences between them.

We've noticed that while our Terraform code has been changing pretty consistently between cloud platforms, our application code and the operating system configuration—either in Packer or Docker—haven't. As we take our final step with Google Cloud, we'll be going through a similar process to the one we went through when we transitioned our application to AWS Lambda and Azure Functions. We'll have to completely refactor the application code.

The chapter covers the following topics:

- Laying the foundation
- Designing the solution
- Building the solution
- Automating the deployment

Laying the foundation

Our skilled team had just finished putting the finishing touches on the final ConfigMap in our Kubernetes configuration when they received a not-so-surprising telephone call. Keyser seems to have had yet another epiphany, this time while hanging out with Larry Page.

While walking through Larry's private terminal at San Jose International Airport to his personal Boeing 767 waiting for them, Keyser and Larry were discussing Keyser's new venture. Larry mentioned in passing, *"Keyser, why are you even investing in infrastructure? These days, everybody is going serverless. Focus on your platform. Let Google Cloud focus on how to scale it."*

"Eureka!" exclaimed Keyser, as he tossed a few warm cashews into his mouth before elaborating. *"Oh man, Larry, you're so right! I need to get my team on this right away! What was I thinking? We don't have time for the plumbing; we need to move fast to stay ahead of the competition!"*

Back at headquarters, the team is adapting to this exciting yet sudden change in direction. Now, thanks to Keyser's bold new strategy, they're gearing up to dive deep into serverless computing. This shift will require more than just repackaging the application—they'll have to completely refactor the code!

Designing the solution

In this section, we will look at the overall design of our solution given the shift from virtual machine- and container-based architectures toward serverless architectures. As we saw in previous transformations, serverless at its core has the quintessential objective of eliminating heavy infrastructure from the stack. Therefore, we will be looking for ways to shed any Google Cloud services that require significant fixed costs, such as **virtual machines** or **Kubernetes clusters**, and replace them with serverless options. This change in our operational context and our technology landscape will likely require us to rethink some things about our solution, including its design, implementation, and deployment strategy:

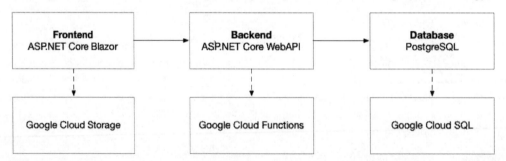

Figure 15.1 – The logical architecture for the autonomous vehicle platform

While our application's architecture doesn't change significantly, we will use different Google Cloud services to host it. In this case, we'll be using Google Cloud Storage to host the application's frontend, and we'll be using Google Cloud Functions to host the application's backend, as illustrated in *Figure 15.2*:

Figure 15.2 – The source control structure of our repository

In this solution, we'll have four parts of our code base: Terraform code that provisions the environment, GitHub Actions code that executes the deployment process, and the two code bases for our application's frontend and backend.

Cloud architecture

In *Chapter 13*, our cloud-hosting solution was a set of dedicated virtual machines, and in *Chapter 14*, it was a set of shared virtual machines within our Kubernetes cluster's node pool. Using virtual machines has the most sunk cost, whether they are standalone virtual machines or part of a Kubernetes node pool.

In *Chapter 14*, our entire solution was executed on containers that allowed the frontend and the backend to coexist as a set of containers on the same virtual machine. This saved some money, but we still needed servers to host the workload. In this chapter, we have a new objective: take advantage of the power of the cloud by leveraging cloud-native services that abstract the underlying infrastructure from us and allow us to truly pay for only what we use. Google Cloud's serverless offerings will be crucial to us in this endeavor.

Frontend

In previous chapters, we hosted our frontend on public-facing servers that return the HTML and JavaScript that composed our web application, and we still required a cloud-hosted solution to host the files and respond to requests.

However, due to the nature of the web application running within the end user's browser, we really don't need to use cloud-hosted virtual machines to host what are essentially flat files. We can use simple cloud storage to host the frontend as a static website and rely on the cloud platform to shoulder the burden of returning the web content.

We can use the Google Cloud Storage service on Google Cloud. This service allows us to host static web content that is internet accessible. As we did on AWS and Azure in previous chapters, most of this functionality is achieved by adding a **Storage bucket** and enabling it to host web content. However, unlike how we handled this on AWS and Azure, we need to add our own load balancer to ensure our web application functions properly, as illustrated in *Figure 15.3*:

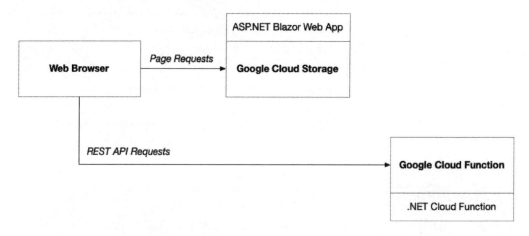

Figure 15.3 – Google Cloud Storage handles web page requests while
Google Cloud Functions handles REST API requests

As we saw on other platforms, we will gain a huge advantage because Google Cloud Storage has absolutely no sunk costs. When you create a Google Cloud Storage bucket, it costs you absolutely zero dollars ($0) per month. Like other serverless offerings, it uses a set of microtransactions to measure your activity and charge you for precisely what you use. In Google Cloud Storage, this can be a bit complicated as there are several measurements that incur costs.

Table 15.1 shows all the costs you will run into when using Google Cloud Storage to host your static websites:

Metric	Unit	Scale	Price
Storage	GBs	1,000	$0.023
Write Transactions	Transactions	1,000	$0.01
Read Transactions	Transactions	1,000	$0.0004

Table 15.1 – Google Cloud Storage micro-transactional pricing

> **Note**
>
> The prices listed are, at the time of writing, for Google Cloud's West US 2 region. Prices may have changed by the time you are reading this, so it's best to check the latest prices for the most accurate cost estimation.

I included these prices to make a point. We can host a static website on a three-node Kubernetes cluster for approximately $300 a month, or we can host a static website on Google Cloud Storage for less than $0.01 a month on the most rock-solid storage tier that Google Cloud has to offer. Which approach would you choose?

Backend

Like our frontend, in previous chapters, our backend was also hosted on virtual machines in two different ways: dedicated virtual machines and shared virtual machines within the node pool on our Kubernetes cluster.

Unlike our frontend, our backend doesn't have the option of running entirely client-side inside the end user's web browser. In the backend, we have custom code that needs to run on a server. Therefore, we need to find a solution to host these components without all the overhead of a fleet of virtual machines. On Google Cloud, we can use Google Cloud Functions to accomplish this. Google Cloud Functions is a managed service that allows you to deploy your code without paying the sunk costs for any of the underlying virtual machines. Like Google Cloud Storage, it has its own micro-transactional pricing model that charges you for precisely what you use.

Table 15.2 shows what costs that you will incur when deploying your code to Google Cloud Functions:

Metric	Unit	Scale	Price
Compute	GHz/s	1	$0.00001
Memory	GB/s	1	$0.0000025
Total Executions	Transactions	1,000,000	$0.40

Table 15.2 – Google Cloud Functions microtransactions pricing

The first thing that you'll probably notice is that, like Google Cloud Storage, these prices are extremely small but they measure a very small amount of activity on the platform.

For example, the **compute** and **memory** metrics have units that correspond to that resource's unit of measure per second. For compute metrics, it's measured in GHz per second, and for memory metrics, it's measured in GB per second. These units of measurement give you the flexibility to adjust the amount of compute and memory resources your cloud functions have access to when they are executed. Given that it measures at a *per second* interval, you don't have to be running your Google Cloud Functions very long to rack up quite a few of these. *Figure 15.4* shows Google Cloud Functions deploying the application code to Google Cloud Storage:

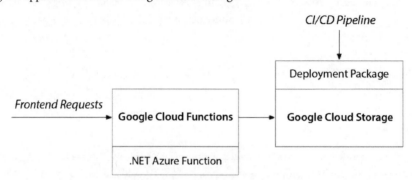

Figure 15.4 – Google Cloud Functions runs the application code
which is deployed to Google Cloud Storage

Previously, our ASP.NET REST API was set up using a traditional ASP.NET project that used Controllers to implement the REST API endpoints. However, when transitioning to Google Cloud Functions, this solution structure is incompatible with the Google Cloud Functions framework. In order to be able to host our REST API as Google Cloud Functions, we need to conform to the framework that Cloud Functions dictates. This means that the ASP.NET controller classes will need to be refactored to conform to this standard. In the next section, we'll delve into the code that makes this possible.

Deployment architecture

Now that we have a good idea of what our cloud architecture for our solution on Google Cloud will look like, we need to devise a plan for provisioning our environments and deploying our code.

In *Chapter 12*, when we deployed our application to virtual machines, we baked our compiled application code into a virtual machine image using Packer:

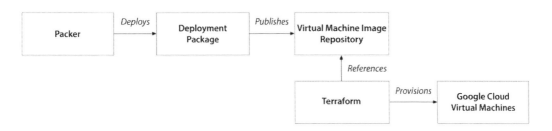

Figure 15.5 – The deployment process for virtual machines using Packer-built virtual machine images

Similarly, in *Chapter 13*, when we deployed our application to containers on our Kubernetes cluster, we baked our application code into container images using Docker:

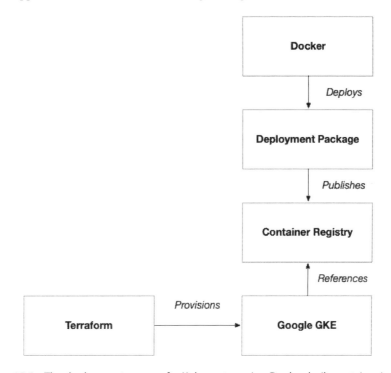

Figure 15.6 – The deployment process for Kubernetes using Docker-built container images

With serverless, this completely changes because Google Cloud's serverless offerings abstract away the operating system. This means that all we are responsible for is producing a compatible deployment package.

Creating the deployment package

As discussed in the previous section, we have two components of our application: the frontend and the backend. Each has a different deployment target. For the frontend, we are going to be deploying as a static website, while the backend is going to be deployed as a Google Cloud function. Since both are .NET projects, we will be using both .NET and Google Cloud Platform-specific tools in order to create deployment packages and deploy them to their target Google Cloud services. The following diagram shows the process we go through to provision our environment, package our application code, and deploy it to the target environment in Google Cloud:

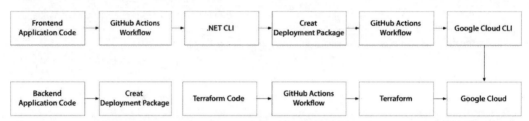

Figure 15.7 – The deployment pipeline to build our .NET application code for deployment to Google Cloud

For the frontend, this means enabling the feature to deploy our ASP.NET Blazor web application as WebAssembly. This will allow the frontend to be hosted as a static website that can run completely client-side without any server-side rendering. This is only possible because of the way we have designed our frontend web application, which uses HTML, CSS, and JavaScript to interact with server-side REST APIs. It's important to note that ASP.NET Blazor supports both hosting options, but we specifically chose to go down the client-side-only path and eliminate any dependency on server-side page rendering. As a result, when we use the .NET CLI to publish our ASP.NET Blazor project, it will emit a folder containing static web content. Then, using a Google Cloud CLI, we can upload the contents of this folder to our Google Cloud Storage bucket to complete the deployment, as shown in *Figure 15.8*:

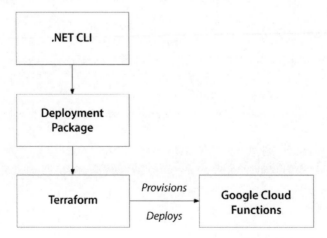

Figure 15.8 – The deployment process for Google Cloud Functions
using custom-built deployment packages

For the backend, unlike on AWS and Azure, the application code on Google Cloud shouldn't be compiled as it needs to be processed by Google Cloud Functions. This means the actual source code files need to be uploaded as opposed to the compiled artifacts, as we have done previously. Therefore, we must zip the source code folder into a ZIP archive. Another major difference is that the Terraform provider for Google Cloud requires this zip archive to be uploaded by Terraform:

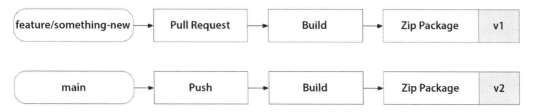

Figure 15.9 – The GitFlow process to create new versioned artifacts

This process will integrate nicely with the GitFlow process discussed in *Chapter 6*. With each new feature we develop, we'll open a new feature branch, and when we're ready to integrate our updates with the main body of work, we'll submit a pull request:

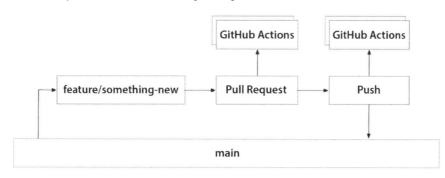

Figure 15.10 – GitFlow process to create new versioned artifacts

This pull request will trigger GitHub Actions that run built-in quality checks on our application code and run a `terraform plan` to evaluate the impact on our long-lived environments. We can do any number of tests before the code is merged, which is good to verify that our updates–both to the application code and to the infrastructure code– won't negatively impact our target environment. Once our pull request is approved and merged, it will trigger additional GitHub Actions that will apply the changes to the target environment.

Now that we have a solid plan for implementing both the cloud architecture using Google Cloud Platform and the deployment architecture using GitHub Actions, let's start building! In the next section, we'll break down the **HashiCorp Configuration Language** (**HCL**) code that we use to implement Terraform, and we'll look at the application code changes we need to make to get our application up and running using Google Cloud Functions.

Building the solution

Now that we have a solid design for our solution, we can begin building it. As we discussed in the previous section, because we'll be using Google Cloud's serverless offerings such as Google Cloud Storage and Google Cloud Functions to host our application, we will need to make some changes to our application code. This is something that we have never had to do in *Chapters 13* and *14*, as we were able to deploy our application to the cloud by packaging it in either a virtual machine image (using Packer) or in a container image (using Docker). Therefore, in order to build our solution, we need to write some Terraform and make updates to our application code in C#.

Terraform

As we discussed in our design, our solution comprises two application components: the frontend and the backend. Each has its own application codebase that needs to be deployed. Unlike previous chapters, where we also had operating system configuration, now that we are using serverless offerings, this is no longer our responsibility as the platform takes care of it for us:

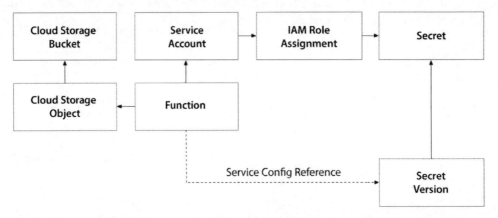

Figure 15.11 – A Google Cloud Functions resource structure

Much of the Terraform setup is very similar to what we have done in previous chapters so we will only focus on new resources needed for our solution. You can check the full source code for this book, which is available on GitHub, if you want to work with the complete solution.

Frontend

As we saw in previous chapters, when working with Google Cloud, we need to activate the required Google APIs to provision resources to our new project. For the frontend, we will mainly use Google Cloud Storage, but we also need a **Cloud Load Balancer**, which requires the compute.googleapis.com API.

First, we need to provision a Google Cloud Storage bucket to which we can deploy our frontend. However, we need to configure our Google Cloud Storage bucket differently using an optional block called `website` to enable the static websites feature:

```
resource "google_storage_bucket" "frontend" {

  project  = google_project.main.project_id
  name     = "${var.application_name}-${var.environment_name}-
  frontend-${random_string.project_id.result}"
  location = "US"

  website {
    main_page_suffix = "index.html"
    not_found_page   = "404.html"
  }

  cors {
    origin          = ["*"]
    method          = ["GET", "HEAD"]
    response_header = ["Authorization", "Content-Type"]
    max_age_seconds = 3600
  }

}
```

To allow anonymous internet traffic to access the content stored within the bucket, we need to set up a binding with the Identity and Access Management service. This will grant `allUsers` access to view objects within the storage bucket:

```
resource "google_storage_bucket_iam_binding" "frontend" {
  bucket = google_storage_bucket.frontend.name
  role   = "roles/storage.objectViewer"

  members = [
    "allUsers"
  ]
}
```

In previous chapters, we've set up Google Cloud Load Balancing, which establishes a load balancer as the frontend and allows you to configure many different types of backends:

Figure 15.12 – Google Cloud Load Balancing routes traffic to
the Frontend hosted on Google Cloud Storage

In this case, the backend for the load balancer becomes extremely simple; it's just a Google Cloud Storage bucket:

```
resource "google_compute_backend_bucket" "frontend" {

  project = google_project.main.project_id

  name        = "${var.application_name}-${var.environment_name}-
frontend-${random_string.project_id.result}"
  bucket_name = google_storage_bucket.frontend.name
  enable_cdn  = true


}
```

The Google Cloud Storage bucket needs to be set up as the backend for the load balancer, which will allow traffic to be routed to the appropriate location.

Backend

Our Backend will be hosted on Google Cloud Functions, so we need to enable `logging.googleapis.com` to allow Google Cloud Functions' telemetry to be accessible from the Google Cloud console.

As we discussed in the previous section, Google Cloud Functions requires our source code to be uploaded, not compiled artifacts; this is because of the way Google Cloud Functions handles the packaging of our application on our behalf. As a result, this creates a dependency on `cloudbuild.googleapis.com`, which Google Cloud Functions uses to create a packaged artifact based on the source code we upload.

For our Google Cloud Functions to execute, we need two additional Google APIs, the Cloud Run API (i.e., `run.googleapis.com`) and the Cloud Functions API (i.e., `cloudfunctions.googleapis.com`). Google Cloud Functions is a layer built onto the Cloud Run API that provides an additional layer of abstraction and additional capabilities to create event-driven workflows, while the Cloud Run API provides a foundational service to run stateless containers that are invocable via HTTP requests.

Google Cloud Functions have a rather simple deployment model. Like AWS Lambda, you must declare a resource for the function itself. The resource has two main configuration components—the build and service configurations—as shown here:

```
resource "google_cloudfunctions2_function" "backend" {

  project  = google_project.main.project_id

  name = "func-${var.application_name}-${var.environment_name}-
backend-${random_string.project_id.result}"
  location = var.primary_region
  description = "a new function"


}
```

The build configuration controls the type of execution runtime (e.g., Python, Java, or .NET), the entry point in the application code, and the location in storage where the application code can be found:

```
build_config {
   runtime     = "dotnet6"
   entry_point = "FleetAPI.Function"

   source {
     storage_source {
       bucket = google_storage_bucket.backend.name
       object = google_storage_bucket_object.deployment.name
     }
   }
}
```

The service configuration controls how many resources the cloud function has access to when invoked. Consequently, this configuration is also the primary driver of costs:

```
service_config {
   max_instance_count = 1
   available_memory   = "256M"
   timeout_seconds    = 60
}
```

The service configuration block also allows you to set environment variables that can be used to pass non-sensitive configuration settings to the cloud function:

```
service_config {

   ...
```

```
    environment_variables = {
        SERVICE_CONFIG_TEST = "config_test"
    }
}
```

Secrets management

As we saw in previous chapters, we can only provision secrets using Google Cloud Secrets Manager once we have enabled the `secretmanager.googleapis.com` API.

First, we need to define the secret with a unique secret identifier that we can use to look up the secret's value from our application code. If we are building multi-region deployments, we can also set the regions to which we want this secret replicated:

```
resource "google_secret_manager_secret" "sauce" {
  secret_id = "sauce"

  replication {
    user_managed {
      replicas {
        location = var.primary_region
      }
    }
  }
}
```

As we saw with the `aws` provider in earlier chapters, the secret is just a placeholder, a unique way to look up our secret's value. We need to create versions of our secret to store the actual secret value:

```
resource "google_secret_manager_secret_version" "sauce" {
  secret = google_secret_manager_secret.secret.name

  secret_data = "secret"
  enabled = true
}
```

After provisioning the secret and a version of our secret, we can access it from our Google Cloud Functions. There are two methods for injecting our secrets into our cloud function; the first is using environment variables:

```
    secret_environment_variables {
      key        = "sauce"
      project_id = google_project.main.project_id
      secret     = google_secret_manager_secret.sauce.secret_id
      version    = "latest"
    }
```

The preceding code demonstrates how we can add a secret to the service configuration block of our cloud function to inject our secrets stored in the Google Secret Manager device using the secret's identifier.

The second approach is probably more secure as it avoids exposing the secret within the process' environment:

```
secret_volumes {
  mount_path = "/etc/secrets"
  project_id = google_project.main.project_id
  secret     = google_secret_manager_secret.secret.secret_id
}
```

The preceding code shows how to set a mount point within the filesystem and drop the secret's value there using the secret's identifier.

Application code

Google Cloud Functions are inherently event-based. Each cloud function is triggered by a different type of event from a wide variety of Google Cloud services. For the purposes of this book, we'll focus on the HTTP trigger only, but if you are interested, I'd recommend you go check out all the other options that Google Cloud Functions has—it's quite extensive:

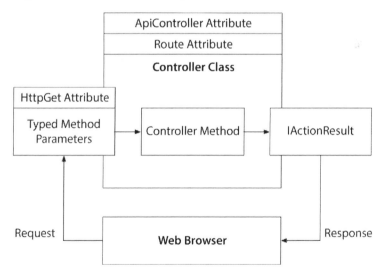

Figure 15.13 – ASP.NET MVC controller class anatomy

In a traditional ASP.NET REST API solution, you have controller classes that embody a specific route and then methods that implement different operations at that route. The controller class needs to be decorated with an `ApiController` attribute informing the ASP.NET runtime that this class should be used to process incoming web requests at the route specified in the `Route` attribute.

Each method is decorated with an attribute that denotes which HTTP verb the method should respond to. In the preceding example, we use HttpGet, but there are corresponding attributes for each of the supported HTTP Verbs. The method can take strongly typed parameters that can either be part of the route, the Query String, or the request body. The method returns IActionResult by default, which allows us to return different data structures depending on the outcome of the request.

In order to implement a REST API using Azure Functions, we need to implement a class using the Azure Function SDK. This requires us to slightly adjust how we implement both our class and our method. We will employ different class and method attributes in order to achieve a similar outcome, defining an endpoint that responds to web requests at a specific route:

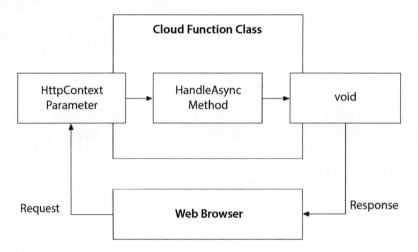

Figure 15.14 – Google Cloud Functions class anatomy

Google Cloud Functions has a very simple method for integrating with the underlying cloud service that drives the runtime. The only requirement is to implement the IHttpFunction interface. This interface has a single requirement to implement a method called HandleAsync that takes an HttpContext object as its only parameter. There is no return object. Therefore, the only way we have to respond to the client is by writing to the response object that is accessible from the HttpContext object.

As we can see, the cloud architecture radically simplifies, but one trade-off is that our backend code needs to be adapted to the Google Cloud Functions framework. This will require development and testing efforts in order to transform our code base into this new hosting model. This stands in stark contrast to what we explored in previous chapters, where we hosted on virtual machines or containerized and hosted on a Kubernetes cluster. While conforming to the Google Cloud Functions model does take work, its benefits are twofold. First, it allows us to take advantage of near-zero sunk cost, and second, it allows us to fully abstract the underlying infrastructure from us and let Google Cloud Platform take care of scalability and high availability. This allows us to focus more on the functionality of our solutions rather than the plumbing of managing the underlying infrastructure.

Now that we have implemented Terraform to provision our solution and made changes to our application code to conform it to the Google Cloud Functions framework, in the next section, we'll dive into YAML and Bash and implement the GitHub Actions workflows.

Automating the deployment

As we discussed in the previous section, serverless offerings such as Google Cloud Functions and Google Cloud Storage abstract away the operating system configuration. Therefore, when we deploy, we only need an application package that is compatible with the target platform. In this section, we'll create an automation pipeline using GitHub Actions that will provision our application to its new serverless home in Google Cloud.

Terraform

The first thing that we need to do is to provision our environment to Google Cloud. This is going to be extremely similar to the way we did this in the previous chapters. In *Chapter 13*, we needed to ensure that our virtual machine images were built and available before we executed Terraform because the Terraform code base referenced the virtual machine images when it provisioned the virtual machines. This means that with our virtual machine architecture, application deployment happens before Terraform provisions the environment, as shown in *Figure 15.15*:

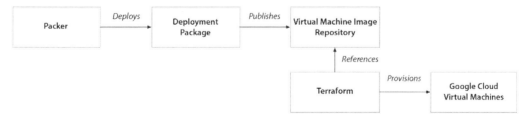

Figure 15.15 – Packer-produced virtual machine images are a prerequisite for Terraform

In *Chapter 14*, we provisioned our Kubernetes cluster using **Google Kubernetes Engine (GKE)** without such a prerequisite. In fact, the application deployment occurred after the Kubernetes cluster was online. This means that with container-based architecture, application deployment happens after Terraform provisions the environment:

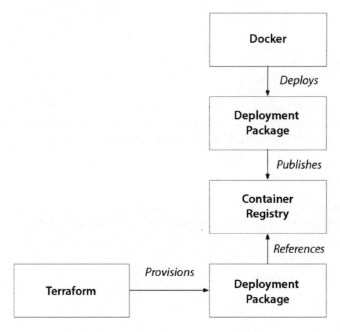

Figure 15.16 – Docker-produced container images are provisioned to Kubernetes after Terraform executes

When using Google Cloud's serverless offerings, the deployment process is split. While both the frontend and backend of our application need a deployment package to be created, the way they are deployed is different. For the frontend, like on other platforms, we simply generate static web content. However, for the backend, due to Google Cloud Functions' unique approach to packaging and deployment, we need to generate a ZIP archive with the application's source code itself. These artifacts share a similar purpose to Docker images in that they are a target service-compatible way of packaging our application for deployment, as shown in *Figure 15.17*:

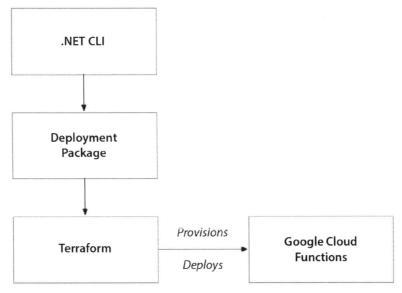

Figure 15.17 – The ZIP archive with the source code acts as the deployment artifacts that are provisioned to Google Cloud when Terraform executes

As you can see, the backend deployment looks very similar to the approach used with the virtual-machine-based architecture. The Terraform code references the packaged artifact and is responsible for deploying it to the Google Cloud Functions that it provisions.

Deployment

Now that Terraform has provisioned the Google Cloud infrastructure we need for our serverless solution, we need to take the final step of deploying both deployment artifacts to the appropriate locations in Google Cloud.

We will use .NET and Google Cloud custom tools to produce the artifacts and deploy the frontend. However, the backend will be provisioned by Terraform.

Frontend

As we saw in other chapters, our .NET application code needs to follow a continuous integration process where the code is built and tested using automated unit testing and other built-in quality controls. Nothing changes there, except that we need to add some special handling to the deployment artifact that these processes produce to ensure it is available to our GitHub Actions job that deploys the workload to the appropriate location:

```
    - name: Upload to Google Cloud Storage Bucket
      working-directory: ${{ env.DOTNET_WORKING_DIRECTORY }}/upload-
  staging
```

```
        run: |
          gsutil -o Credentials:gs_service_key_file=../gcp-terraform.
json -m cp -r . gs://${{ needs.terraform.outputs.frontend_bucket_name
}}
```

We need to ensure that we authenticate with Google Cloud and target the right Google Cloud project with the right Google Cloud Storage bucket. The Google Cloud command-line tool that we are using is called `gsutil`. It can be configured to obtain credentials in several ways, but it is probably the safest to specify the path to a Google Cloud credentials file. We can use the GitHub Actions secret to generate a file that we then reference when we call `gsutil`. Once done, we can execute `gsutil` to recursively upload all the files within the staging directory.

Backend

In order to deploy the Google Cloud function, we need to modify our Terraform to provision a location for the zip archive to be uploaded to and specify the ZIP archive containing the source code of our application code:

```
resource "google_storage_bucket" "backend" {

  project  = google_project.main.project_id
  name     = "${var.application_name}-${var.environment_name}-backend-
${random_string.project_id.result}"
  location = "US"

}
```

After the Google Cloud Storage bucket has been provisioned, we must upload the deployment package:

```
resource "google_storage_bucket_object" "deployment" {
  name   = "deployment.zip"
  bucket = google_storage_bucket.backend.name
  source = "deployment.zip"
}
```

The preceding code will reference the `deployment.zip` file in Terraform's root directory and upload it to the Google Cloud Storage bucket.

That's it! Now, our application has been fully deployed to Google Cloud Functions!

Summary

In this chapter, we designed, built, and automated the deployment of a complete end-to-end solution using serverless architecture using Google Cloud Functions. To accomplish this, we finally had to make some major changes to our application code to conform to the requirements of the serverless runtime. When adopting serverless offerings, one must make this distinct and considerable decision, as it tightly couples your application code with the target cloud platform.

As we conclude this chapter and this Google Cloud-centric narrative, we have successfully implemented cloud architectures on three different cloud platforms—**Amazon Web Services** (**AWS**), Microsoft Azure, and Google Cloud Platform.

Throughout our journey with our enigmatic CEO, Keyser Söze, we saw many similarities that cross from one cloud platform to another, but we also saw distinct differences between the cloud platforms, spanning from small naming convention differences, design and implementation variations up to large structural changes within the entire taxonomy of the cloud platforms. In addition to exploring these three cloud platforms, we witnessed the journey that many organizations face when navigating their journey to the cloud—whether to stick with what they know or to leap into new capabilities and service offerings that pose challenges due to the learning curve while also granting potential opportunities to streamline operations and better take advantage of the economies of scale that the public cloud has to offer.

In the next chapter, we'll switch gears and look at the distinct challenges when we aren't starting from scratch but trying to adapt existing environments and architectures to bring them into an infrastructure-as-code world.

Part 6:
Day 2 Operations
and Beyond

In this part, we explore the challenges and common pitfalls when working with existing environments using Terraform, either importing existing environments that were provisioned initially outside of Terraform or managing environments long-term with Terraform.

This part has the following chapters:

- *Chapter 16, Already Provisioned? Strategies for Importing Existing Environments*
- *Chapter 17, Managing Production Environments with Terraform*
- *Chapter 18, Looking Ahead – Certification, Emerging Trends, and Next Steps*

16

Already Provisioned? Strategies for Importing Existing Environments

The previous nine chapters of this book have focused on implementing new cloud architectures across multiple clouds using multiple cloud computing paradigms. Now, we're going to shift gears a bit and focus on how to work with existing environments. Unfortunately, sometimes (actually, a lot of the time), the cloud environments that you will manage weren't originally provisioned using **Infrastructure-as-Code (IaC)** using via Terraform. They could've been provisioned using other tools, or even manually provisioned, and now you're trying to consolidate your cloud operations using Terraform.

The chapter covers the following topics:

- Importing individual resources
- Identifying resources to import
- Importing existing environments
- Best practices

Importing individual resources

Terraform supports two ways of importing resources into state. One is inherently imperative and procedural and is typically executed outside of a GitOps process using Terraform's **Command Line Interface (CLI)**. There is also another, newer option that allows us to declare import operations in code and follow our standard GitFlow process to shepherd these changes into production.

The import command

The `import` command allows you to import an existing resource that has already been provisioned outside of Terraform by some other means:

```
terraform import [options] ADDRESS ID
```

The `Terraform import` command (`https://developer.hashicorp.com/terraform/cli/commands/import`) takes two key parameters. The various options fall outside of the scope of this book. I recommend that you check the documentation for more details on all of the available options.

The first parameter, the address of the resource within the Terraform code base, is crucial. It's the same reference that we use to access resources in our Terraform workspace. Unlike when we're in the HashiCorp Configuration Language code base, we're not limited by the current Terraform module's scope. The address follows your Terraform provider's naming convention. For instance, you'd need the resource type and object reference to import a virtual machine.

The second parameter is the resource's unique identifier on the target cloud platform. This unique identifier will look very different between different clouds. In the next section, we'll look at how this differs for each cloud platform.

The `import` command is great for individual resources that might have failed due to transient issues during a `terraform apply`. If you had to import an entire solution, it would be extremely tedious to put together an `import` command for every resource. Even a simple virtual machine might consist of a dozen or so resources.

Import block

The `import` command is useful and available, but it requires you to introduce change to your IaC code base through outside influence from a human operator through the command line. The import block was introduced in version 1.5.0 of Terraform to allow these changes to be made through source code changes, which is important to maintaining a GitFlow process. This, in turn, is a key component of a GitOps model.

Rather than executing a command using the Terraform CLI, you'll need to embed an import block in your code base that looks like this:

```
import {
  to = ADDRESS
  id = ID
}
```

It looks very similar to the parameters of the `import` command but it utilizes the existing context in which you execute Terraform. It also uses HashiCorp Configuration Language to define the import action.

This technique not only allows us to perform state management operations as part of our GitOps process but also streamlines the process. Importing resources only requires two pull requests: the first to introduce the import blocks for the resources we wish to import, and the second to remove the import blocks after a successful `Terraform Apply`, when the resources are imported into Terraform state.

Importing multiple resources

The `Import` command and the import block support importing resources using the `for_each` and `count` meta-arguments.

To import resources provisioned with a `for_each` block, you simply need to define a map with the unique identifiers for the resources you wish to import:

```
locals {
  resources = {
    "zone1" = "ID-for-zone1"
    "zone2" = "ID-for-zone2"
  }
}
```

The import block's unique identifier will come from this map that you define. Then, use a matching `for_each` in the import block, which references your resource block using the same map and references the corresponding resource using `each.key`:

```
import {
  for_each = local.resources
  to = ADDRESS[each.key]
  id = each.value
}
```

Likewise, when importing resources provisioned using the `count` meta-argument, we must declare an array with unique identifiers:

```
locals { resources = [ "ID-for-zone1", "ID-for-zone2" ] }
```

Finally, we can use the `count` meta-argument on the import block and iterate across it just as we do with the resource block:

```
import {
  count = length(local.resources)
  to = ADDRESS[count.index]
  id = local.resources[count.index]
}
```

Using the `import` command is a bit more difficult. You'll need to execute a `terraform import` command for each item within the map, referencing the correct `key` and mapping it to the corresponding value:

```
terraform import 'ADDRESS["key"]' ID
```

A similar technique is used for importing resources that are provisioned using `count`:

```
terraform import 'ADDRESS[index]' ID
```

When working with `for_each` provisioned resources, we need to execute the `terraform import` command for each item within the array and manually correlate the index with the correct unique identifier.

Although it is technically possible through some pretty advanced bash scripting, the recommended approach is to use the import block within the HashiCorp Configuration Language, as this is much easier and less error-prone to implement.

We have examined the imperative and declarative ways of importing existing resources into Terraform using the `import` command and the import block, respectively. Now, let's examine how to identify the correct unique identifier for each of our existing resources across the three cloud platforms we have covered in this book: **Amazon Web Services** (**AWS**), Microsoft Azure, and Google Cloud Platform.

Identifying resources to import

Just as there were subtle differences in each of the cloud architectures we developed in the previous chapters of this book, the way in which existing resources are imported into Terraform is affected by the structural and not-so-subtle differences between the cloud platforms.

AWS

The naming convention used by AWS for EC2 instances tends to look like this: `i-abcd1234`. It typically consists of two components: the prefix and the identifier, with the prefix varying across AWS services.

The `i-` prefix indicates that this is an **Elastic Compute Cloud** (**EC2**) instance. Other prefixes might be used for different types of resources, such as `vol-` for volumes or `sg-` for security groups.

In this case, the `abcd1234` identifier is a unique identifier for the instance. AWS usually assigns a hexadecimal string to each instance to differentiate it from other resources. This naming convention helps users and AWS services identify and reference resources within the AWS ecosystem. You'll need to recognize the correct unique identifier for whatever resource you are trying to import into Terraform from AWS and the other cloud platforms.

When using the import command on AWS, it would look like this:

```
terraform import aws_instance.foo i-abcd1234
```

The corresponding import block would look like this:

```
import {
  to = aws_instance.foo
  id = i-abcd1234
}
```

It's important to understand the distinction between the address, which is the internal object reference within Terraform, and the unique identifier, which is the external reference to the resource on the target cloud platform. This understanding will help you navigate the import process more effectively.

Azure

In Azure, the unique identifier is called the **Azure resource ID**. It takes on a radically different format that is composed using several different landmarks in a cloud resource's location within Azure. It follows a structured format that includes several components: the subscription, the resource group, the resource provider, a resource type, and a localized resource name:

```
/subscriptions/{subscription-id}/resourceGroups/{resource-group-name}/
providers/{resource-provider}/{resource-type}/{resource-name}
```

For example, the Azure resource ID for an Azure virtual machine would look like this:

```
/subscriptions/00000000-0000-0000-0000-000000000000/resourceGroups/rg-
foo/providers/Microsoft.Compute/virtualMachines/vmfoo001
```

In this example, we can see the concrete values for each component of the resource ID's path:

- **Subscription ID**: This is the unique identifier for your Azure subscription: a **Globally Unique Identifier (GUID)**. In our example, we just use an empty `00000000-0000-0000-0000-000000000000` GUID for the subscription.

- **Resource group**: This is the name of the resource group that contains the resource. Resource groups are used to organize related resources. In our example, the resource group is `rg-foo`.

- **Resource provider**: This indicates the type of service or resource in Azure. In our example, `Microsoft.Compute` is the resource provider for Azure compute services, which includes Azure virtual machines.

- **Resource type**: This specifies the specific resource type within the service. In our example, `virtualMachines` is used for an Azure virtual machine. Together, the resource provider and the resource type create a fully qualified Azure resource type: `Microsoft.Compute\virtualMachines`.

- **Resource name**: This is the resource's name. In our example, the virtual machine is named `vmfoo001`.

Each resource type within a resource provider has subtypes as well. These are delimited with additional slashes (such as a virtual machine extension: `Microsoft.Compute/virtualMachines/`{vm-name}`/extensions/`{extension-name}`). This naming convention for Azure resource ID uses a resource path strategy instead of AWS's prefix and unique identifier strategy. As a result, Azure resource IDs can get rather long, but they do have a sensible way in which they can be deconstructed to gather valuable information about the deployment context of a particular resource, making additional lookups unnecessary.

When using the import command on Azure, it would look like this:

```
terraform import azurerm_linux_virtual_machine.foo "/
subscriptions/00000000-0000-0000-0000-000000000000/resourceGroups/
rg-foo/providers/Microsoft.Compute/virtualMachines/vmfoo001"
```

The corresponding import block would look like this:

```
import {
  to = azurerm_linux_virtual_machine.foo
  id = "/subscriptions/00000000-0000-0000-0000-000000000000/
resourceGroups/rg-foo/providers/Microsoft.Compute/virtualMachines/
vmfoo001"
}
```

It's important to remember that the address is the internal object reference within Terraform. The unique identifier is the external reference to the resource on the target cloud platform.

Google Cloud Platform

In Google Cloud, the unique identifier for a resource is called the **resource path**, and like Azure, it is composed of some important landmarks in the cloud resource's location within Google Cloud. These landmarks differ from Azure's due to the structural differences between the two platforms and other design considerations:

```
projects/{{project}}/zones/{{zone}}/instances/{{name}}
```

For example, the Google resource path for a Google compute instance would look like this:

```
projects/proj-foo/zones/us-central1-a/instances/vmfoo001
```

In this example, we see the concrete values for each component of the resource path:

- **Project ID**: This is the name of the resource group that contains the resource. Resource groups are used to organize related resources. In our example, the resource group is `proj-foo`.

- **Zone**: This indicates the physical location of the resource within a Google Cloud region and zone.

- **Resource Name**: This is the resource's name. In our example, the virtual machine is named `vmfoo001`.

While Google Cloud does have higher-level organizational structures, such as the Google Cloud organization and the folders within that organization, a resource path only includes the Google Cloud project ID. This is similar to Azure's resource ID, which includes the Azure subscription and resource group, as these are logical containers of the resource within the platform. Google opted for a more simplistic path by only including the project ID. A major difference between Google Cloud's resource path and Azure's resource ID is the inclusion of the zone within the resource path. The zone indicates the resource's physical location within one of Google Cloud's regions. Azure's resource ID only includes logical structures such as subscription, resource group, resource provider, and type, not physical locations such as Azure regions or availability zones.

When using the import command on Google Cloud Platform, it would look like this:

```
terraform import google_compute_instance.foo "projects/proj-foo/zones/
us-central1-a/instances/vmfoo001"
```

The corresponding import block would look like this:

```
import {
  to = google_compute_instance.foo
  id = "projects/proj-foo/zones/us-central1-a/instances/vmfoo001"
}
```

It's important to remember that the address is the internal object reference within Terraform and the unique identifier is the external reference to the resource on the target cloud platform.

Now that we know a bit about how to identify the existing resources and the unique identifiers that we need to map to the resources defined within our code base, we are fully equipped to start manually importing resources into our Terraform code. However, is this the only way? Is there potentially a more cost-effective or time-sensitive approach that would allow us to import resources en masse? In the next section, we'll explore some tools that allow us to find and import existing resources and generate their corresponding Terraform code.

Importing existing environments

As we saw in the previous sections of this chapter, Terraform contains extensive import mechanisms that allow us to import individuals and a multitude of existing resources into our Terraform code base. These tools can help us overcome transient errors that result in orphaned resources that need to be managed with an existing Terraform code base and Terraform state file.

However, what happens when we don't have any Terraform code written and many existing resources already provisioned within our cloud landscape? Manually reverse engineering all the Terraform code from scratch doesn't seem like a useful way to spend our days. That's why there are tools that help automate this process!

In this section, we'll examine a couple of the most popular open-source tools for solving this problem.

Terraformer

Terraformer is an open-source tool developed by Google that helps with the process of importing existing cloud infrastructure into Terraform configuration and state. It supports various cloud providers, including the ones we've explored in this book. Naturally, Google Cloud is well-supported, including its main competitors (AWS and Azure), but a myriad of other Terraform providers also have support. Unlike the built-in capabilities of Terraform, this tool was designed to generate Terraform code and state based on the existing resources spread across your cloud landscape.

This tool, and others like it, works by leveraging the cloud provider's REST APIs in order to gather information about the various resources that have already been provisioned. You just need to point it in the right direction and give it some guardrails in order to narrow its field of vision. You simply pick up the resources that you want to bundle together into the same Terraform workspace and state file.

The key command line arguments that allow you to scope Terraformer to just the resources you are interested in are resource types, regions, and tags. Depending on the provider, there may be limitations in resource type support, so it is best to check the current list of supported resources by using the following command:

```
terraformer list --provider=aws
```

This will help you inform how you will query the particular cloud platform. For example, when importing resources from AWS, we can determine that s3 and ec2_instance are supported resource types:

```
terraformer import aws --resources=s3,ec2_instance --regions=us-west-1
```

On Azure, we'll be using Azure-specific resource types and will often use the --resource-group argument to specify this Azure-specific logical structure to import resources:

```
terraformer import azure --resources=resource_group,vm --resource-group=your-resource-group
```

Likewise, on Google Cloud, we'll use the Google Cloud Project, which is the logical structure that corresponds to Azure resource groups, to narrow the field:

```
terraformer import google --resources=gcs,compute_instance --projects=your-project-id --regions=your-region
```

Tags play an important role, as they provide a very fine-grained way to import exactly what we want into our Terraform workspaces:

```
terraformer import google --filter="Name=tags.Environment;Value=Production"
```

We can specify a very specific collection of tags that we pre-seed in our environments to get the most efficiency during the import process.

The Azure Export Tool

There are other commercial and platform-specific tools that might do a better job than general-purpose tools like Google's Terraformer. One example of this is the **Azure Export Tool** for Terraform. This tool provides greater query-ability to the Azure platform and allows you to customize code generation to leverage both the `azurerm` provider and the `azapi` provider, which are two Terraform providers that can be used to provision and manage Azure resources.

Like Terraformer, the Azure Export Tool has several mechanisms for querying existing resources that should be included in the code generation process. It supports additional import options, such as a subscription-wide import, and eliminates the need to specify resource types. This can help speed up the process for Azure code generation by using a combination of `azurerm` and `azapi` providers. Since the `azapi` provider enables full support of every Azure resource, there are no resource type-based compatibility concerns that can't be filled by using the `azapi` provider as a poly-fill when the `azurerm` resources are unavailable.

The command to import all the resources within a given Azure resource group would simply be as follows:

```
aztfexport resource-group rg-foo
```

It can be run in an interactive or non-interactive mode. The interactive mode allows the end user to review the resources that will be imported and mapped to their corresponding references in the Terraform code.

While the Azure Export Tool isn't as widely known as the Terraformer project, it does have some interesting features that are useful within the context of Azure and the broader Terraform community as well. One example is the **append** feature that allows you to perform targeted code generation and append existing resources into an existing Terraform workspace.

Limitations

The allure of an efficient code generation tool for IaC and Terraform is very real. However, it is not without its limitations and common pitfalls that you should be aware of when venturing into this territory.

The biggest challenges with code generation tools for Terraform are not unique problems within the realm of Terraform and IaC, but ones that affect the approach of reverse engineering or code generation in general. Code that is generated using reverse engineering tools often lacks the craftsmanship that handwritten code has engrained within it from day one. This can result in not only functional defects that need to be ferreted out but also countless occurrences of code quality and readability issues that need to be resolved before the code base can really be used for its intended purpose: to maintain cloud environments via IaC.

One functional problem that often crops up in imported Terraform code bases is over-zealously defined explicit dependencies using the `depends_on` meta-argument. The `depends_on` clause is a valuable tool for resolving implicit dependencies between resources that Terraform can't otherwise pick up automatically. However, in most cases, an explicit definition of these dependencies between resources is unnecessary, adds additional bloat and complexity to the code base, and can be detrimental to readability.

Another example is that when the resource configuration is extracted from the cloud platform, its values are largely imported as hard-coded values that are scattered across all the resources declared. This creates an immediate backlog of technical debt to rationalize related constant values and extract a sane and then desirable set of input variables that can be used to define relevant configuration settings.

Lastly, there are often write-only attributes on Terraform resources that will not be returned by the cloud platform's REST APIs because they contain sensitive or secret information. This is by design to protect against secret leakage and would not be a problem if the resource was originally provisioned from Terraform, as those sensitive values would be stored in the state. However, this creates a bit of a refactoring process because it means that in most cases, your Terraform code base will not pass `terraform validate`, let alone `terraform plan`, without errors that need to be resolved.

Running `plan` immediately after you generate the code and import the resources can help you pick up on subtle differences and irregularities in the import process. This can happen, as the terraform code generation is far from 100% accurate.

As we can see, there are some pretty good options in the realm of tools that can automate the code generation and terraform state file creation of large landscapes of cloud resources across the multitude of Terraform providers available, including the three major cloud platforms that we focused on in this book. However, while code generation can expedite some parts of the process, it can also bring its own challenges that need to be addressed. In the next section, we'll weigh the tradeoffs and discuss some best practices and alternatives for bringing existing environments under Terraform management.

Best practices

We've looked at the built-in capabilities within Terraform to import individual resources and at how we can identify the existing resources that we want to import on different cloud platforms. We recognized some of the limitations of the built-in capabilities and looked at 3rd party alternatives that offer options of importing entire environments en masse, as well as the current limitations of such options. Now, we'll look at best practices for how and when to use these different approaches to import existing resources and environments to bring them under the management of Terraform.

Blast radius

When importing existing resources and bringing them under management using Terraform, it's important to think carefully about the organization of those resources and how you want to compartmentalize them into working IaC solutions in the long term. This is the design principle of minimizing the **blast**

radius of your Terraform modules. When we are importing resources, we are essentially establishing the boundaries of our root modules or Terraform workspaces.

This is the ideal time to perform this design, as the workspaces have yet to be organized. It's important to think this through, as it will affect how easy it is to manage, update, and replicate parts of your infrastructure, depending on how you group resources together.

You should consider the function that the resources will play and who will be responsible for managing them. Suppose a central team is responsible for maintaining a certain part of the architecture. In that case, you may want to consider organizing these resources together within the same Terraform workspace to make it easier to control access and reduce friction between teams.

Use tags to narrow your resource filter as you use Terraformer or other tools to generate code within your Terraform workspaces. Pre-seeding the cloud resources with tags that are fit for purpose will help you maximize the effectiveness of the Terraform import tools you use. This is especially important in AWS, where you lack logical containers for resources like those that are present on Azure and Google Cloud with resource groups and projects, respectively.

Sometimes moving slowly is moving fast

As an alternative to using an import tool to import resources on masse, you could use a lightweight technique using built-in import tools. This process is a bit tedious, but moving slowly sometimes allows you to be more purposeful and thoughtful. This process involves simply using querying techniques to identify the resources that you plan on importing and then scaffolding them using the most bare-bones Terraform resource definition. This resource definition is merely a placeholder and is very unlikely to match the configuration of the previously provisioned resource—but that's not the point.

The point is to import the existing resource into the state and then run a `terraform plan` to determine the configuration differences. You can then use the resulting plan to adjust the resource definition's configuration in code to match the output from the plan until there are no more changes required.

With this approach, you are taking the opposite approach to bulk tool-based import. Rather than wielding a machete and traipsing through the jungle, you wield a scalpel and make extremely thoughtful cuts. You will have to manually configure it, but it will give you a more systematic and step-by-step understanding of the components you are importing and bringing under management. This deeper understanding can help you identify dependencies and flaws in your design that might get swept under the rug when following a bulk import process.

Blue/green deployment

Another option is to consider alternatives to importation. Importing is a messy and very error-prone business. If you have critical infrastructure that was manually provisioned, you might want to consider replacing it with newly provisioned environments that are already under Terraform management.

This approach is called a **blue/green deployment**. It is a well-known release management strategy whereby the existing **blue** environment is replaced through the construction of a new **green** environment. After the green environment is fully tested and ready to go, we perform a cutover operation to transition from the blue environment to the green environment.

You can set up new environments and transition workloads and applications into those. This will allow you to have a clean separation between environments that were provisioned manually without proper governance in place and those for which you followed best practices. Slowly transition your workloads, a piece at a time, to the new well-organized environment until the legacy environment is simply shut off.

Using code generators will likely produce code of extremely poor quality that will require extensive refactoring. While some of this will be simple input variable extraction, moving resources into modules will become extremely tedious as the complexity of the environment increases. The effort to perform an import, refactor, and transform process might actually be greater than writing from scratch and cutting over gradually.

When you weigh the cost of putting the legacy environment into a "keep the lights on" mode while you build out the new world order, this allows your organization to maintain some normalcy and slowly adapt to the change of using IaC-managed environments over time rather than in one fell swoop.

In this section, we discussed some important rules of thumb for importing existing resources and environments under Terraform management. If you plan on performing bulk imports, first recognize the limitations of the tool that you will use and build in ample time for refactoring. Most importantly, make sure that you narrow the focus by defining a focused blast radius around your deployments.

If combing through a mountain of junk code and cleaning it all up through extensive refactoring doesn't sound like your cup of tea, consider moving slowly by either reconstructing the environment through a highly focused step-by-step import process or going all the way and planning a blue/green deployment. My preferred method is blue/green, but you must carefully assess the impact on production environments to determine whether this is the best option for you.

Summary

In this chapter, we looked at Terraform's built-in capabilities for importing existing resources into Terraform state using imperative and declarative approaches. While the built-in import capabilities lack any sort of code generation, we looked at a few open source tools that analyzed existing environments and generated HashiCorp Configuration Language code to manage the resources and provide for them to be imported into the state. We discussed the relevant trade-offs between these different import techniques and when to consider each, which should help you decide the best course of action for your organization and teams. In the next chapter, we'll look at how to manage and operate existing environments using Terraform.

17

Managing Production Environments with Terraform

It is fitting that the capstone of this book is managing your environments with Terraform as that is probably the most important operational aspect of our solutions' infrastructure: managing it. All too often, infrastructure as code is used as an expedient way to turn meters and blast solutions into the cloud without a thought given to what would happen the next day and every other day going forward.

This *day 1 ops* mindset is rampant, and while understandable from a psychological standpoint, the people working with infrastructure as code are inherently builders. We love building new things and are constantly looking for ways to improve how we do so. But I would argue that one of the most important (and often neglected) design considerations for infrastructure-as-code solutions is not scalability, performance, security, or even high availability—it's operability.

Can we effectively operate our environments without outages and delays that can impact the health of our environments and ultimately the commitments we make to our customers? If the answer is no, then we have failed as infrastructure-as-code developers, cloud engineers, and cloud architects.

In this chapter, we will look at how we can infuse infrastructure as code with processes and techniques empowered by Terraform to achieve these goals.

The chapter covers the following topics:

- Operations models
- Applying changes
- Breakfixing

Operating models

In this section, we'll delve into the different operating models that fit common usage patterns for teams and organizations employing Terraform to provision and manage their infrastructure. Let's start with the basics of Terraform operations: **state management**. We'll then explore how teams can incorporate Terraform into their operating models. Depending on a team's role within an organization and the cloud infrastructure they are managing, the team's dynamics may vary. This can also affect how they collaborate with other parts of the organization that may or may not use Terraform in their workflow.

State management

When starting to manage long-lived environments using Terraform, whether they are just for development, testing, or actual production workloads, the foundational change to your operating model is the introduction of **Terraform state**. We discussed Terraform state in *Chapter 1* of this book when we delved into Terraform's architecture, so we already know the value it brings as the arbiter of what the environment should look like, but creating state and managing it is part of the day-to-day operations of managing environments with Terraform.

Just say no to manual state manipulation

As we have established, Terraform state files are essentially just JSON text files that contain an inventory of the resources as they were provisioned during the last Terraform Apply. It might be tempting to manually manipulate the state file just by opening it up in a text editor and changing things around. However, this is ill advised. The Terraform CLI has many commands that provide a safe way to perform state manipulation operations, and HashiCorp is even starting to aggressively roll out HashiCorp Configuration Language features to enable state manipulation through the code base itself rather than bespoke administrator tinkering through the CLI. Besides transitioning from an imperative approach to a declarative one, it also has the added benefit for module authors to make version upgrade paths more seamless by building a safe way to update without costly blue-green deployments or implementing short-term *fixes* that become long-term problems.

Access control

Due to Terraform's nature of being this extensible chameleon of an infrastructure-as-code tool that adapts to each target platform through its provider plugins, it also adapts to the target platforms by way of the backend provider that is used. By default, Terraform uses the local filesystem for the state, but this, of course, is not used when managing long-lived environments. As we discussed, when we implemented the solution across each of the three cloud platforms covered in this book, we used a different backend provider to store the state on the corresponding cloud.

In AWS, we used the s3 backend, which stored our state on AWS's **Simple Storage Service (S3)**. By default, only users with sufficient identity and access management permissions are able to access the data. This allows us to have fine-grained control over the users (and the machines) who can access the state files. Likewise, on Azure, when we used the `azurerm` backend, and on Google Cloud Platform, when we used the `gcs` backend, Terraform stored the state files on the corresponding storage service for each of these cloud platforms. Like AWS, the other cloud platforms implement similar access controls to prevent unprivileged access. On Azure, this takes the form of Azure **Role-Based Access Controls** (**RBACs**) specified at either the resource group or the subscription level. On Google Cloud, this takes the form of access control lists that are driven at the project level.

Encryption

In addition to identity-based access controls that we can apply on the cloud services that are hosting our Terraform state files, we can also employ built-in capabilities of these services to leverage various levels of encryption. The simplest level is the built-in transparent data encryption that protects us if the cloud provider has a physical data breach. This is a nice insurance policy but it's one of the more unlikely attack vectors.

The more likely way our Terraform state files will become vulnerable is if we have leaky identity and access management controls. One method for adding an additional layer of security is by leveraging encryption of the data within the storage service itself. When you do this, access to the files is not enough; you need access to the encryption keys themselves.

On AWS, this is done using AWS **Key Management Service** (**KMS**), which allows you to create and manage your own keys that can be used to encrypt your Terraform state files. Similar capabilities exist on both Azure and Google Cloud. On Azure, you would employ customer-managed keys created in Azure Key Vault, and on Google, you would employ the same approach but, of course, use the equivalent Google Cloud service called Google Cloud KMS. If you want a cloud-agnostic approach, you could leverage a multi-cloud key management solution such as HashiCorp Vault.

Backup

In the previous chapter, we looked at how to import an existing environment into Terraform and saw that even while there are built-in tools to do this, it can be tedious and error-prone. Unfortunately, the only thing keeping your environment in the classification of environments *managed by Terraform* is the state file. If you lose your state file or if it becomes corrupted or out of sync beyond all recollection, your clean environment that was provisioned by Terraform could very easily become an orphaned environment, no longer managed by Terraform and requiring you to consider your options when it comes to importing or re-provisioning.

Don't let that happen! You should keep backups of your state files. Most of the Terraform backends that we looked at support this out of the box in several different ways. First, it does this by enabling version tracking so you actually have a versioned history of the state file within the storage service itself. This is a very convenient and cost-effective way to help you overcome small issues such as human error or transient deployment failures.

However, you should also consider more advanced cross-region replication features of the cloud storage service hosting your Terraform state backend to help you in case of a broader outage. Terraform state going temporarily offline or unavailable doesn't impact your solution's availability, but it does impact your ability to exert control in the environment in the case of an outage. So, it's important to think about implementing cross-region replication and a backup strategy to ensure all scenarios are covered.

Organization

One of the easiest things you can control is where your Terraform workspaces are stored. It doesn't take a whole bunch of bells and whistles to protect your state files if you properly segment your Terraform workspaces and work within the security boundaries that your cloud has to offer.

On AWS, you may want to create more S3 buckets and place those buckets in different AWS accounts to ensure there isn't secret leakage due to overly benevolent IAM policies.

Likewise, on Azure, more storage accounts can be provisioned and placed in Azure subscriptions to isolate them more effectively against overly generous subscription-level permissions.

On Google Cloud, consider carefully what project the Google Cloud Storage service should be provisioned within and opt for an isolated project for Terraform state. This will ensure that the application and its administrators don't necessarily have access to the secrets that may be in the Terraform state file.

Standalone application

For most of this book, we have been operating as a small team at the elusive billionaire magnate Keyser Söze's firm building a next-generation fleet operations platform. In these scenarios, we worked across multiple clouds and implemented our solution using three different cloud computing paradigms along the way:

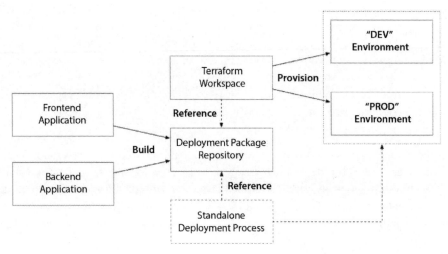

Figure 17.1 – Small team operating model for a small team deploying a standalone application

In this scenario, we saw an application development team that was working on a typical N-tier architecture application. The team consisted of probably 6-8 people who were software developers or software testers. The ultimate goal was not to provision infrastructure but to facilitate a release process for the application software the team is developing.

In these types of teams, it's not uncommon for both the application code and the infrastructure as code to be maintained within the same source code repository. This simple approach recognizes the natural dependencies between the infrastructure and the application as a result of the deployment process. The presence of well-known secrets is provisioned by the infrastructure as code but referenced by the application during its initialization. Keeping it all in our source code repository allows us to minimize the mechanics of making changes that cascade across the infrastructure and application code base in a single feature branch, pull request, and ultimately merge into `main`.

We have a single Terraform root module that we use to deploy our environments, and we alter the input variables to configure it appropriately for different instances of the environment: DEV and PROD. This allows us to manage a multitude of environments simply by changing which workspace we point at either using the `terraform workspace` command or by changing the backend key that we use to partition the workspace within the backend.

The solution that we built and deployed was an end-to-end solution with multiple architectural components that made up the entire application—in this case, an application with a web frontend and a REST API as its backend, which is not an uncommon scenario. Because our solution was so simple, we were able to operate in a completely self-contained manner. This isn't always the case, as we'll see later, in larger teams and larger environments—particularly in the enterprise.

During the solution development that we did in *Chapters 7* through *15*, we didn't really address how those environments would be managed in production. In a normal product development process, we would need to provision multiple environments for various purposes and manage our release life cycle across these environments until we finally ship the product by deploying it into production.

As we saw along this journey, in addition to the subtle and sometimes not-so-subtle differences between cloud platforms, depending on the cloud computing paradigm, we would use different mediums for packaging our application deployment, which sometimes allowed us to integrate the deployment artifact into our Terraform configuration by referencing the virtual machine image or the container image; but sometimes, as with serverless, we had to implement an additional standalone deployment procedure that would execute after Terraform provisioned our environments.

Shared infrastructure

Unlike the application development team that we followed along on their journey through the multiverse of cloud platforms and cloud computing paradigms, there is an entire engineering group that isn't building application code, but they are still heavy users of Terraform. These teams manage an organization's shared infrastructure. These teams might be made up of traditional infrastructure engineers who may have managed the on-premises virtualization environment, network security, or other similar realms within IT infrastructure. Depending on the size of the organization, this can be a big job, spanning many teams and organizations, each with its own scope and realm of responsibilities, or it could be a single team:

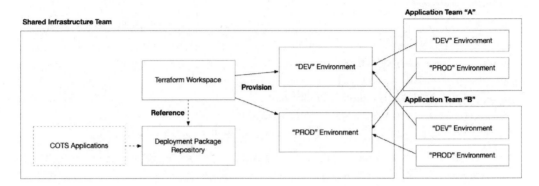

Figure 17.2 – Shared infrastructure team operating model for a shared infrastructure team deploying infrastructure that supports one or more application teams within an organization

This operating model differs from a simple project with stand-alone application development in that there are some inherent dependencies between what this team and other teams in the organization provision. Those external teams draw their dependencies without committing to any type of operating model that conforms to the shared infrastructure team's. Therefore, these teams might not be using Terraform or any automation for that matter.

The environments that they are managing could be a shared network, centralized monitoring and logging, databases, data lakes, data warehouses, or even pools of shared compute, such as Kubernetes clusters. In most scenarios, they won't have their own application code, but they will often have their own deployment packages—whether these are virtual machine or container images of their own creation or third-party **Commercial Off-the-Shelf (COTS)** software packages provided to them by software vendors through either a commercial or open source relationship.

In large organizations, virtual machine and container image repositories themselves are usually built and managed as shared infrastructure that is built and maintained by a platform team to be reused across the organization.

These workloads will likely also have multiple environments but may not have as many as an application development team and may opt to delineate environments simply by a non-production/production dimension. This approach enables maximum reuse for non-production workloads and reduces the overhead of further fragmenting the shared infrastructure for every use case that dependent teams might have.

The deployment process is simplified due to the absence of application code, but shared infrastructure teams should carefully consider how to organize their Terraform workspaces to minimize friction between the external teams, which draw dependencies on them. This is where blast radius plays an important role in the design and segmentation of shared infrastructure workloads into discrete and manageable Terraform workspaces.

Shared services

Finally, the most complex operating model is that of a **shared service**. In this scenario, we are combining aspects of both our standalone application and our shared infrastructure. Shared services not only have the application code base that they need to build and deploy but also have other teams within the organization that draw dependencies on them. However, unlike the shared infrastructure team, where those dependencies might be at the network or configuration layer, shared services often have dependencies at the application interface layer, embedded within the message-based protocols that the two systems use for interoperability. The shared services team is likely made up of developers and testers responsible for maintaining one (or more) services within a portfolio of microservices:

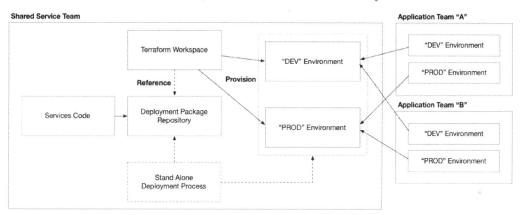

Figure 17.3 – Shared services team

Shared services teams are commonplace at large organizations and, as a result, often operate in an environment where they may draw their own dependencies on both other shared services and shared infrastructure teams within their organization. This helps reduce the scope of responsibility of the shared services team as they can shed responsibilities that are picked up by shared infrastructure teams operating lower-level infrastructure, such as the wide area network, security, and logging and monitoring, as well as higher-level infrastructure such as Kubernetes or even shared Kafka or Cassandra clusters.

While the distribution of this responsibility helps focus a shared services team's energy on the development and maintenance of their service, it also creates additional coordination effort to synchronize changes and release processes as well as versioning compatibility between both downstream and upstream services.

Now that we've looked at several different operating models for using Terraform to manage existing environments, we'll take a deeper look at some of the common operations that you'll need to perform as you manage your environments. No matter what your team looks like and what type of workload you are managing with Terraform, these scenarios are bound to come up!

Applying changes

When we manage a long-lived environment, it's inevitable that we will have to eventually make changes to that environment—whether they are large or small. Change happens. It can be a change related to our solution itself, or it can be a change needed due to upgrades to our tools and the underlying platform itself. It can be expected—such as planned releases—or unexpected—such as zone or regional outages. In this section, we'll look at all of the different types of changes that often happen to our environments and how we should best handle them while managing our environments using Terraform.

Patching

When using Terraform, there are several places within our code that we will need to make conscious decisions about what versions of what components we want to use. These places include the version of Terraform's executable and the providers and modules that you use within your configuration.

Upgrading the Terraform executable

The first thing we need to consider is what version of Terraform we want to use. This may seem surprising—I mean, why wouldn't you always want to use the latest and greatest version of Terraform? However, there are some pretty important reasons why upgrading the version of Terraform you are using is something you should be careful about when managing existing systems.

The version of Terraform you are using could impact the versions of the providers you are using that are supported, which could result in cascading upgrade requirements that may require you to take on more change in your code base than you were originally planning.

While new versions of Terraform often bring exciting new features, capabilities, and bug fixes, they can also bring deprecations and backward incompatibilities. This is something that HashiCorp has historically done an excellent job of managing, minimizing the impact of the change, but it is nonetheless something to keep an eye on as it does occasionally happen. The most recent example of where the version of Terraform had major implications was with version `0.12` of Terraform. In this situation, if you were using the `aws` provider, if you upgraded to version `0.12` of Terraform, you would need to upgrade to version `2.20.0` of the `aws` provider.

The version of Terraform is often referenced in the `required_versions` block of both root modules and reusable modules alike. Therefore, you should also evaluate the upgrade's implications on your Terraform-managed environments and any modules that you are referencing.

Upgrading providers

Like Terraform itself, each of the providers we use to provision resources to various clouds and other platforms has its own version. This compounds the issues we experienced when upgrading Terraform itself across every provider we use within our Terraform solutions. However, most Terraform deployments use the provider for one cloud platform but also might include other providers for different control planes that the solution targets.

The cloud platforms, in particular, are problematic just because they move so fast and are so far-reaching. For example, the AWS, Azure, and Google Cloud resource providers have over 700, 600, and 400 different resource types, respectively! Now, you probably won't be using all of those resource types in one of your Terraform solutions, but with so many different resource types offered by a provider, there is an opportunity for change anytime one of those services adds a new feature. Hence, they change frequently, with new versions of the provider released weekly and sometimes even faster!

It's a good idea to be purposeful about upgrading the versions of your providers. While you shouldn't necessarily follow the provider's weekly release cadence, it's best not to let the version of your provider stagnate, as this just builds up technical debt until it becomes an emergency. Emergencies can arise in one of two ways. First, you could be leveraging deprecated resources, blocks, or attributes within your configuration that will eventually have their support removed. Second, you might want to take advantage of a new feature or capability of one of the resources you are using, but it's unsupported in your current version.

Upgrading modules

Modules are another place where you need to think about versions. When you reference a module from the Terraform Registry, you explicitly set the version you want to use. If you are using modules stored in other, less structured locations, such as Git repositories, you should be careful to reference them using a specific tag.

The impact of upgrading a module version, like each of the resource types within a provider, depends on the breaking changes—or lack thereof—within the module's new version. Sometimes, modules can differ radically between versions, and this can result in a significant negative impact on consumers of these modules who naively upgrade, assuming everything will work out okay.

For modules, Terraform Plan is usually sufficient to detect whether there is a major change being introduced, but when provider and module version changes overlap, it is often a good idea to perform test deployments in order to verify upgrades. This can be done for any type of change you are trying to introduce into the environment.

Refactoring

As we develop more advanced configurations, we can often find ourselves in a situation where there are components of our module—whether it's a root module or a reusable module—that can ideally be extracted into their own module because they implement a repeatable pattern that could be reusable in a more granular context in other modules and other deployments.

It is in these situations that we will likely need to move resources from one module to another. If we do this within our code, any new environments that we provision immediately can reap the benefits, but our existing environments will suffer because they will detect the change. The resource that we moved from one module to another will now have an entirely new path when Terraform does its plan. From Terraform's perspective, the resource at the old location was deleted, and a new resource needs to be created at the new location. This drop-create motion creates a tremendous amount of disruption when managing existing environments.

Like with the importing of resources, we have two methods for moving resources. There is the `terraform state mv` command-line operation and the `moved` block, the latter of which we can define in our HCL configuration:

```
moved {
    from = module.foo.azurerm_network_security_rule.nsg_443
    to   = module.bar.azurerm_network_security_rule.main[0]
}
```

The command-line operation is quite simple and is structured how you would expect:

```
terraform state mv SOURCE DESTINATION
```

The SOURCE and DESTINATION command-line parameters correspond to the `moved` block's `from` and `to` attributes, respectively.

Let's look at a specific example. In the chapters where we built solutions using Kubernetes, we saw several resources get repeated with nearly identical configurations for both the frontend and backend components of our application architecture. These resources were `kubernetes_deployment`, `kubernetes_service`, and `kubernetes_config_map`:

Root Module

Frontend Kubernetes Deployment	**Backend** Kubernetes Deployment
Frontend Kubernetes Service	**Backend** Kubernetes Service
Frontend Kubernetes ConfigMap	**Backend** Kubernetes ConfigMap

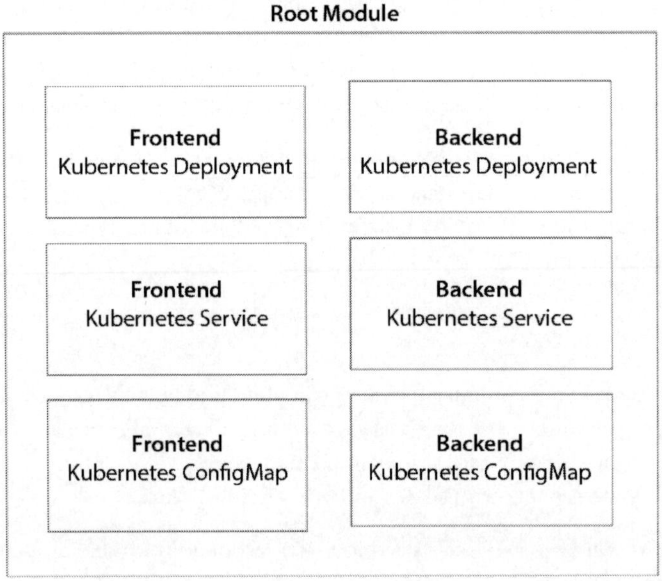

Figure 17.4 – Visible repeating pattern of resources

Before we can refactor this solution, we need to create a module that will replace the three repeating resources:

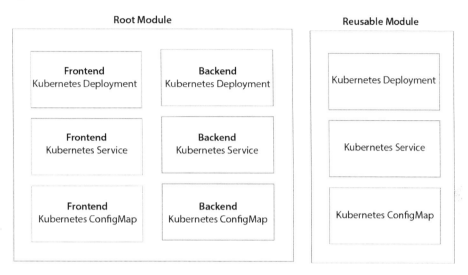

Figure 17.5 – Refactor step 2 – construct a reusable module that can be
configured to replace each of the instances of the repeating pattern

Now that the module has been created, we need to create an instance of the module in the root module and delete the previous resources within the repeating pattern:

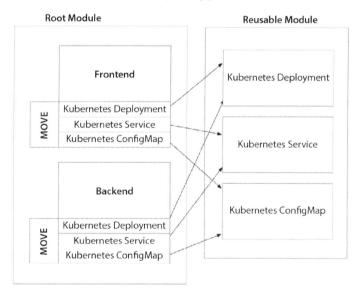

Figure 17.6 – Refactor step 3 – replace the loose resources with module references and moved blocks

Finally, we create `moved` blocks that will facilitate Terraform recognizing that the resources don't need to be destroyed and recreated because they have already been provisioned but the path has changed.

Planning for failure

Sometimes, the unexpected happens and part of our infrastructure is impacted due to an outage of some kind on the target cloud platform. In these situations, we need to be able to react and bring change to our existing environments in order to minimize the damage or recover from the outage.

Active-passive

First, let us look at the active-passive workload deployed within a single Terraform workspace:

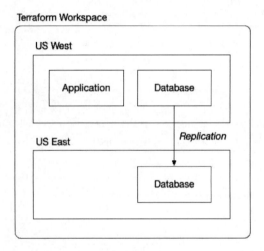

Figure 17.7 – Active-passive workload deployed within a single Terraform workspace

Here is what it looks like during an outage:

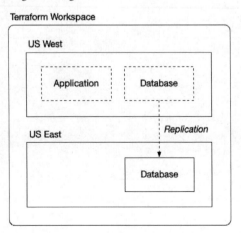

Figure 17.8 – Active-passive workload when disaster strikes!

The application and database in US West are unavailable. Luckily, we have the database in US East that we were replicating to. However, we need to create an online environment to start serving our customers using this database:

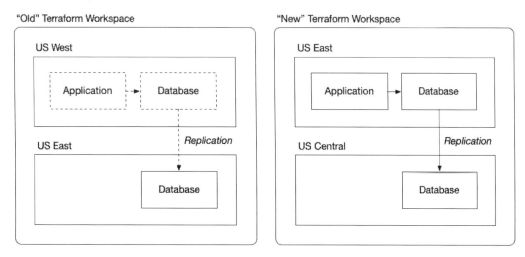

Figure 17.9 – Recovery step 1: Provision a new environment in a different region

We use Terraform to provision a new environment in a new Terraform workspace. We configure the new root module to use the US East as the primary region and the secondary region as another healthy region nearby, in this case, US Central. This environment is healthy, but it's missing our data.

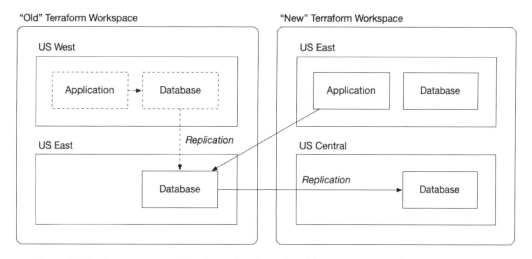

Figure 17.10 – Recovery step 2: Replicate data from the old environment to the new environment

We reconfigure our new workspace to reference the *old* database by importing it into the state, essentially replacing the new empty database with the old database. This will also likely cause a replacement of the replication configuration to start replication from the old database to the new disaster recovery database in the US Central region:

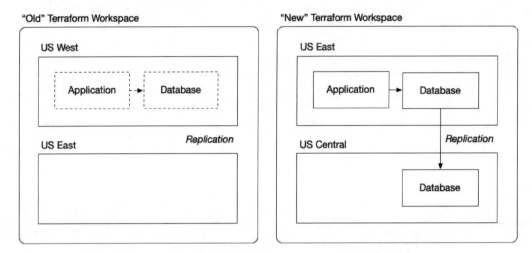

Figure 17.11 – Recovery step 3: Cut over to new environment
and decommission the old environment entirely

Now, the old disaster recovery database in US East is our main production database, and we have a new disaster recovery site in US Central in case we need to perform this same operation again. At this point, we are ready to resume service with our customers by allowing traffic back to our application. The database will be up to date because of the previous replication that was in place from US West to US East. There might be minor data loss for some customers during the small window when the requests were recorded in US West but may not have made it over to US East through the replication.

Active-active

Now, here's an active-active deployment in a single Terraform workspace without using any modules:

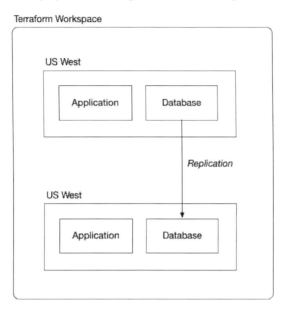

Figure 17.12 – Active-active deployment in a single Terraform workspace without using any modules

To achieve higher levels of system availability, we can opt for an active-active cross-region deployment. In this situation, we will have two instances of our application deployed across two regions and replication between the databases. This will ensure that in case of an outage in one region, our customers will continue to be served by routing traffic to the healthy region.

In the preceding approach, we created our multi-region deployment in a single Terraform workspace, which means both regions will be updated on a single Terraform application. This can be problematic because if one region is down, then half of our deployment will potentially be unresponsive, thus impacting our ability to enact change across the entire environment. This could impact our ability to failover, increase capacity, or adjust auto-scale settings in the unaffected region.

In order to start moving away from deploying all of our regions into a single Terraform workspace, it is a good idea to encapsulate an entire regional deployment into a single reusable module. In doing so, we make it much easier to segment our Terraform workspaces across regions and easily add additional regions as we scale out:

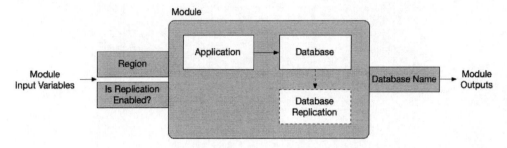

Figure 17.13 – Module design to encapsulate our application deployment within a single region

The module will have everything that needs to be deployed into a single region. In addition, there may be optional components, such as the database replication configuration, which may not need to be enabled depending on whether this region is the primary or one of the secondary endpoints. Therefore, our module needs to take two input variables. First, there is the region that this instance of our application will be deployed into. Then, there is a feature flag to enable or disable database replication. This will be enabled when the region is our primary, but it will be disabled when it is set up as a secondary.

This is an example; your mileage may vary depending on the database or technologies that you are using, but it's important to recognize that it is a common scenario in such modules to leverage feature flags to allow the customization of each instance of the module to fulfill its specific role:

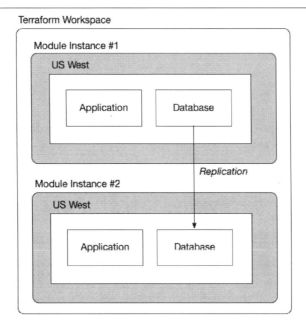

Figure 17.14 – Active-active deployment in a single Terraform
workspace using modules to provision each region

Now that we have our module, we can use it within our single Terraform workspace to provision both regions. This approach allows for additional regions to be provisioned quite easily within a single Terraform Apply, but it is susceptible to operational impact when an outage occurs. If you have designed your failover mechanism and secondary regions to be self-sufficient, then this approach may not be unreasonable, but just remember that you may lose the ability to perform Terraform Apply operations during the outage.

Even when performing a targeted apply, it will execute a plan across the entire workspace. So, even though, in theory, a targeted `terraform apply` will only change resources that you target because it has to perform a full plan, if the control plane you are targeting is impacted in certain regions or zones, then you will be unable to do so.

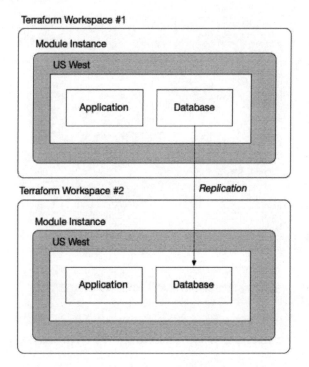

Figure 17.15 – Active-active with separate workspaces

Transitioning to completely separate workspaces for each region can help you maintain control over your environments through Terraform because you will be performing a `terraform apply` operation within the context of each region. This adds additional operational overhead during steady state as it creates additional Terraform workspaces to manage and additional mechanics when performing day-to-day maintenance of your environment, so many might still opt for a single workspace to manage multi-region environments.

As we saw in this section, even when change is planned, things can be challenging. There are changes to the modules we build and consume in our solutions, there are changes to the design and capabilities of the cloud services we employ, which translates into changes within the individual resources we use, and finally, there are changes to the Terraform executable itself. And these are only changes that we plan and control! Additional changes can come in the form of unexpected outages within the availability zones or regions where our solutions are deployed. In the next section, we'll look at how we can respond to unexpected errors and perform some routine **breakfixing**.

Breakfixing

Now that we've looked at the change we know is coming, and the change that we know is coming but we can't control when, we need to take a look through a more tactical lens to help us respond to the inevitable *little* bumps along the way of our journey of managing existing environments with Terraform. These are going to be smaller issues that are not massively impactful but can definitely become a burden if we are ill prepared. But once you get used to them—and how to respond—they become easy to manage!

Apply-time failures

While `terraform plan` provides us with excellent intelligence on what changes (or lack thereof) need to be made to our environments, sometimes things can go wrong in unexpected ways during the `terraform apply` operation even for the most well-intentioned plan. There are some things that you can do to try to stay ahead of these issues and lessen the frequency of encountering them.

As we know, Terraform executes under an identity on whatever cloud platform we are targeting, and as a result, whatever permissions or privileges that identity has—so does Terraform. Being aware of what permissions Terraform's identity has and what your code is doing well helps you identify whether there are gaps that will result in authorization failures, as these are often implicit and hard to detect by Terraform. Some cloud platforms even require you to explicitly enable entire categories of cloud services before you use them. As we saw in *Chapters 13* through *15*, Google Cloud is notorious for this and we were required to enable each of the relevant Google Cloud APIs within our Google Cloud project before we could even attempt to provision something. On Azure, most common services are enabled by default, but some more obscure resource providers need to be explicitly enabled.

Beyond simply enabling the services you want to use, all cloud platforms implement default quotas that will restrict how much you can provision within certain contexts. These contexts are usually region- or SKU-based. They provide joint protection for the cloud platform from a capacity planning standpoint but also for us as customers to prevent us from accidentally provisioning extremely expensive resources or too many of one kind of resource. Quotas are not the only limits imposed by the cloud platforms, there are often resource limits set for each service within a given deployment context, such as within an AWS account, an Azure subscription, or a Google Cloud project.

In addition to quotas and service limits, often, when working with cloud services that employ private networking, you may run into issues if network settings are misconfigured, such as incorrect virtual network and subnet configurations, or security group rules that prevent resources from being created or accessed. Sometimes, Terraform operates on a cloud service's data plane, which might become unavailable when you configure it with private networking. Ensure that Terraform has the proper private networking in place to have a line of sight for necessary data planes.

Other issues can arise with implicit resource dependencies that Terraform can't determine through the configuration and plan. This can occur when a resource relies on another resource, but that relationship or dependency is not known to Terraform through direct references between the resources within the configuration. There could also be conflicts with existing resources, such as trying to create resources that already exist with the same name or other settings that can't exist in more than one resource within the given scope—be it at a networking level or at the cloud platform's control plane level.

Operations might take longer than expected, and other transient platform errors lead to timeouts. Timeouts can result in the resources eventually being successfully provisioned, but because it happened after the operation timed out, Terraform won't know about it. This can happen when large resources are being provisioned or when there are network delays.

Removing from state

In the previous section, we discussed apply-time failures and their impact on Terraform infrastructure management. Another common situation that can arise when managing environments with Terraform is the need to remove a resource from the state. As we've discussed in previous chapters, this can be achieved both imperatively using the `terraform state rm` command or declaratively by using the `removed` block in your HashiCorp Configuration Language code.

One such scenario is when you need to decommission resources. If you manually delete a resource outside of Terraform, it needs to be removed from the state file to prevent errors during the next `terraform apply`. Similarly, if a resource is accidentally imported into the wrong location in your Terraform configuration, it can be removed before re-importing it correctly.

When working in a team, if someone else has already removed a resource but your local state file is not yet updated, resolving the discrepancy may involve removing the resource from your state file. Cleaning up orphaned resources is another important use case. If a resource becomes orphaned (no longer managed by Terraform) due to manual changes or configuration errors, it can be removed from the state file.

Another place where you may need to remove resources is during the refactoring process. Of course, as we've discussed, it's more common to move resources in this scenario, but there are cases where removal might be necessary as well, such as splitting a large configuration into smaller modules; that is, resources might need to be removed from the state file before re-importing them into their new locations. Additionally, if a resource needs to be replaced with a new one (for example, due to a change in the resource's configuration that requires recreation), the old resource might be removed from the state file before creating the new one. During testing or debugging, temporarily removing resources from the state file can help isolate issues or test specific scenarios. If you're consolidating multiple similar resources into a single resource (e.g., merging several security groups into one), the old resources might be removed from the state file.

Importing into state

In *Chapter 16*, we delved into the intricacies of importing existing environments that were provisioned outside of Terraform. As we continue our exploration of managing existing environments in this chapter, we will encounter situations where importing resources becomes essential for breakfixing within environments already under Terraform's management.

One common situation where importing resources becomes necessary, even in environments initially provisioned with Terraform, is when transient errors occur during the `terraform apply` process. These errors can lead to a peculiar state where resources are provisioned but reported as unhealthy to

Terraform, causing the `terraform apply` process to fail. However, these resources may eventually finish provisioning or be recovered by the cloud platform later. In such instances, we are faced with the decision to delete these resources and rerun `terraform apply` or import them into the state.

Importing resources in this context serves as a form of breakfixing, akin to patching up a leak in a well-oiled machine. It allows us to reconcile the discrepancies between the actual state of our cloud environment and Terraform's understanding of it, much like how we would address apply-time failures by ensuring proper permissions, quotas, and network configurations.

Another scenario where importing might be necessary is when dealing with resources that have been manually or by an automated process created or modified outside of Terraform. This can lead to a drift between the Terraform state and the actual infrastructure, similar to how unexpected changes in cloud service limits or network settings can cause issues. This can arise from human operators working outside the bounds of our infrastructure-as-code process, or it could arise from automated systems enforcing enterprise governance standards. By importing the newly created or modified resources back into the Terraform state, we can realign our configuration with the current state of the infrastructure, ensuring that subsequent Terraform operations proceed smoothly.

Summary

In this chapter, we explored how to manage existing environments using Terraform. We began with a comprehensive examination of the various operating models employed by teams with differing roles and responsibilities within organizations of varying sizes. We investigated how these teams integrate Terraform into their day-to-day operations—from managing a simple standalone application to navigating the complexities of shared infrastructure services, such as a centralized network, and addressing the nuances of building shared services that intertwine across the enterprise. We discussed the challenges of interdependencies experienced with shared infrastructure, coupled with their own application development release processes.

A significant portion of this chapter was dedicated to simply applying changes to our existing environments. This included the seemingly mundane process of upgrading our Terraform tools—ranging from the Terraform executable itself to the Terraform providers we use and the modules we consume within our solutions. We also discussed the refactoring that may be necessary with our own code and addressed how to handle unplanned changes—such as when disaster strikes. This discussion was akin to preparing for a storm; just as one would secure their windows and doors, we explored how to use Terraform to prepare our environments for when we needed to take action during an outage.

We concluded the chapter by discussing the more common break-fixing scenarios that you will encounter in your day-to-day operations of managing existing environments with Terraform.

In the next chapter, we'll be looking to close out the book by discussing some important things to consider as you take your next steps in mastering Terraform.

18

Looking Ahead –
Certification, Emerging
Trends, and Next Steps

We are at a place in our journey where we have to stop and ask ourselves, *What's next?* Before we do that, let's think about where we've been.

We've learned what Terraform is and how to use it. We've learned some basic concepts of cloud architecture that transcend the particular cloud platform you might be using at the moment. We've built three sophisticated architectures on each of the three major hyperscalers—AWS, Azure, and GCP—and finally, we've learned how to work with existing environments, either importing them into Terraform or managing them with Terraform as long-lived environments in production or otherwise.

That's a lot! It's been quite a journey, so where do we go from here? Well, the answer is in you. I hope that means you have learned something along this journey, and you'll take that into your day-to-day work to build amazing systems that solve real-world problems and are better equipped to build and manage them with the power of Terraform.

In this chapter, before we close, I'd like to discuss some potential next steps, both for your personal growth and extended learning. You have invested a tremendous amount of time in reading this book and have begun your journey of mastering Terraform. You may want to consider certification as a way to validate your skills and knowledge and to demonstrate your expertise to potential employers.

Additionally, there may be other technologies that you may want to consider as you continue to deepen your mastery of Terraform. We'll explore some of these options, including tools and platforms that complement Terraform and how they can enhance your **Infrastructure as Code (IaC)** capabilities. By the end of this chapter, you should have a clear roadmap for your continued learning and a solid foundation for your future endeavors in the world of cloud infrastructure management.

The chapter covers the following topics:

- Preparing for the exam
- Terraform Cloud
- What's next?

Preparing for the exam

On your journey through this book to mastering Terraform, you've gained a wealth of knowledge and practical experience. But how do you showcase your expertise to the world? One of the most effective ways is through certification. In this section, we'll delve into the intricacies of preparing for the Terraform certification exams. We'll cover the key topics you need to master, the format of the exam, and strategies to optimize your study time and approach. By the end of this section, you'll be well equipped with the tools and confidence needed to tackle the certification exam and take a significant step forward in mastering Terraform.

Scope and topics

The **HashiCorp Terraform Associate Certification** is an entry-level certification that will test you on general concepts of IaC, Terraform's competitive position against other tools, working with code using the **HashiCorp Configuration Language** (**HCL**), and using the core Terraform workflow as well as other workflows that are supported through various sub-commands within the **Command-Line Interface** (**CLI**).

There is a new exam that is coming soon called **Terraform Authoring and Operations Professional**. This exam is designed for seasoned practitioners who have extensive experience in managing production systems, developing reusable modules, and operating within a mature enterprise IaC environment. It aims to validate the advanced skills and deep understanding required to efficiently author and manage Terraform configurations at scale. Candidates can expect to be tested on their ability to implement complex infrastructure architectures, optimize workflows, and ensure best practices in an enterprise environment. This certification is an excellent opportunity for those looking to demonstrate their expertise in leveraging Terraform's full capabilities in a sophisticated and dynamic infrastructure landscape.

This book is designed to help you go beyond many of the foundational concepts covered in the Associate exam and help you prepare for the Professional exam. As a result, our journey in this book has been taking a hyper-practical approach to building actual cloud architectures using Terraform and implementing collaborative flows with Terraform and an automation pipeline tool, which, for the entirety of this book, was GitHub Actions.

As you can see in the following diagram, I map chapters within this book to actual topics covered within the Associate exam:

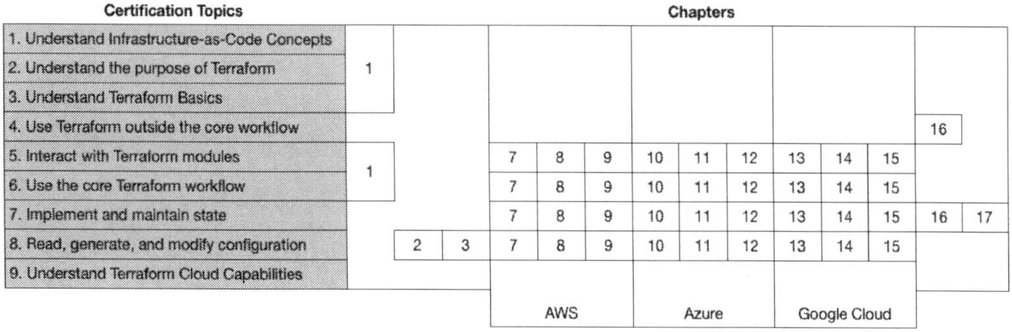

Certification Topics				Chapters										
1. Understand Infrastructure-as-Code Concepts														
2. Understand the purpose of Terraform	1													
3. Understand Terraform Basics														
4. Use Terraform outside the core workflow														16
5. Interact with Terraform modules	1			7	8	9	10	11	12	13	14	15		
6. Use the core Terraform workflow				7	8	9	10	11	12	13	14	15		
7. Implement and maintain state				7	8	9	10	11	12	13	14	15	16	17
8. Read, generate, and modify configuration		2	3	7	8	9	10	11	12	13	14	15		
9. Understand Terraform Cloud Capabilities														
				AWS			Azure			Google Cloud				

Figure 18.1 – Map of Associate certification topics to chapters in this book

We breezed through the foundational conceptual layers of IaC, Terraform's architecture, and HCL in the first three chapters of this book. This was by design, as this book is intended for an intermediate to advanced audience and not a beginner's guide.

This allowed us to dedicate some time, in *Chapters 4* through *6*, to the conceptual layer that most Terraform practitioners actually spend their time in—the cloud architectures that they are designing and provisioning when we set the bases for the cloud computing paradigms we would be working with across all three clouds.

Then, we hit the ground running, getting our hands dirty and building three real-world solutions for each cloud. As you can see, we spent most of our time in the book working on implementing HCL code across all three clouds—AWS, Azure, and GCP—and across three cloud computing paradigms—virtual machines, containers, and serverless. In these nine solutions, we implemented Terraform modules and delved deep into configuration using three corresponding Terraform providers: `aws`, `azure`, and `GCP`.

In *Chapters 16* and *17*, we focused on the non-core workflows involving advanced topics in state management and configuration importation that are common and necessary when working with existing environments—whether or not they were originally provisioned with Terraform.

In the Professional exam, this is still significant coverage of all the key topics with one key exception:

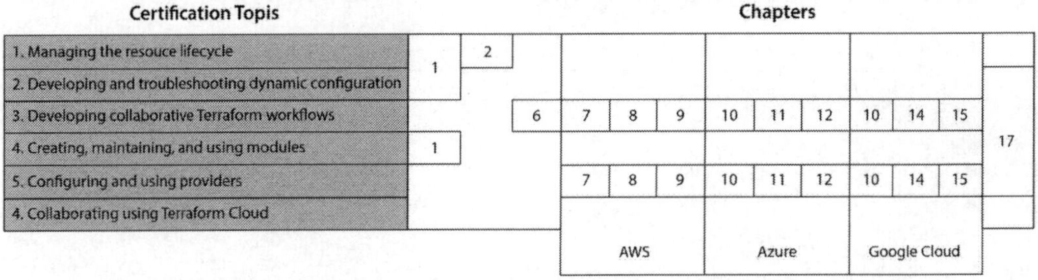

Certification Topis	Chapters										
1. Managing the resouce lifecycle	1	2									
2. Developing and troubleshooting dynamic configuration											
3. Developing collaborative Terraform workflows		6	7	8	9	10	11	12	10	14	15
4. Creating, maintaining, and using modules	1										17
5. Configuring and using providers			7	8	9	10	11	12	10	14	15
4. Collaborating using Terraform Cloud											
			AWS			Azure			Google Cloud		

Figure 18.2 – Map of Professional certification topics to chapters in this book

The notable exception is **Terraform Cloud**, which I chose to omit as a main focus of this book since I don't think knowledge of it is required to master Terraform at this time. We will look at Terraform Cloud in the next section of this chapter, as I think it is an interesting topic area for further study if you want to leverage some of its capabilities to streamline your organization's collaborative workflows.

Preparation

Go and check out the study guides for both the Associate and Professional exams. The study guides have helpful links to the official documentation, which should augment the contents of this book. Remember, this book was intended to be a practical guide for those who want to master Terraform to provision cloud architecture. That doesn't necessarily mean memorizing every nook and cranny of the Terraform CLI. I specifically chose to focus on skills that will help you start developing real-world solutions no matter what cloud and cloud computing paradigm you'll be working with.

The exam will likely have tricky edge cases or obscure commands that are seldom used, so be ready for that, but I wouldn't dedicate a tremendous amount of time to it. Make yourself a quick cheat sheet of some of these obscure commands and how to use them. Employ flashcards to help you memorize them if you feel like you need to. If you have a solid understanding of Terraform's architecture and are hands-on with it, you should do well.

My best advice is to study through hands-on experience. Take the projects in this book, and feel free to clone them from my GitHub repositories, but to maximize your own mastery, develop them from scratch in your own repository on GitHub. Recreate them, provision yourself and the environment, and then improve upon them. Think about how you would like to modularize components within them to be more reusable. Go ahead and implement those modules, and then refactor your environment to use your new modules. Treat your environment as if it were production and try to minimize the impact on your environment by making sure you avoid replacing resources in your existing environment while trying to refactor to use your new modules.

I sat for the exam while I was at HashiConf in October 2023. I didn't study, I didn't prepare, I didn't even read the study guide. I passed with a score of 84.21%. I was pretty happy about it. Am I telling you this to brag? No. Well, maybe a little, but seriously, my point is that the best way for you to prepare is by doing. How was I able to pass without studying at all? Because I've been hands-on with Terraform for several years and know it inside and out. Did I know every obscure command within the Terraform CLI? Absolutely not. Had I ever used Terraform Cloud? Not for one New York minute. You have to ask yourself, do you want to pass an exam, or do you want to upskill yourself and become a dangerous force in the cloud automation space with one of the most powerful automation tools in the world? I think the answer is clear. Focus on the primary objective with gazelle-like intensity and augment it with a bit of studying more obscurities, and you will do well.

Now that you are energized, feeling empowered by all that you have learned from this book, and ready to take the Terraform Associate or upcoming Professional exam, let's look forward to some interesting topics that every Terraformer (not just the Azure ones) should know about.

Terraform Cloud

In this section, we'll explore Terraform Cloud, a powerful platform designed to enhance Terraform's capabilities in team-based and enterprise environments. Terraform Cloud provides a centralized hub for managing and automating Terraform workflows, offering features such as version control integration, remote state management, and collaborative IaC development.

We'll take a brief look at the core components of Terraform Cloud, including advanced features such as workspace management, private module registry, cost estimation, and policy enforcement.

By understanding Terraform Cloud's features and use cases, you'll gain insights into how it can streamline your infrastructure management processes and foster collaboration among team members. It's definitely something to consider if you are looking to scale up your organization's IaC maturity quickly.

Features

Terraform Cloud's mission is about streamlining the process of managing environments with IaC. This will include features that handle day-to-day operation concerns of using Terraform, as well as more advanced capabilities related to empowering teams and scaling across larger organizations within the enterprise. The following is a diagram showing the grouping of these capabilities:

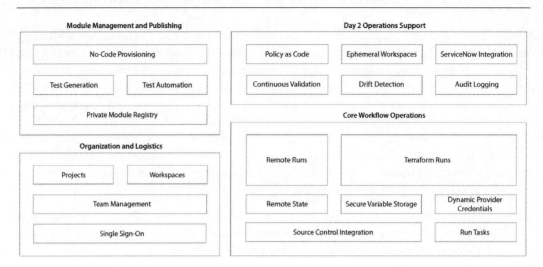

Figure 18.3 – Terraform Cloud capabilities

These groupings are across four functional areas:

- Core workflow operations

- Organization and logistics

- Module management and publishing

- Day 2 operations support

We'll explore each of these functional areas individually to get a better idea of what Terraform Cloud brings to the table.

Core workflow operations

As we know, Terraform, itself is a simple command-line tool that processes HCL code and leverages a multitude of providers to generate a plan and then execute that plan by orchestrating resource creation across multiple providers. Terraform Cloud is a multi-tenant SaaS offering that encapsulates the functionalities of the command-line tool and hosts it as a managed service offering.

As a result, a significant portion of the value of Terraform Cloud comes from, well, Terraform itself— that is, the command-line tool that does all the work. However, Terraform Cloud provides many things beyond what is built into the command-line tool. As a hosted service, it sits atop our version control system and acts as a pipelining tool that executes the Terraform `plan` and `apply` commands. In this book, we worked with GitHub Actions to integrate the Terraform command-line tool into our workflows to run the core Terraform workflow, which includes `plan` and `apply`.

Terraform Cloud's capabilities in the *Core Workflow Operations* category focus on providing Terraform as a service, similar to what pipeline tools such as **GitHub Actions** do for general-purpose pipelines, but Terraform-specific. This means Terraform Cloud is essentially an automation-hosted platform that specializes in executing Terraform configurations. As a result, the service is tailored to Terraform's specific needs, including things such as remote state management. However, it also includes essential features found in general-purpose pipelining tools, such as source control integration, cloud platform credential management, and secure variable storage. It also offers extension points for integration with external tools, allowing it to be integrated into broader automation orchestration.

Organizational and logistics

The organizational and logistics aspect of Terraform Cloud is designed to facilitate collaboration and management by teams within organizations large and small. It provides a structured environment to organize users, roles, and permissions across logical projects, leading to the creation and operation of Terraform workspaces—ensuring that team members have the appropriate access and permissions to perform their tasks effectively. Like other more general-purpose automation platforms such as **Azure DevOps** and **GitHub Enterprise**, maintaining order and control in these collaborative environments is baseline functionality.

Module management and publishing

Terraform Cloud's capabilities within module management and publishing enable teams and organizations to build, maintain, and share their own libraries of Terraform modules across their organization. As we've discussed, Terraform modules often encapsulate organizationally approved best practices and are often maintained by a central organization responsible for their implementation and built-in quality. Terraform Cloud supports this publishing process by integrating Terraform module testing and validation to ensure quality before new versions of Terraform modules are distributed across an organization. Additionally, these modules can be made available in no-code environments, providing a service catalog-like experience for end users. This empowers teams to standardize and scale their infrastructure management efforts but also makes the solutions that they build available to parts of the organization that are unfamiliar with IaC or Terraform in general.

Day 2 operations support

The Day 2 operations support functionality in Terraform Cloud is geared toward managing and maintaining existing systems in production. It includes continuous validation to ensure environments remain up to date with the desired state described within the code and drift detection to identify changes made outside of Terraform code. There are also more advanced enterprise features, such as audit logging, to help larger organizations meet regulatory compliance standards and implement risk management policies to detect and prevent unplanned changes to the environment. Another key feature is the policy-as-code capabilities provided by **Sentinel**, which enables governance and security controls over the environments managed by Terraform Cloud.

Pricing tiers

The *Free* tier provides all IaC capabilities of Terraform as a hosted service out of the box and all of the core workflow operations capabilities—including remote state, secure variable storage, dynamic provider credentials, and source control integration. It's a great way to get your feet wet exploring the platform and learning the new way of working with Terraform Cloud as the foundation as opposed to a general-purpose pipeline tool. As expected, it is pretty limited with a single concurrent job and limited access to more advanced enterprise features such as Policy-as-Code and run tasks that are designed to help you scale Terraform Cloud into a larger, more sophisticated IaC-powered organization. The Free tier allows you to provision up to 500 resources.

The *Standard* tier adds team management and increases the number of concurrent jobs from one to three, which probably makes sense in a team environment. The pricing model is per hour per resource, which means every resource you declare in your Terraform configuration will count toward your usage. The price per hour per resource, at the time of writing, was $0.00014. To give you an idea of how much this would cost to operate, one of the environments that I manage is an environment with a small Kubernetes cluster and all the surrounding supporting infrastructure. I provisioned exactly 110 resources in this environment using Terraform:

110 resources x $0.00014 per resources per hour = $0.0154 per hour

$0.0154 per hour * 24 hours per day * 30 days per month = $11.088 per month

So, for roughly 11 dollars per month, I can use Terraform Cloud to manage my environment. This is in addition to what I pay for my source control management system and the cloud hosting costs of the environment.

The *Plus* tier introduces Day 2 operations support scenarios such as audit logging, drift detection, continuous validation, ephemeral workspaces, ServiceNow integrations, and unlimited Policy-as-Code to help you better manage your environments and integrate with your day-to-day operations.

The *Enterprise* tier is essentially the hosted offering that allows you to deploy Terraform Enterprise into your own data center, which can be important to large enterprises that are not interested in taking advantage of the lowered operating cost of utilizing HashiCorp's multi-tenant offering, Terraform Cloud.

In this section, we looked at Terraform Cloud, including what it offers in terms of capabilities and recognizing that, unlike more general-purpose automation platforms, it is tailored specifically for IaC management and collaboration using Terraform. Compared to these more general-purpose pipeline tools, Terraform Cloud stands out by offering features specifically designed for Terraform workflows, such as remote state management, secure variable storage, and integrated module management. This focus on Terraform-specific functionality makes it an ideal choice for teams looking to take their IaC processes to the next level. Next, we'll look at some other key trends to be aware of that are out of the scope of this book but should be on the radar of anyone looking to truly master Terraform.

What's next?

In this section, we'll explore some emerging trends within the Terraform community that are essential for anyone working with Terraform to be aware of. While these topics are technically outside the scope of this book, including upcoming features that have not even been finalized and may evolve over time, understanding these emerging topics can provide valuable context into the future direction of Terraform and help you stay ahead of the curve in your journey to mastering Terraform.

CDK

The Terraform **Cloud Development Kit** (**CDK**) is a method for developing Terraform configuration using imperative programming languages that you already know and use within your application development. Any language can be used, from Python to C# and from TypeScript to Java. Any Terraform provider and Terraform modules can be used as well. It's essentially the same thing as working with HCL but using the programming language of your choice.

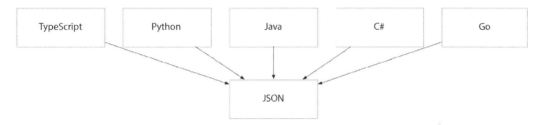

Figure 18.4 – Use the programming language of your choice

Whatever language you choose will ultimately compile down into a Terraform-compatible JSON file that is then interpreted by Terraform in a similar way as HCL files are processed.

This option is great for existing development teams that already work with a programming language of choice and don't want to invest energy in learning the HCL. However, for non-developers, the HCL is definitely the way to go as it provides a simple, functional language that is easier to adopt and already has a massive ecosystem of practitioners that are using it, asking and answering questions about it, and sharing code on public GitHub repositories that can help you along on your way.

Terraform Stacks

Terraform Stacks, a highly anticipated feature on the horizon for Terraform, promises to revolutionize the way we design and manage complex architectures across multiple control planes. This innovative feature is expected to provide a seamless and integrated experience for users working with Terraform Cloud and the **Terraform Community Edition** (the command-line tool). By allowing for more sophisticated organization and modularization of IaC, Terraform Stacks aims to streamline the process of deploying and managing large-scale, multi-tiered environments. We'll dig into what we know right now based on what was made public by HashiCorp at the time of writing and how it's supposed to work when it's eventually released.

Current state

In the current landscape of Terraform usage, a singular root module serves as the cornerstone of infrastructure deployment. This root module encompasses the provider configuration and engages with various Terraform resources, either directly or via module references. The versatility of these root modules is heightened by supplying them with distinct input parameters tailored to the desired environment for deployment. To further segregate the deployment of each root module instance, Terraform workspaces are employed, resulting in individual Terraform state files. These state files are then uniquely associated with specific environments, such as DEV, TEST, or PROD, effectively encapsulating the configuration and status of the deployed infrastructure within each environment:

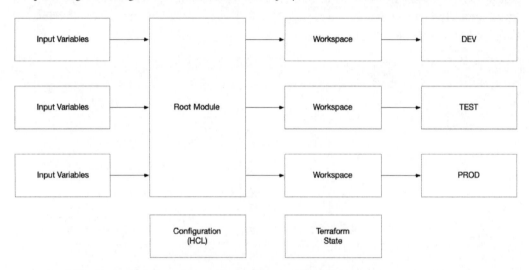

Figure 18.5 – Current state: Terraform workspaces and root modules

In the realm of provisioning complex environments with Terraform, it is often necessary to employ multiple root modules to delineate layers of architecture based on their dependencies, such as blast radius considerations or concrete control plane dependencies such as those between a cloud platform and a Kubernetes control plane. This is not the only scenario where you will run into control plane dependencies within the providers, but it is a common one as the use of managed Kubernetes offerings continues to grow in popularity. The dependency can arise anytime you are provisioning resources with two or more providers and one provider provisions a resource that is then used to configure another Terraform provider. Depending on the way this dependent provider initializes, you might see a conflict arise because providers that rely on their control plane to be provisioned in another provider's resource can experience deadlocks in both `terraform apply` and `terraform destroy`. This is because Terraform cannot plan resources on the control plane, which doesn't exist yet.

Some other common scenarios that I have encountered are with the **Azure Managed Grafana Service**, which provisions a hosted **Grafana** instance on Azure. Although this is an Azure service, it is fully compatible with the Grafana endpoint, which means you can use the `grafana` provider for Terraform to provision resources for it. This mirrors the dependency created by **Azure Kubernetes Service** (also an Azure resource) and the `kubernetes` provider. It doesn't matter what cloud platform you are working with. Many cloud platforms have similar managed service offerings that are provisioned through their corresponding provider, which produces an endpoint that can be automated by a Terraform provider designed for that control plane. This is even the case with something as fun as the `minecraft` provider—whether you are using EC2, Azure VMs, or GCE!

While there are two main approaches to this, both necessitate executing `terraform apply` multiple times. The first approach involves provisioning each stage of our deployment independently and then linking the upstream dependency to the downstream stage using data sources, with values provided by input variables. This method allows different stages to be deployed relatively independently by various teams, but it introduces additional configuration management overhead, as each downstream dependency must explicitly reference the previously provisioned upstream stages. Consequently, this approach results in a highly serial deployment pattern, requiring each upstream dependency to be deployed and stabilized before progressing to the next downstream dependency:

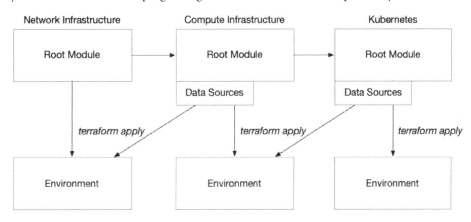

Figure 18.6 – Current state: independent deployments with data source dependencies

An alternative approach to provisioning complex environments with Terraform diverges from independent deployments and instead adopts a monolithic pipeline that sequentially executes `terraform apply`. In this model, the dependencies are seamlessly integrated by piping the Terraform outputs from the upstream dependency directly into the inputs of the downstream dependency. While this method streamlines automation, it also results in a tighter coupling of the environments. Irrespective of the approach—whether it involves independent deployments or a monolithic pipeline—there is an inherent necessity to implement a substantial amount of *glue* to stitch together multiple `terraform apply` steps. This entails writing Bash scripts or similar automation to act as the connective tissue, ensuring the correct values are passed from one pipeline job to the next, thereby maintaining the integrity of the deployment process across various stages:

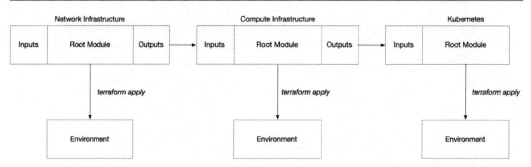

Figure 18.7 – Current state: integrated deployment with output-based dependencies

Stacks

Defined in a .tfstack file, Stacks allow you to declare one or more component blocks that essentially define what is currently a root module. These components represent discrete and deterministic provisioning stages within a deployment:

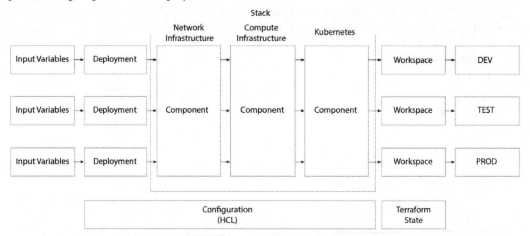

Figure 18.8 – Future state: Terraform Stacks

In the preceding diagram, we see three components that make up our stack:

- Network infrastructure
- Compute infrastructure
- Kubernetes deployments

This would be defined in a .tfstack file in this manner:

```
component "network" {
  source = "./network"
```

```
    inputs = {
      region = var.region
    }

    providers = {
      aws = providers.aws.this
    }
}
```

The compute infrastructure would be defined in the same file but, this time, referencing outputs from the network component that it draws a dependency on. This informs Terraform to provision the network component first and resolve that stage of the deployment first before attempting to deploy the compute infrastructure component next:

```
component "compute" {
  source = "./compute"

  inputs = {
    region = var.region
    network_name = component.network.network_name
  }

  providers = {
    aws = providers.aws.this
  }
}
```

After the compute component is provisioned, we will have a Kubernetes cluster that is ready to deploy our applications and services to. Therefore, we declare the final component of our stack, the application component:

```
component "app" {
  source = "./app"

  inputs = {
    region = var.region
    cluster_name = component.compute.cluster_name
  }

  providers = {
    aws = providers.aws.this
    kubernetes = providers.kubernetes.this
    helm = providers.helm.this
  }
}
```

This allows us to initialize the kubernetes and helm providers only after the necessary steps have been taken to provision the Kubernetes cluster, which is absolutely required before we can even begin to execute a plan.

Deployments

Defined in a .tfdeploy file, deployments allow you to declare one or more deployment blocks that essentially define a Terraform workspace that manifests itself once provisioned into an individual Terraform state file that represents a provisioned environment. The introduction of deployments allows us to declaratively establish different environments that we provision in our configuration rather than implicitly through the organization of our Terraform workspaces and the context in which we execute Terraform core workflow operations such as plan and apply.

Deployments act as the central place where provider configuration is established. This includes linking the preferred method of authentication with each provider. This is done using a new block called identity_token, which would be defined in this manner for AWS:

```
identity_token "aws" {
  audience = ["aws.workload.identity"]
}
```

This would be defined in a .tfdeploy file in this manner:

```
deployment "dev" {
  variables = {
    region = "us-west-2"
    identity_token_file = identity_token.aws.jwt_filename
  }
}
```

As you can see, the deployment block allows us to establish multiple instances of our Stacks and configure them with their own input variables and provider context, including relevant authentication and authorization context.

Terraform Stacks is an exciting new capability in preview on Terraform Cloud and is planned to be released for both Terraform Cloud and Terraform Community Edition. As you can see, with this approach, we'll be able to eliminate a tremendous amount of *plumbing* that we currently put into our pipelines (i.e., **GitHub Actions**, **Azure DevOps**, **Jenkins**, etc.) and replace it with Terraform configuration that we can manage with the **Gitflow** standards we learned about in *Chapter 6*. If you plan on managing complex solutions with Terraform, this is a feature to watch for in future releases!

Summary

In this final chapter of *Mastering Terraform*, we've explored the next steps for those of you looking to deepen your mastery of Terraform and stay abreast of emerging trends in the community. We discussed the importance of Terraform certification, highlighting the Associate and Professional level exams.

We also delved into Terraform Cloud, which can enhance automation and collaboration in your IaC process, building upon the workflows and concepts we've covered throughout this book.

The Terraform community is vibrant and continuously evolving, with new trends and alternative pathways emerging regularly. We explored some of the latest developments, including the Terraform CDK, which allows you to use Terraform with familiar programming languages, and finally, we looked at some exciting upcoming features in Terraform, such as Terraform Stacks, which promises to revolutionize the way we manage environments through IaC by providing more flexibility and modularity in defining and deploying sophisticated and layered cloud architectures.

Closing statement

We have traveled long, and we have traveled far. We have explored Terraform, its architecture, its capabilities, and its form and function. Beyond just learning Terraform, to truly become masters of Terraform, we need to ground ourselves in the architectures and work patterns expected of us as IaC practitioners. That means we need a deep understanding of cloud architectures to effectively use Terraform to its fullest potential. This includes the various flora and fauna we will find in the wild—from virtual machines to containers to serverless—and all the surrounding ancillary resources that support those architectures. Once we have this core conceptual knowledge, we'll be able to better navigate the multi-cloud world that we live in today and truly transcend our current cloud provider of choice to be ready for the future—whatever may come.

Thank you for coming on this journey with me. I hope you enjoyed my very focused and practical approach to mastering Terraform. I think the best way to learn is by doing, so I encourage you to go to GitHub, clone any or all of the solutions described in this book, and get to work on finishing your journey of mastering Terraform!

Index

packtpub.com

Subscribe to our online digital library for full access to over 7,000 books and videos, as well as industry leading tools to help you plan your personal development and advance your career. For more information, please visit our website.

Why subscribe?

- Spend less time learning and more time coding with practical eBooks and Videos from over 4,000 industry professionals

- Improve your learning with Skill Plans built especially for you

- Get a free eBook or video every month

- Fully searchable for easy access to vital information

- Copy and paste, print, and bookmark content

Did you know that Packt offers eBook versions of every book published, with PDF and ePub files available? You can upgrade to the eBook version at packtpub.com and as a print book customer, you are entitled to a discount on the eBook copy. Get in touch with us at customercare@packtpub.com for more details.

At www.packtpub.com, you can also read a collection of free technical articles, sign up for a range of free newsletters, and receive exclusive discounts and offers on Packt books and eBooks.

Other Books You May Enjoy

If you enjoyed this book, you may be interested in these other books by Packt:

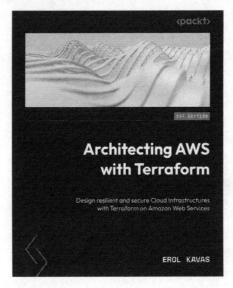

Architecting AWS with Terraform

Erol Kavas

ISBN: 978-1-80324-856-1

- Get to grips with Terraform frameworks and best practices
- Use Terraform providers and modules
- Develop your first AWS resource in Terraform
- Build an infrastructure project with Terraform
- Govern an infrastructure project in Terraform
- Deploy Terraform projects to AWS with CI/CD

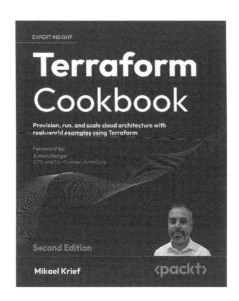

Terraform Cookbook

Mikael Krief

ISBN: 978-1-80461-642-0

- Use Terraform to build and run cloud and Kubernetes infrastructure using IaC best practices
- Adapt the Terraform command line adapted to appropriate use cases
- Automate the deployment of Terraform configuration with CI/CD
- Discover manipulation of the Terraform state by adding or removing resources
- Explore Terraform for Docker and Kubernetes deployment, advanced topics on GitOps practices, and Cloud Development Kit (CDK)
- Add and apply test code and compliance security in Terraform configuration
- Debug and troubleshoot common Terraform errors

Packt is searching for authors like you

If you're interested in becoming an author for Packt, please visit authors.packtpub.com and apply today. We have worked with thousands of developers and tech professionals, just like you, to help them share their insight with the global tech community. You can make a general application, apply for a specific hot topic that we are recruiting an author for, or submit your own idea.

Share your thoughts

Now you've finished *Mastering Terraform*, we'd love to hear your thoughts! Scan the QR code below to go straight to the Amazon review page for this book and share your feedback or leave a review on the site that you purchased it from.

https://packt.link/r/1835086012

Your review is important to us and the tech community and will help us make sure we're delivering excellent quality content.

Download a free PDF copy of this book

Thanks for purchasing this book!

Do you like to read on the go but are unable to carry your print books everywhere?

Is your eBook purchase not compatible with the device of your choice?

Don't worry, now with every Packt book you get a DRM-free PDF version of that book at no cost.

Read anywhere, any place, on any device. Search, copy, and paste code from your favorite technical books directly into your application.

The perks don't stop there, you can get exclusive access to discounts, newsletters, and great free content in your inbox daily

Follow these simple steps to get the benefits:

1. Scan the QR code or visit the link below

https://packt.link/free-ebook/9781835086018

2. Submit your proof of purchase

3. That's it! We'll send your free PDF and other benefits to your email directly

Made in United States
Troutdale, OR
11/03/2024

24386933R00275